Memories of Chicano History

Memories of Chicano History

The Life and Narrative of Bert Corona

Mario T. García

UNIVERSITY OF CALIFORNIA PRESS
Berkeley · *Los Angeles* · *London*

University of California Press
Berkeley and Los Angeles, California

University of California Press, Ltd.
London, England

© 1994 by
The Regents of the University of California

First Paperback Printing 1995

Library of Congress Cataloging-in-Publication Data

García, Mario T.
   Memories of Chicano history : the life and narrative of Bert
Corona / Mario T. García.
     p.   cm. — (Latinos in American society and culture; 2)
   Includes bibliographical references and index.
   ISBN 0-520-20152-3
   1. Corona, Bert N. 2. Labor leaders—United States—Biography. 3. Alien labor,
Mexican—United States—History. 4. Mexican Americans—Politics and government.
I. Title. II. Series.
   HD8037.C67G37 1994
   323.1'16872—dc20
   [B]   92-41578
                                                    CIP

Printed in the United States of America
9 8 7 6 5 4 3 2 1

All photographs are from the collection of Bert Corona

When I read the book, the biography famous
And this is then (said I) what the author calls a man's
    life?
And so will someone when I am dead and gone write my
    life?
(As if any man really knew ought of my life)
Why even I myself I often think knew little or nothing of
    my real life,
Only a few hints, a few diffused joint clues and
    indirections
I seek for my own use to trace out here.

                    Walt Whitman (1867)

You don't have anything if you don't have the stories.

                    Leslie Marmon Silko (1977)

Contents

Illustrations follow page 192

Foreword

"One thing I learned from my days with the CIO and my later political experiences," says Bert Corona, "is that any labor, political, or community organization takes time and commitment. There are no short-cuts." Corona's life has spanned three-quarters of a century. During that time, his efforts to organize fellow Chicanos and other working people have never flagged. But constantly changing social and political circumstances have guided those endeavors into such a variety of different forms that Corona's narrative retraces much of the history of our times.

Woven through the fascinating chronicle of struggles and insightful sketches of the men and women of varied organizations and generations with whom he has collaborated is the conviction that most people—those who do not occupy society's positions of power, wealth, and prestige—can influence the circumstances in which they find themselves only by conscious and concerted action. To be an organizer of such action requires total immersion in those people's everyday needs, frustrations, and hopes. And it requires persistence.

Mario García's introduction offers astute insights into the character of Bert Corona and of his narrative. García takes advantage of his long collaboration with Corona to reflect on the scope and trajectory of the history of Chicanos in the twentieth century and also on what it means to write oppositional history and to present a life in narrative form.

Corona's account of his own relentless struggle, however, also provides important lessons for readers who wish to understand the social and political development of the United States during this century, as well as for those who wish to improve the lives of its people during the future. Some brief observations on three of those lessons may be in order.

First, Corona shifts the focus of the controversy over multiculturalism from the level of academic discourse to that of everyday experience and conflict. His own elementary and high schools were cultural battlegrounds, as were such schools throughout the length and breadth of the United States during the 1920s. African-Americans and Euro-American immigrants also encountered systematic tracking away from higher education, described by Corona, as well as the demeaning images of their own histories and cultures presented in the textbooks, vocabulary, and even maps used in the classrooms. They felt the effects of the brutal role sometimes played by physical education teachers in enforcing racial hierarchies and disciplining rebellious students. At times these students also encountered a certain unforgettable teacher, who provided at least some particular children with intellectual nurturing, even in that hostile pedagogical environment. Later, those high school graduates who, like Corona, went on to college found that they had not left the cultural wars behind. At the University of Southern California, Corona joined with other students of varied ethnic backgrounds in the Non-Org Association, to combat the stranglehold of the elite fraternities and sororities on campus life.

The encounters of *mexicano* children with the schools, however, had distinctive characteristics and intensity, which these memoirs have captured vividly and which suggest important lines of inquiry to historians who would understand the meaning of the ubiquitous experience of schooling to the children of the twenties. The schools were theaters of much harsher confrontations than one would imagine from reading much of today's historical writing about the encounter between mass culture (or consumerism) and ethnic traditions. Classroom conflicts over pedagogy and language were rooted in the local society's patterns of domination and exploitation, which were evident for all to see.

Moreover, for Chicanos, the battle of the schoolroom has persisted long after the 1920s. Corona's first strike prevented the expulsion of fellow *mexicano* students who had objected to the content of their history lessons and had clashed physically with the coach. His first experience with political organizing arose out of a successful attempt to elect a popular athlete as the first *mexicano* president of the student body. Fifty years later, Corona was involved with the Raza Unida Party, whose rapid rise to power in Crystal City, Texas, also grew out of Chicano protests against the way youngsters were treated in the public schools.

The intersection of culture with social power is underscored in Corona's reflections on the 1930s. He threw himself into the cause of industrial unionism, organizing workers of many races and nationalities into the Longshoremen and Warehousemen's Union of the new Congress of Industrial Organizations. The union mobilization, in turn, infused vitality into Mexican-American communities. To unionize Latino workers required a tireless battle against the harassment and deportation of noncitizens by the immigration authorities. The Spanish Civil War as well as the quickening of social reform and the nationalization of foreign oil companies in Mexico under President Lázaro Cárdenas blended with the rise of industrial unions to produce El Congreso Nacional del Pueblo de Habla Española, the National Congress of Spanish-Speaking Peoples. In its view, the worldwide cause of democracy was inseparable from the empowerment of workers and from the unification of Latinos as a political force within the United States.

A second historical insight suggested by Corona's life and recollections is that the domain of effective political organizing for social reform has changed several times during the past six decades. The dynamics of Mexican-American mobilization that had been evident in the 1930s did not survive the coming of the Cold War. Although unions (especially the Mine, Mill and Smelter Workers) continued to play decisive roles in galvanizing political movements in many localities, the decline of labor militancy, the purging of the left from the CIO, and governmental repression directed with special intensity toward individuals and groups who clung to the political vision that had earlier been embodied in the Congreso (and was now widely denounced as "Communist") combined to elevate ethnic, racial, and neighborhood organizations to dominant roles in the social struggles of the twenty years that followed World War II.

An enduring legacy of the New Deal, however, was the tendency of all such movements to promote candidates for political office through the Democratic Party. Corona's reflections on the Mexican American Political Association (MAPA) and the Viva Johnson clubs reveal much about the endemic tension between political officeholders and grassroots activists that characterized these efforts.

By the end of the sixties, the growing importance of the Chicano student movement, the reintegration of union and cultural struggle through the United Farm Workers, the emergence of civil rights councils stressing the common interests of people of color, the assassination of Robert Kennedy, and the fight to end the war in Vietnam (whose bloody denouement in the National Chicano Anti-War Moratorium Corona analyzes so perceptively) had reshaped the context of Chicano movements for political power. Corona's role in the leadership of MAPA positioned him well to record, as well as to participate in, this process of incessant change.

Finally, Corona offers the provocative observation that President Lyndon Johnson's "Great Society program . . . was not anything like the New Deal. It was not something that released the force and strength of the great body of poor and working people." It did not "provide poor people with the means to work themselves out of poverty."

The most radical and controversial feature of the Wagner Act of 1935 was the encouragement it gave to workers to group themselves into a power with which employers and government would be obliged to deal. As the organizing techniques that Corona learned from his mentor Lloyd Seeliger reveal, the Wagner Act's encouragment was often most effectively utilized by activists who ignored the formal procedures it prescribed. The endless political meetings in the working-class halls and neighborhoods of Los Angeles, the widespread sense of sympathy with workers outside of one's own workplace (which first drew Corona himself into CIO activity), and the level of community involvement that developed around the 1941 strike in the city's waste-material industry all bore witness to the ability of working people to empower themselves during the New Deal.

The Great Society channeled money and direction from Washington and from foundations into poor neighborhoods. While it accomplished far more than is often recognized in improving living standards for many people, the Johnson administration remained the manager of its own reforms. Nevertheless, it was challenged, in Corona's words, by "college-age youth of all races, seeking a new lifestyle and at the same time combatting some of the atrocities of the time." In addition to the fierce confrontation of students with what they called "the power structure," which had produced segregation and the war in Vietnam, opponents of the administration were encouraged by the Great Society's own patterns of funding to group themselves under the banner of community power for people who had been subjugated by American racism. Corona's recollections of the Chicano movement of the epoch illuminate many aspects of this paradox. They also help us understand both the creativity and the limitations of those rebellious years.

In the course of his reflections on the organizations with which he has been involved since 1945, Corona returns several times to the influence of outside funding on popular movements. As early as 1949, when the Community Service Organization mobilized the first successful campaign to place a Chicano on the city council of Los Angeles, Corona became aware of the way fund-raising and a paid staff can shape the relations between an organization and the constituents in whose name it speaks. During the 1960s, when protest organizations unhesitatingly solicited grants from foundations established by corporations and wealthy individuals, these funding agencies established links to the directorates of the very organizations that were challenging the social order through which the wealth of the foundations had been accumulated. Corona's observations about the relationship of the Ford Foundation to the Southwest Council of La Raza should be required reading for those social activists of our own time who automatically set out to solicit grants.

It is difficult to find an effective alternative. La Hermandad Mexicana Nacional (the Mexican National Brotherhood), through which Corona now helps undocumented immigrants organize for their own defense against employers and the immigration service, revived the heritage of workers' mutual-benefit societies. Small dues paid by every member and abundant volunteer work have taken the place of a staff funded by a foundation. Close collaboration with the more progressive unions of the locality and with service agencies operated by professional, clerical, and student volunteers have helped to make this style of work, drawn from a bygone era, effective in the 1990s.

One cannot help but note, however, that Corona's own work has in one respect returned to the point at which it began. From the days of his childhood, the international boundary that divides people of Mexican ancestry left its imprint on his every action. In the year he graduated from high school, he witnessed thousands of refugees of the Great Depression passing through El Paso. Traveling from North to South were Mexicans, driven out of the United States by lack of work and often by coercion. Traveling from East to West were Anglo and African-American victims of the great droughts of 1932–1934 and of massive evictions from the land. In 1954, Operation Wetback required more than a million Mexicans to leave the United States, in response to the efforts of migrants to improve the terms under which they worked, beyond the conditions established by the *bracero* program. In the 1990s, the mobility of both capital and people across that border, under the surveillance of authorities on both sides, sets severe limits to the empowerment of working people, not only along the border but now throughout North America as well.

Bert Corona is, as always, in the thick of the fight. The rest of us are deeply in his debt, not only for what he has done over the years but also for making available these reflections on what he has done and the circumstances under which he did it. They help us understand how people make their own history.

David Montgomery
Yale University

Acknowledgments

First and foremost, I want to thank Bert Corona for his support for this project. Despite his many commitments and work on behalf of Latino immigrant workers and their families, Bert always managed to find the time and patience for our interviews.

I also want to thank Blanche Corona for sharing her story with me.

A special acknowledgment goes to Professor Jeffrey Garcilazo of the University of Utah, who, as my graduate assistant during the course of this project, accompanied me on our numerous visits to the Corona home in Los Angeles. I wish him much success in his career as a historian.

For transcribing and typing the narrative, I wish to thank Jim Viegh and Carole MacKenzie.

I also express my gratitude to David Oberweiser for conducting an earlier, unpublished interview with Corona, dealing with the CIO years, that I was able to utilize.

Funding support for this project initially came from the Interdisciplinary Humanities Center at the University of California, Santa Barbara. I thank Professor Paul Hernadi, who was then director of the center, for his endorsement of the project. Additional support came from the Faculty Research Fund of the UC Santa Barbara Academic Senate and the Provost's Office of Yale University.

Thanks are also owed to those scholars who read earlier versions of the manuscript and who provided valuable recommendations for changes. These include Professors Nell Irvin Painter, Genaro Padilla, Carl Gutiérrez-Jones, Zaragosa Vargas, Julie Leininger Pycior, George Sánchez, and Francisco Lomeli. A special thanks goes to Professor Richard A. García, colleague and brother, whose reading of the manuscript and lengthy discussion of it led to significant revisions.

I want to acknowledge Professor David Montgomery, my best friend at Yale, who graciously agreed to write the foreword for this book and who likewise provided helpful comments on the manuscript. In addition, David and Marty Montgomery shared their home and hospitality during my two years at Yale.

I must also thank the Special Collections Department of the Stanford University Library for their assistance in my research of the CASA Collection.

The Freedom of Information/Privacy Office of the Department of the Army provided censored documents on the surveillance of Corona by Army Intelligence and by the FBI.

At the University of California Press, I want to thank Jim Clark, Lynne Withey, and especially Mary Renaud for her sensitive and thorough editing.

I give my very special and affectionate thanks to Professor Ellen McCracken, my colleague and wife, whose love, support, and advice have sustained me and my work over the years.

Finally, to my children, Giuliana and Carlo: If you can come anywhere close to emulating Bert Corona's commitment to social justice, you will make me very happy.

Introduction

Redefining American History:
Bert Corona and Oppositional Narrative

Who is Bert Corona? His is certainly not a household name or a name readily identified by most Americans—indeed, not even by most Mexican-Americans in the United States, who have been denied their own heroes in American history.

To put it simply, Bert Corona is a Mexican-American labor and community activist, whom I have admired for many years. After collaborating on the writing of his life history, I admire him even more. Bert Corona is a Mexican-American whose life and political career correspond to many of the key themes and periods of twentieth-century American history, in particular those of the Mexican-American experience. His life and work embody the changing character of the Mexican-American communities in the United States.

Bert Corona was born in 1918 in El Paso, Texas, a child of the Mexican Revolution of 1910. Through his family, Corona symbolizes the thousands of Mexican immigrants and refugees who crossed the U.S.–Mexican border—a border created by nineteenth-century U.S. expansion—seeking jobs and safety. Having grown up along the border as the child of Mexican immigrants, Corona represented by the 1930s a new generation of Mexican-Americans who had been born or raised in the United States and who began to distinguish themselves from their immigrant roots. They were still *mexicanos*, but they were also American citizens. They became aware of an identity that resembled what

1

W. E. B. DuBois referred to as the "double consciousness" of black Americans: the consciousness both of being black and of being American.[1]

As part of what I and others refer to as the Mexican-American Generation, which came of political age between the 1930s and the 1950s, Corona joined in the renewed struggles for social justice and first-class citizenship identified with this political generation. In Corona's case, the workplace became the main site of struggle. In the late 1930s and the early 1940s, he played a key role in union drives conducted by the CIO (the Congress of Industrial Organizations) among the varied ethnic communities composing the Los Angeles working class. Within the Mexican-American community, Corona joined and worked in the youth-oriented Mexican American Movement (MAM) and in the National Congress of Spanish-Speaking Peoples, a radical Popular Front group influenced by the Communist Party.

In 1942 Corona volunteered, along with thousands of other Mexican-Americans, to fight the "Good War" against fascism. Returning from World War II, he entered the expanding urban and suburban worlds of Mexican-American veterans and their families, who struggled to meet the challenges of a postwar environment that was still too often characterized by racism. In the late forties and through the fifties, Corona participated in and led groups such as the Community Service Organization (CSO) and the Asociación Nacional México-Americana (ANMA).

Anticipating a new decade with the hope of greater changes, Corona was one of the founders of the Mexican American Political Association (MAPA) in 1960. In the early 1960s, through MAPA, Corona more closely linked his earlier labor and civil rights struggles with electoral politics. As the decade progressed, he became a quintessential transitional figure. Although not without doubts concerning the dogmatic ethnic nationalism of the developing Chicano movement, Corona participated in movement politics and contributed significantly to the movement through his work on the issue of extending protection and organization to Mexican and Latino undocumented workers.

Today, in his mid-seventies, Corona is still struggling on this and other fronts. From this committed and lengthy career, Corona provides

1. See Arnold Rampersad, *The Art and Imagination of W. E. B. DuBois* (New York: Schocken Books, 1990), pp. 68–90.

a memory of history, or a "social memory."[2] In contrast to the case presented by Richard Rodríguez in his controversial 1981 autobiography *Hunger of Memory*, in Bert Corona there is no hunger of or for memory. Rather, we find memory, history, and identity, rooted and shaped by the struggles of Mexicans in this country to combat oppression and discrimination. "The context of that 'memory,' " as Ramón Saldívar notes of Ernesto Galarza's Mexican-American autobiography *Barrio Boy*, "is undeniably historical and discursive."[3]

Oppositional History and Bert Corona

This book therefore concerns much more than the life of Bert Corona. It is not only about one individual but also about many individuals and communities. Personal history, as Barbara Harlow observes about many Third World narratives, becomes transformed into historical narrative and analysis. It is a story—a collective story, if you will, or what Ronald Takaki refers to as a "community of memory"—about the struggles by people of Mexican descent in the United States, who have at different times and even within families referred to themselves variously as *mexicanos,* Mexicans, Mexican-Americans, Chicanos, Latinos, or Hispanics or by more regional designations such as *tejanos* in Texas or *manitos* and Hispanos in New Mexico.[4]

This is a story of Mexican-Americans—or those described by whatever name one chooses to use to designate people of Mexican descent in the United States—struggling to overcome barriers of racial discrimination, social injustice, economic exploitation, inferior educational opportunities, and prejudice that caused them to be regarded as less than American. Both individually and collectively, this is an oppositional text, based on Corona's memories of history.[5] By oppositional, I mean

2. See Peter Burke, "History as Social Memory," in *Memory: History, Culture, and the Mind,* ed. Thomas Butler (London: Oxford University Press, 1989), pp. 97–113.

3. Ramón Saldívar, *Chicano Narrative: The Dialectics of Difference* (Madison: University of Wisconsin Press, 1990), p. 164. See also Richard Rodríguez, *Hunger of Memory: The Education of Richard Rodríguez* (Boston: Godine, 1981).

4. Barbara Harlow, *Resistance Literature* (New York: Methuen, 1987), p. 96; Ronald Takaki, *Strangers from a Different Shore* (Boston: Little, Brown, 1989), p. 493.

5. James Clifford refers to this type of oppositional text as a "postcolonial

that Corona's life and narrative are centered on a fundamental opposition both to social injustice and to an American historical narrative that has excluded the roles, struggles, and even contradictions of diverse racial and ethnic groups such as Mexican-Americans from the making of American history.[6] The history of Mexican-Americans and of Bert Corona is in fact a very American story—a part of U.S. history, although not often acknowledged as such.

Mexicans first became part of the United States as a conquered people, following the U.S. invasion and conquest of Mexico's northern frontier, *el norte,* during the U.S.–Mexican War (1846–1848). Those Mexicans who remained in this territory—an estimated one hundred thousand, scattered from Texas to California—were granted American citizenship, but this was often in name only. Despite class differences between Mexicans of the working class and the lower classes as opposed to land-owning and (in some cases) quite wealthy frontier Mexicans, most people of Mexican descent were relegated to a subaltern political, economic, and cultural position within the first decades of Euro-American rule.[7]

Yet by the turn of the century the great influx of Mexican immigrant workers into the Southwest had augmented the nineteenth-century communities and revitalized Mexican culture north of the border. Brought in and coveted as cheap labor by the key emerging industries of the Southwest—railroads, mines, smelters, ranches, and agriculture—Mexican immigrant workers formed the labor foundation for the

---

ethnographic representation"; see Clifford, *The Predicament of Culture: Twentieth-Century Ethnography, Literature, and Art* (Cambridge: Harvard University Press, 1988), p. 10.

6. See Angie C. Chabram, "Chicana/o Studies as Oppositional Ethnography," *Cultural Studies* 4 (October 1990): 228–247.

7. See, for example, Albert Camarillo, *Chicanos in a Changing Society: From Mexican Pueblos to American Barrios in Santa Barbara and Southern California, 1848–1930* (Cambridge: Harvard University Press, 1979); Arnoldo De León, *The Tejano Community, 1830–1900* (Albuquerque: University of New Mexico Press, 1982); Richard Griswold del Castillo, *The Los Angeles Barrio, 1850–1890: A Social History* (Berkeley and Los Angeles: University of California Press, 1979); Robert J. Rosenbaum, *Mexicano Resistance in the Southwest: The Sacred Right of Self-Preservation* (Austin: University of Texas Press, 1981); Douglas Monroy, *Thrown Among Strangers: The Making of Mexican Culture in Frontier California* (Berkeley and Los Angeles: University of California Press, 1990).

development of the southwestern economy and its integration with the rest of a newly industrializing America. The nearly one million Mexican immigrant workers who arrived between 1900 and 1930 were accompanied by Mexican political refugees fleeing the destruction and dislocation of the Mexican Revolution of 1910. It is in this context that the Corona family saga north of the border commences.

Mexican immigrants and their offspring, who would form the Mexican-American Generation, did not reap the full fruits of their labor. Mexicans began their search for America under severe handicaps, relegated to what were termed "Mexican jobs" (the worst jobs), paid "Mexican wages" (the lowest wages), living in "Mexican barrios" (congested, impoverished, and segregated), and forced to attend "Mexican schools" (the worst schools available).[8]

But this history—what has become known as Chicano history—is not merely a history of victimization. Chicanos, or Mexican-Americans, also possess a history of struggles, both personal and collective, which have been manifested in different ways. Mexican-Americans as a people have participated in oppositional struggles to survive as an ethnic group and to oppose second-class treatment. Some of this opposition has been overtly political, whereas some has been more personal and subtle.

I stress the theme of opposition not to glorify or to romanticize or to exaggerate the concept of struggle in Chicano history, and certainly not to essentialize or suggest a monolithic Mexican-American experience (although I agree with critic Ramón Saldívar that in the experiences of oppressed minorities in the United States, essentialism, or generalization, has in fact represented a form of resistance to the dominant culture).[9] Rather, I stress opposition simply to note that most people of Mexican descent—whether their politics are liberal, conservative, moderate, radical, or nothing in particular—have resented and

8. See, for example, Mario T. García, *Mexican Americans: Leadership, Ideology, and Identity, 1930–1960* (New Haven: Yale University Press, 1989); Richard A. García, *Rise of the Mexican American Middle Class: San Antonio, 1929–1941* (College Station: Texas A&M University Press, 1990); Guadalupe San Miguel, *Let All of Them Take Heed: Mexican Americans and the Quest for Educational Equality in Texas, 1918–1981* (Austin: University of Texas Press, 1987).

9. Ramón Saldívar, "The Politics of Culture," in *Rearticulations: The Practice of Chicano Cultural Studies,* ed. Ellen McCracken and Mario T. García (forthcoming).

reacted to being treated as subordinates. Hence, diverse struggles have characterized Mexican-American resistance movements. In an earlier text, *Mexican Americans: Leadership, Ideology, and Identity, 1930–1960,* I focused on the history of Mexican-American struggles against racism and class exploitation from the perspective of key liberal groups such as the League of United Latin American Citizens (LULAC) as well as radical groups such as the National Congress of Spanish-Speaking Peoples.[10]

Because both racism and the exploitation of Mexicans in this country have deep roots and have persisted throughout this century, each generation of Chicanos has taken on the struggle in its own way. Both liberals and radicals in the Mexican-American Generation, Corona's generation, challenged the system, but they did so mostly based on the premise that the system was capable of being reformed to allow the full integration of Mexican-Americans. They believed that it was possible to achieve a pluralistic synthesis—or what Werner Sollors refers to as "consent"—between what is Mexican and what is American.[11]

In contrast, in the late 1960s and early 1970s, a new generation of Mexicans in the United States more boldly and militantly challenged the system, its years of prejudice against Mexicans, and the historical and cultural amnesia that relegated Chicanos to mostly marginal historical roles and stereotypical cultural contributions. At the same time that they resurrected the civil rights struggles of their parents and grandparents, members of this Chicano Generation rejected earlier themes and goals such as integration, pluralism, and acculturation. Instead, the Chicano Generation asserted the right of Mexicans in this country to political self-determination and proposed an anti-colonial struggle that suggested the future secession of Chicanos and their historical homeland, the Southwest, now called Aztlán after the mythical original homeland of the Aztecs. Although the Chicano Generation felt it necessary to re-create or invent its own version of a tradition of resistance, with corresponding myths, its general discourse and actions were in fact rooted in a collective memory of Mexicans who had been struggling against prejudice since the American conquest during the nineteenth century.

10. García, *Mexican Americans.*
11. Werner Sollors, *Beyond Ethnicity: Consent and Descent in American Culture* (New York: Oxford University Press, 1986).

Despite the demise (and some would say cooptation) of the Chicano movement and the more conservative general political climate in the 1980s and 1990s, elements of resistance and opposition still remain, although they are less focused and more sporadic. Even those upwardly mobile Mexican-Americans who have benefited from the discourse of "multiculturalism" and "diversity" in the eighties and nineties have not succumbed fully to the forces of cooptation, as Rosa Linda Fregoso notes in her study of recent Chicano cultural productions and artists such as Luis Valdez. For example, within what appear to be assimilationist-oriented films, such as *La Bamba* by Valdez, lie various subtexts of political and cultural opposition based on alternative readings of American history and culture.[12]

It is this history of Mexican-American struggles against injustice that, in a larger sense, this book is all about. "Identity politics," Lourdes Torres observes about women of color, "has never meant bemoaning one's individual circumstances, or ranking oppressions, or a politics of defensiveness around one's issues. Rather, identity politics means a politics of activism, a politics which seeks to recognize, name, and destroy the system of domination which subjugates people of color."[13] The same is true of Corona's case. It is a story of the struggle to maintain in a constructive way some form of ethnic and cultural integrity—the redefinition and reinvention by each generation of the meaning of being Mexican-Americans—against those forces which seek only to valorize Mexican-Americans for the labor that can be exploited from them.

Yet at another level, it is also a history of struggles to assert Mexican-American rights to being American, to occupying a discursive space within an American context—and not solely on a standard set by Euro-Americans, or Anglos, but also on Mexican-American terms. This involves the redefinition of what it means to be an American, what it means to be a citizen. This means changing, for example, traditional views of American development as simply an East-to-West movement

12. Rosa Linda Fregoso, "Re-membering the Border Through Chicano Cinema," in McCracken and García, *Rearticulations.*

13. See Lourdes Torres, "The Construction of the Self in U.S. Latina Autobiographies," in *Third World Women and the Politics of Feminism,* ed. Chandra Talpade Mohanty, Ann Russo, and Lourdes Torres (Bloomington: Indiana University Press, 1991), pp. 275–276.

of peoples, from civilization to frontier. It means reinterpreting American history also from a South-to-North perspective, from Spanish/Mexican to Mexican-American to Chicano and to a viable definition of multiculturalism, from frontier to border—borders both real and mythical, both political and cultural—and to the intersections of borders, as suggested by Chicana writer Gloria Anzaldúa.[14] It involves producing and accepting what Edward Said refers to as "new objects for a new kind of knowledge."[15]

Is Corona's Life Representative of Other Mexican-Americans?

The answer to this question is both yes and no. It is yes in the sense that aspects of Bert Corona's life conform to the shared experiences of other Mexican-Americans. For example, Corona, like many other Mexicans, became American as the result of his parents crossing the border as immigrants and refugees during the Mexican Revolution of 1910. Most Mexicans in the United States descend from the immigrant experience—great-grandparents, grandparents, parents, or they themselves have crossed the Rio Grande or the *linia,* the borderline, somewhere between Brownsville and San Diego. As a child of the Mexican Revolution and as a child of what I call the Immigrant Generation in Chicano history, Corona shares this historical experience with many other Mexicans in this country.

Corona's own coming of age in a Mexican-American world, in a world of literal borders (the El Paso–Ciudad Juárez area) as well as cultural borders, parallels the experiences of others who also came of age during the era of the Mexican-American Generation. This generation, distinct in both a political and a biological sense, was forced to confront more individual and collective borders than any generation before it. What did it really mean to be Mexican and American (Mexican-American)?

14. Gloria Anzaldúa, *Borderlands/La Frontera: The New Mestiza* (San Francisco: Spinsters/Aunt Lute, 1987).

15. Said is quoted in Harlow, *Resistance Literature,* p. 116. Also see Claudia Salazar, "A Third World Woman's Text: Between the Politics of Criticism and Cultural Politics," in *Women's Words: The Feminist Practice of Oral History,* ed. Sherna Berger Gluck and Daphne Patai (New York: Routledge, 1991), pp. 93–106.

Writing of the literal border implications of the term "Mexican-American," William Anthony Nericcio observes: "The hyphen in the name 'Mexican-American' serves, in effect, both as a symbol of the bridges that span the nations of the United States and Mexico and, also, a minus sign (−) symbolizing the negation of the peoples forming the culture around that very boundary."[16]

Like the lives of most other Mexican-Americans, Corona's life has been one of crossing new, symbolic personal, political, cultural, and social borders. The concept of the border is a metaphor for Mexican-American life. This border life and culture are today moving from the margins to the center of American culture and society, as Third World peoples such as Mexican-Americans and other Latinos increase in numbers and influence in the United States.

On a larger scale than ever before, the Mexican-American Generation had to explore these and other issues. Moreover, this search for a new ethnic identity had to be carried out within the context of a changing Mexican-American social reality that was affected on the one hand by the threats and dislocations of the Great Depression and on the other hand by opportunities for social improvement, especially for those who joined the CIO labor struggles of the late 1930s, as Corona did.

Corona's generation, of course, also shares the memories of World War II. Like thousands of other Mexican-Americans—predominantly men, but including some women—Corona volunteered to participate in the struggle against fascism. And, like most other *veteranos,* Corona came back to discover that although America had changed, not everything had changed. As he and others rediscovered racial and cultural exclusion in their hometowns, this ignited various community and even regional efforts by Mexican-Americans to wage still another war, this time on the homefront. This war was against discrimination and for the integration into U.S. society of Mexican-Americans, many of whom had risked their lives in a conflict to preserve democracy.

All these experiences Corona shares with other Mexican-Americans —or at least with other Mexican-American males, for women were still too often segregated in the more private sphere of the home within

16. William Anthony Nericcio, "Autobiographies at *La Frontera:* The Quest for Mexican-American Narrative," *Americas Review* 16 (Fall-Winter 1988): 169.

Mexican-American culture. Corona's life and career certainly parallel those of other Mexican-Americans in a broad historical sense. Yet he is not an Everyman. He possesses exceptional qualities, and I have no misgivings about portraying him as an exceptional Mexican-American leader.

Despite those postmodernist critics who applaud the end of the subject and the author in history, racial minority groups such as Mexican-Americans who have been excluded, marginalized, and dehistoricized still need subjects, authors, leaders, heroes—figures of whom we have been deprived, figures we didn't even know existed. Many of my generation grew up in the 1950s believing that true heroes and leaders came only from the ranks of the Anglos and not from among Mexicans.[17]

As someone who early recognized the need to struggle against injustice, as a key labor and community leader, and as an activist whose leadership has extended and survived over various historical periods in Chicano history, Bert Corona is without question exceptional. He clearly is not a follower. He is a leader in the best and most progressive tradition of that term. Yet he is not so exceptional that he stands by himself. As is evident in the memories of his life, Corona places his leadership within the context of what some critics refer to as the "collective self"—that is, his memories of struggle are social and collective rather than individualized. Unlike the leadership described in the traditional Western male autobiography, his is instead a social leadership, for the many rather than for the few.

Moreover, Corona's leadership is part of a larger expression of leadership that emanates from the Chicano communities of his own Mexican-American Generation, as well as those of earlier and later generations. Corona's cohort of Mexican-American leaders also represent oppositional figures in American history. They symbolize disjuncture, rupture, and interruption of a social process and a historical

17. In this sense, I would agree with Regeina Gagnier (although I would place more stress on the "collective self") when she writes concerning the emergence of the female oppositional voice: "In literary critical terms, women who have never possessed the authorial signature are not ready to give themselves over to the deconstructive or postmodern 'death of the author,' and they cling more tenaciously to individualism" ("Feminist Autobiography in the 1980s," *Feminist Studies* 17 [Spring 1991]: 140).

narrative that has largely relegated Mexican-Americans to the margins of second-class citizenship, to the status of what poet Pat Mora terms "legal aliens."[18] Corona and his cohort participate in the "politics of memory" by constructing oppositional memories, or what Michael Fischer calls a "counter rhetoric," against the dominant side of American history, which is centered on the advancement of some by the exploitation of many others.[19] "Memory recovers history," Genaro Padilla asserts, "and in recovering reshapes it, revises it, reassigns meaning to it, reinvents and repossesses it for the individual."[20]

Bert Corona and American History

We can learn a number of things about American history through Bert Corona's narrative. At a general level, one of these is certainly the perspective that American history not only is the result of the specific types of victimization that people of color have experienced but also is the result—and this is perhaps more important—of the role that minorities themselves, male and female, have played in constructing history. Corona exemplifies at a leadership level the importance of historical agency in the making of Chicano history. From his initial involvement in the struggle against injustice when he was in grade school and participated in a school strike to protest the maltreatment

18. Pat Mora, "Legal Alien," in Mora, *Chants* (Houston: Arte Publico Press, 1984), p. 54.

19. See E. San Juan, "The Cult of Ethnicity and the Fetish of Pluralism: A Counterhegemonic Critique," *Cultural Critique* 18 (Spring 1991): 224; Michael M. J. Fischer, "Ethnicity and the Post-Modern Arts of Memory," in *Writing Culture: The Poetics and Politics of Ethnography,* ed. James Clifford and George E. Marcus (Berkeley and Los Angeles: University of California Press, 1986), p. 213.

20. Genaro Padilla, " 'Yo Sola Aprendi': Contra-Patriarchal Containment in Women's Nineteenth-Century California Personal Narratives," *Americas Review* 16 (Fall-Winter 1988): 93. "Counter-memory," George Lipsitz notes, "looks to the past for the hidden histories excluded from dominant narratives" ("History, Myth, and Counter-Memory: Narrative and Desire in Popular Novels," in Lipsitz, *Time Passages: Collective Memory and American Popular Culture* [Minneapolis: University of Minnesota Press, 1990], p. 213). Also see David Thelen, "Memory and American History," *Journal of American History* 75 (March 1989): 1117–1129; and David W. Blight, " 'For Something Beyond the Battlefield': Frederick Douglass and the Memory of the Civil War," *Journal of American History* 75 (March 1989): 1156–1178.

of Mexican-American students by the teachers, Corona has actively labored to change conditions both for Mexican-Americans and for others.

Rather than waiting for someone else to better the conditions of Mexican-Americans, Corona has always taken the initiative to bring about change. This struggle has been strategically modified over time, from the initial years of organizing CIO unions in Los Angeles to his current work in helping to protect and assist undocumented workers and their families. Despite the common stereotypes—or what ethnographers Clifford and Marcus refer to as "visualisms"—of Mexican-Americans as lazy, passive, and fatalistic people, Corona's life and narrative challenge these images. By engaging in what Octavio Romano terms "historical confrontation," Corona provides counter-images of Mexican-Americans as active, engaged, and future-oriented people whose oppositional stance is not itself intended to destroy but rather to build—in this case, to build a better and more just America.[21]

Along these lines, Corona's narrative also emphasizes a second theme: a sense of continuity within the struggle for social change in American history, specifically in the Mexican-American experience. One of the impressive aspects of Corona's career has been his consistent commitment and dedication to social change. He is in essence a "man for all seasons," seeking to engage and to organize the widest possible circle of people. Strongly influenced by the CIO unionizing efforts and the Popular Front politics of the 1930s, Corona has always been anti-sectarian and anti-dogmatic. Although clearly a man of the left, he has always interpreted this position in the most general of ways in order to include in the fight against injustice as many people as possible, regardless of their political views.

And he has done this consistently through several periods in Chicano history. Although centered within the Mexican-American Generation, Corona has not been completely tied to his own generational position. As a classic transitional figure, he has adjusted and helped to shape the politics of later periods. This is most clearly seen in his transition to involvement with the more militant and certainly more separatist-

---

21. Clifford and Marcus, *Writing Culture*, p. 11; Octavio Ignacio Romano, "The Historical and Intellectual Presence of Mexican Americans," *El Grito* 2 (Winter 1969): 32–46.

oriented ethnic nationalism of the Chicano Generation during the 1960s and the early 1970s.

In the post-movement years, Corona has further adapted, or "crossed over," without ever giving up his political principles. While remaining true to his commitment to achieving social justice, he has been able to work with more moderate groups and leaders in this more conservative period in order to achieve gains and protections for undocumented immigrants. "Latino experience in the U.S. has been a continual crossover," Juan Flores and George Yudice argue, "not only across geopolitical borders, but across all kinds of cultural and political boundaries."[22]

Although some might label these transitions as opportunism, I believe that instead they represent an approach which is basically pragmatic, yet which remains at its core oppositional. A man of principles, Corona is also a man of action who stresses results. He does not view this combination as contradictory. Corona answers the question of how to achieve social justice in the United States by organizing both around his own humanistic beliefs and in a pragmatic fashion based on inclusion rather than exclusion. Ideological purity is not enough. For example, as he notes, Corona warned Chicano movement activists against such ideological purity, but many refused to listen, only to find themselves isolated from most grassroots Mexican-Americans.

For Corona, ideology must be wedded to sound and effective organizing principles. His approach to organizing over the years and through different political periods has been based on including entire families—men, women, and children—and on helping them to develop their own organic leadership. Although clearly a leader, Corona has never believed himself to be indispensable. Consequently, leadership training at the grassroots has been of major importance to him. His ability and that of many others of his generation to continue *la lucha,* the struggle, over the years reveals a basic theme of continuity centered on the quest for social justice.

Despite ups and downs, this quest has persisted in Chicano history and in the histories of other American minority groups. It sets a goal that has been interpreted in different ways, one that has accommodated

---

22. Juan Flores and George Yudice, "Living Borders/Buscando America: Languages of Latino Self-Formation," *Social Text* 24 (no. 2, 1990): 71.

various political tendencies and cultural changes. Yet it remains based on a fundamental agenda shared by Mexican-Americans and other Americans, an agenda for achieving equal treatment and equal opportunity. This is a basic human goal, an American goal, and a Mexican-American goal. It has been Corona's goal.

A third theme in Corona's narrative that links memory to history concerns the multiple identities, or multiple selves, that characterize the American ethnic experience. Corona has had to confront or reconcile multiple levels of both self-identity and group identity.[23]

Corona's initial identity, as he observes, was based on growing up *mexicano,* on being a young boy of Mexican descent. Yet this sense of being *mexicano* is framed within the context of growing up in the border city of El Paso, where being *mexicano* is also shaped by the close intersections of crossing and recrossing the border. Being *mexicano* is further defined in childhood as children incorporate a sense of "otherness." As a schoolchild, Corona became aware of the disparate and hostile treatment Mexican-American children received from Anglo teachers in the segregated "Mexican schools."

For Corona, this sense of "otherness" was reinforced, but in a positive way, by the active community involvement of both his grandmother and his mother, especially among Mexican immigrant Protestants. Yet growing up Protestant, in contrast to most other Mexican-Americans, who were Catholics, provided the young Corona with still another level of identity. Although he does not recall any tensions between Protestants and Catholics in El Paso, he acknowledges that his disciplined, community-oriented, and education-oriented Protestant upbringing was influential in developing his own character and self-identity.

Ethnicity, as Werner Sollors and others propose, is not a given.[24] It is always changing and being adapted to new environments. It is invented and reinvented by different ethnic generations. Michael Fischer

23. Philippe Lejeune notes that a person is always several people not only when writing but "even all alone, even [in] his own life" (*On Autobiography* [Minneapolis: University of Minnesota Press, 1989], p. xvii). Michael Fischer adds that "assuming an ethnic identity is an insistence on a pluralist, multidimensional, or multifaceted concept of self: one can be many different things, and this personal sense can be a crucible for a wider social ethos of pluralism" ("Ethnicity," p. 196).

24. Sollors, *Beyond Ethnicity.*

observes: "Ethnicity is not something that is simply passed on from generation to generation, taught and learned; it is something dynamic, often unsuccessfully repressed or avoided."[25] In Corona's case, he moved from a sense of being a *mexicano* to recognizing that he was also a Mexican-American in the United States. As part of the Mexican-American Generation, Corona reflects the dual cultural characteristics of his more bilingual and bicultural generation.

Most Mexican-American children of this period, whose parents were immigrants and refugees, first became acquainted with English only when they entered school. Corona and his siblings, however, learned English at home before entering school, as a result of his mother's English skills. This, as Corona admits, gave him a literal head start in school and distinguished his superior academic performance from that of many other Mexican-American children.

Yet this dual cultural identity—being Mexican and being American, or what Ramón Saldívar describes as the "dialectics of difference"— does not appear to have produced in Corona a great deal of anxiety, alienation, or fragmentation.[26] Perhaps because he had already been exposed to a dual cultural existence (a "dialogue between cultures," as Ramón Gutiérrez characterizes it) within his own home, Corona appears to have been spared what has been a source of alienation for many other Mexican-Americans.[27]

It may also be that this sense of alienation, based on dual cultures, has been somewhat overstressed by scholars, particularly Chicano intellectuals. For many within Corona's generation, especially those in circumstances similar to his, acculturation or transculturation—adapting and inventing a Mexican-American tradition—may have been a somewhat positive strategy in adapting to one's position in the United States (although not without its tensions). That is, this dual identity, or dual consciousness, possesses its creative side and has provided a positive sense of self for some Mexican-Americans.

All this, of course, is not a single process. In a revealing discussion

---

25. Fischer, "Ethnicity," p. 195. See also Stuart Hall, "Ethnicity: Identity and Difference," *Radical America* 23 (October–December 1989): 9–22.

26. See Saldívar, *Chicano Narrative*, pp. 1–9.

27. Ramón A. Gutiérrez, *When Jesus Came, the Corn Mothers Went Away: Marriage, Sexuality, and Power in New Mexico, 1500–1846* (Stanford: Stanford University Press, 1991), p. xvii.

of group identity, Corona recalls his involvement in what was initially called the Mexican Youth Conference, in which the issue of ethnic labeling was paramount. This appears to have been the first time that Corona consciously faced this question. Although Corona, like the other members of this 1930s college-age group, saw himself as a Mexican in the United States who possessed American citizenship, he did not at first care for the term "Mexican-American," nor did he choose to simply call himself an American. He believed that the term "Mexican-American" was redundant because the term "American," as he understood it, encompassed all peoples of the Western Hemisphere, including Mexicans. Hence, to be a Mexican, on either side of the border, was to be an American.

Yet, having been raised to be proud of his Mexican heritage and his father's participation in the Mexican Revolution, Corona never sought to shed his identity as a *mexicano*. Consequently, in the 1930s he preferred the term *"mexicano"* or "Mexican" as a form of ethnic identity. At the same time, as his nondogmatic but principled pragmatism developed, Corona accepted the majority opinion that favored using the term "Mexican-American" for what then came to be called the Mexican American Movement.[28] He adopted and utilized the term "Mexican-American," which in essence signified what he was. In 1960, for example, Corona helped to organize the Mexican American Political Association.

Multiple identities, or multiple selves, continued to characterize Corona's later adult experiences as well. Being a male, for example, even a minority male, allowed him certain privileges and authority not available to Mexican-American women. As a man, Corona found it easier to develop as a community leader in a Mexican-American cultural environment still largely dominated by males.[29] Yet, having been raised by strong and independent-minded women who were well educated and trained as professionals (his mother was a teacher and his grandmother a physician/nurse), Corona grew up with an appreciation of female leadership. His memories, therefore, suggest an equitable relationship with female colleagues, in particular with equally strong

28. For a discussion of MAM, see Carlos Muñoz, Jr., *Youth, Identity, Power: The Chicano Movement* (London: Verso, 1989).

29. See Torres, "Construction of the Self," pp. 271–287.

community and labor leaders such as Luisa Moreno, Josefina Fierro, and Chole Alatorre. This does not mean, of course, that Corona did not continue to enjoy certain privileges and access by virtue of being a male; other Mexican-Americans, both men and women, were more inclined to accept his leadership than the leadership of a woman.

Moreover, within his own marital relationship, Corona participated in a symbiotic but at the same time uneven relationship with his wife, Blanche. Unlike Bert, who spent most of his time working as a community and political organizer, Blanche throughout most of their relationship had to be not only the more involved parent in caring for their three children but also the main breadwinner when she had to work outside the home to help sustain the Corona household. Blanche recalls that, despite Bert's progressive politics, he possessed what she refers to as a traditional Latin male perspective toward marriage and family. Blanche attributes this to the influence of Bert's grandmother, who despite her own sense of independence, believed that women belonged in the home. Blanche's ability to take care of her family clearly provided Bert with the domestic support system necessary to sustain his political work. Bert acknowledges Blanche's critical role, and both agree that in time, despite certain domestic tensions, they established a more equal relationship.[30]

Still another level of multiple identities confronted by Corona involves the relationship of class to race and ethnicity. The discourse on such a relationship in American history is expansive. Do members of racial and ethnic minority groups such as African-Americans, Mexican-Americans, and Asian-Americans identify primarily with their ethnic affiliation or with their class position? Often the suggestion is that the two are almost irreconcilable extremes. Yet, as David Montejano notes in his prize-winning history of Mexican-Americans in Texas, in reality this polarity is not always the case.[31]

As Corona describes his life, we do not find a sharp tension between his identity as a Mexican-American and his decision to join the CIO and to promote left-oriented, working-class unity. For Corona, the additional dualities of being Mexican-American and being working-

30. Blanche Corona, interview with Mario T. García, Los Angeles, July 17, 1991.

31. David Montejano, *Anglos and Mexicans in the Making of Texas, 1836–1986* (Austin: University of Texas Press, 1987).

class are in fact two sides of the same coin. Most Mexican-Americans in the United States have been part of the working class. Consequently, the movement of many Mexican-Americans such as Corona into the struggles for CIO unionization in the 1930s did not represent a major break with their history as working people. Joining the CIO was seen as furthering their interests as Mexican-American workers.

In Corona's case—and here I believe that his orientation toward leftist politics, through his connections with the Communist Party and Popular Front groups, is important—he felt comfortable organizing and working in the CIO not only with Mexican-Americans but also with workers of other ethnic backgrounds. As labor historian David Montgomery noted after reading initial drafts of Corona's narrative:

> Above all, I admire the way Corona's memories and career demolish the whole attempt of historians to argue that ethnicity was more important than class, or vice versa. His union activity dealt with workers of all nationalities: those who were on the same jobs. His work with [the National Congress of Spanish-Speaking Peoples] organized Latinos as such: those who shared language and ethnic experience. His activities mock the notion that one activity could be reduced to the other or was opposed to the other or was superior to the other. They were two basic dimensions of a single life. Corona comes through as such a believable human being.[32]

This coalition-minded approach to labor organizing and to politics in general characterizes Corona's later activities. Although working predominantly with Mexican-American organizations such as CSO, ANMA, MAPA, and the Hermandad Mexicana Nacional, Corona has never accepted a sectarian nationalist or ethnic chauvinist line. He is a nationalist to the extent that he has always been proud of being of Mexican descent, has always believed in retaining one's ethnic and cultural traditions (though in an adaptive way), and has anchored his struggle for social justice in his own community, the Mexican-American community. At the same time, his left and working-class politics have led him to synthesize his moderate nationalism with a commitment to working-class struggles and to a more democratic and egalitarian society—an American democratic socialism. Rather than being in opposition to each other, these multiple political identities have in Corona's mind been complementary.

32. David Montgomery, letter to Mario T. García, New Haven, January 18, 1990.

Indeed, Corona's own personal life displays this synthesis, most clearly in his marriage to a young Jewish-American woman in 1941. Their three children, Margo, David, and Frank, were raised in an ethnically mixed but politically united family environment. Corona's mixed marriage and his family situation do not appear to have ever been a source of profound alienation or tension for him or for his relationship with the Mexican-American community.

During the tumultuous period of the Chicano movement of the late 1960s and early 1970s, Corona identified with the goals of the movement, despite his own positioning within the Mexican-American Generation and despite his misgivings about the extreme nationalism of the movement. Corona recognized that the Chicano movement was advancing, among a new generation, the historic struggles of Mexican-Americans against injustice, including opposition to assaults on Mexican-American culture and identity. He had no problem becoming a Chicano and participating in the movement.

Where Corona can perhaps be criticized in his relationship to the Chicano movement concerns his apparent lack of understanding that one of the movement's contributions was in identifying culture as part of the arena of political contestation, as described by Antonio Gramsci, Italian political critic of the early twentieth century. Chicano activists, perhaps more so than Corona, acknowledged Gramsci's contention that before major political changes could take place in a society, the issues of cultural and ideological hegemony had to be confronted by subaltern groups.[33]

In recent years, with the addition of new terms of identity such as "Latino" and "Hispanic," Corona, ever the pragmatist, has further adapted to a post-movement generation. For example, although he calls it ludicrous to use a term such as "Hispanic" when addressing issues in the Southwest, where a predominantly Mexican-American community exists, he at the same time accepts the need for a coalition term such as "Hispanic" or "Latino" in order to recognize certain ties

---

33. On Gramsci, see John M. Cammett, *Antonio Gramsci and the Origins of Italian Communism* (Stanford: Stanford University Press, 1967); Carl Boggs, *Gramsci's Marxism* (London: Pluto Press, 1976); Jerome Karabel, "Revolutionary Contradictions: Antonio Gramsci and the Problem of Intellectuals," *Politics and Society* 6, no. 1 (1976): 123–172; and David Forgass, *An Antonio Gramsci Reader: Selected Writings, 1916–1935* (New York: Schocken Books, 1988).

between Mexican-Americans, Puerto Ricans, Cuban-Americans, and other people of Latin American extraction in the United States. It is within the interplay of all these multiple identities or selves, which transform themselves over time, that Corona has functioned and through which he has evolved.[34]

Oral History, Genesis of Study, and Methodology

American historiography has expanded considerably over the past twenty-five years. The development of ethnic studies programs and the entrance of significant numbers of students of color into Ph.D. programs have created a critical mass of historians who are exploring the history of racial minorities in the United States. The results have been a solid scholarly body of work.[35]

In recovering, re-creating, and redefining this history, one of the key sources has been oral history. Although Chicano history, for example, spans eras from the early Spanish settlements in the Southwest to the current century, most of the historiography has focused on the twentieth century, when the Mexican-American communities grew dramatically as a result of mass migration from Mexico. Consequently, historians have had access to a wide range of people from previous generations. Oral history has been particularly important because Mexican-Americans and other racial minorities in the United States have generally been poor, working people who historically have not produced a vast array of documents or other written matter. This is not to say that archival sources documenting the minority experience are not available to historians but only to suggest that such sources have been limited.

Oral tradition has been a rich cultural resource. In the Mexican-

34. As Stuart Hall notes of African-Americans (and the same can be said for Corona and Chicanos): "The end of the essential black subject also entails a recognition that the central issues of race always appear historically in articulation, in a formation with other categories and divisions, and are constantly crossed and recrossed by the categories of class, of gender, and ethnicity" ("New Ethnicities," in *Black Film/British Cinema,* ed. Kobena Mercer [London: ICA Documents, 1988], p. 28).

35. For a review of recent Chicano historiography, see, for example, Alex M. Saragoza, "Recent Chicano Historiography: An Interpretive Essay," *AZTLAN* 19 (no. 1, 1988–90): 1–78.

American communities, families and community groups reproduce family life histories, *cuentos* (stories), *corridos* (folk songs), *chistes* (jokes), *dichos* (proverbs), and other forms of oral tradition that have been told and retold over generations. Hence, oral history has helped to fill many important gaps.[36] "Oral history," Asian-American scholar Gary Okihiro recognizes, "is not only a tool or method for recovering history; it is also a theory of history which maintains that the common folk and the dispossessed have a history and that this history must be written."[37]

Although oral history has been one of many research tools used in producing a variety of studies such as community histories, scholars of the Mexican-American experience have not utilized oral history to construct autobiographical texts along the lines of the Latin American *testimonio* or the slave narratives found in the African-American historical tradition. This is unfortunate because the genre of life histories would add another rich dimension to Chicano history. It is also becoming a critical need, for many of the older generations are passing away, and now is the time to record their experiences in full autobiographical form.

For some time, I had imagined compiling a life-history narrative of Bert Corona. For me, there is something exciting about getting a personal response to history. Autobiographies represent the best of two worlds I love: history and literature. These worlds, of course, are not disconnected, and we have come to appreciate the importance of interpreting history as a literary text. In 1988, then, on a rather cool and overcast Cinco de Mayo celebration at the University of California, Santa Barbara, I broached the possibility of an oral history project with Corona, who had been invited to be the keynote speaker that day.

I have known Bert—as everyone refers to him—for some years, having first met him when we were both serving as lecturers in Chicano Studies at San Diego State University in the early 1970s. I later par-

36. See, for example, the work of Américo Paredes: *With His Pistol in His Hand: A Border Ballad and Its Hero* (Austin: University of Texas Press, 1958); and *A Texas-Mexican Cancionero: Folksongs of the Lower Border* (Urbana: University of Illinois Press, 1976).
37. Gary Okihiro, "Oral History and the Writing of Ethnic History," in *Oral History: An Interdisciplinary Anthology,* ed. David K. Dunaway and Willa K. Baum (Nashville: American Association for State and Local History, 1984), p. 206.

ticipated in some of the large marches in Los Angeles organized by Bert and the Hermandad Mexicana Nacional to protest the raids and deportations carried out by the Immigration and Naturalization Service against the growing number of undocumented Mexican immigrants who were working in southern California.

When I began teaching at the University of California, Santa Barbara, in the mid-1970s, I arranged to have Corona come and teach a course on Mexican immigration to the United States. Into the 1980s, I encountered him in other, related activities—for example, when he worked for several weeks in Santa Barbara unionizing hospital workers. I also compiled a short oral history of Corona after one of his classes at the university. In addition, in researching my book on Mexican-American leadership, I interviewed him regarding the activities of the National Congress of Spanish-Speaking Peoples.

Knowing Bert through some of these experiences, as well as having a general notion of his life history, I developed a strong admiration for him. When I saw him again at that Cinco de Mayo celebration, I almost spontaneously asked whether he would be willing to allow me to interview him for the purpose of writing his life history. Without even pausing—and, as always, willing to be helpful—Bert agreed.

Within about a month, I arranged to go to Los Angeles to begin the project. This also began the development of a special relationship between Bert and me, a relationship that had its own particular character. We began a ritual that usually involved my driving once a week to Los Angeles from Santa Barbara, often accompanied by my graduate assistant and friend Jeff Garcilazo. I came to know the route of that two-hour drive very well. We would meet Bert at his modest home in the Silver Lake district of L.A. Jeff and I would arrive around noon, frequently before Bert, who seems to work day and night, had returned from his morning activities.

Before sitting down to do the interview, Jeff and I often treated Bert to a nice lunch at a favorite and convenient restaurant. During lunch, Bert would talk about a whole range of issues, mixing contemporary issues—politics, immigration, labor—with historical references. I often thought of turning on my tape recorder at lunch, and in fact I did so on a couple of occasions in order to be sure not to lose a point Bert had made. But generally, it seemed more important to simply enjoy Bert's and Jeff's company.

Following lunch, we would return to Bert's home and begin the interview, which on the average lasted between one and two hours. It was rare for us to go beyond this limit, primarily because Bert tired after this time or had to go back to work. And, of course, Jeff and I wished to avoid the always heavy traffic out of Los Angeles.

Our interviews were as enjoyable and relaxed as our lunches. I have fond memories of sitting on Bert's couch with my notes, the tape recorder on the coffee table, Bert in his favorite chair to my right, and Jeff taking notes or just listening to my left. It is a quiet house—the sounds of our voices were only occasionally interrupted by the noise of a passing car or the sound of someone cutting their lawn with an electric lawnmower. Through all of the interviews that I conducted, some fifty-five hours in total, the interior of Bert's house never appeared to change. Everything seemed to always be in the same place, from the yellowing documents on his coffee table to the newspapers on another table near the kitchen.

I appreciated the quiet and sedate environment of the Corona home. We also enjoyed the occasional times when Blanche, Bert's wife of some fifty years, would be at home. Sometimes she joined us at lunch.

In these enjoyable surroundings, we re-created memories and history. This re-creation was not spontaneous; rather, it was organized and deliberate. Knowing the general outline of Corona's life and career, I had a sense of the different chapters I wanted to organize. Hence, each meeting was structured by a tentative outline of questions. We never rushed through anything; it would often take several weeks before we completed what would amount to one chapter.

What was remarkable about this experience was Corona's wonderful command of narration. He is a natural storyteller. Perhaps this comes partly from his childhood, when he used to hear his mother, his grandmother, and other refugees from the Mexican Revolution tell of their exploits or those of others such as Pancho Villa. Corona possesses an incredible memory, recalling minute details. He remembers remarkable and varied facts as well as anecdotes.

I had begun the project somewhat fearful that Bert might meander during the interviews, but I was pleasantly surprised at how disciplined his narrative structure remained. Corona represents a "chronicler of history through memory," to borrow José Saldívar's characterization of Ernesto Galarza.[38] Of course, I was not passive during this process. One should keep in mind that this form of oral history—referred to as *testimonio* in Latin America—is a cooperative process. It represents a joint authorship between a scholar and a grassroots activist.

Unlike anthropologist Elisabeth Burgos-Debray, who claims (perhaps too modestly) in her testimonial text *I, Rigoberta Menchú* that she was only a listener, I intervened in the narrative through my outline, questions, and follow-up inquiries.[39] I represent to a certain extent what Philippe Lejeune identifies as an "ethnobiographer." Perhaps critics, in order to fully appreciate the Corona text, will thus need to deconstruct me and my previous work as well. As Lejeune suggests of his own involvement with autobiographical texts: "I chose to work, academically, *on* autobiography, because in a parallel direction I wanted to work *on* my own autobiography" (his emphasis).[40]

Although I am much younger than Corona, my own life has some parallels with his. My maternal family came north from Mexico, from Chihuahua to the United States, fleeing the Mexican Revolution. Like Corona's family, they settled in El Paso among Mexican immigrants and political refugees. Like Corona, my mother, Alma Araiza, came of age as a Mexican-American along the border. She attended El Paso High School, as did Corona.

I particularly appreciate the El Paso connection because this border city not only is my hometown but also has served as a key research subject and site for me. Although I became a scholar and not a community leader like Corona, my research interests in the Mexican-American working class and the civil rights struggles of Mexican-Americans correspond to Corona's career involvements. In a historical sense as children of the Mexican Revolution, as products of border life, and as students of history, Bert Corona and I have been drawn together.

By acknowledging my intervention in Corona's narrative and my particular perspective on it, however, I do not mean to say that the process was rigid. As the interviews progressed, I had to be prepared

38. See Saldívar's analysis of Galarza's *Barrio Boy* in José David Saldívar, *The Dialectics of Our America: Genealogy, Cultural Critique, and Literary History* (Durham: Duke University Press, 1991), p. 140.

39. See Elisabeth Burgos-Debray's introduction to *I, Rigoberta Menchú: An Indian Woman in Guatemala* (London: Verso, 1984), p. 22.

40. Lejeune, *On Autobiography*, p. xxiv.

to flow with Corona's narrative, and sometimes it took me to places I didn't expect. "The relationship between interviewer and interviewee involves a reflexive process by which the interviewee's view of history is developed in relation to the historian's view," Okihiro observes of oral history, "while the historian's questions, in turn, are developed in response to the interviewee's answers."[41]

We proceeded in this fashion through the first summer and completed the narrative covering the period from Bert's childhood in El Paso to his experiences during World War II. Our interviews were interrupted for the next few months, when I left for a post as a visiting professor at Yale. During this time, my secretary and friend Jim Viegh, from the Chicano Studies program at UC Santa Barbara, ably transcribed the interviews. I began to go over the transcripts (documents Okihiro refers to as "conversational narratives") by myself at the same time, listening to the tapes of the interviews.[42]

In the fall of 1988, I wrote the first chapter based on the corrected transcripts. I remember the excitement of commencing that first chapter one night in a guest suite at the Yale Law School, where I spent the fall semester. I mention this only because it seemed so strange and so distant to write this narrative in New England; it made me homesick for California and anxious to resume my work with Bert.

During that academic year, I managed to write the first several chapters. Corona is such a wonderful narrator and natural storyteller that his narrative for the most part flowed. I have generally kept his language and the structure of his narrative. Occasionally, I have added or deleted certain words and even paragraphs to enhance the logic and readability of the story. I have also edited materials from different parts of the transcripts in order to maintain a logical or chronological order.

Upon returning to Santa Barbara the following summer, I renewed the interviews with Bert, again accompanied by Jeff. From June 1989 to August 1990, we worked to complete the project, or at least the interviews. Usually we met once a week, sometimes once a month. At the end of this period, we had completed approximately fifty-five hours of interviews, with several hundred pages of transcripts. Jim Viegh continued to transcribe the interviews, and I continued to correct the

41. Okihiro, "Oral History," p. 204.
42. Ibid., p. 203.

transcripts and write the narrative. During the summer of 1990 and into 1991, Carole MacKenzie in Santa Barbara finished transcribing the interviews. The final manuscript was completed in the fall of 1991.

In July of 1991, Bert read the entire manuscript, and we spent two days in Santa Barbara going over his corrections, which were minimal, mostly involving more precise dates for certain events and additional names of colleagues. I also set up a final interview to fill in particular questions that remained. It was during this time that I also interviewed Blanche Corona and was led to pose additional questions to Bert concerning his personal and family life. The final manuscript was then corrected by Carole MacKenzie.

Conclusion

Working on the life history and narrative of Bert Corona has repre-sented a rare privilege for me personally. In interviewing Bert and working with him for more than four years, I have become deeply immersed in his life story. It is a life that I very much admire. Bert Corona is many things, but above all he is an honorable and decent person who believes that social justice can prevail. I admire that, and I believe in that. Working with Bert not only has taught me much about American history, particularly about the Mexican-American experi-ence, but also has reinforced for me the importance of linking one's life and work to the common good. It is my hope, one that Bert shares, that this narrative will inspire others in the same way. We agree with Michael Fischer that "ethnic memory is thus, or ought to be, future, not past, oriented."[43]

43. Fischer, "Ethnicity," p. 201.

CHAPTER ONE

Child of the Revolution

My memories of history begin with the Mexican Revolution of 1910. My father, Noe Corona, was a child of the Revolution. This major turning point in Mexico's long history set the stage for my father's own life history, which began in Chihuahua, in the north of Mexico. Although far from the center of power in Mexico City, Chihuahua, like most of Mexico, felt the oppressive hand of Porfirio Díaz, Mexico's dictatorial president from 1877 to his overthrow in 1910—the Age of the Porfiriato.

My father joined the revolutionary forces at a very early age, possibly twelve or thirteen, because some of his relatives had been killed in the massacre that took place at Tomochic around 1892 in the mountains of Chihuahua. The people from the Sierras, the mountain people of Chihuahua, were resisting the attempts of the federal troops to take their land, destroy their fences, and steal their cattle—common violations against the Indians and the poor. And so the people of Tomochic armed themselves and, for the first time, significantly resisted and defeated the federal army that had been sent to seize the town and destroy the army of *campesinos* and cattlemen that had been formed there.

The *federales*—Díaz's troops—were unable to move up into the mountains where the people were protected, and so they resorted to deception. They manipulated a priest, who convinced the people to attend a Catholic mass of reconciliation. Believing in the sincerity of the priest, hundreds participated in the mass at Tomochic. They were surrounded by the *federales,* who set fire to the church. More than a thousand people were killed.

Following the massacre, my family, on my father's side, hid in the Copper Canyon of Chihuahua, the Barranca de Cobre. Ten times deeper and broader and fifty times longer than the Grand Canyon, it stretches all the way down to the state of Durango. Within this huge canyon, which is impossible to reach by road, lives an entire nation of Indians, the Tarahumaras. My family stayed there for five or six years, and my father learned the language of the Tarahumaras fluently. My paternal grandmother, a *mestiza,* who had married my Spanish grandfather after he arrived in Mexico in the 1850s, always insisted until she died that we were Tarahumaras.

Out of that period of oppression arose famous folk heroes. Enrique Parra, for example, was considered a bandit by the government but a Robin Hood by the people of that region. He defended their right to keep their land and their cattle, and he helped the mountain people resist the incursions and raids of the land grabbers and cattle robbers, who were Díaz's henchmen. And then, of course, there was the mythic figure of Pancho Villa, who was seen in the same light as Parra and who retrieved the people's stolen lands and cattle and avenged the political murders committed by the federal troops.*

This period of Chihuahua's history saw the people resist Díaz and his mercenaries, who were in league with U.S. capitalists. These capitalists built huge ranches by stealing property from the poor. William Randolph Hearst, for example, built an enormous estate called El Rancho de la Babicora, something like two million hectares. Hearst's *mayordomos* [managers and foremen] pushed back and sometimes murdered the indigent *campesinos* and small landowners. Hearst also built a big ranch of about a million and a half hectares up in the northern end of Chihuahua, in Palomas. Other American as well as English capitalists bought additional lands that Díaz had taken away from the original settlers.

---

*There were in fact two Pancho Villas: One was an older man who gave his name and the stature of his leadership to his young follower Doroteo Arango, who fought as Pancho Villa in the Mexican Revolution of 1910.

As a young boy, my father knew Pancho Villa—the Villa of the Mexican Revolution, Doroteo Arango—and joined his movement. By 1910 my father had also become a member of the Partido Liberal Mexicano, led by the anarcho-syndicalist Ricardo Flores Magón, as well as a member of the Junta Revolucionaria Mexicana, headed by Abraham González in Chihuahua City.

Despite the violence of the Revolution, my father was a peace-loving man who disliked military trappings. He refused, for example, to pose in uniform or with firearms. The *magonistas* themselves opposed violence even though they were anarchists. They believed instead in an intellectual approach to winning over the people.

My father considered himself more of an anarchist/populist. He worked with the syndicalist movement, but he was not a trade unionist, nor did he gravitate in that direction. He was more of an agrarianist. He was more involved with the *campesinos* and *rancheros—gente de la tierra* and *gente de la Sierra*—the peasants and ranchers, who formed the biggest part of Mexico's population. The revolutionary movement in Chihuahua was composed of small-time cattle ranchers and orchard farmers, not big hacienda owners.

My father's friends later told me that he was a good planner and manager and that he could organize the common folk. He was also strongly influenced by *villismo,* the social philosophy of Pancho Villa, which was essentially justice for the common people. I remember reading some of my father's letters in which he quoted the liberal Mexican constitution of 1857 and then observed that those same democratic ideals were being fought for in 1910.

My father believed in local autonomy and the right of the people to govern themselves through their popularly elected *cabildos* or *municipios* [city governments]. He further believed in the right of the people to arm and protect themselves against anyone who would take away their rights and property, whether it was the police, the federal army, or the American companies.

My father fought in the first battles of the Revolution. He participated in the initial conflict around San Andres, in Chihuahua, in November 1910 and in all the battles leading up to the capture of the entire railroad line that extends from Chihuahua City to Ciudad Juárez on the border. They captured every town, after fierce battles where sometimes the only people who were there to fight were just a handful of *magonistas* or other brave people against the well-established and fortified federal troops. My father had found the Revolution. He later became a colonel in Los Dorados and the División del Norte [Division of the North], commanded by Villa.

My father also represented Villa as an agent for the revolutionary forces in Juárez and El Paso around 1911, before the fall of Juárez.* He smuggled ammunition both to the revolutionary forces headed by Francisco Madero, which were gathering just outside Juárez, and to the rebels within the border city. He even convinced some of the *federales* to support the Revolution by dismantling their cannons. Because of his activity in El Paso, American officials arrested my father for violating the U.S. neutrality laws. He served about two months in the El Paso county jail.

After the overthrow of Díaz and the election of Madero as president in 1911, General Victoriano Huerta led a counterrevolution that overthrew and assassinated Madero in 1913. My father participated in the struggle led by Villa first against Huerta and then against Venustiano Carranza and Alvaro Obregón, who were seen by the *villistas* as betrayers of the Revolution and of the poor and oppressed.† After Villa's defeats in Celaya, Silao, and Leon in the north, my father, who had been wounded in battle, crossed the border to El Paso, around 1915 or 1916. At that time, he married my mother.

My Mother and My Grandmother

Like my father's, my mother's early history is also set in Mexico's revolutionary years. Her maiden name was Margarita Escápite Salayandía. She became a schoolteacher after being educated at La Filomática and at El Colegio Chihuahuense, both of which were part of a bilingual school system organized by American Congregational teachers, missionaries, and ministers who had come to Chihuahua from Wellesley and Harvard. Americans such as Dr. Howard Eaton and the Misses Hammond, Scott, and Smith had founded the schools.

*The Battle of Juárez took place in early May of 1911. The defeat of Díaz's forces in this strategic border town caused Díaz to flee Mexico and helped to bring Francisco Madero to power.

†Victoriano Huerta ruled Mexico from 1913 to 1914, when he was overthrown. Venustiano Carranza ruled from 1914 until 1920, when he was assassinated. Alvaro Obregón, who overthrew Carranza, was president of Mexico from 1920 to 1924.

My maternal grandmother, Ynes Salayandía de Escápite, had been converted by these often very wealthy missionaries when they were working in Parral, to the south of Chihuahua City. My grandmother, unlike most Mexicans, was not raised a Catholic. She attended the first nonreligious private school in Chihuahua in the 1870s. This girls' school was opened by her aunt, who had been educated in Europe. Her aunt's husband was accused of being a Mason and a heretic, but the girls' school was acknowledged as being very good.

My grandmother went to her aunt's school through the grammar grades and graduated with some ideas that were very new at that time, that women could do other things with their lives besides being wives and mothers. She did not share the passive resignation of many Mexican women.

My grandmother's family was part of the silver-mining aristocracy of Chihuahua. Although she married a highly respected rancher when she was still very young, she did not like being a wife or living on the ranch. Being more or less a freethinker, she left her husband and came to Chihuahua City with my mother. She put her child in this modern Protestant school, where my mother became a very dedicated student.

My mother attended La Filomática from the first grade through normal school and then studied at the Colegio Chihuahuense, where she learned to be a teacher. She first taught in the mountains of Chihuahua, after which she returned to the city and taught in the elementary school, in the high school, and finally in the teachers' college, where she became vice-director.

About this time, around 1911, my father was commanding a regiment that was attempting to seal off Chihuahua City in preparation for an attack by Villa's forces. His mission was to block Díaz's reinforcement troops. During this siege, he first encountered my mother and her family.

My grandmother by then was a medical doctor. She had graduated with the first class of Mexican women to be trained as nurses and medical practitioners, although they could not become surgeons and were restricted to working as nurses and midwives.

She was working in a Chihuahua City sanatorium with three German doctors and two other Mexican doctors when the revolutionary forces opened up the assault on the city. My grandmother boarded the last train out, along with the other doctors and refugees who were fleeing the city.

My father captured the train outside Chihuahua in order to get medical attention for his wounded and dying men. My grandmother and the other doctors tended to the men who needed attention, and my father was very grateful. He promised that he would look her up when he got to Juárez, which was by then under the control of the revolutionary forces.

After the rebels captured Chihuahua, my father made a trip to Juárez and sought out my grandmother. She had set up a clinic and a small sanatorium with Dr. Wenceslao Olvera, and my father offered to help her. At this time, he met my mother, and a courtship followed, with the approval of my grandmother. Although my grandmother did not support the Revolution as strongly as my mother did, she thought my father was a wonderful person and liked and respected him very much.

My father and mother were engaged throughout the remaining time he fought in the Revolution. Before the defeat of the División del Norte, my parents were married in both Juárez and El Paso. Pancho Villa was my father's *padrino* [best man].

My parents were married in El Paso in the Methodist church by the Reverend López, the father of Ignacio López, who later and for many years edited the newspaper *El Espectador* in the Pomona Valley of southern California. They also had a civil marriage in Juárez at the customs house. It served on occasion as a ballroom and a reception room for the revolutionary army occupying Juárez, and it was there that they gave their wedding party.

El Paso

My parents settled in El Paso. I was their second child, born May 29, 1918. My older sister, Aurora, was born in 1917, my brother Orlando in 1919, and Horacio in 1921. We were all born in El Paso at home. Since my grandmother was a doctor and a midwife, she delivered each one of us.

Our first home was located in East El Paso, one of several Mexican barrios in the city. The largest one, El Segundo Barrio [the Second Ward]—or El Pugido [the Grunt], as it was also called—was downtown. Every available room and every available structure was occupied by immigrants and refugees fleeing the Mexican Revolution. We lived on Frutas Street in East El Paso, in an area where a lot of homes were built for the new immigrants who were coming out of Mexico.

Our house was not a brick tenement of the kind found in El Segundo Barrio, but rather a one-family unit. There were some tenements in East El Paso, but they were not the same as the *presidios* [tenements] that existed in El Segundo Barrio. The *presidios* were built to take care of the *enganchados,* laborers who were contracted in Mexico by the Great Western Sugar Beet Company and the Union Sugar Beet Company— the big sugar beet companies in the Midwest—and by the American railroads, who would bring the workers to the border and outfit them. The *enganchados* were housed in two-room apartments and taken care of by commissary companies that had their warehouses on Kansas, Oregon, and El Paso streets in El Segundo Barrio.

As more immigrants arrived, they found newer and better housing, and the *presidios* were occupied by permanent residents. My great-aunt, who worked for Villa's forces during the Revolution, lived in one of the *presidios*. They were good, safe places to live during the revolutionary period because they were in the middle of an all-*mexicano* area that could effectively be sealed off. The buildings themselves were like penitentiary blockhouses.

There were also other kinds of tenements from the previous century that were called *vecindades*. These were stripped houses made of adobe and were located on the streets below Second and Third streets in South El Paso, which ran all the way down to the river. These and the *presidios* housed those Mexicans who would come to El Paso only if their families could join them.

Most preferred the *presidios,* where each family could have two rooms with an outdoor toilet at the end of the row of rooms. Some of the *presidios* were three stories high and some two stories. This was very desirable housing because the buildings were made of brick and, since they were off the ground, could not be flooded.

Living communally, the people helped each other when someone became sick, and they alerted and hid those sought by the police. The Mexicans used their great numbers as a shield. Many revolutionary refugees liked to live there for the protection. Pancho Villa, for example, at one point stayed with my great-aunt in her *presidio* apartment, and no one except a few of the people around knew that he was Pancho Villa.

Other *villistas* occupied key places in those *presidios* for several years. I remember that when I was a youngster famous *villista* generals still lived in the *presidios*. They liked to live together because they knew that other families would alert them if the police or their enemies in Mexico attempted to arrest or even to assassinate them.

In El Paso, my father sustained his family by pursuing the trade he had learned as a young boy. In the mountains of Chihuahua, he had learned about logging and had worked for the Pearson Lumber Company, an American firm with a box factory in El Paso. Pearson harvested timber in Chihuahua under a partnership with the Madero family. My father learned to set up a complete sawmill. Later, when he was not working with the revolutionary groups, he earned his living this way.

He also learned how to extract and bring down rock. Those mountains have a lot of granite—*cantera*—and some of the finest construction-grade granite mines are in Chihuahua. That's why in Chihuahua City both the cathedral and the Teatro de los Héroes [Theater of the Heroes] are built of granite. My father helped to build the *teatro*. He cut and hauled stone for that structure. In El Paso, my father hauled rock from Mount Franklin, which overlooks the city, and he helped to construct Fort Bliss, the federal military base in El Paso, as well as the embankments on the Rio Grande. He was a contractor of building materials.

Return to Mexico

However, despite my father's job in El Paso and his young family, he—like most other Mexican immigrants and refugees at the time—still hungered to return to *la patria,* to his homeland Mexico. In 1921, he petitioned to be granted amnesty by the Obregón government so that he could return to Mexico.

My father distrusted and disliked Obregón. He especially did not care for Obregón caving in to U.S. pressures and conceding to American business interests. Still, my father wanted to return.

His petition, along with many others submitted by *villistas* in the U.S., was granted, and he convinced my mother and grandmother to return to Chihuahua. We returned sometime in 1922 and for a time lived right behind Pancho Villa's house, which is still standing today. Señora Villa resided there for many years.

I liked Chihuahua City. We lived on the outskirts of the city, and there were *caballerizas* [horse ranches], barns, and cattle yards. Although my father had a car, he still traveled on horseback. He raised horses, and we had several. One time in El Paso, right after World War I, he bought three hundred horses from the U.S. Army. They were called remounts, and he got them for five dollars a head. He sent those horses with his brother to Chihuahua on the hoof—that is, herded—about two hundred twenty miles.

Living in these surroundings in Chihuahua was a pleasant experience. Everywhere we went, we went on horseback. If you wanted to go to the grocery store, you got up on the horse rather than riding a buggy or driving an automobile.

After several months in Chihuahua, my father was asked by Adolfo de la Huerta,* a friend of Pancho Villa, to transport a trainload of farm implements to Villa and his troops, who at that time were occupying a big hacienda called Canutillo in northern Durango state. My father agreed and, after delivering the implements, stayed a month with Villa.

I'm not sure what they discussed, but it was decided shortly thereafter that my father and some of his friends from Chihuahua would move to Mexico City and apply for federal jobs. This, I suppose, was Villa's way of infiltrating the government in the hope of still gaining power.

My father and the other *villistas* secured jobs as forest rangers. They surveyed El Desierto de los Leones [Desert of the Lions] and then were quartered at the Hacienda Chapingo to survey and stake out the Bosque de Texcoco [Forest of Texcoco] as well as other wooded areas in the federal district around Mexico City. Besides preserving trees and cutting older growth, my father and his men located sites for both sawmills and forest preservation. They did this for several months. My father was a staunch conservationist and understood the value of preserving Mexico's natural resources.

On one of their forest expeditions, a fire was spotted, and while they were attempting to put it out, my father and his men were assassinated—shot in the back by unknown assailants. We believed the assassins were agents of President Obregón, who feared that the *villistas* were planning to reorganize and overthrow the government. We later heard from friends that this had indeed been Villa's goal. My

---

*Adolfo de la Huerta, who was from Sonora, served for a brief period as interim president of Mexico in 1920, after the assassination of Carranza. De la Huerta had been part of the effort to overthrow Carranza.

father was killed in 1924, the year after Pancho Villa himself was assassinated.

Memories of the Revolution

When my father left to work in the federal district, my mother and my grandmother brought us back to El Paso. There we received news of my father's death.

The memories of my father and of the Mexican Revolution had a strong influence on me and my own later political and social views. The Revolution, my father's role in it, and his martyrdom symbolized the struggle for social justice. This would be the same struggle I would later pursue.

These memories of my father and of the Revolution were kept alive in my family by the stories told to us by both my mother and my grandmother. My mother, especially, would tell us about our father's commitment to the Revolution. While my grandmother had differences with the Revolution, still she admired the dedication and selflessness exhibited by many of the revolutionaries. After the assassination of Pancho Villa, for example, my grandmother, who had known Villa, told us that he was a good man and not a thief or a killer or a *bandido*.

Memories of my father and of the Revolution were also transmitted to us through other sources. Many of our Protestant ministers in El Paso had supported the Revolution; some were *magonistas*. They had opposed the Catholic church at a time when the church was very reactionary.

Many friends of the family likewise visited and recalled episodes of the Revolution. One *compadre* and good friend, José Tapia, who became an important railroad official and mayor of Chihuahua City after the Revolution, visited us often in El Paso and dined with us. He had been an intimate friend of my father and of Pancho Villa. My father and he had early on joined Villa's forces in the mountains of Chihuahua. Other friends in El Paso and Juárez also remembered their involvement with the Revolution.

After we returned to El Paso, we moved into El Segundo Barrio on Ochoa Street between Second and Third streets, where we lived for about two years. Our home was not one of the tenement buildings, but a double bungalow that served as a duplex. Each bungalow had its own door, and rooms, and a toilet. The toilets were back to back, so you could hear the other user's water running. The two units shared a common backyard.

For a time, my grandmother rented the unit next to us, which served as her medical clinic. Later, after one of my aunts moved to El Paso, her son, Dr. José Perches, opened up a separate sanatorium on Oregon Street, where he and my grandmother treated patients. My aunt then lived in the adjacent duplex.

With my father gone, my mother, who had not worked in Chihuahua during our return, resumed her teaching profession to help provide for the family. She taught English in both the Juárez and El Paso schools. In Juárez, she instructed students first in the public schools and later in two private schools. In El Paso, she worked for the School Adult Program and taught English to Mexican immigrants in the barrio. Later she instructed students at the Houchen Methodist Settlement House.

In 1926 she got a job at the Mexican customs house in Juárez, where she worked until about 1945. She had the honor of becoming the first female director of a customs house in Mexico. Unlike most customs directors on the border, who were corrupt and took bribes, especially from American companies doing business in Mexico, my mother was thoroughly honest. She hated the smell of American exploitation and rebuffed any effort to corrupt her.

Since I barely got to know my father, the key parental influences on my life came from my grandmother and my mother. My grandmother in many respects filled the seat vacated by my father. She was the ultimate authority in the family and a real matriarch. In some ways I'm like my grandmother, but I also have some of my mother in me. I get some of my discipline and drive from my grandmother. My mother was a friendlier and warmer person than my grandmother, and more forgiving. From both of them I received a sense of right and wrong and a sense of duty about helping others, especially those suffering injustices.

I think that being raised by women of the caliber of my grandmother and my mother helped in my later social and political relations with women. Both my grandmother and my mother possessed what would later be considered feminist ideas. Because of them, we rejected what was thought of as macho behavior for men. My grandmother, for example, never accepted the idea that women had to forgo education simply because they got married.

Although I was not devoid of certain traditional attitudes toward women, including my own wife later on, still I think that I came to have a greater appreciation for women's rights because of my family's sense of independence regarding women. It helped in my later relationships with strong female leaders such as Luisa Moreno and Josefina Fierro. I never saw such women as a threat.

Another factor here was that my grandmother and my mother belonged to the Protestant community of El Paso, which allowed Mexican women more authority and independence than the Catholic church did. I noticed years later that some of the stronger Mexican-American female leaders I worked with had Protestant backgrounds.

Although we lived in better conditions than other Mexican immigrants and refugees, we were in close proximity to the big *presidios.* Because of this, I really got to know how the barrio operated. I especially recall the excitement during the Prohibition years in the twenties when it was a common sight to see chases through El Segundo Barrio as federal prohibition officers chased *contrabandistas,* Mexican bootleggers. Every night there would be running gun battles and police raids on homes in search of liquor. Bootlegging was a big business in the barrio, and much border folklore accompanied this activity. Every time I hear the *corrido* [folksong] "El Contrabando de El Paso," I'm reminded of those years.

It was also a time when El Segundo Barrio became partly converted into a refugee colony, as many continued to flee Mexico because of political and religious persecution. Besides El Segundo, there was another refugee colony in Sunset Heights, in the western part of El Paso, where many of the rich ex-*porfiristas* settled. They had their own church, schools, and cultural life there.

My aunt, who had moved in with us, left for Sunset Heights as soon as her son's clinic began to make some money. She disliked living in El Segundo. She had been on the opposite side of the Revolution from my mother and father. I don't know how she and her son got along with my mother, but they did. I guess family love is thicker than water. Both sides of the family continued to assist each other and to retain family ties and loyalties.

But the real center of refugee activity remained in El Segundo. It hosted a number of key individuals such as Mariano Azuela, who in 1915 wrote *Los de Abajo* [The Underdogs], one of the major novels of the Mexican Revolution.* Rodolfo Uranga and Dr. Alberto Rembao, who wrote for Mexican newspapers in the United States such as *La Prensa* of San Antonio and *La Opinión* of Los Angeles, also lived for a time in El Segundo.

Many ex-generals, many of them *villistas*, found refuge in the barrio. They would often get together and retell stories of the Revolution—how they had fought the battle of El Cerro de La Bufa or the battle of Tierra Blanca and how they had witnessed the exploits of Pancho Villa.

I heard some of these stories as a kid, and I particularly remember the one about how Pancho Villa killed a traitor. It seems there was this General Tomás Ornelas, who had commanded Villa's troops in Juárez. This was at the same time that my father was commander of one of the garrisons in Juárez. Rumors abounded that the U.S. was going to allow Carranza to move troops against Villa through El Paso. Believing that such an attack was imminent, Ornelas defected to the *carrancistas*. A year or so later, Villa captured a train near Ojinaga on the Mexican side of the Texas border and discovered Ornelas on the train.

As one of these ex-*villista* generals told the story, Villa, upon encountering Ornelas, exclaimed, *"¡Mira nomás que sorpresa verte. Que bien vestido vienes!"* [What a surprise! How well you look!]

To which Ornelas replied, *"Sí general, pues sí he estado bien. ¿y Ud., como ha estado?"* [Yes, General, I have been fine. And how have you been?]

"Bien, bien, compadre, nomás que lo hemos echado de menos. ¿Pero ha estado bien Ud?" [Fine, *compadre*, except that we have missed you. But you have been okay?] inquired Villa.

Ornelas responded, *"Sí, sí estoy muy bien."* [Yes, I am just fine.]

Villa then says, *"Pero mire nomás qué bien ajuariado estás, a ver voltéase para verlo. Mire qué bien vestido está."* [But just look how well dressed you are. Just turn around and let me see you.]

So Villa turns Ornelas around, and in a flash he pulls out his gun and shoots him, declaring, *"Así se matan a traidores como Ud., por la espalda."* [That's the way traitors like you are shot, in the back.]

The fact that these refugees were living side by side with the Mexican

*Mariano Azuela (1873–1952) is considered the major writer of the Mexican Revolution. Azuela's work began a new age for the Mexican novel, characterized by an emphasis on Mexican social themes and writing that reflected the colloquial language of the Mexican masses.

immigrant workers had quite an effect on the consciousness of the workers. The *obreros*—the immigrant workers—learned what the Revolution had been all about through an episodic richness that was hard to replace. Through the refugees, they learned tales of valor, of weakness, of cowardice, and of sacrifice.

This lore added immensely to the lives and culture of the workers. Of course, they had their own lore about working and living in the United States. But the stories of the Revolution they heard the refugees recount in El Paso only added to their sense of social justice. It encouraged them to fight for their rights.

One of the most popular stories retold by members of Villa's raiding party into Columbus, New Mexico, in 1916* was of how yellow the Americans had been, of how they had begged for their lives, how they had shit and pissed in their pants, crying, *"No me mates, no me mates, yo soy amigo de los mejicanos."* [Don't kill me, don't kill me, I'm a friend of Mexicans.]

Stories such as this one were told and retold over and over again. It must have had an impact on the minds of the immigrant workers on the railroads, those who went to Chicago to work in the stockyards or in the beet fields and cotton fields, different places where Mexicans were working. Such stories had the effect of linking folk ideology to struggles for social justice.

Family and Religious Influences

Besides the stories of the Revolution told by the *villista* generals, our social and cultural life revolved around family-related activities. My family was close-knit. We had three aunts in Juárez who were cousins of my mother. We often visited them along with some of my grandmother's and my mother's close friends who also lived in Juárez. We spent much time in Juárez. I remember going over there every day to visit my mother at work, to visit friends, and to do shopping. It cost

*Villa's raid on Columbus, New Mexico, occurred on March 9, 1916, in retaliation for the U.S. recognition of Carranza as the legitimate authority in Mexico. Villa's raid in turn provoked an American military intervention headed by General John J. Pershing, who crossed the border in search of Villa. After several months of frustrated searching, Pershing's troops left Mexico on the eve of America's entry into World War I.

only five cents to go across the border by streetcar and only two cents if you walked. Living in El Paso, we lived a kind of dual but related border existence.

Our family's social culture expanded through my grandmother's and my mother's associations with other Mexican Protestants. Besides their own relatives, my grandmother and my mother had all of these spiritual brothers and sisters through the various congregations they participated in. My grandmother and my mother had started as Congregationalists, but in El Paso they became ecumenical. They attended other Protestant churches such as the Presbyterian, Methodist, or Baptist. They had many friends—friends in the faith, as they called them.

Another form of social life involved the alumnae associations of the Congregational school my mother had attended in Chihuahua. Since she had taught in that school, my mother knew a lot of the families. Many of them, like her, had fled Mexico and come to El Paso and other places in the United States. These graduates of the Congregational La Filomática and El Colegio Chihuahuense then formed alumnae groups in places such as El Paso and Los Angeles. They kept in touch with one another and often met socially.

Also important were the Conferencias Hispanas formed by the various Protestant churches. There was in particular a Conferencia Hispana Feminil, composed of women members of the different Mexican Protestant churches. They raised funds for the churches and for the schools sponsored by the churches. They held conferences in El Paso, Los Angeles, San Antonio, and other places, where more social contacts were made.

My grandmother and my mother participated in these *conferencias*. Later, when I moved from El Paso to Los Angeles, I recall being warmly received by many members of these religious associations who knew my grandmother and my mother.

Religion, specifically Protestantism, was also very significant in my socialization and in influencing my own later political activity. It is important to understand just how religion played a role in my family's life. In their own upbringing, both my grandmother and my mother had been exposed to liberal Protestant social thought through American missionaries in Mexico, especially Congregationalists from Wellesley and Harvard and Methodists from Princeton. They were attracted to Protestantism because of its more liberating views, especially concerning women, in comparison to the Catholic church. Neither of them supported the more fundamentalist forms of Protestantism, including such things as a literal interpretation of the Bible.

I remember once asking my grandmother how in the world Jesus Christ had taken seven loaves of bread and seven fishes and with them fed the multitude. How did he do it? Did he have a knife and cut them into little pieces?

"Oh, no," she responded, "that's just figurative. That's just an expression. The lesson here is that those with more should help those with less."

My grandmother had a terrible time with the Baptist ministers. They wouldn't let her get up in Sunday School classes to explain the parables. Unlike the fundamentalists, my grandmother believed that Christ intended for each one of us to interpret his words. She couldn't swallow the evangelicals and fundamentalists. She thought that they were crazy, backward people. She was more inclined to be a Universalist, Unitarian, or Congregationalist. My mother was the same way.

My family didn't require us to read the Bible, but we did so in Sunday School. I appreciated those principles from the Bible and from my church experience that centered on the social doctrine, which implied that religious beliefs, to have any real meaning, had to be applied to social relationships. This meant engaging in social and political struggles.

I also appreciated the historical foundations of Protestantism from the 1600s and 1700s, when the first Protestants took on the whole question of the divine right of kings. They rebelled and struggled for freedom. We learned these things in Sunday School, and my family reinforced them. In a sense, I'm a product of the Protestant Reformation.

I attended church until I went into the military during World War II. I stopped going to church regularly after the war. My stopping had little, if anything, to do with religion per se. What I all along had gotten from the Protestant churches was not theology but the practice of social doctrine. That I never abandoned. Although I later considered myself an agnostic, I have continued to go to various churches in the Mexican-American communities, including Catholic ones, in order to help organize our people, many of whom still attend church regularly.

Besides family and religious events, my family also took my sister and brothers and me to other Spanish-speaking cultural activities. Our favorite place was the Colón Theater, which presented vaudeville and traveling theatrical groups and performers such as Virginia Fabregas, who was famous all over Mexico and the Southwest. I remember seeing *The Merry Widow* and *The Chocolate Soldier* in Spanish at the Colón.

Mexican impresarios organized still other Spanish-language festivities in the larger Liberty Hall in downtown El Paso. They brought legendary opera singers such as Caruso, Tito Schipa, Angela Peralta, Adelina Patti, and others, but I wasn't old enough to attend. El Paso was considered part of the Mexican tour of many of these artists because it had such a big Spanish-speaking community.

CHAPTER TWO

Border Education

I started school in the barrio, in the pre-kindergarten of the Houchen Methodist Settlement House. After one semester, I transferred to El Divino Salvador, the Mexican Presbyterian church on Fourth and Ochoa, also in El Segundo Barrio. These were sort of "headstart" programs. Later my mother enrolled me in the regular public kindergarten at the Alamo School.

Since my mother spoke fluent English, we also learned how to speak it, as well as read and write it, at a very early age. For that reason, I didn't have many problems when I went to Alamo. I didn't encounter the kind of harassment faced by the children who spoke mostly Spanish. In fact, the teachers gave awards to my brothers and sister and me because we could speak and write English so well. Mother taught us at home, so we were always ahead of our classes, and that made it very easy for us to stand out and excel.

My initial school experience was very different from that of the Mexican kids who weren't so lucky, who were never taught English before school. Teachers would spank them and wash their mouths with soap if they spoke Spanish in the classrooms or halls and on the playground. Of course, the parents resented their children being treated this way and complained to the school authorities; some even kept their kids at home.

The school district responded not by changing the schools but by assigning truant officers to the barrio to catch the kids who were being kept home. The truant officers roamed the streets in their little cars, which were called *flivers,* hunting for the missing kids. There was one officer who was especially feared and hated by all the children. He prowled around the alleys, the *presidios,* and the backyards, over the banks of the canal, and all along the river, hoping to catch some poor little kid who was afraid to go to school because he'd get whipped for speaking Spanish.

Even though my brothers and sister and I were spared, my mother resented these actions as much as if they had happened to her own children. As a teacher herself, educated by North American standards, she knew what a good education was; and she knew that we just weren't getting it. She abhorred the atmosphere and reluctantly sent us away to school to escape the racism and discrimination.

Harwood Boys School

I was sent to the Harwood Boys School in Albuquerque, where I spent two years, in the fourth and fifth grades. A boarding school for boys operated in conjunction with a girls' school, it went from the second grade to high school. Because I had never been away from home, it was a challenging time for me, and I had to mature quickly to get by.

We lived in dormitories, where I learned to keep my belongings organized and protected. A whistle woke us up early every morning, and we got dressed, made our beds, and rushed outside to do calisthenics. We then changed into our work clothes and carried out our assigned chores. Like a prison or a monastery, the school operated a truck farm and a dairy, where we worked part of every day except Sunday. We all had important responsibilities, and this taught me discipline and independence at an early age.

Despite the many good and healthy things about the Harwood School, we still did not escape racism on the part of the teachers. The overwhelming majority of the students were Mexicans, either from the Southwest or from Mexico. During my second year, a crisis developed, touched off by the violent behavior of a coach whose job it was to discipline students who talked back to their teachers.

Talking back was a daily occurrence. It wasn't that the students were troublemakers; rather, they could not let some of the teachers' statements about Mexican and U.S. history and culture pass unchallenged. The most outspoken students were the brightest, and they were better acquainted with the facts surrounding the issues than the instructors were.

These students insisted that Mexico had not simply given away its lands in the Southwest, but that this territory had been stolen by the United States. They also vehemently defended the Mexican Revolution and argued that Pancho Villa was not a bandit, as he was being portrayed, but a soldier and a hero to his people. They defended a history and a culture that they honored and were proud of.

This, however, provoked the Anglo teachers who, despite good intentions, harbored their own versions of the "white man's burden" and the racist feelings and beliefs that went along with it. It got to the point where some of the older students who were physically assaulted by the coach fought back, and blows were struck.

We complained to the Mexican pastor at the church where we went every Sunday in Albuquerque, but he couldn't help us. The situation came to a boiling point when some of the more outspoken students were threatened with expulsion.

We responded to this threat and called a meeting during the night, where we planned a strike. We organized the entire student body. In the morning at roll call, we just sat down and refused to go to class. We didn't budge for the entire day.

Not surprisingly, the administration was stunned and at a loss for what to do. They feared that the newspapers would get wind of what was going on and that there would be a scandal. Because of this, they backed down, and we won our demands: The expulsions were rescinded, and the coach was forced to apologize and to stop attacking the students for speaking their opinions. This was my first strike!

The problems at the Harwood School, however, convinced my mother that we might as well return to El Paso, since this kind of discrimination could occur anywhere. She enrolled us in the San Jacinto School, which was on the northern outskirts of the barrio.

I was supposed to be in the sixth grade by now, but the teachers felt I was too advanced for that grade, and so I was double-promoted to the seventh, even though I was only ten years old. When I turned eleven, I could have gone directly into high school, but my teachers felt it might be better for me to repeat the seventh grade since I was so small. It made no sense for me to repeat the seventh grade at San Jacinto, so my mother enrolled me at the Bowie School, which had both a junior and a senior high school.

The "Mexican Schools"

Bowie was a "Mexican school" located in the barrio. Bowie Junior High was largely a vocational school, where students took shop and other similar classes that were designed to prepare them for semiskilled jobs. It practically took an act of Congress for any of these youngsters to be able to go to El Paso High School or Austin High School, the regular and academically oriented schools in the northern part of El Paso.

It was my good fortune that the year I attended Bowie, in 1929, it became an academic as well as a vocational institution. This was a period of tremendous change. Many of the Mexican parents had insisted that their children receive the same academic training as the Anglos. A great power struggle ensued, and some of the most racist teachers were forced to leave Bowie. Eventually, the academic movement won over the vocational status quo, and Bowie became a more academic school.

In all, I did very well in my early school years. I succeeded because of my unique and fortuitous background. Besides the tutoring I received from my mother, I also benefited from a Protestant heritage that encouraged education. At least a half dozen Protestant churches served the barrio, and every one of them had a type of "headstart" preschool that operated throughout the year. There was even a bilingual Protestant elementary and high school in El Segundo Barrio, the Lydia Patterson Institute, which was administered by the Methodists. Its alumni did very well when they went on to the public high schools. It was generally understood that Mexican youngsters who had these advantages did better in school.

Many other Mexican children didn't succeed because they were poor and also victims of racism. Kids were simply sent home from school on some occasions; at other times, they were beaten by the teachers. Some of the teachers shifted the responsibility for these shameful actions by turning the students over either to truant officers to be whipped or to the physical education instructors, who were only too happy to give them a few belts.

When the teachers administered the punishment, they would take out a rod the length of a yardstick and whip the children's open hands or their rear ends. On one occasion, my grandmother, who was standing on our porch directly across from the San Jacinto schoolyard, saw a teacher strike a Mexican child for throwing rocks. She marched straight up to the teacher and publicly bawled him out for his behavior.

Another type of racism that was prevalent in the Mexican schools was the curriculum itself. Parents often complained that the presentation of the Mexican side of the U.S.–Mexican War of the 1840s was not an honest one, that blatant racism was expressed in the classrooms every day. The curriculum was not enriching; it was bare bones.

Although there was no formal tracking, in fact the schools did divide the pupils. Teachers subjectively chose certain students whom they recommended for high school and ignored the rest. Interestingly, those Mexican students selected to go on to high school, especially to the mostly Anglo El Paso High School, for the most part had parents who were either clerical employees, in business, or professionals. They usually came from families whose complexions were lighter than those of most other Mexicans. I remember that in some families whose children were dark-complected, the parent who was lighter than the children would go to the school to protest that the children were being shunted aside to vocational school or to Bowie High in the barrio rather than to El Paso High with the Anglos and a few chosen Mexicans.

But as far as the majority of Mexican students were concerned, the teachers didn't give a damn. This helps to explain why prior to 1940 so few Mexican youngsters, including those at El Paso High, ever went to college. They simply were not encouraged or even allowed to go.

Another example of racism had to do with the physical conditions in the Mexican schools. Most were severely overcrowded, especially in the first, second, and third grades. Unlike the Anglo schools, where the playgrounds were well-kept lawns, the Mexican schools had playgrounds that were covered with gravel and left untended. Indoors, the classrooms were cold in winter and stifling hot in the summer.

Many students simply didn't make it and dropped out. The dropout rate was phenomenal, especially by the third grade, and little effort was made to retrieve these students. There were no remedial classes for the children who spoke no English.

Some of the better-off families took their children out of public schools altogether and sent them to Mexico. Others sent their kids to other Texas cities such as Austin or Brownsville, where they thought there might be a more enlightened school system and less discrimination. Some sent their children to Los Angeles or Chicago, where they had relatives.

Many parents, on the other hand, refused to accept such discriminatory school conditions and organized to protest. A lot of friction existed between the school authorities and the Mexicans who lived in the *presidios*. In some instances, older Mexican youngsters or parents fought back physically against the truant officers. Of course, some of the parents, like my mother, were educated political refugees who knew what a good education should be, and they became community activists.

Not all the teachers were racists. Some were outstanding and were highly regarded by the Mexicans, and especially by the Mexican middle class, but these were few in number. You could perhaps find one or two in each school. They were not representative of the majority of teachers, who didn't care and who consistently failed the Mexican children in their classrooms. After two or three failures of this kind, there was no interest in keeping the children in the school system. By then, they were too old for their grade level and would be kicked out.

El Paso High School

From my grandmother and my mother, I and my brothers and sister got the idea that it was important to get an education and to prepare yourself to make an honest living. As part of this orientation, they influenced us to choose our friends carefully. Both my grandmother and my mother were very careful in this regard. They rejected relationships with those whom they considered to be morally corrupt. This included not only poor people engaged in crime but wealthy ones as well. This left a big impression on me. We chose our friends not because they were of a certain social class but because of the way they conducted themselves and how they treated others.

In 1930, at the very young age of twelve, I became one of those fortunate Mexicans who attended El Paso High School. I entered high school at this age as a result of the acceleration I had been given in my earlier school years. I had been recommended by my teachers, and, in addition, we lived just inside the district limit reserved for El Paso High.

Unlike the Mexican schools south of the tracks, El Paso High was becoming integrated. About one-third of the student body was *mexicano*. These were not the children of the poor immigrant families but instead were youngsters from the more well-to-do Mexican families whose parents were white-collar workers or skilled mechanics in the railroad yards—in general, those *mexicanos* who had better jobs and who had moved north of the railroad tracks and lived in a new Mexican buffer area. My family lived here. Also, many children of prominent Juárez families attended this school. We did not constitute the majority at El Paso High, but there were a lot of Mexicans at the school.

While the education at the high school was good, we still found racism toward *mexicanos*. I had teachers who would tell us: "You people will never make it because you're Mexican."

I remember the case of two brothers, the Prado brothers, who were outstanding students. Miguel graduated with an average of 96.5; Enrique had a 98 and won a Rhodes scholarship. But because that scholarship had a clause stating that only candidates who furthered the advance of Anglo-Saxon values were eligible, Enrique was disqualified. There were many other excellent Mexican students and athletes, including those from Juárez who had dual-citizen status.

I attended El Paso High as a transition was taking place. Mexicans of the middle class were beginning to attend high school in larger numbers and were excelling in academics and in sports. Some of the instructors resented this change. Some tried very hard to discourage us by giving us low grades whenever possible. Some *mexicanos* did fail, but many didn't. For the ones who succeeded, it was always an uphill battle.

I succeeded in high school not so much because of my teachers but because of my mother and my grandmother. They encouraged my brothers and sister and I to take strictly academic courses and not the more vocationally oriented curriculum. I took four years of math, four years of English, four years of science, and four years of language—the so-called sixteen solid courses.

In high school, I enjoyed trigonometry and solid geometry as well as chemistry and physics, and I did well in these classes. My interest in these subjects was partly a result of my mother's influence. In Mexico, she had taught logarithms and trigonometry, and she had brought some of her texts to El Paso. She tutored students at our home in these subjects, and so I knew a lot of this terminology even before I got to high school. My grandmother's medical practice also influenced me toward scientific topics. Besides these subjects, I enjoyed reading history. I can't say that there was any subject I didn't like.

The history taught in school was a traditional approach to U.S. history. It contained nothing on Mexico or Latin America that was laudatory. This might have been an alienating influence, except that my grandmother and my mother countered such history with their own version of the histories of the United States and of Mexico.

My grandmother, who disliked the growing economic and cultural penetration of Mexico by the U.S., possessed a very skeptical view of U.S.–Mexican relations. When we would discuss U.S. history, especially anything that touched on relations with Mexico or Latin America, she quickly corrected us or commented. "Well," she would say, "you have to understand that the United States writes its history to its own convenience. It always has, and these people always will."

Because of this type of socialization at home as well as discussions with some of my friends, I and other Mexican-American classmates often clashed with our teachers. As had been the case at the Harwood School in Albuquerque, we disputed certain historical interpretations, especially those that put Mexico and Mexicans in a bad light. This even led to fistfights in some classes between our teacher and some of the students, although not with me.

Some of these teachers we referred to as "honkies." They were out-and-out racists. They were from East Texas or South Texas, and they held racist versions of the Alamo and of race relations. But they wouldn't last long because there would be protests by the Mexican-American students. The better teachers understood the clash and remained quiet.

Extracurricular Activities and Acculturation

Anglos dominated social life at El Paso High. Mexicans, for the most part, were left out of formal activities. Class parties, for example, were always held at the El Paso Country Club. Not many Mexicans had ever seen a country club, much less gone to a party at one, although there were a couple of notable exceptions.

I remember two Mexican families who lived in the exclusive part of

the city. The head of one family, Tomás Fernández Blanco, was a
Spaniard who had married a Mexican woman. At one time they had
lived on San Antonio Street near us, but later on they moved further
north. They were red-headed and freckle-faced, and, because of their
wealth and appearance, they were accepted by the Anglos. Another
rich family, the Revillas, were from Chihuahua and were also light-
complected. They too moved close by the country club and were accepted by the Anglo elites.

Such families were rare, however, and for most of us social life
remained distinctly split. The Anglos had theirs, and we Mexicans
had ours, which was outside the campus and revolved around the
churches—in my case, the Protestant ones. My family went to church
activities and mixed with Protestant families, in addition to socializing
with members of our extended family who were Catholic.

I also associated with neighbors whom I had known for a few
years, and I recall parties and socials organized by the Logia Hispano-
Americana. These affairs were held either at one of the Masonic halls
or at the Catholic Community Center adjacent to Cathedral High
School on Stanton Street, just north of the downtown area.* On occasion, we attended dances and other activities sponsored by the Casino
Español, which had been organized by families of Spanish descent but
with Mexican membership. I would say that about ninety-five percent
of our social life was with Mexican families, although I had a few
Anglo friends.

I dated very little in high school. I was still quite young, graduating
at age sixteen. I began to date more seriously the year or so after I
graduated. I saw a girl by the name of Orlena Lucero, who was the
daughter of the pastor of the Mexican Presbyterian church. My family
didn't object to this relationship, especially because they knew that she
was from a good family. My grandmother, however, did express some
concern that I not get too serious and go and get married before I had
a chance to go on to college.

I was not rebellious as a teenager. I would describe myself as a pretty
obedient kid, both as a child and as a teenager. This was largely because
of the strict discipline and motivation provided by my grandmother and
my mother. One of the few pranks I remember engaging in was swim-

---

*Cathedral High School was and still is an all-boys' school operated by the
Christian Brothers order.

ming across the Rio Grande with some of my friends to the Mexican side, against the orders of the U.S. Border Patrol officials. After taunting them, we would swim back.

I don't recall the process of growing up Mexican in the United States—and often feeling the tensions between both cultures through a process of acculturation—as a particularly alienating experience. I think this was because, in our family, my grandmother and especially my mother had already themselves become somewhat bicultural before coming to the United States. Both had gone to schools taught by Americans. Both understood English, and my mother spoke good English.

As we attended schools in El Paso and spoke more English, my family wasn't particularly concerned about us losing our Spanish. We continued to speak Spanish at home and with family friends. The only thing my mother and my grandmother worried about was that we not speak poor Spanish. They corrected our improper composition, improper spelling, or improper pronunciation. I never took a lesson in Spanish, and I don't know how I learned to read it and write it, but I learned the accents. My mother, at the same time, corrected our English. They had no trouble with us speaking English at home.

As for other "Americanizing" influences, my family was not especially concerned. At home, we had our culture, which was essentially Mexican; and out in the business or work world, we dealt with English and U.S. customs and rules. I attribute this lack of direct alienation to my family's earlier experiences with U.S. cultural traditions in Mexico.

This doesn't mean, however, that my mother and my grandmother weren't concerned about certain tendencies in U.S. culture that would denigrate or discriminate against Mexican culture. Their concern was obvious from the way they reacted against examples of racism and prejudice and from their objections to the way history was taught in the schools. What they were not afraid of was our becoming effectively bilingual and bicultural. They saw this as an asset.

Acculturation, of course, was unavoidable, even in such a Mexican-oriented border city as El Paso. One clear example early on was how teachers Americanized our names. I went from being Humberto to Bert. Others went from Francisco to Frank, from Tómas to Tommy. My family tolerated this practice. Although my mother called me Bert, my grandmother never did, but she didn't make a big deal of it.

Besides my academic studies, I participated in sports along with other Mexican boys. I played some football and baseball, but my favorite and best sport was basketball. I was on the varsity team for three years. Most of the stars of that and the other major sports teams were *mexicanos*. The teams were integrated, and I don't recall any racial tensions that accompanied playing at El Paso High.

I do remember, however, that on certain game trips outside El Paso we encountered quite a bit of harassment. Once when we played in the Panhandle area, either at Big Springs or Pampa, we got booed and called all kinds of dirty names. These places where Mexicans weren't liked hated seeing their home teams beaten by Mexican athletes. In other cities such as Tucson, Phoenix, or Albuquerque, we didn't encounter problems, since as many Mexicans played on those teams as on ours. I enjoyed basketball and later was given a chance to play college ball in either Texas or California.

Teachers and Graduation

Although I was not particularly close to any of my teachers, I became friends with my drama teacher. She was a graduate of Mills College in Oakland and would often give me a ride to my afternoon job at the Warner Drug Company. She talked to me about how I should consider leaving Texas for college. "You know," she said, "things are much different in California." She resented the racism in El Paso and especially the aggressively racist character of Texas men. She was very liberal for those times, and I think it was partly because of her that I decided to go to school in California when I had the opportunity.

My English teacher also encouraged me to consider going west. "I've been out in California," she told me. "There are great opportunities for Mexican students, and you'll do well over there." On the other side, my basketball coach, Ed Price, whom I liked and respected a great deal, felt that I could get a basketball scholarship at his alma mater, the University of Texas at Austin.

All of these things were on my mind when I graduated in 1934. I was open to the idea of either going to Austin or going to the West Coast, especially if I could get a basketball scholarship. However, Coach Price convinced me that at age sixteen I was still too young and not physically developed enough to be seriously considered for such a scholarship. He thought it would be best for me to stay a couple of years in El Paso and play in the amateur city league. Then he would help me get that scholarship later.

I took his advice, with which my mother also agreed, and I remained at home and worked at the Warner Drug Company. It was during this time, as well as during my high school years, that the Great Depression and its effects on the border made such vivid impressions on me.

CHAPTER THREE

Border Depression

I remember the 1929 crash. I didn't understand what people meant by "crash." I didn't understand what radio and newspaper accounts of the crisis meant for the daily life of people. But I recall that as 1930 came on, the layoffs began in El Paso.

Half of the shift was laid off at the ASARCO smelter, which operated only half-time. They laid off part of the people at the Peyton Packing Plant, at the Pearson Lumber Company, at the Phelps Dodge Refinery, and at the two railroad roundhouses run by Southern Pacific and the Texas Pacific. People began to lose their homes. Some moved to apartments or tenements. In time, I began to understand *la crisis*—the crisis.

Soon, efforts were made to boost the declining morale. Parades were held, and patriotic thinking was promoted. But no matter how many parades they had, no matter how many sermons they preached, no matter how many times they promised that good times were just around the corner, good times didn't come, and happy days were not here again.

Instead, I heard of cases where people died of starvation inside railroad cars. People also began to arrive in El Paso, riding the rails in large numbers. They left the railroad cars and wandered the streets pandering, asking for a dime or asking for something to eat. You also saw thousands of people leave El Paso and go to Mexico.

People's wages were cut. Banks failed. People thought El Paso National Bank and the First National Bank were going to close. Jobs became harder and harder to find; there were many unemployed. By the end of 1930 and the beginning of 1931, we saw all the manifestations of a severe economic crisis in El Paso.

The New Deal in El Paso

In the 1932 election and with the coming of the New Deal, Franklin Roosevelt campaigned very openly for change and attacked the Republican policies and Hooverism. I remember the big "Bonus Armies" coming from California through El Paso, heading for Washington.* I think there were two such armies, one calling for a bonus for veterans and the other for help for the unemployed. They walked through El Paso. The authorities, who were very reactionary, didn't want the marchers to stay in El Paso.

The election of FDR, however, changed the political climate. I recall a big victory parade for Roosevelt. With Roosevelt's election, you heard more of a political evaluation of the crisis rather than just the lamentation and a listing of all the country's ills. People began to discuss fascism, communism, and socialism.

The New Deal opened up programs such as the CWA in El Paso.† These work programs provided single men with dormitories and camps where they were housed and fed. The men kept the places clean. They

*In the summer of 1932, two "Bonus Armies" traveled from the West Coast to Washington, D.C. On the way, many adherents and supporters joined the marches. The first army represented World War I veterans, who were demanding promised bonuses that had not been provided. When this army reached Washington, D.C., it was brutally suppressed by the government's use of military force. The second army represented the unemployed, who demanded relief. It was organized largely through the efforts of the Communist Party. For more information, see Franklin Folsom, *Impatient Armies of the Poor: The Story of Collective Acts of the Unemployed, 1808–1942* (Niwot, Colo.: University Press of Colorado, 1991), pp. 310–318.

†The Civil Works Administration (CWA) was created by the federal government in October 1933 to provide work relief on projects of civic value. By January 1934, more than four million men were at work in CWA projects. They repaired roads and streets, improved school buildings, and constructed stadiums, swimming pools, parks, and airports. The program was not renewed during the winter of 1934–1935.

worked if there was work. In the camps, they had recreational activities. They also had discussion groups.

Two or three of those camps were opened in El Paso not very far from where I lived, on Angie and Missouri streets above the second layer of railroad tracks. We lived adjacent to the tracks in a row of houses. This was between 1931 and 1935, the pit of the depression. Besides being close to one of the CWA camps, we were in close proximity to an NYA center that had been set up out of a large converted warehouse on Missouri Street.*

We would often go to the NYA center because they had guest speakers. Some were comedians, but some were very serious. They weren't going to bring in a banker who would say conditions were getting better. The speakers, who lectured on the causes of the depression, awakened and sharpened my own political interests and whetted my appetite for learning more about what had caused the depression.

Dust Bowl Migrants

My strongest recollection of the Great Depression in El Paso was the plight of the Dust Bowl migrants, the "Okies" and "Arkies." Thousands passed through El Paso, fleeing the ravages of drought and bankrupt conditions in Oklahoma, Kansas, Nebraska, North and West Texas, and Arkansas. Whole families came through on freight cars, both inside and on top of the cars, on their way to California.

We were eyewitnesses to all of it because our backyard faced the tracks. If you lived within two or three blocks, you saw these masses of people passing through every day. It was said that a hundred-car freight train could carry a thousand Dust Bowlers. Three trains came through every morning and three more in the evening, so you can just imagine the huge numbers of Okies and Arkies and other Dust Bowl refugees who arrived—five or six thousand a day—and that was just from the East. The Rock Island and Santa Fe lines came down from Chicago and brought more. It was like the population of a small town coming in every single day. People sometimes stayed over either because they were sick or because they missed the trains leaving El Paso.

*The National Youth Administration (NYA), established in 1935, was a New Deal effort to provide jobs, especially for young people.

On top of everything else, there was a certain amount of the criminal activity you'd expect from such a huge mass of humanity: holdups, rapes, and petty theft. My mother, who was working in Juárez at the customs house, left early in the morning and returned at night. My grandmother stayed home and was very cautious in looking after us, with so many desperate transients milling around.

Yet both my mother and my grandmother sympathized with the migrants and helped them. My grandmother, for example, never threw out any edible leftovers or stale bread. She continued to practice medicine, and whenever she went out on calls, she returned with food to feed the steady stream of hungry people coming to our front door and back door asking for something to eat. My grandmother wouldn't think of throwing out an old tortilla or cold oatmeal from breakfast. This was a feast for these sad and miserable people.

My grandmother also offered medical care to the Okies and Arkies. She had her regular clientele, but people arriving and in need soon knew where to find her. She put a sign outside our house that said something like *doctora, partera,* or *enfermeda titulada* [physician, midwife, or licensed nurse]. She treated persons who had fallen off the railroad cars or who were sick from fever. The sick and dying migrants asked the Mexicans living alongside the tracks, "Can you help us? Can you tell us where to get medicine? Where can we get help? My wife is dying in this railroad car, my baby is dying," or, "My husband is dying."

It was horrible. I remember my mother and grandmother treating them; they laid the sick and injured out in the backyard. People were there, on our porch, or in the ditch next to the tracks. I remember children being born in these same places. My grandmother treated thousands, literally, during this time. Although she kept records, she didn't even know the names of some of these patients.

Los Repatriados

In addition to the problems of the Okies and Arkies, El Paso witnessed the plight of those Mexicans who repatriated themselves to Mexico because of the depression and deportation pressures. By 1932 and 1933, you saw *los repatriados* passing through the Juárez Customs House and declaring everything they had brought with them. Some came from California and other parts of the Southwest, and some from as far away as Chicago, Minnesota, and Detroit. They came and found temporary shelter in El Paso while they waited to be processed by the Mexican authorities.

Some of our own relatives from Los Angeles left California because there was no work in the orchards, packing sheds, canneries, or factories. Despite the amount of agriculture there, my relatives just couldn't make it. They came to El Paso and lived with us for a while before returning to Mexico. People doubled and tripled up in the barrios as the *repatriados* arrived on the border.

Even more arrived after the election of Lázaro Cárdenas as president of Mexico in 1934.* Cárdenas was very different from his predecessors. He was a true champion of the people and embodied the best ideals of the Mexican Revolution of 1910. He issued a call to all Mexican nationals in the United States to return to their homeland. He promised them land and government support. They could also bring back whatever possessions they could transport, including automobiles.

With Cárdenas's promises, the *repatriado* migration became a caravan. Some of the *repatriados* arrived with only the shirts on their backs. They entered El Paso on the trains. Those who were better off drove their cars and pickup trucks to the border.

While waiting to be processed across the border, those *repatriados* who could not find a haven with families in El Paso resorted to living in different locations. Some lived in parks, some in vacant lots. Others lived in makeshift camps along the Rio Grande, where they parked their cars in clusters. Every hundred or so yards along the riverbed where there was a tree or an indentation, the *repatriados* camped. Federal officers kept a close watch to ensure that they would not try to cross the river with liquor or other undeclared goods.

Their living conditions were terrible. Those who couldn't find temporary work begged for food. Still others, who were more acquainted with desert terrain, collected and ate *nopales* and *tunas* [cacti and the fruit of the cacti] as well as mesquite beans. They also gathered mesquite wood to warm themselves and to cook or sell.

Even when they finally crossed into Juárez, their living conditions

---

*Lázaro Cárdenas served as president of Mexico from 1934 to 1940. One of the most populist presidents following the Mexican Revolution, Cárdenas carried out significant social reforms. These included agrarian reform and the nationalization of foreign oil companies.

remained horrible. Finally, the Cárdenas administration opened up a couple of big yards where they let the *repatriados* park their cars and stay temporarily. This at least helped to prevent the goods brought by the *repatriados* from being stolen. Here they lived for a time and helped each other out, until they could move further south.

Adapting and Reacting to the Depression

The depression, of course, also created hard times for the Mexicans who were already living in El Paso. Fortunately for us, my mother remained employed at the Juárez Customs House. Less fortunate ones lost their jobs. In a border town like El Paso, with the economy being what it was, this meant a dead end. Consequently, hundreds of Mexican families left every year, steadily from about 1930 to 1936. When I went to Los Angeles in 1936, I was amazed at the number of people from El Paso living there.

Those who stayed in El Paso, as some of our relatives did, couldn't find jobs. It was also hard to find local sources of food. Truck farms in the Rio Grande Valley of the El Paso area produced only a limited amount.

Fortunately, starvation was prevented by the greater availability of food in Juárez, where vegetables, fruits, and cheese from the Valle de San Buenaventura in northern Chihuahua—along with food from the Mormon and Mennonite colonies, also in northern Chihuahua—would be transported to the border.* Poor people in El Paso could cross over to Juárez and purchase two big bags of food for only twenty-five cents.

But at times even this food supply dwindled, and Mexicans in El Paso resorted to begging or gathering food from the desert. Of course, this lack of food affected all of the poor, both Mexicans and Anglos. But those who survived best were the native Mexicans and Indians, who foraged *nopales* and *tunas* and even mesquite. The Anglos didn't know how to do this, and the worst-off of all were the Dust Bowlers— they could starve in a field of *tunas!*

Conditions in Juárez were also bad. The Juárez economy was significantly affected because of its dependence on the El Paso economy.

*In the early twentieth century, American Mormon and Mennonite settlers established colonies in northern Chihuahua, around Casas Grandes. These American religious settlers reproduced their communities and survived by farming.

The economy of northern Mexico in general was very dependent on the U.S., especially in mining, ranching, and logging. Yet, while the export economy of Mexico went into a depression, the internal economy produced enough for local consumption. In those sectors not totally dependent on the U.S. economy, Mexicans were not as seriously affected by the depression. This was the situation in Juárez, so less hunger and poverty were evident in that neighboring city.

As the depression set in and unemployment increased in El Paso, the workers, both Mexicans and Anglos, reacted. Before I left in 1936, and even before the significant CIO organizing drives of the late 1930s,* workers along the border had attempted to unionize and had engaged in strikes to protect themselves in a city long known for its anti-union and anti-labor practices.

The major newspapers of El Paso, the *Times* and the *Herald-Post*, didn't devote much space to the efforts of labor organizers. However, we would hear from neighbors who worked in the railroad shops that the men were going to the union meetings and that the union might strike, or that the workers were on a slowdown, or that the shops were laying off more workers and instituting a speedup for the remaining ones. This informal information network kept people aware of the labor situation.

I recall that prior to 1936 the International Union of Mine, Mill and Smelter Workers had unsuccessfully attempted to organize the hundreds of Mexican workers at the El Paso smelter. Red-baiting and accusing the workers who were sympathetic to the union of being Communists complemented the company's anti-union efforts. There was much talk about getting the "commies" out of El Paso. All this, of course, was before the enactment of New Deal labor laws such as the National Labor Relations Act, the NLRA, which extended federal protection to workers who wanted to unionize.

Not until 1935, when electrical workers from the American Federation of Labor—predominantly Anglos, like most in the AFL—went on strike in El Paso, did the newspapers pay attention to the plight of labor

*The Congress of Industrial Organizations (originally the Committee for Industrial Organization) was formed in 1935 with the aim of organizing unskilled and semiskilled industrial workers into large-scale industrial unions for the first time. The CIO in El Paso first focused on the garment, packing, smelter, and refining industries.

on the border. The strike was broken, however, when the sheriff and local police arrested the strikers and held them incommunicado. Subsequently, the plants blacklisted them. Shortly thereafter, some unionizing efforts succeeded as a result of the passage of the NLRA. But in the first part of the thirties, such activity failed because workers had no rights.

The depression era witnessed several important new Mexican-American organizations. The most prominent, though limited in influence, was LULAC, the League of United Latin American Citizens, which had been formed in Texas in 1929. We had a good friend, Fred Ponce, who was one of the early members of LULAC in El Paso.

He and the other members of LULAC came under attack by *mexicanos* who resented the use of the term "Latin American." LULAC members explained that they chose to call themselves Latin Americans because the term "Mexican" was given no respect in Texas. That still didn't set well with the other *mexicanos* who regarded the members of LULAC—unfairly, I believe—as *vendidos* [sell-outs]. I don't recall much about early LULAC activities; they didn't as yet have a youth group, so I couldn't join.

LULAC was attacked at the same time by those Mexican-Americans who were engaged in the local Democratic Party and who had for years served as ward bosses. They opposed the idea of Mexican-Americans organizing their own people. These politicos formed a kind of courthouse gang. While they had played important roles when the Mexican population was smaller and composed mostly of immigrants, they had begun to lose their influence by the 1920s and 1930s, when the population of El Paso was well over one hundred thousand. More Mexicans were U.S. citizens and were therefore less susceptible to the manipulations and favors of the politicos.

Despite the decline of the ward bosses and the birth of LULAC, the political leadership among Mexicans in El Paso still consisted largely of the mutual-benefit societies [*logias*] and the church groups. Few leaders inspired the Mexicans to participate in formal politics or to use political action to redress grievances. Nothing was being done to build a political base in order to elect Mexican candidates to office.

Even the churches weren't playing that role. The Protestant pastors, for example, played the role of intermediaries between Mexicans and the Anglo power structure represented in the city council. Council

members gave talks at the churches or at church picnics, but that was
about all. It was similar to the days before the civil rights movement in
the South, when white politicians would go to the black church congregations, make their spiel, and the minister would then recommend
supporting a given white guy. That's about where it was in El Paso.

Ethnic and Political Consciousness

Coming of age in El Paso during the depression, I underwent various
changes, especially concerning my self-identity. In my early childhood,
I had a sense that I was a *mexicano* exclusively. Since we had also lived
in Juárez and in Chihuahua, I essentially viewed myself as a child of
Mexico and considered Mexico my homeland.

But as I grew up and went to school in El Paso, I began to feel that
here, after all, was where I had been born and raised and that we as
Mexicans also had a historic and rightful claim to El Paso and the
Southwest. I learned more about the U.S.–Mexican War of the 1840s,
in which the U.S. conquered half of Mexico's northern territory. And
I learned when I attended school in Albuquerque about the struggles of
the *manitos*—the people of New Mexico—to protect themselves and
their lands after the U.S. conquest.*

By the time I was about twelve, I saw myself belonging to a people
who possessed a right to be in the Southwest and who believed that this

*Following the U.S.–Mexican War (1846–1848), the United States annexed
lands that had been Mexican territories, stretching from Texas to California. The
most populated area was the New Mexico settlement. Primarily a pastoral people,
composed of both small landholders and families who owned large amounts of
land, the New Mexicans—the *manitos,* also called Hispanos—were able to maintain most of their lands for several decades following the American annexation.
Beginning in the 1880s with the penetration of the railroads, however, New
Mexico was opened up for Anglo-American ranchers and land speculators. A
Court of Private Land Claims set up in the 1890s challenged many of the land grants
belonging to the original New Mexicans. Some New Mexicans defended themselves in the courts, whereas others resorted to more direct action. Las Gorras
Blancas (the White Caps), for example, were night-riders who in the late 1880s and
early 1890s tore up railroad tracks and cut the new barbed-wire fences put up by
Anglo ranchers. The *manitos* later shifted to electoral strategies to hold on to their
land. Into the twentieth century, however, more and more New Mexicans lost land
as a result of legal challenges and economic problems. Still, some families, especially in the more remote areas, continued to work family and communal lands.

was our land too, despite the Anglo invasion. I felt that we had to redress our grievances here and not in Mexico and that the Anglos owed us at least equal treatment and recognition. I suppose I thought of myself as a Mexican from the United States with full rights; this represented a change from the way I felt when I was younger.

Although I was experiencing this change of consciousness, I never heard the term "Mexican-American" used in El Paso. When I left in 1936 for Los Angeles, there was no question in my mind but that I was a Mexican. Even when I arrived in Los Angeles, I joined what was called the Mexican Youth Conference. It wasn't until about 1937 that such groups began to use the term "Mexican-American."

But even though this term was not used in El Paso, the fact was that Mexicans in the U.S. were becoming increasingly bilingual and bicultural. We spoke English at home only in regard to schoolwork. At El Paso High, we spoke English, but after classes we reverted to Spanish. All of the Mexicans there were bilingual.

One of the other ways in which I was changing was in regard to my political consciousness. This was partly a result of the economic and social conditions affecting El Paso during the depression, but it was also because of my participation in a study group formed by several Mexican students at El Paso High. Some of these students were older than me and had done much more reading. They guided the rest of us. We met because we wanted to understand the crisis of the 1930s, both in our own country and in the rest of the world.

I also attended meetings of the Sociedad Anarcho-Sindicalista, which was composed of the followers of Ricardo Flores Magón. This was a very small club, but I thought that it merited respect. It moved me to think and to read further, as did the discussions in our study group.

The study group met at Houston Park on Angie and Yandell boulevards, not far from my house. Some of the older guys had read about fascism, others about socialism, another about the Russian Revolution, and they would lead discussions on these topics. It really started me thinking about all of these things in an organized way.

The writers who inspired us the most were the American muckrakers and progressives: Upton Sinclair, Lincoln Steffens, Thorsten Veblen, Jack London, and others. I read quite a few of Jack London's books, especially at the encouragement of my English teacher. I became interested in London's life because he had been in El Paso during the time of the Mexican Revolution and had written a story about a man who at one time had delivered ice to our home. The man's name was Joe Rivers. London's story about Rivers was called "The Mexican," and it was later made into a screenplay and a film.

In the story, London depicted Rivers as a *campesino* from Mexico who, after his wife is raped and killed by the *federales,* joins Pancho Villa's forces. Villa sends Rivers to the border to acquire guns and ammunition. In El Paso, he comes into contact with the Junta Revolucionaria Mexicana, a group my father worked with.

Rivers remained on the border and became a prizefighter. He fought for the welterweight and lightweight championship and then donated all his prize money to the Junta. He later retired from fighting and became an ice delivery man in El Paso.

At the same time that we were becoming politicized through our study group, we also felt the need to become active politically. We didn't run for public office, of course, but in school we organized the Mexican students to achieve certain goals, such as greater recognition. For example, we organized a campaign to elect Moisés Flores, one of our star football players, as president of the student body at El Paso High. Our group formulated a strategy to get Moisés elected. We brought together the Mexican athletes, the scholarly types, and the service clubs. Two of the older guys in the study group served as campaign managers, and they were very astute in determining what had to be done.

Moisés won. He was the first *mexicano* to get elected as student body president. This was my first lesson in waging and organizing a political campaign.

CHAPTER FOUR

Welcome to L.A.

I left El Paso in 1936. I probably never would have left had it not been for the opportunity to receive a basketball scholarship. Basketball had been my favorite sport at El Paso High. Following my graduation in 1934 at age sixteen, my coach, Ed Price, had advised me to play in the local commercial league for two years before college, to give me time to mature physically and to improve my game.

Although I was unaware of it at the time, various college scouts had been watching me since my senior year, as I played in the local league. El Paso was a hot basketball town, and scouts came through from the University of Texas, Texas Christian, Southern Methodist, and the University of Southern California. After graduation, I was in close contact with Coach Price, who wanted me to accept a scholarship to play for either Texas or USC. Two of my other coaches, Mike Brumbelow and Ed Martin, however, urged me to go to their alma mater, Texas Christian.

I wanted to play basketball, and, seeing this as an opportunity to attend college, I finally decided to go to USC. I was affected partly by Coach Price's support for USC and by the good things that some of my teachers had told me about California. But there was also my family to consider. My mother, grandmother, brothers, and sister weren't too happy about the idea of my leaving home; they of course didn't want the family to break up. They realized that this was an important opportunity for me to attend college, so they agreed with my decision. But as long as I was leaving home, they felt better about my going to Los Angeles, where we had relatives who could watch over me and help me out.

Arriving in Los Angeles

I left El Paso in late summer of 1936 to enroll for the fall semester at USC. Train travel was fairly cheap, and, since I had been working and had a little money, I bought a Pullman ticket from El Paso to Los Angeles. I think the price of a Pullman berth was about twenty-two dollars then. I didn't have a full Pullman, so I had to share it with someone else.

The chair cars, on the other hand, were loaded with Okies and Arkies carrying their big bundles and with a lot of poor Mexicans carrying their baggage on their way to California. Since they didn't have the money to buy food on the train, they brought their food with them. The Mexicans getting on in El Paso had sacks of groceries, which they had purchased in Juárez. I felt fortunate that I could afford the luxury of eating in the dining car.

Not being used to traveling on the train, I had no idea of particular practices, and this led to a funny experience on my first night. I didn't know where to put my shoes when I went to bed, so I left them outside the curtain. The next morning, I discovered that they had been shined. I put them on and forgot about it.

About ten o'clock that morning, a black porter comes by and says to me, "Those sure are sharp-looking shoes." It didn't dawn on me as he stood there and jived with me that he had no real interest in my appearance but simply wanted to be paid for shining my shoes.

Finally he said, "Ain't you going to show your appreciation, son? You know, I'm the one who polished your shoes."

I gave him a dime because that's what shines cost in El Paso. "You can do better than that," he responded. I was embarrassed, and I gave him a quarter.

It wasn't until later when I became involved with the CIO in Los Angeles that I realized how tough times were then for black porters. Pullman porters and redcaps received only two dollars a day and had to rely on tips to make a decent wage. This arrangement was written into their union contract, which was a lousy one—Who in the hell tipped during the depression?

We finally arrived at the old Central Station in Los Angeles. My aunt, Juanita López, picked me up. She had a little Model A Ford, which she soon taught me to drive. After I started working in L.A., and because she didn't want me to ride the streetcars late at night, she suggested that I buy the Model A from her. I paid her a hundred dollars. The car was in such good shape that three years later I sold it for two hundred.

My Aunt Juanita and her husband, Uncle Guillermo, lived in a house on Echandia and Brooklyn in Boyle Heights. At that time, this was still a Jewish neighborhood, northeast of the downtown area and across the Los Angeles River. We were the only Mexicans on the block. Uncle Guillermo had a good job as a photo supply salesman, and Aunt Juanita worked as a clerk at a downtown store on Third Street.

I had other aunts, uncles, and cousins in other parts of L.A. They were all very popular and knew many other *mexicanos,* including some of the Mexican movie stars in Hollywood such as Dolores Del Río and Lupe Vélez, who helped other Mexicans get work as movie extras to make additional money during the depression.

The Barrios

Although my aunt and uncle lived in a mixed neighborhood, I quickly discovered the barrios, where thousands of Mexicans resided. At that time, and even today, a number of areas were predominantly Mexican. There was a little barrio called Sonoratown near the railroad depot, where Chinatown is today. Another barrio was located above Angel's Flight, bordered by Grand, Olive, Flower, and Figueroa streets. Here a number of families lived in broken-down old homes. This area is now Belmont, central Los Angeles.

Compton originally started out as an all-white retreat from Watts, but when I arrived, Mexicans were moving into little houses there in greater and greater numbers, as they were also doing in Watts and Gardena. *Colonias* had grown up around the Bethlehem Steel and U.S. Steel plants in Maywood, Bell, Gardena, and Torrance. As you went further south toward the ocean, near Torrance and Long Beach, there were more barrios, adjacent to the refineries in Harbor City and Lomitas. Wherever there were industries, you would find *colonias* and little *capillitas* [shrines], tiny, sanctuary-type churches.

Moving up from downtown Los Angeles, you could find pockets of Mexicans along Main Street and what they called Dogtown and Santa Rita. At the intersection of Main, Mission, and North Broadway, a *colonia* existed directly underneath the bridge.

All along the Red Car line, the electric train run by Pacific Electric, east from downtown Los Angeles, were *colonias:* Alhambra, San Gabriel, El Monte, Temple City, Colton, Ontario, Pomona, Ramona, La Verne, all through the San Gabriel Valley to San Bernardino. A Mexican fellow once told me that he never experienced discrimination from whites, because once he entered the U.S. at Calexico, he could stop and work in one of the series of Mexican *colonias* that existed all along the route to Los Angeles and never have to deal with Anglos.

Then, of course, there were the growing Mexican barrios of Belvedere and East Los Angeles, just across the L.A. River. Part of East L.A. was called the Flats. It was on the opposite side of the river from the big meatpacking plants operated by such firms as Cudahy, Swift, Wilson, and Armour. The stench there was horrible. They just poured the guts and stuff into the river. Many of the *mexicanos* who worked in those plants lived in the Flats or on Mission Street, next to the San Antonio Winery.

Some time after I arrived, I began work as a volunteer at El Salvador Church on First and Mission. The church was in the heart of a horrible slum. Mexicans lived in cheap clapboard structures. Some of these houses contained many more than the two families they were at best suitable for. The congestion was horrible. Replacing the Molokan Russian Jews who had initially lived in these areas,* *mexicanos* also lived in garages, ten to a room, ten families to one structure, a whole family to one room.

Working with the Reverend Kendrick Watson and other social workers, we formed a committee to find better housing. We photographed the houses and did our own door-to-door survey. This succeeded in getting the slum houses leveled and replaced by the new Aliso

---

*The Molokan Russians were a Jewish sect, whose members began to leave Russia around 1905. These refugees began to form a community in Los Angeles at about the same time. See Ricardo Romo, *East Los Angeles: History of a Barrio* (Austin: University of Texas Press, 1983), pp. 65–67.

Village housing project. Unfortunately, many of the existing residents did not get into these new homes, especially when the war broke out and soldiers, sailors, and marines were given preference.

Beyond the Flats was Boyle Heights, where my aunt and uncle lived. When I first arrived, there was a growing influx of *mexicanos* moving in there to replace the Jews, who were moving west to the West Adams area. Mexicans were also moving into the City Terrace area. So, for a time, Mexicans and Jews lived in mixed neighborhoods in both Boyle Heights and City Terrace.

Further east was Belvedere, which started out to be multiracial but very quickly became Mexicanized in the 1920s and 1930s. At the edge of Maravilla, which was also becoming Mexican, was one particular barrio called El Hoyo [the Hole], which was a gully where a number of Mexicans had lived for many years with their pigs, chickens, dogs, and donkeys.

Los Angeles and El Paso

Despite the poor housing and the congestion in the barrios, the conditions faced by Mexicans in L.A. were not as rough as those faced by Mexicans in El Paso during the depression, because L.A. offered more opportunities to find food and jobs. Poor people, for example, went to the big produce markets and came back with bags of ripe and overripe fruit and vegetables that had been purchased at bargain prices from the surrounding agricultural areas. At the loading docks in the port towns, the longshoremen purposely dropped sacks of sugar and crates of squash and other foods to allow hungry people to pick up what was dropped.

There was just as much unemployment in L.A. as in El Paso, but L.A. had more industries than El Paso, which meant more opportunities: in auto assembling; at rubber tire manufacturers such as Firestone, Goodyear, Goodrich, and others; in the steel mills, such as U.S. Steel, Bethlehem, and Republic; and in the meatpacking plants. Mexicans worked in the tire retreading plants along Alameda and Main streets; they did the heavy work in the waste-material industry, which collected old rags, newspapers, bottles, and scrap iron that was shipped to Japan. Mexicans worked in all of these and other industries as well as on the surrounding farms and ranches.

Los Angeles differed from El Paso in other important ways too. By moving from El Paso to L.A., I left a city of one hundred thousand people and came to a metropolis of about eight hundred thousand with a totally different social and cultural climate. For example, racial and ethnic relations were different. In El Paso, whites were either very friendly and helpful to Mexicans, or they were very hostile and racist. The existence of overt racism eventually led to many confrontations, especially over educational discrimination and police abuse, and it also led to efforts to ensure the extension of New Deal relief and work programs to the Mexican population.

In L.A., however, I didn't find such sharp divisions initially. This may have been because social services in California were more generous and federal programs were being implemented in the poverty-stricken barrios. There were, of course, many complaints on the part of the Mexican community, but these complaints were not raised as aggressively as in El Paso.

Another interesting characteristic of the Mexicans of Los Angeles was that many seemed less proud of their heritage than those who lived in El Paso. Some Mexicans in L.A. shied away from speaking Spanish and from defending Mexican culture against its detractors and outright bigots. It was the first time that I had met Mexicans who would say, "I'm proud to be an American." I thought that they were using the most contradictory terminology imaginable—of course we were all Americans!

In El Paso, we saw Mexico and Mexicans as being inhabitants of the American continent and therefore Americans. In fact, we felt even more American because of our Indian heritage, in contrast to the Anglos, who were Europeans—and relative newcomers, at that. But I knew that when Mexicans in L.A. said they were proud to be Americans, they meant that they were proud not to be Mexicans. I was shocked that so many were ashamed to speak Spanish.

I'll never forget an incident that happened to me on a bus ride to Hollywood. The car was nearly filled with white people. When I got on, I sat next to two Mexicans and asked them in Spanish if they knew where Fairfax Avenue was.

They completely ignored me. I thought that perhaps the noise of the streetcar had prevented them from hearing what I said, so I tapped one of them and asked again in Spanish which stop was for Fairfax.

This time, one of them acted very annoyed and answered in English, "I don't speak or understand Spanish."

"Oh, my God," I thought, "maybe this guy's a Samoan or something." So I got up and went to the conductor and asked for directions in English. He told me to ride all the way to the end of the line, which I did.

When I got off, so did the other two Mexicans. As I passed them on my way to Fairfax, I said in English, "Oh yeah, I found out that Fairfax is over there."

And they replied, "We could have told you that in English."

"Do you mean you understood what I said in Spanish?" I asked.

And one of them tells me in perfect Spanish: "*Sí, pero aquí no se habla español. Aquí es mejor que no crean que eres mexicano. Te tratan mejor.*" [Yes, but here it's best not to speak Spanish. It's best if they don't know you're Mexican. They treat you better.]

I looked at them, and I couldn't understand that attitude. It was totally different from what I had been taught by my family in El Paso. They had instilled in me a pride of being *mexicano* and of speaking Spanish. The Mexicans I encountered here in L.A. wanted to pass for non-Mexicans, a situation similar to that of blacks who tried to hide their blackness, their social and ethnic identity. This insecurity and assimilationist tendency became less noticeable, however, as more *mexicanos* arrived in California from Mexico as well as from Arizona, New Mexico, and Texas in the late 1930s.

Unwanted Mexicans and Relief Efforts

There was, of course, another major reason why Mexicans were afraid to call themselves Mexican during the early 1930s, and this was the direct result of the deportation drives. Thousands of *mexicanos* were either deported or forced to repatriate themselves to Mexico because of the crisis of the depression and the opposition to their inclusion on the county relief rolls. Where once they were seen as essential to the economy, they now were treated as liabilities.

Yet some *mexicanos* spoke about the deportations in a very quixotic way. They assumed a philosophical attitude: After all, despite the circumstances, they were being sent back to their homeland, to Mexico. It was not like they were going to some foreign country or to the

North Pole or to hell—they were going to be reunited with their families.

Others, quite correctly, held the attitude that what was happening was a terrible injustice. They regretted and deplored the situation in which families were divided and forced to leave friends behind. Because they were not U.S. citizens, they had to uproot their kids, pull them out of school, and return to towns in Mexico which might not have a school. A spectrum of conflicting sentiments existed among the *repatriados*.

But, not being able to do very much about their fate, the *repatriados* also expressed themselves in an ironic and humorous manner. There were all kinds of jokes, *chistes,* surrounding the situation. Poor people laugh at their sad life because, when they run out of tears, that's all that is left to do; humor helps to ease the sadness. You would hear *chistes* about things that the *repatriados* would forget to take with them or about mistaking someone else's belongings for their own.

One joke was about a young *repatriada* who worked for a very rich employer in Beverly Hills. When the domestic gave notice that she would have to leave, she received a brand-new set of luggage and a hundred-dollar bill as a gift.

The *repatriada* goes to the train station with her two kids and asks someone waiting there where the repatriation train is. She is told that she can catch the train on Fifth and Mateo or Alameda.

So she marches up there and gets on the train with her kids. When they get to Glendale, the last stop out of Los Angeles, the conductor begins walking down the aisle collecting tickets. He says, "Where're your tickets, ma'am?"

She answers, "*Yo soy repatriada. Me voy para San Francisco del Oro en Chihuahua.*" [I am a repatriate. I'm going to San Francisco del Oro in Chihuahua.]

"San Francisco?" the conductor says. "Okay, it'll be ten dollars for you and five dollars for each of the kids."

She asks, "*¿Que dijo?*" [What did he say?] One of the other Mexicans on the train translates, "*Que tiene que pagar diez dólares por Ud. y cinco dólares por cada uno de los niños.*"

She answers back, "*¡Uy lo van a repatriar a uno y hasta le cobran!*" [Wow, they're going to repatriate you, and you still have to pay!] But she pays the conductor.

When they arrive in San Francisco, California, she exclaims: *"¡Pero este no es San Francisco del Oro!"* [But this isn't San Francisco del Oro!]

Many such incidents and others far worse did happen. The *chistes* reflected a courageous attempt to make light of a truly shocking and frightful experience.

For those who faced being deported or repatriated as well as for those who remained, relief assistance was a major problem. I knew a fellow who had been in the U.S. since 1919. During the depression, he lost his job, a good job in a factory. To survive, he went out to the fields and gleaned discarded fruits and vegetables that the growers had not gathered. But things got worse and worse for him, and he couldn't pay his rent. So one day he and his family, with five kids, moved in with another family. His wife got a job cleaning houses for two dollars a day, and it was very tough for them.

They finally received some local relief, but it was not nearly enough to meet even his family's most basic needs. They gave him just so many pounds of flour, of beans, and of powdered milk; but with a wife, five kids, and his mother to feed, the county relief allocation simply wasn't enough. He and his family were forced either to starve or to repatriate themselves to Mexico. It was a sad situation.

The problem with relief aid was so bad that it sparked two big demonstrations in front of the state relief administration headquarters. At one of the demonstrations, the people—including many Mexicans— broke down the doors and took all the flour and other food that was stored there.

These demonstrations, which occurred in 1936, were organized by the International Workers Order, a coalition of Jews, Anglos, blacks, and Mexicans. It had headquarters on Brooklyn near Soto, where it assisted people on welfare or relief or those who simply didn't have enough to eat. I later learned that the Communist Party had helped to start the IWO, and prominent Communists served as IWO officers.

It was groups such as the IWO who, through their demonstrations, obtained more state relief for the poor and also helped to terminate the deportation and repatriation of *mexicanos*. The IWO also struggled to establish the Social Security system, pressed for the National Labor Relations Act, and pushed for New Deal agencies such as the WPA and the CCC camps to open and expand in L.A.* The majority of the people in the IWO were not Communists; they were poor people such as Jewish workers in the waste-material industry, who were very poorly paid, or Jewish women working in the needle trades, also poorly paid.

Another group that assisted Mexicans and other poor people in Los Angeles during the depression was the Workers Alliance. Several chapters existed, including one for Mexican and other Spanish-speaking workers. The Alliance helped people with relief allocations and helped them to fight evictions from their homes if they couldn't make the rent. The Alliance also had a considerable number of Communists as leaders and members. It attacked the capitalist system as the cause of the depression, unemployment, and hunger. I didn't belong to the Alliance, but a number of Mexicans supported it.

Many of these groups such as the Alliance and the IWO attempted to reach and organize greater numbers of Mexicans by proselytizing in places where large numbers of Mexicans congregated, such as La Placita near downtown Los Angeles. There had been a free-speech tradition in La Placita going back to the period of the Mexican Revolution and the Emma Goldman and IWW days before World War I.† On Sundays, speakers at La Placita got up on a box and addressed the unemployed and the other people who gathered to listen.

Most spoke in Spanish, and of these most were Mexicans. Some pushed the anarcho-syndicalist line in the tradition of Ricardo Flores Magón. They attacked the labor unions, the Communist Party, and the Socialist Party for being nonrevolutionary. These *magonistas* were very sectarian.

*The Works Progress Administration (WPA) was established in 1935 and provided work-relief jobs in a variety of projects for skilled, semiskilled, unskilled, and even white-collar workers who were unemployed. The Civilian Conservation Corps (CCC) was another effort by the New Deal to provide jobs for the unemployed, especially young men, who were put to work clearing forests, planting trees, improving roads, and erecting dams.

†Emma Goldman was a leading anarchist in the United States during the 1890s and the early years of the twentieth century. The Industrial Workers of the World (IWW) was a labor organization founded in 1905 on the principle of class conflict. The "Wobblies," as they were called, sought to create "one big union" through which workers would own the means of production and distribution. The IWW carried out a variety of militant strikes and other direct actions during the first two decades of the century. Although heavily persecuted during World War I, the IWW continued to function in some parts of the country until the 1930s.

The remnants of the IWW were also represented at La Placita. Of course, the Communist Party and the various activist groups in the CIO movement were there. They all drew very large audiences.

University of Southern California

It was within this new social and community setting that I began my studies at USC. Although my grandmother and other relatives had wanted me to go into medicine, by the time I entered USC, I was more inclined to go into either merchandising or law. I finally decided to sign up for a five-year B.A. program in law.

When I went to the campus on registration day, I was nervous and unsure of what to expect. I very quickly discovered the nature of my athletic scholarship. When I came to the financial assistance table, I showed them the letter offering my athletic scholarship. They looked at it and told me to pay whatever I could toward my registration fee and that I would be interviewed the following day for work assistance. Tuition was low in those days, but I still needed financial aid.

The following day, I received an interview. Based on my prior work experience with Warner Drugs in El Paso, they quickly placed me with a large drug warehouse in L.A., the Brunswig Drug Company. This is what an athletic scholarship at USC meant in the 1930s—not an all-expenses-paid scholarship, but a job in order to pay tuition and expenses while you participated in sports. Football players worked at Coca-Cola or places like that and received good pay, while basketball players got lighter types of jobs provided by supportive firms. I received thirty-five dollars a week, including overtime. You could live decently with that.

Unfortunately, I had bad luck with basketball at USC. Shortly after starting practice that fall, I injured my heel when another player spun around, knocked me down, and ruptured the ligament. I missed the entire season. But the coaches supported me and kept me on scholarship, which meant I could remain at my job. Forced to sit out games and practices, I concentrated on my classes and on extracurricular activities on campus.

I was one of only four Mexican-Americans in the entire USC student body. Gil Kuhn, one of the other three, was part Mexican and part German and was an All-American center on the football team. Once, during my first year, Kuhn and I called a meeting of all the Spanish-surnamed students on campus. We were inspired by the initial organization of the Mexican Youth Conference in L.A., which was attempting to organize Mexican-American college students. We wanted to see about the possibilities of perhaps establishing a chapter at USC.

However, most of those who came to our meeting were students from Latin America. They were from rich Mexican, Venezuelan, and Argentine families. They didn't stay long, but before they left they told us that they had no interest in Mexican-Americans or in the kind of social issues we were concerned about. They were *malinchistas* from the word go.*

Racism certainly existed at USC, although, with so few minority students, it was not very visible. Kuhn, despite his All-American stature, was not allowed to join a fraternity once it was known that he was part Mexican. The teachers, once they knew that you were Mexican, were either patronizing or hostile. I did not have a single inspirational professor during my time at USC.

But the bigger issue and conflict at USC in the thirties was based more on class than on race. In addition to the students from very wealthy families, the school was beginning to admit an increasing number of white students from very distressed middle-class families and even working-class families. Because their parents didn't have the money to send them to USC, many of these students found themselves working at the CCC camps one year to save money to attend college the next. They would even drop out of USC for a year to work so that they could save for another year of school. With enrollments declining in the thirties, USC willingly admitted these students, although it had once restricted enrollment to only the very wealthy.

These new students often wore the army boots and CCC jackets that they had worn in the camps. These were the students who initiated what was called the Non-Org movement at USC. Lower-middle-class and working-class students were never invited to participate in the key campus organization that controlled student funds, and this created a

---

*The term *"malinchista"* is used to mean a traitor to one's race. The word is derived from the name of Doña Marina (sometimes also called Malinche), an Indian woman who aided the Spanish conqueror Hernán Cortés in his conquest of the Aztec empire in 1521. Doña Marina has been unfairly treated in Mexican history as a traitor to her people for aligning herself with Cortés.

great deal of resentment. Many of the students who had participated in the CCC camps also became quite political and began to put together the Non-Org Association.

I joined the association, and we took on the fraternities and sororities, besides shaking up the administration. Because the Non-Orgs represented the majority on campus and because of their level of organization, the association soon controlled student politics. It also captured the student newspaper.

Controlling student funds, the Non-Orgs stressed funding for social issues rather than for fraternities and sororities. They forced the administration to purchase or rent whole blocks of homes for student housing adjacent to the campus, which was critical for those with little money. The Non-Orgs endorsed major political issues such as support for Republican Spain, the National Labor Relations Act, and the rest of the New Deal programs to alleviate the suffering of the depression.

I admired their commitment, although I was only nominally active in the Non-Orgs because by 1937 I had become involved with the CIO. The only other time I've witnessed militant actions, or even radical ones, on the part of USC students was during the 1960s and the struggle to end the war in Vietnam.

By the start of my second year at USC, my injury had healed, and once again I came out for basketball practice. By then, however, I was becoming more active with the CIO, and I finally decided that labor organizing was more important to me than basketball. I didn't quit USC, but I did transfer to the evening campus in downtown L.A., on Seventh and Los Angeles, where I took some courses.

A particularly memorable one was a course on the National Labor Relations Act, which was also known as the Wagner Act. The class was taught by an extremely good professor, Dr. Towne Nylander. Dr. Nylander had been involved in drafting the bill and, at the time he taught the class, was working for the National Labor Relations Board in Los Angeles. He was a rather conservative man but an excellent professor. He explained the law and encouraged people to learn how to use it. His main weakness was that he didn't accept a political interpretation of the NLRA. He saw it only in legalistic terms.

This contrasted and clashed with many of the students in the class, some of whom were also taking political science and sociology courses, besides being labor activists. Some were either Marxists or were study-

ing Marxism, and they engaged in some lively discussions ignited by
Nylander's refusal to interpret the NLRA in light of class conflict, as
many of the students did.

He asked the class: "What would you predict to be the future of the
NLRA?" And one of the students spoke out that it would increase class
conflict because workers were sick and tired of being exploited by the
capitalist class and were now organizing as a class under the banner of
the CIO.

Nylander frowned and said, "Well, there's much more to it than
that." Despite—and because of—the differences, the class was packed
with interested students, and I learned a great deal.

Unfortunately, the more I personally became involved with the CIO,
the less time I had for my education. By 1938 I was no longer a student.

The Mexican American Movement

While still at USC and while I was just beginning to become involved
with the CIO, I also participated in the development of what came to
be called the Mexican American Movement, or MAM. MAM originated as a result of the efforts of a unified group of college students,
Protestant ministers, Catholic priests, and social workers. The initia-
tors of MAM included Paul Coronel, Félix Gutiérrez, Juan Acevedo,
Esteban Reyes, Manuel Ceja, and Manuel Avila and his brother Art.
These young people represented a small number of Mexicans attending
colleges such as Chaffey College, Compton College, Occidental, UCLA,
Redlands University, USC, and Santa Barbara City College. Other key
organizers were Guadalberto Valadez, who headed a neighborhood
center in Placentia; Dora Ibáñez, a teacher from La Verne; Socorro
Moreno, who was a buyer at the May Company department store; and
Kendrick Watson, the minister of the El Salvador Baptist Church.

They came together as a result of a series of meetings sponsored by
the YMCA, which was attempting to promote Mexican-American
youth leadership throughout the Southwest. These meetings led to a
series of Mexican Youth Conferences in Los Angeles.

I attended one of the conferences, the theme of which was education
and Mexican-Americans. People raised concerns about educational opportunities and about how to combat discriminatory practices in the
schools, which relegated Mexican youths to vocational and nonaca-

demic careers. No adequate support system existed in the Mexican schools to discourage dropping out or to promote the idea of college as a way of obtaining better employment and career possibilities. Another major issue was youth gangs in the barrios. Gangs composed of high school dropouts had already formed in various communities.

Besides focusing on educational problems, the conference expressed concerns about a variety of other issues: employment discrimination, the state of health services for the Spanish-speaking communities, the barring of Mexicans from public swimming pools and other recreational facilities, segregation in housing, the lack of job opportunities, the conditions of Mexican youth in the state prisons, and adequate political representation. The conference concluded with the formation of the Mexican American Movement as an organization dedicated to encouraging Mexican-American students in colleges and high schools to complete their education and to begin working together to break down barriers to full opportunities.

MAM met in various regional areas on a fairly regular basis. Sometimes we met in Los Angeles, other times in San Bernardino, Pomona, or Santa Barbara. We also established a small newspaper, *La Voz* [The Mexican Voice], edited by Félix Gutiérrez.

I helped to organize MAM chapters. I remember being on an organizing committee and going to Orange County several times to form a chapter there. That area had a lot of problems with segregated schools and swimming pools in towns such as La Modena, Westminster, and Placentia. We particularly encouraged Mexican college students, along with *mexicano* social workers and teachers, to form a club. We also worked with similar groups in Duarte, Pomona, and La Verne in the San Gabriel Valley.

We contacted churches and even probation officers who were *mexicanos,* encouraging them to join MAM. We succeeded in establishing a number of chapters. At one point between 1938 and 1940, we had almost a thousand members—not all active, but at least subscribers to *La Voz.*

We also organized annual conferences and smaller regional ones in places like San Bernardino, Pomona, and Oxnard. At first, men and women functioned separately within MAM, but by our third annual conference the groups had merged. Key women within MAM were people such as Dora Ibáñez and Socorro Moreno, who was a very dynamic organizer. We didn't have a MAM office, so business was conducted out of the homes of the officers.

Because MAM was mostly made up of young men and women attending college, we focused predominantly on educational issues. We tried to bring the greatest attention to those schools with the highest dropout rates.

We met a couple of times with the principal of Roosevelt High School in East Los Angeles. He tried to soft-soap us at first by telling us how much he loved Mexicans. But we found out through the investigations of Jess Aguirre and the Avila brothers that Roosevelt deliberately directed Mexican youngsters into vocational classes. Roosevelt and various other Mexican schools failed to encourage their students to stay in high school, much less go to college. We confronted the principals with these facts, but they became defensive and unwilling to talk.

We took a similar approach in Orange County and organized community meetings to get the facts to Mexican parents, in the hope of promoting action. We also took up issues of police brutality against Mexican youngsters, plus discrimination in public facilities.

MAM's activities did not end these problems, but they did call attention to them. Perhaps more important, MAM symbolized the coming of age of a new generation of Mexicans in the United States. Many of us saw ourselves as a new generation. A lot of MAM members came from very poor families, many from the rural agricultural areas of California; but they viewed themselves as a generation with better opportunities than their parents and with a better understanding of how to function in this country and of the role they could play in their communities. MAM was just the beginning of this new generation of leadership, which some historians are now calling the "Mexican-American Generation."

Although we identified with the idea of a new generation, at first we did not fully agree on what term to use to describe ourselves—the problem of ethnic labels. We first came together as the Mexican Youth Conference. Some believed that we should refer to ourselves as "Mexican-Americans." The objection to this, which I shared, was that it was a redundant term since Mexicans were, by definition, Americans. The term "Mexican-American" acceded to the Anglo view that the only true Americans were Anglos or whites and that the rest were not really Americans. The debate within MAM on this issue was intense.

I remember Juan Acevedo and Esteban Reyes, in particular, supporting the use of the term "Mexican-American." They argued that racism
toward Mexicans was deeply rooted and that we had to confront the
reality of our situation, that we had to call attention to our U.S.
citizenship. Using the term "Mexican" exclusively would imply that we
were interested only in issues germane to Mexico. In the end, more
members favored "Mexican-American," and so we became the Mexican American Movement.

But if there was a difference of opinion over what to call ourselves,
there was little if any difference on the direction of MAM and on the
goals we pursued. We were not assimilationist per se. To us, assimilation meant picking up the technical and employment skills we needed
and obtaining full rights and opportunities. But it did not mean giving
up our culture or forgetting our language—we never even considered
such assimilation. Our meetings were always bilingual.

Although MAM disbanded during World War II, as many members
joined the armed forces or engaged in war-related work, it represented
an important development in the Mexican communities of the L.A.
area. In a sense, MAM was a precursor of the later Chicano student
groups such as MECHA.* We didn't have the number of students then
that we have today, but we had people who were very militant and very
committed. Some of the children of these activists later became quite
involved in community and educational issues. I think that, historically
speaking, MAM represented a burning desire by young Mexican-
Americans for a better and more advanced education and for the
elimination of discrimination and segregation.

Family Reunion and Social Life

During these first two years in Los Angeles, I adjusted quite well,
primarily because part of my family followed me to California. After
I had been in L.A. for about six months and saved some money, I
decided to rent an apartment in Lincoln Heights and to invite my
grandmother in El Paso to join me in California. She felt sad about her
family beginning to break up, and I knew I could support her. My
grandmother was seventy-two and no longer practicing medicine, although she was in pretty good health. But she couldn't stand the heat

*El Movimiento Estudiantil Chicano de Aztlán. MECHA was begun during the
1960s, with chapters at many colleges and universities; see Chapter Thirteen.

in El Paso—or the altitude, because of her high blood pressure—and, for these additional reasons, she welcomed the invitation to join me.

Her doctors had actually told her that she had only a few years to live because of her blood pressure. But she lived a disciplined life and maintained a strict diet, never overeating. The only stimulant she ever took was coffee; she never drank or smoked. She ate maybe three tortillas a day plus fruit, vegetables, and grains. She lived to be ninety-five and had perfect eyesight!

After my grandmother arrived, I also invited my brother Orlando to come to L.A. because I heard that he had quit high school. Orlando was a happy-go-lucky person. He came out, started school again, quit, got a job, and then returned to school. He loved California.

Soon after Orlando came out, our younger brother Horacio decided that if his brothers and grandmother were in L.A., he would join us. So he too arrived. My sister Aurora remained with my mother in El Paso, but after the war they would also come to California. Orlando went to Lincoln High School, while Horacio attended Franklin. Both of them played football.

My grandmother periodically left and returned to visit my mother and sister in El Paso. She sometimes felt that there was not much for her to do since I was going to school, working, and beginning to get involved with the CIO. My grandmother remembered how involved my father had been during the Revolution, and she saw me following in his footsteps. Sometimes she despaired and threw her hands up in the air and said, "You are just like your father!"

While she was in L.A., she kept herself busy visiting all our relatives in the area. I think one of the important characteristics of Mexican communities has been the close family ties, even if in some cases family members disagreed politically, as was true in our family. Relatives were relatives, as my grandmother insisted.

My grandmother was very diligent about her family visits; they were to her almost obligatory. She visited that niece, that cousin, this second nephew, and all other family members, no matter how distant. She visited all of them because she thought it was her duty to keep in touch, to see how they were doing. If she could help them in any way, she wouldn't hesitate to do so. On Sundays, we often accompanied her to visit a relative, a ritual practiced by countless other Mexican families across the land.

Besides the Sunday visits to the houses of relatives, *mexicanos* in Los

Angeles engaged in a lively social life, despite the depression. Many of these activities revolved around the churches. This was especially the case during certain religious celebrations, such as the one associated with Our Lady of Guadalupe.

Theater and vaudeville also attracted thousands of Mexicans. The family of Hollywood actor Ramón Navarro—the Samaniegos—used to perform legitimate theater at the Mason Theater. My grandmother particularly enjoyed going there because she knew the Samaniegos. They presented either modern or classical plays.

Actress Rita Hayworth's father, José Cansino, put on one or two dance festivals a year at the Philharmonic Auditorium. These were community events, and the community turned out to see the Ballet Folklórico or marimba bands. Musicians such as Lydia Mendoza and Los Madrugadores [the Early Risers] were quite popular in the 1930s. They performed at the Mason or at the California Theater.

An even more impressive affair would take place when a big travel-ing group such as the Orquesta Sinfónica Típica de Lerdo de Tejada appeared at the Hollywood Bowl. This orchestra from Mexico con-sisted of musicians playing the typical instruments of Mexico, along with dancers and comics. My grandmother's brother-in-law, Pedro Escápite, managed the *orquesta*. The whole community turned out for an event like this and packed the Hollywood Bowl. My grandmother loved to attend these performances.

There was a lot of interest in boxing and other sports among *me-xicanos* in the thirties. Two or three world champions from California, such as Bert Colima, often fought at the Olympic Auditorium or at Gilmore Stadium in Hollywood, where as many as twenty-five thou-sand would attend one of these fights.

The Olympics in 1932 had also attracted many *mexicanos,* especially to see the Mexican and Mexican-American athletes who participated in the running events. In the Los Angeles area, Chicanos dominated cer-tain events such as the five thousand and ten thousand meters. We had runners from Compton Junior College and Watts, such as Manuel Ceja, Manuel Banda, Arturo Avila, and Juan Acevedo, who won the Compton and UCLA relays.

While these types of spectator activities usually occurred without racial incidents, problems arose when *mexicanos* used public facilities such as swimming pools. One incident happened to me and a friend of mine, involving the Bimini Bath House. It was a huge and beautiful building on Third and Vermont. Since I was working indoors at this time and, when I wasn't working, my classes and labor activities kept me inside nearly all day every day, I lost my "El Paso tan"—I got very light, comparatively speaking. I liked to swim and started going to the Bimini Baths, where I never encountered any problems.

However, I took Henry Nava to the baths with me one Saturday morning. Henry was the older brother of Julian Nava, who was on the L.A. school board years later and also became ambassador to Mexico. We went in and checked out towels and a key to a locker.

As we entered the dressing room, I heard a question coming from behind me: "Health certificate?" I turned around and saw Henry get a strange expression on his face, sort of uptight. I took two steps back, and the attendant repeated to Henry: "You've gotta have a health certificate to come in here."

Both Henry and I knew immediately what was happening. Even though many dark, sun-tanned whites were there, Henry was a Mexican with black eyes and black hair and was very sun-tanned. We raised a big stink, and they backed off and let Henry enter. He was so humiliated that he didn't want to ever go back. But I convinced him that we had to go back and test them. We did, and they didn't bother us again.

The exclusion of *mexicanos* from southern California public swimming pools was widely practiced. During the summer of 1938, *mexicanos* filed lawsuits in Norwalk, Westminster, and Montebello. MAM, and later the National Congress of Spanish-Speaking Peoples, took on such issues.

Another area of recreation where Mexicans encountered racism involved dance halls. Like many young people during those days, *mexicanos* enjoyed going to dance halls such as the Palomar Ballroom, next to the Bimini Baths, where for a buck and a half you danced to many of the top bands, such as Benny Goodman's. Yet very dark Mexican kids, as well as those wearing the popular zoot suit, were often excluded. We found out that such exclusion also occurred in other downtown ballrooms.

As a result, groups such as the National Congress of Spanish-Speaking Peoples complained and generated enough publicity to force these facilities to stop discriminating. These developments opened many people's eyes as to what was going on in California and the fact that it was not as liberal as some believed.

CHAPTER FIVE

Working for the Union

While I was in high school in El Paso and after I graduated, I worked at the Warner Drug Company. My cousin Benigna Prats was a bookkeeper there, and she arranged the job for me. I first worked as a bicycle delivery boy and then was promoted to inventory clerk and then to be an assistant to the chief buyer, a Mr. Aguirre. He took an interest in me, and soon I became chief inventory clerk and assistant buyer. I learned all about the drug business, especially about taking stock. I learned to distinguish all the varieties of drugs and medicines.

When I applied for a job through USC, I showed them letters of reference written by my employer in El Paso. USC sent me out to the Brunswig Drug Company, which had a big warehouse next to La Placita near downtown Los Angeles, where many Mexicans congregated on weekends. Brunswig was owned by a wealthy Frenchman, Lucien Napoleon Brunswig, and carried his name. After examining my credentials and realizing that I had some valuable experience in the drug industry, they hired me as a checker.

I was surprised, because a checker was one of the higher-paid employees. And here I was, at age nineteen, starting closer to the top than many others; the next youngest checker was about thirty-five. My appointment generated some resentment from guys who held lower positions and had been working there a few years. I think I got the job primarily because of my USC connections.

In any event, it was a job that I could handle because I was well acquainted with the ordering and pricing of pharmaceuticals. I received thirty dollars a week, plus overtime for weekends. I cleared about thirty-five dollars a week, which, for me as a student, was not bad for that time. I enjoyed my job and did it effectively.

Brunswig was a big operation. It employed about eighteen hundred workers in all of its divisions. Where I worked, there were about nine hundred. I was one of a handful of Mexicans in this labor force. Almost no blacks worked there. Mr. Brunswig had recruited many French employees from France, and there were also many other white ethnics.

The Longshoremen's Union

During my second month at Brunswig, representatives from the Longshoremen's Association, the predecessor of the Longshoremen's Union, came around during our lunch hour and asked for our help in the big dock strike the longshoremen were waging in Los Angeles.* I and several others from Brunswig agreed to help. During our spare time and our lunch hours, we formed picket lines to prevent scab merchandise from being transported into the big warehouses on Los Angeles Street, on San Pedro, and on Central, in close proximity to Brunswig.

We also participated in dawn patrols organized by the longshoremen. We met about five o'clock in the morning in the warehouse district, where the truck drivers bringing in or picking up merchandise often stopped to have coffee in nearby cafes. We talked to the drivers in the cafes and tried to convince them to stop breaking the strike. The strike lasted about one hundred days, with the longshoremen winning.

We were impressed with the longshoremen and their union, and so when they talked about organizing the drug industry, we listened attentively. The first formal meeting to organize Brunswig was conducted in secret in the basement of Local 47 of the Musicians Hall. About one hundred fifty of us heard Jack Tenney, the president of Local 47, talk

---

*The International Longshoremen's and Warehousemen's Union (ILWU) is heir to a long tradition of waterfront unionism and left politics. It was first established as the International Longshoremen's Association in 1853. In 1937, after it moved to organize both docks and inland warehouses, the union voted to join the CIO. It was chartered as the ILWU, with Harry Bridges as its president. The ILWU constitution prohibited discrimination based on political beliefs, promoted a strong role for the union rank and file, and opposed racial discrimination.

about the importance of unionization. In later years, Tenney unfortunately became a red-baiter; as a state senator during the 1940s and 1950s, he persecuted many CIO activists.

The main motivation at Brunswig for joining the longshoremen and establishing a union was that the workers in the drug industry were badly underpaid. Despite the depression, the drug industry in Los Angeles had prospered as it expanded into the big discount and high-volume drugstores that sold everything from medicines to bicycles. Consequently, workers in the industry who had once dealt with fifteen thousand items now checked out forty-five thousand items. At the same time that they worked more and had more responsibilities, they received no comparable wage increases.

Being a stocker in a drug warehouse, for example, was not like being a stocker in a grocery warehouse. Drug stockers had to know and distinguish between thousands of items, not just a few basic ones as in the grocery warehouses. Stocking pharmaceuticals was not like stocking sacks of beans. Yet unionized grocery stockers received almost double the wages of those in the drug industry.

The organizers from the Longshoremen's Association stressed these disparities. They also pointed out the vacation plans, the grievance procedures, and the job security that workers in these other industries had won as a result of unionization. Many of the drug companies unilaterally fired workers. Brunswig rarely did, but its more paternalistic policy also worked to the disadvantage of the workers. The main argument at Brunswig was that, although we were highly skilled, we were being treated like ordinary warehousemen, as if all that was needed was a strong back and muscles to load beans. This argument caught on.

We began to organize Local 26 of the newly constituted International Longshoremen's and Warehousemen's Union, the ILWU, by the fall of 1937. Because I was attending college and was therefore considered educated, I was elected recording secretary.

We met not only with workers at Brunswig but also with those working at some of the other warehouses, such as those owned by McKesson and Thrifty. To organize within the plants, we devised a variety of secret code words transmitted by the various checkers such as myself. We organized by first talking to workers inside the plant and during the lunch hour. We recruited a number of workers in this way.

With workers who expressed stronger reservations about the union, we made a point of riding with them, either in the same car pool or on the same bus. Los Angeles at that time had very good public transportation—the red cars and the yellow cars that went everywhere. So we boarded the bus with the workers, sat down next to some, and started a conversation.

"Where are you going?"

"Temple City."

"You are? What have you guys been doing? Have you heard of the union?"

In this way we recruited many more. We recruited the last group of workers by going to their homes. In about six months, we had organized about ninety-five percent of the workers at Brunswig as well as at the McKesson's and Thrifty Drug warehouses.

Lloyd Seeliger

While I didn't particularly care for my position as recording secretary, I enjoyed meeting, talking with, and organizing workers. This was a wonderful experience that taught me some valuable lessons and techniques about labor organizing.

One guy who taught me a lot was Lloyd Seeliger. He was a big Norwegian—a huge guy, with hands as big as baseball mitts. He had a big rough voice and swaggered like a big gorilla. He was six foot six and must have weighed about three hundred pounds, with not an ounce of fat on him. He had joined the Wobblies, the IWW, when he was thirteen years old, and for some years he had worked and organized in the Pacific Northwest as a logger. Many of the Wobblies in the Northwest, like Lloyd, were Norwegians, Finns, or Swedes; and they were all very militant union people.

Lloyd knew all the tricks of organizing, and he took me on as his apprentice. He stopped the workers as they were driving out of the plant, and before they could say anything, he planted his huge foot on the running board of the car. He planted it with such authority that the driver couldn't easily drive on. Lloyd then said, "My name is Lloyd Seeliger, and I'm with the Longshoremen's Union. I want to talk to you about signing your union card. I know you work here. I've seen you in one of the departments. We really would like to see you with us because we think you're a pretty good fellow."

No one dared to speed up and avoid Lloyd. He recruited a number of workers in this way. I also tried my hand at this technique. I put my foot down on the running board and told them, "I'm Bert Corona, and I'm organizing for the union. How are you, brother?" The first thing you did was get their hands off the wheel by offering a handshake.

Another technique Lloyd used was to rig a loudspeaker to his car. During the lunch hour, as the workers ate outside, he talked to them from outside the plant: "Brothers and sisters, this is the CIO International Longshoremen's and Warehousemen's Union talking to you about joining the union. You shouldn't be out here in the hot sun eating your sandwiches. The company should provide you with a decent facility." And he talked about the other conditions. Once in a while, the police showed up and arrested Lloyd because he was operating a loudspeaker without a permit. He was ingenious in his approach to the workers.

On other occasions, he talked himself into a job with one of the much smaller warehouses that sometimes employed fewer than a dozen people. At first, the owners were not aware that Lloyd belonged to the union. Instead, they were impressed with his boast that he could throw a sack of beans or whatever from inside the plant all the way to the trucks.

The first thing Lloyd would do in this job was to arrive early and talk union to the workers. On one street in the warehouse district, he organized every plant with this method. Eventually, the big owners caught on and complained to Lloyd's boss. But by then his organizing had been completed.

Perhaps the most lasting lesson I got from Lloyd was never to ask anyone if they wanted to join the union. He never asked a single worker if he or she wanted to join. Instead, he would confidently thrust out an endorsement card and a pencil and instruct the workers to just write their name and address and to sign the card. To this day, as I still help to sign up workers for the unions or register them to vote, especially Mexican workers, I use Lloyd's technique. I never say, "Do you want to sign this card?" Rather, I say, "Have you signed your card? Well, what are you waiting for? Sign it. Okay, who's next?"

Lloyd always operated as if everyone agreed about the union and we were all in this together. He was a natural: "Everybody wants to build a union; just sign your name right here. We're building a union."

He completely disagreed with the National Labor Relations Act, which was passed in 1936 and which many consider the Magna Carta of the American labor movement because it sanctioned union elections in industries, under the supervision of the National Labor Relations Board. Lloyd couldn't understand the idea of holding an election to decide whether or not workers wanted to have a right that, he believed, inherently belonged to them. Lloyd felt that it was a mockery to debate this right. In his years of organizing, he never participated in an election. He just showed the bosses that he had signed up almost all of their workers and insisted that if they didn't agree now to a contract, the union would strike. The bosses generally agreed.

Union Recognition

When we organized at Brunswig, we employed all of Lloyd's techniques because the workers were at first afraid of joining the union. Los Angeles had a history of being anti-labor and of being an open-shop town where unions were not tolerated. All of the industries in Los Angeles belonged to the Merchants and Manufacturers Association, which had been organized in the twenties to fight unions. It wrote up blacklists to deprive union activists of work, and it propagandized against the unions—especially the CIO unions in the thirties—by calling them Communist and Bolshevik.

Still, despite such opposition, we successfully organized Brunswig and the rest of the drug industry. Using Lloyd's techniques, the organizing committee at Brunswig, of which I was a member, simply went to the manager of the plant, a Mr. Folsom, and informed him that we had signed up ninety-five percent of the workers into Local 26 of the Longshoremen's Union. We said that we didn't need an election, which would be costly for the company and which they would in the end lose. We told Folsom to call a meeting that evening of the workers on the plant grounds and ask for a show of hands in support of the union.

Folsom responded, "But how will the workers determine their rights unless we have an NLRB-sanctioned election?"

"They already have their rights, Mister Folsom," Lloyd replied. "We have them all signed up, so what are we arguing about?"

Mr. Folsom and Mr. Brunswig capitulated and agreed to call a meeting at seven-thirty that evening. Out of eight hundred fifty workers, seven hundred ten came out and raised their hands in support of the union.

After we secured our contract at Brunswig, I, in my spare time, helped to organize other industries for Local 26 of the Longshoremen's Union, including the hardware, paper, and waste-material industries and the milling warehouses. Between 1937 and 1940, I served on various organizing committees and, in 1940, was head of the strike committee for Local 26. As an organizer, I never dealt just with Mexican workers. I liked to work with them and organize them, but as an officer, I represented all of the local and organized workers of different ethnic backgrounds.

Some of these other warehouses proved to be more difficult and more sophisticated in employing the NLRA to contest us. In the paper plants, we also ran up against the competition of the Teamsters Local 208. Employers in Los Angeles favored the more opportunistic and less militant Teamsters. Still, we succeeded in a number of these places, even though in many cases we participated in long and bitter strikes.

By 1941 we had over six thousand members in Local 26, representing not only the drug industry but also many other warehouses. In addition, we organized dozen of factories in other industries besides the warehouses, including furniture plants, die-casting plants, molding plants, and metal-fabricating plants. The workers came and asked for our help, and we gave it to them. However, after we organized these workers, we turned many of them over to other unions—such as the unions for the clothing, oil, auto, electrical, mining, and rubber workers—at the orders of Harry Bridges, the head of the ILWU and of all the CIO in the West.* Everyone looked to the ILWU for leadership and assistance.

---

*Harry Bridges (1901–1990) was born in Australia and came to the United States as a young man. He began working as a longshoreman in San Francisco in 1927, joining the San Francisco local of the International Longshoremen's Association in 1933 and rising rapidly to leadership in the union. Bridges worked closely with Communist Party members to develop a militant longshoremen's union. In 1937, he led the West Coast ILA into the CIO as the ILWU. He became ILWU president and CIO regional director.

Labeled a Communist by business and government officials, Bridges was subjected to deportation threats for several years. He became a U.S. citizen in 1945. In 1949, however, Bridges was charged with lying on his naturalization papers regarding Communist affiliations. The Supreme Court ruled in his favor in 1955. See Robert W. Cherny's entry on Bridges in *Encyclopedia of the American Left*, ed. Mari Jo Buhle, Paul Buhle, and Dan Georgakas (Urbana: University of Illinois Press, 1992), pp. 106–107.

Political Education

Besides learning about the labor movement during the late 1930s, I also expanded my political education. Here again Lloyd Seeliger was my teacher. Lloyd was a walking political machine. He always carried copies of the latest *Daily People's World,* which was the paper of the Communist Party on the West Coast; socialist magazines; and a variety of other political publications—all of which he made sure that I and others received. He also took me to a number of political forums on weekday nights and weekends.

Lloyd was totally a political animal. We went to forums in support of Republican Spain, against Hitler, on Latin America, and on defending Jews in Nazi Germany. These forums were sponsored by a number of organizations. One was called the League Against War and Fascism, which was essentially a radical Jewish forum. The Committee in Support of Republican Spain received support from many ethnic groups, but its biggest support came from both the Communist Party and the Socialist Party. The Sixth Street Town Meeting every week emphasized New Deal and CIO issues.

Another active group was the Hollywood Committee to Aid Farmworkers, led by people such as author John Steinbeck. It was established to support the big agricultural strikes, including those by hundreds of Mexican workers, in the Imperial Valley and elsewhere in California.

Every Sunday, the Grace Methodist Episcopal Church in East Los Angeles sponsored a town forum. Bishop Harry F. Ward, a prominent leader of the Methodist church, was an ardent peace advocate and was committed to educating people to the threat of Hitlerism and fascism. He also sent speakers to talk about conditions in the South, where lynchings and persecutions of blacks were rampant.

Some of the speakers that I particularly recall were Carey McWilliams, speaking on the plight of the Dust Bowl refugees; the environmentalist Scott Nearing, who was very strong for peace and cooperative socialism and against fascism; Upton Sinclair on his EPIC movement, which favored turning over unused factories and land to the unemployed; and the widow of Lincoln Steffens, the old Progressive muckraker.* All of this represented a type of politicized subculture in

*Carey McWilliams was a lawyer and author who investigated farm labor conditions in California during the 1930s. In 1939, he published an exposé about

Los Angeles, to which Lloyd introduced me and which raised my own political consciousness and commitment to social justice.

I, of course, didn't come to the union movement or to left politics in a vacuum. Besides being influenced by the memory of my father's role in the Mexican Revolution and my early family and religious socialization in El Paso, which was based on the idea of standing up against injustice, I had also been influenced by the New Deal. I was very much affected by the terrible conditions of the depression and the failure of the capitalist system to provide a decent existence for all Americans, including the Mexicans who were being deported. As part of our informal study group in El Paso, we had read socialist literature, as I mentioned. I didn't have any predisposition to being anti-labor or anti-socialist.

So when the Longshoremen's Union organized the drug industry, I wasn't shocked. I knew some labor history. Some of the Mexicans who had entered the United States around World War I had migrated to big cities like San Francisco that had strong union movements. Some joined the unions. During the depression, many of these workers returned to El Paso and spoke about their experiences in church meetings or in homes. They talked about the big strikes in San Francisco and about the impact of labor unions. They talked about key

---

the exploitative conditions in California agriculture, *Factories in the Fields: The Story of Migratory Farm Labor in California* (1939; reissue, Santa Barbara: Peregrine Press, 1971). He also served as chief of the Division of Immigration and Housing for California in the late 1930s. McWilliams was the first to write a history of Mexican-Americans; this work is titled *North from Mexico: The Spanish-Speaking People of the United States* (Philadelphia: Lippincott, 1948). From 1955 to 1975, McWilliams was editor of *The Nation*.

Scott Nearing was a socialist writer who in the 1930s critiqued the wasteful nature of industrial capitalism and its effects on the environment. See Scott Nearing, *The Making of a Radical: A Political Biography* (New York: Harper & Row, 1972).

The End Poverty In California (EPIC) movement was headed by Upton Sinclair, the socialist author who had written *The Jungle* (1906), a fictionalized exposé of the Chicago meatpacking industry. In 1934, Sinclair organized EPIC as a political action group in California, and it won control of the machinery of the state Democratic Party. Opposed by the Communist Party but supported by a coalition of the unemployed, trade unionists, and professionals, Sinclair was narrowly defeated in the race for governor of California in 1934. See Eric Homberger's entry on Sinclair in Buhle, Buhle, and Georgakas, *Encyclopedia of the American Left*, pp. 701–702.

legal cases such as that of Tom Mooney and the Sacco-Vanzetti trial.*

In addition, some of our Protestant pastors in El Paso had spent time in California ministering to the Mexican farmworkers in the San Joaquin Valley and in the Imperial Valley. They returned and talked about their experiences there, the plight of the Mexican workers, and the big agricultural strikes such as the one in Oxnard around 1935. And, of course, many of our family friends in El Paso had been *magonistas,* and they continued to read and discuss socialist and anarcho-syndicalist literature.

I was further attracted to socialist ideas because of my sense that socialism could solve many of the problems created by capitalism. The Communist Party always stressed the example of the Soviet Union and of the significant progress there since the Bolshevik Revolution. Closer to home, we had the example of the *cardenistas* in Mexico, where President Lázaro Cárdenas in the 1930s had brought about agrarian reform under a quasi-socialist system and had nationalized the oil industry.

Despite my more middle-class family background, I considered myself working class when I joined the Longshoremen's Union, because I was now on my own and working. I figured that joining the union was in my best interest as a worker. My livelihood depended on how I was being treated at Brunswig and on what I was being paid.

When I joined Local 26, I wasn't conscious that this would turn out to be a career pattern. I didn't really view it that way because we had so much work to do. I saw it as a challenge to try to organize the unorganized, and if I could do this and still be able to continue school, it was okay with me. If I had to delay my schooling, that was all right.† But I didn't really envision myself as being a labor leader all my life. My thinking was more constrained by the immediate task, which was vast.

---

*Tom Mooney, a labor organizer in San Francisco in the years before World War I, was unjustly convicted and sentenced to death for a bombing incident in 1916. After a number of years of international protest by labor and radical groups, Mooney was finally pardoned and freed in 1939.

Nicola Sacco and Bartolomeo Vanzetti, two Italian immigrants who were outspoken anarchists, were convicted of robbery and murder in 1921 in Massachusetts, in a trial marked by weak evidence and contradictory testimony. Despite a public outcry and numerous appeals over the next six years, Sacco and Vanzetti were executed in 1927.

†Corona stopped taking classes at the USC downtown evening campus by 1939.

Union Politics

In 1940, our contract with the drug industry came to a close. It had been a good contract, but the drug owners were preparing to put up a tough fight in the renegotiations. This led to a heated dispute within Local 26.

The president of the local was Marion Phelps, who was an old Wobbly and the founder of Local 26. He believed that we should strike immediately and put the owners on the defensive. Others, like myself, believed that we needed more time to prepare for the strike. We knew that our officers, including myself, had been so busy organizing other industries that we had neglected our own workers in the drug warehouses, and we had not laid down the foundation for a protracted struggle. We argued for a ninety-day period to organize the strike. Harry Bridges supported us, but he couldn't convince Phelps to delay the strike.

Phelps felt that he could win the strike with only a week's preparation, and he got carried away with his own rhetoric. Inside of a week's time, the owners were tougher than ever. As head of the strike committee, I and others couldn't bring the bosses to negotiate a decent contract. So we settled the strike under very tough conditions. We won some concessions, but lost on other issues.

In early 1941, Phelps was ill, and he decided not to run for reelection as president of Local 26. I ran for his position and was unanimously elected. But no sooner was I elected than I was confronted with a challenge by Charlie Pfeiffer, the secretary-treasurer of the local and a Phelps supporter. Pfeiffer was very power-driven, and he wanted to have his position designated as the chief executive officer of the local.

To assert his authority and to challenge me, he organized a slowdown at Brunswig to try and force more concessions from the management. But we had just come off a tough strike, and I as well as my supporters opposed the slowdown. Still, the word got out inside the plant that a slowdown was planned.

The secretary-treasurer had his guys place calls to me on the checking floor, and they'd say, "We're really cutting down production up here on the third floor." But the company was recording all of this. I would respond, "Brother, that's nice, but you're not supposed to be doing this." The secretary-treasurer even called me on the house phone and told me "to keep up the slowdown."

The company, believing that I was behind this action, fired me and threatened reprisals against others. Bridges asked my advice on how to handle the situation with management, also recognizing that another strike would be disastrous. I told him that he should go in and talk to management, since they obviously didn't want to talk to me, and the secretary-treasurer would only make matters worse.

Bridges did so and on returning told me, "Bert, they have agreed not to lay off anybody else if we do not pursue a slowdown, and they will negotiate grievances with our stewards; but they are adamant about not taking you back. They just don't want you back."

So I was out of Brunswig after more than four years of working there—plus I was a non-paid president of Local 26. Bridges later called me up and said, "I'll put you on the payroll of the CIO, and you'll be an organizer." Since I was out of a job, I accepted but remained as president of Local 26.

Organizing the Waste-Material Workers

As an organizer for the CIO in Los Angeles, I participated in unionizing a number of other industries. One of my more memorable experiences concerned the work we did in the waste-material industry. These were very large operations that included the waste-paper and waste-bottle plants, the waste-rag plants, and the companies that processed waste rubber tires and scrap metal.

These industries had been started up by Jewish refugees from the Russian Revolution of 1917. Actually, many of them had remained in Russia following the revolution and had participated in the waste-material industry in Lenin's New Economic Program, which combined some capitalist industrial practices with the new socialist economy. After Lenin died in the early 1920s, most of them left and came to the United States.

Some of those who arrived in California established new waste-material plants. Some of the plants included Eureka Iron and Metal, Berg Iron and Metal, Newmark Bag, U.S. Bag, Friedman Bag, California Mill Supply, and Finklestein Iron and Metal. Many of the owners had also recruited a large number of other Russian refugees, such as Molokan Russians, as workers. Some of these workers had labored in the same kind of plants in Russia.

Although some men worked in this industry, the labor force con-

sisted predominantly of women. I visited one of these plants and saw
Russian women wearing beautiful kerchiefs on their heads and beautiful blouses and skirts. Alongside the Russian women in the used-bag
plants, Mexican women also worked, sewing the reclaimed bags. The
Russian and Mexican men who worked there did a lot of the more
back-breaking type of work.

Conditions were very bad in the waste-material industry for all the
workers. In the plants that processed used grain bags, the idea was to
clean the bags by using machines that sucked the remaining grain and
dust out of the bags, get the bags absolutely clean, and then have the
women stitch them up again so the bags could be reused. This cleaning
process created very unhealthy conditions for the workers. The old
machines dispersed a great deal of dust into the plant. Sometimes there
was so much dust in the air that it resembled a fog bank. You couldn't
see inside, and the workers would be constantly coughing. They suffered all kinds of allergies. It was horrible. Wages were very low, fifteen
to twenty cents an hour. The Russians and Mexicans received the same
pay.

The Jewish Russian owners pitted the Molokans and the Mexicans
against each other. They believed that these two ethnic groups would
never join together to resist bad working conditions. The Russian
owners communicated with the Russian workers in Russian or Yiddish,
while a Mexican foreman spoke in Spanish to the Mexicans. Because
of the language barrier, little communication existed between Russians
and Mexicans.

The International Ladies Garment Workers Union, known as the
ILGWU, and the Textile Workers Union had earlier tried but failed to
organize the used-bag industry. But conditions were so bad in these
plants that the workers themselves initiated another effort to form a
union. During the time we were waging our questionable strike in the
drug industry, representatives of the workers at the used-bag plants
came to us and requested our help. "You just stand by us, and we'll
organize ourselves," they insisted.

We put together a rank-and-file organizing committee of Yiddish-
speaking and Russian Jews, Mexicans, blacks, and Anglos. During the
time that we were on strike, this organizing committee pulled off a
couple of quickie strikes. Lloyd Seeliger worked with them while I was
still with the drug strike.

One day, about a week before we ended our strike, a huge crowd of workers from the used-bag and other waste-material plants came to our union headquarters on Second and Los Angeles. Our hall could hold only about a thousand, but three thousand workers came. They stopped working that day and marched to our headquarters to ask for union membership.

Some of our officers, however, expressed skepticism about organizing such a poor industry. Our secretary-treasurer even condemned the workers as "lumpen." He erroneously believed that the term "lumpen" simply meant poor rather than describing an underclass.

Fortunately, better heads prevailed, especially after we counted about thirty-three hundred workers, and we signed them into the union. Since we were still on strike against the drug industry, we instructed the used-bag workers to go back to work but promised that we would in time deal with the poor conditions in their plants.

Five or six months later, after I went to work with Harry Bridges and the CIO, Lloyd Seeliger and I worked to organize the waste-material industry. At the used-bag plants, the initial problem involved how to communicate with both the Russians and the Mexicans together. The Russians spoke only Yiddish or Russian, and the Mexicans spoke only Spanish.

We finally devised a method at our meetings in which one of us, as CIO representative, spoke in English and then paused to have our words translated first into Yiddish, then into Russian, and then into Spanish. The meetings would last three or four hours because of the translations. It was also frustrating for the non-Russians because we prohibited smoking during the meetings; the Molokan Russians, because of their religion, didn't smoke. I always thought it was quite amusing that the Russians could stand working with all of that horrible grain dust but still objected to cigarette smoking.

As we got to know the workers better, I discovered that, especially among the Russians, there existed a tremendous amount of political savvy. One of the men would say, "Well, we haven't been active since the 1905 revolution in Russia, but when I was in Smolensk, I stood on the top of a temple and shot at Cossacks from there. I guess I can do the same again." Some of the Russians were very militant as a result of their experiences in the Russian Revolution.

We explained to them that such militant action as taking up arms wasn't necessary to get improved working conditions in the plants. But some didn't believe us. "Oh, yes," they replied, "a company's a company, a boss is a boss, a capitalist is a capitalist—they're all bad."

They also understood that in order to succeed in this labor action they needed to seek unity with the Mexicans. For their part, the Mexicans also understood this. On the basis of the common plight of these poor workers, we built the union and forced the owners to recognize it.

In organizing the waste-material industry, I again applied many of the techniques that Lloyd had taught me. Of key importance was that after we signed up over ninety percent of the workers, we refused to have an NLRB election. If the owners refused to recognize the union, we struck right there and then. I particularly remember an encounter in 1941 with the owner of the Eureka Iron and Metal Company. We signed up all the workers, and then I went with Blanche, my wife of just a few months, to see Jerry Miller, the owner.

"We represent the people, Mister Miller. The majority have signed up," we informed him.

But he refused to believe this: "No, they haven't. Now get the hell out of my office."

"We were just trying to tell you that unless we can come to an agreement today, we're going to strike tomorrow morning."

"The hell you are. I've got my attorneys, and I'm going to have an election."

"You can have all the elections you want," I replied, "but we're not going for no election. Either you agree to bargain with us or we're going out tomorrow morning."

Blanche and I walked out of Miller's office. We had about four hundred workers, mostly Mexicans, on our side. We went back to the workers and spread the word: "¡Mañana en la mañana huelga!" [Tomorrow in the morning—strike!]

Blanche and I arrived the next morning about six. Lloyd was organizing four more plants a few blocks down from Eureka. The idea was that all of the waste-material plants would be struck that day. We organized the workers into picket lines and blocked all of the entrances.

The little old Russian Jews who gathered old metal, tires, and sacks in their horse-drawn carts and delivered them to the plants found that on that morning they couldn't make their deliveries. We told them, "There's a strike here, brother." Many of them were also refugees from

Russia and possessed memories of militance: "Oh, it's a strike; we can't break this." They'd turn around and go back.

When Mr. Miller arrived in his big Cadillac, we let him through as the workers hooted at him. Upon arrival in his office, he realized that not only was his plant being struck but so was the entire industry. He walked out of his office and called down to me, "Mister Corona, can you come here? I want to talk to you."

Blanche and I went up to his office. After inviting us to sit down, he pulled out his desk drawer and took out a gun.

"You know I could kill you right now."

"Well," I responded, "I know you could, but I don't think you will."

"Goddamn it! This gun tells you how determined I am to keep the union out. At least we have to have an election."

"No, we don't need an election. We're ready to bargain right now. If you want to spend all of that money to fight us, go ahead. But we're going to strike because conditions are so bad in your company."

He argued that he treated his workers well. So I said, "Well, we're ready to negotiate now. If you refuse, we'll not go back to work."

We started to get up to leave, but he prevented us and asked if we knew his lawyer in San Francisco. I said that I knew he was a big-time lawyer who represented the warehouse industry.

"That's right," Miller stated. "He represents the Zellerbach Corporation, but he's also my attorney. I would like for you to talk to him by phone. If he has a solution to this problem, will you guys go back to work?"

"Well, it all depends. I'll be happy to talk to him."

So Miller rang up this attorney and informed him of the situation. He then asked me to take the phone.

"What's the problem, Mister Corona?" I heard the attorney ask.

"Well, we've got ninety-five percent of the people signed up for the union, and we're waiting to bargain. We don't see that there's any point in delaying recognition. We've struck the entire industry this morning."

"What!" the attorney exclaimed. "You've struck the entire industry?" He then got back on the phone with Miller, who, after some argument, wrote down some lines on paper. After he hung up, Miller called his secretary in and dictated a letter to her in which he agreed to recognize the union and to commence bargaining. He signed the letter and gave it to me.

"Fine," I said and went outside to inform the workers. We started the talks that day. Soon the other plants also fell into line.

Youth Gangs and Union Organizing

While organizing the waste-material industry, the CIO developed a very important relationship with the growing number of Mexican youth gangs in the barrios. Many of the youths who belonged to gangs were children of Mexican men and women who worked in the waste-material industry. Paid wages as low as ten to fifteen cents an hour, these Mexican workers were forced to live in old and dilapidated housing in what was then called the Flats, below Pecan and Clarence streets, down near the Los Angeles River along Mission Street, in Boyle Heights, along the river in shacks, in what was called Dogtown along North Main Street, or toward South Central below East Olympic and East Tenth. These were very poor areas with inferior schools and few recreational facilities.

Alienated in the schools and unemployed, Mexican youths formed gangs—the Dogtown Gang, the Flats Gang, the Clanton Fourteen, the Clanton Eighteen, and various others. While some delinquency and crime were associated with gangs, many gangs served as mini-communities for youth. Some of these gangs had actually originated in El Paso and had been brought to Los Angeles as whole families migrated to the West Coast. In El Paso, gangs in El Segundo Barrio had included Los de la Siete [the Seventh Street Gang], Los de la Quinta [the Fifth Street Gang], and Los de la Hill [the Hill Street Gang].

Many of the Mexican youths—from ages thirteen to twenty-two—who joined gangs represented dropouts from the public junior and senior high schools. As a result of language problems, racism in the schools, and a pattern of sending Mexican kids to continuation schools, which were like detention centers, many kids simply dropped out of school. Gangs represented a way of dealing with their alienation and providing a support system outside of the family among their peers.

Many gang members—referred to as *pachucos*—worked part-time at odd jobs. They were not really an underclass. Unlike many of today's gangs, the gangs of the 1930s had few turf wars and did not deal in drugs. Friction sometimes developed between gangs over girlfriends, but not the kind of warfare one sees today.

One of the reasons gang members eagerly sought jobs was to have enough money to buy the type of clothes that became a form of identity for them. There were at first two particular types of dress for male gang members. One type originated in El Paso and consisted of high-waisted pants and bell-bottom trousers. Another style involved fully draped pegged-bottom pants, a long jacket, and a porkpie hat. The latter style in time became more popular and became known as the zoot suit.

Young women also belonged to the gangs and possessed their own distinctive dress. Some wore very short skirts, while others favored pegged skirts. Hairdos were also distinctive. At first, the young women wore their hair very straight, with bangs and Buster Brown side cuts. Later, however, they began to let their hair grow and piled it on top of their head. This longer hair style became associated with the girlfriends of zoot suiters. Because many of the youths, both male and female, worked during the week, they sported their distinctive dress only on weekends when they'd go to parties and dances.

The CIO came into contact with the gangs as a result of the organizing work we did with their parents in the waste-material industry, the meatpacking plants, and various other industries where Mexicans worked. Organizing these plants, of course, was not easy. We encountered tremendous opposition, not the least being goon squads and police, who attacked our picket lines. We noticed that many of the kids of the workers joined their parents on the picket lines. These kids were members of the gangs.

So we approached the gangs and solicited their help in getting more of their members to join the picket lines. The gangs agreed to assist us, and large numbers of their members came out to picket the plants. Many of them were attacked and even hurt by the strikebreakers and police who attempted to break our strikes. But the kids, like their parents, held fast. Some were arrested, and we had to bail them out.

A real alliance was formed, and the youths proved invaluable because of their courage and commitment. Some of them actually had jobs in these industries and participated in the strikes. We developed an official relationship with some of the gangs.

As part of our effort to align the gangs with the CIO, we once organized a big dance in 1940, in a huge empty garage in what is now the Chinatown area. We hired a big Mexican band and invited all of the gangs. About fifteen hundred youngsters attended. Many of them came with a lot of reluctance and trepidation. They didn't know what to expect. At first, each gang congregated apart from the others, and they eyed each other suspiciously.

But the ice broke when a very personable CIO leader by the name of Chili Duarte spoke to the kids. Duarte, a dark-looking Portuguese from San Francisco, told the gang members that the reason the CIO had sponsored the dance was to inform them about what the CIO was doing for their parents and for the Mexican people. He stressed that the CIO fought against discrimination and racism and against police brutality. He appealed to the gangs to join us in the struggles. He also encouraged them to participate in politics as a way of forcing city and county officials to upgrade the schools, to build better recreational facilities, and to provide more job opportunities for youth.

Our appeal was well received by the gangs, and these kids provided important help as we organized in the waste-material, meatpacking, steel, furniture, and garment industries. We reciprocated by making special efforts to get jobs in these industries for gang members. Since we controlled the hiring process in some of these plants, we ensured employment for many of these kids.

Race, Ethnicity, and Class

Although I worked to unionize workers from different ethnic backgrounds, I did participate in some efforts that were specifically directed toward organizing Mexican workers. A Committee on Spanish-Speaking Workers was formed through the leadership of Luisa Moreno, the only Latino officer of the state CIO. It combatted any form of discrimination against Mexican and other Latino workers. I remember Luisa standing up at our state CIO conventions and informing members about the particular conditions affecting many Mexican and other Spanish-speaking workers, including the fact that many couldn't speak English, were not U.S. citizens, and didn't even possess permanent residency. Consequently, she argued, we needed a special outreach to these workers. The committee functioned mostly during the 1940s.

Other Mexican-American unionists besides myself and Luisa participated in the committee, such as Frank López of the Furniture Workers Union. The committee was comparable to a similar CIO committee aimed at black workers. It raised money to assist in its work of putting out materials in Spanish, informing workers of their rights and about the importance of unionization. It also sponsored citizenship classes. Besides its work in Los Angeles and other urban areas, the committee went into the fields and packing sheds. The National Congress of Spanish-Speaking Peoples served as an important ally to the committee.

Race discrimination was, of course, a major issue confronted by many groups at this time. We were getting ready to go to war to protect democracy, and at the same time certain Americans faced discrimination and segregation. It was a contradiction. One particular fight against racial discrimination in which I participated concerned Fetus Coleman, a black man unjustly accused of rape in San Francisco. Coleman one day was walking through Golden Gate Park and stumbled upon a white policeman who was having sex with a white woman. Startled by Coleman's appearance, the cop quickly put on his pants and proceeded to arrest Coleman for raping the white woman, who so testified in court. Although he proclaimed his innocence, Coleman was sentenced to San Quentin.

Enraged at this injustice, civil libertarians, including the NAACP, the Urban League, and the National Congress of Spanish-Speaking Peoples, quickly formed a statewide defense committee to free Fetus Coleman. I joined the committee and spoke at meetings and churches appealing for support. As a result of the committee's work, Coleman was finally freed.

These early experiences with the CIO not only represented my baptism in the labor movement but also reflected a major watershed in the history of American labor. For me, the CIO constituted the only viable effort to bring organization and protection to large numbers of workers. Although in Europe most workers were organized into unions, in the United States only a small percentage were unionized. This had resulted from the mistaken policies and strategies of the AFL, which since its formation in the 1880s had concentrated only on organizing skilled workers by trades. This not only excluded vast numbers of unskilled workers but also led to a ridiculous situation where in particular industries as many as fifteen or twenty unions represented different skilled trades. This split even the skilled labor force and often prevented a unified front against employers.

What was needed, especially in the crisis of the depression, was industrial organization in which all workers, skilled and unskilled, would be represented by one union. This is what the CIO was all about. This was particularly important in bringing organization and protection to the unorganized, many of them ethnic workers such as blacks and Mexicans. I had a sense of the historical importance of the CIO, and I viewed the CIO as a movement whose time had come. Nothing could stop it, and—for a time—nothing did.

The CIO developed some of the major unions of our time, such as the ILWU, the United Mine Workers, the United Steel Workers of America, the United Auto Workers, the Mine, Mill and Smelter Workers, and many others. And it also developed some of the great labor leaders, such as John L. Lewis and Walter Reuther. I was privileged to have worked with one such leader—Harry Bridges, the head of the Longshoremen's Union.

I was not a close friend of Bridges, but we had a very good working relationship. Not only did he support our various labor struggles, but he also gave support to important Mexican-American community groups such as the National Congress of Spanish-Speaking Peoples. He always supported the rights of Mexican immigrant workers, whether they possessed documents or not. He was not a dictatorial type of leader. He tolerated diversity of opinion and acknowledged the contributions of others. He was very receptive to the rank and file, and I could reach him whenever I needed to. I trusted him, and he trusted me.

CHAPTER SIX

The Mexican-American Left

Besides my involvement with the CIO union drives in the late 1930s and early 1940s, I also participated in some of the activities of El Congreso Nacional del Pueblo de Habla Española [the National Congress of Spanish-Speaking Peoples]. El Congreso was a militant organization formed in 1939 to fight for the basic rights of all Spanish-speaking people in the United States. I first heard of El Congreso through my association with the Mexican American Movement. We received reports about El Congreso from Juan Acevedo, Jess Aguirre, and others who attended early organizing meetings in Los Angeles.

What impressed me was that El Congreso was going to carry out a program that addressed a variety of issues affecting the Spanish-speaking: police repression, racial discrimination, increased educational opportunities, better jobs, barrio improvements, lower rents. El Congreso's program mirrored—but in a more impressive fashion—what MAM had hoped to do. Consequently, it seemed natural to gravitate toward El Congreso.

MAM and other Mexican organizations were invited to participate in the organizing meetings. News of El Congreso also began to appear in newspapers such as *La Opinión* and the *Los Angeles Daily News*. Many of us assisted in the preparations for calling the first national convention. I further became interested and involved with El Congreso because of the strong CIO support for it. Local 26, for example, along with other unions, sponsored the first national convention.

The National Congress of Spanish-Speaking Peoples

The idea of El Congreso originated with a remarkable Latina labor organizer, Luisa Moreno. She worked for the United Cannery, Agricultural, Packing and Allied Workers of America, known as UCAPAWA.* However, believing in the need for a broad civil rights organization for all of the Spanish-speaking in the United States, Luisa took a year off from the union in 1938. With her savings of about five hundred dollars, she visited a number of Spanish-speaking communities throughout the country.

She went to Florida and spoke to Cuban and Spanish cigar workers. She went to the East Coast, where she met with Puerto Ricans, Dominicans, and other Latin Americans, as well as with recent refugees from the Spanish Civil War. She of course traveled throughout the Southwest, speaking to Mexican-American educators, political figures, trade union leaders, priests, nuns, and any self-help, mutual-aid organizations that were receptive. As a result of Luisa's efforts, various Pro-Congreso clubs were formed in preparation for the establishment of the National Congress.

The first national convention of El Congreso was scheduled to meet in Albuquerque in March 1939. Regrettably, the convention was canceled because of heavy red-baiting. My understanding of the problem was that Luisa Moreno had made an agreement with Professor George I. Sánchez and Professor Arthur L. Campa, both of whom were teach-

---

*One of the more militant CIO unions, UCAPAWA was organized in 1937 to assist in unionizing agricultural workers. The formation of UCAPAWA brought together a diverse group of field workers who were mainly racial minorities. UCAPAWA also organized in fisheries, canneries, and processing sheds. One of its key characteristics was its policy of nondiscrimination, important in industries dominated by women and minority workers. Union locals were organized on an interracial basis. In 1944, the union changed its name to the Food, Tobacco, Agricultural, and Allied Workers (FTA). See Bob Korstad's entry on the FTA in *Encyclopedia of the American Left*, ed. Mari Jo Buhle, Paul Buhle, and Dan Georgakas (Urbana: University of Illinois Press, 1992), pp. 234–235.

ing at that time at the University of New Mexico, to host the national convention.* However, as preparations proceeded, representatives of the House Un-American Activities Committee in Washington got wind of the convention and red-baited it and the participants.†

The House Committee accused El Congreso of being a radical movement that wanted to separate the Mexicans of the Southwest from the rest of the United States and either form a new republic or return the Southwest to Mexico. It further charged that El Congreso would foment violent riots and revolutionary activities. In all, the committee created such hysteria that the University of New Mexico pressured both Sánchez and Campa to rescind the invitation to host the convention or possibly lose their positions. The Albuquerque meeting was canceled and transferred to Los Angeles.

I remember the excitement associated with the national convention of El Congreso, which was finally held in late April 1939 in downtown Los Angeles. We had never had a gathering like this before in Los Angeles, where one could hear about the struggles of Spanish-speaking people throughout the country: in the meatpacking plants, the mines, the canneries, the mills, and the cotton fields. There was also much discussion of Mexico's recent expropriation of the American oil companies, which had aroused the nationalist feelings of many Mexicans in

---

*For more information on Sánchez and Campa, see Mario T. García, *Mexican Americans: Leadership, Ideology, and Identity, 1930–1960* (New Haven: Yale University Press, 1989), pp. 252–290.

†The House Un-American Activities Committee (HUAC) had its origins in the early 1930s but had become more active and prominent by 1938 under the leadership of its chair, Congressman Martin Dies. Dies used the committee and unproven charges of Communist subversion to attack and intimidate the newly organized CIO unions as well as Popular Front groups. In 1946, HUAC became a permanent standing committee, mandated to investigate "subversive and un-American propaganda activities." During the late 1940s and early 1950s, HUAC, as part of the McCarthy red scare, persecuted hundreds of labor and social activists. Using the power of subpoena, HUAC forced or attempted to force "friendly" and "unfriendly" witnesses to testify about Communist membership in labor unions and other progressive organizations. As Richard Criley notes about HUAC: "Since guilt was ideological, it mattered little to the inquisitorial committees whether a person was an actual member of the Communist (or other Left) Party, or a 'fellow traveler' who participated in a CIO union or other progressive cause." See Criley's entry on HUAC in Buhle, Buhle, and Georgakas, *Encyclopedia of the American Left*, pp. 334–336.

the U.S. toward Mexico and against U.S. intervention. Labor representatives from Mexico attended the Los Angeles meeting.

The convention reflected the militant and activist spirit of the time. Representatives came from various parts of the country—from Arizona, Florida, New York, El Paso, San Antonio, Brownsville, Chicago, Pittsburgh, Kansas City, and midwestern communities. California was well represented, with delegates from San Francisco, Sacramento, Stockton, and other locations, including Los Angeles and many of the small towns surrounding it.

Although Mexican-Americans made up the majority of participants—perhaps about three-quarters—there were also Puerto Ricans from the East as well as Cubans, Spaniards, and other Latin Americans in attendance. Labor people, educators, religious leaders, and community organizers attended. Anglo representatives came from the CIO unions such as the Mine, Mill and Smelter Workers, the Longshoremen's Union, and the Steel Workers. There were people from the movie industry as well as writers. Several black representatives attended the convention.

Above all, the congregation of so many Spanish-speaking people stamped in my mind, and in the minds of many others, that we were a national minority and not just a regional one. It became obvious to me that there were Mexicans and other Latinos all over the United States.

The convention itself was organized into large plenary sessions and topical panels. It met for about four days and nights. I was there for three of the four days, primarily attending the panels concerning youth and education. At these particular forums, much alarm was raised about police brutality against Latino youths. Complaints against police actions were voiced not only by California delegates but also by those from other parts of the Southwest as well as New York and Chicago. I also attended a panel dealing with agricultural strikes and the need to support efforts by farmworkers to unionize themselves.

The discussions were carried out mostly in Spanish, but if Anglo delegates or other persons could not express themselves in Spanish, then somebody translated their statements for them. In this way, everyone participated.

Many women attended the convention. I was impressed by how advanced, capable, and militant many of the women were. Some of the women at the convention worked in the motion picture industry, some were secretaries in law firms, others were college students, and still others were active in civil rights organizations. Besides Luisa Moreno and Josefina Fierro, the principal organizers of the convention, other notable women who attended included Linda Silva and Marta Casares. Women from California, Texas, New York, Florida, and elsewhere contributed to a strong women's contingent at the convention and to ensuring a female voice in El Congreso. In fact, women continued to be very visible in El Congreso throughout its history, playing leading roles and working on committees alongside the men.

Various resolutions were advanced by the panels and adopted by the general body at the founding convention. The convention voted support for Republican Spain and condemned the fascist powers for supporting Franco. One resolution criticized the Roosevelt administration for maintaining a blockade against Spain and for not crying out louder against the arming of Franco by Hitler and Mussolini. Other resolutions supported the extension of the National Labor Relations Act to agricultural and domestic household workers, while still others focused on minimum wages and low-cost housing.

One key concern involved defending the Mexican immigrants living in the United States who had come to work on the railroads, in the cotton fields, and in the sugar beet fields, to name a few of the industries that employed Mexican immigrant workers. Resolutions opposed the deportation of these workers and other forms of unjust harassment by the U.S. Immigration Service and the Border Patrol. Unlike some of the moderate Mexican-American organizations such as LULAC, which at the time differentiated between Mexican-Americans and Mexican immigrants, El Congreso opposed such differentiations and instead stressed the unity of all the Spanish-speaking, U.S. citizens or not. An attack on one Spanish-speaking group was an attack on all.

That sense of unity was one of the beautiful things about El Congreso and was why it captivated so many people even though it was a relatively small movement with very little money. Despite its limitations, it had an impact and provided an opportunity to mobilize the protests of many. No one at the convention even questioned the need for a national association such as El Congreso; it was viewed as a given.

"We're getting together for the first time in our history," speaker after speaker would rise to say. "The problems of the Mexicans may have begun in the Southwest, but now we're present throughout the country, including all Latinos. We need to multiply our strength by also getting into the labor movement. We have to organize to protest bad laws that seek to do away with Social Security or the National Labor Relations Act. We have to protect against attacks on the foreign-born as well as on the constitutional rights of all Americans."

El Congreso spoke out on such issues. And the delegates understood that El Congreso was speaking very boldly and openly on behalf of the Spanish-speaking people of the U.S., as no one had before.

But the convention was not all just politics. Various social functions complemented the proceedings. El Congreso sponsored dances and cocktail parties throughout Los Angeles. On the last day—a Sunday—I accompanied Josefina Fierro and several of the younger delegates to a cocktail party and dance at the Club Mocambo on the corner of Hollywood and Vine. It was a big, elaborate club; how Josefina arranged to reserve it for El Congreso, I don't know. Some of the delegates actually opposed the socializing, including some of the ministers who didn't like the idea of a social function on a Sunday afternoon. They thought it was in bad taste. But I guess that Josefina, who herself was married to a Hollywood writer and partied with the Hollywood crowd, figured that more young people would rather go to the Club Mocambo than go to church.

El Congreso and Praxis

After its formation, El Congreso worked on a number of fronts. One area concerned helping to recruit Mexican workers into the CIO. Since I was already involved with the union, this was something that I personally became associated with in El Congreso. Luisa Moreno, of course, who became a top CIO official, organized agricultural and cannery workers through UCAPAWA. In Chicago, Refugio Martínez, who was later unjustly deported, was a key labor organizer among packinghouse workers.

Other Mexican-American labor organizers affiliated with El Congreso also played key roles in organizing industries that contained large numbers of Spanish-speaking workers. In the furniture industry in Los Angeles, for example, Armando Davila successfully organized for the CIO, as did Frank López in the shoe-manufacturing plants and Tony

Salgado of the Laborers Local 300. El Congreso also assisted the unions among longshoremen, electrical workers, packinghouse workers, and garment workers.

Congreso members helped the unions reach into the community and locate past and present Mexican-American labor leaders who proved to be crucial links in the success of the CIO. El Congreso and the CIO worked very well together. Josefina Fierro, as the executive secretary of El Congreso and its most dynamic leader, was always welcomed at CIO headquarters. Luisa Moreno became a state vice-president of the CIO. El Congreso's support of CIO organizing and strikes helped to promote awareness within the CIO of job discrimination against Mexicans, of racism, and of police brutality against Mexicans and other nonwhite minorities.

El Congreso also became actively involved with issues relating to youth and public discrimination. The organization protested the exclusion of Mexican-American youth from certain public swimming pools in Los Angeles and in surrounding areas such as Pasadena, Ventura, and Orange County. El Congreso likewise protested the lack of public swimming facilities in Maravilla Park in East Los Angeles as well as in the Mexican *colonias* of Riverside, San Bernardino, San Diego, Santa Barbara, Oxnard, and Orange County. In most of these cases, after struggles lasting from two to four years, El Congreso won the establishment of such facilities.

These victories encouraged the Mexican communities to believe that if they demanded better public services, they would get them. Other actions included protesting the racist treatment of Mexican students by teachers in the public schools such as Lincoln and Roosevelt high schools in East Los Angeles.

In a related area, El Congreso—or at least those members who hadn't by then left for war service—took on the issue of police brutality, especially against Mexican-American youth. The most celebrated incident involved the Sleepy Lagoon case. This was the trial of seventeen youngsters for the alleged killing of one youth in 1942. Although little evidence linked the accused Mexican-Americans to the killing, they were denied bail and deprived of their constitutional rights to adequate legal counsel and to a fair trial. El Congreso organized the Sleepy Lagoon Defense Committee to bring public attention to these injustices.

Although I was in military service at the time, Josefina Fierro asked me to serve on the committee, which included various Mexican-American activists along with writer and civil rights leader Carey McWilliams; Hollywood film star Anthony Quinn, who had been born in Chihuahua; and several members of radical groups in L.A., including the Communist Party. Most of the youths were convicted, but the committee persisted in their defense until, through appeals, the convictions were overturned. It is unfortunate that playwright Luis Valdez in his recent play and film *Zoot Suit* fails to note the Mexican-American leadership of the committee and instead makes a Jewish female member of the committee, Alice Schecter, the main protagonist.

Other actions by El Congreso included supporting the expropriation of American and foreign oil companies in Mexico, carried out by President Lázaro Cárdenas in 1938. These companies for years had unfairly exploited Mexico's oil resources. El Congreso organized a march against possible U.S. military intervention to regain the oil concessions. Eight or nine thousand people marched up Broadway Street in downtown Los Angeles in a protest that concluded at the Mexican consulate. The march scared the hell out of the city establishment—Mexicans had never before marched in Los Angeles in such numbers.

When World War II broke out in 1941, El Congreso supported the war effort against the fascist powers. Around 1942, it organized a big rally at the Embassy Auditorium, where speakers such as Harry Bridges, Carey McWilliams, and the actor Orson Welles inspired the Mexican people to participate in the war effort in any way possible.

As part of its own contribution to this struggle, El Congreso singled out the danger of Mexican fifth-column subversives operating in California and in the rest of the Southwest. These were the fascist Sinarquistas, who had originated in Mexico in the late 1930s and who during the early war years organized branches in El Paso, Los Angeles, San Francisco, and several other cities where large numbers of Mexicans lived.* El Congreso clashed with the Sinarquistas, physically as well as

*Founded in León, Guanajuato, in 1937, the Sinarquista movement in Mexico copied the Spanish Falange, a fascist organization. Under the slogan of "Country, Justice, and Liberty," the Sinarquistas voiced populist-sounding positions defending property, capitalism, and Catholicism. They attacked the Mexican government for implementing "collectivization" at the expense of private ownership and for

politically. At community meetings organized by El Congreso, Sinarquistas attempted to disrupt the proceedings, only to be confronted by
Congreso members and run out of the hall.

The Sinarquistas tried to stage rallies and marches, especially on
Catholic feast days. Some Mexican priests went along with them.
Fortunately, the community quickly saw what the Sinarquistas were up
to and realized that their movement was a fraud. In the name of being
Catholic and loyal to Mexico, the Sinarquistas were, in fact, being used
as pawns for Hitler, Mussolini, and Franco. They never recruited
Mexican-Americans who were active with the CIO.

Unfortunately, the war led to the demise of El Congreso. The organization restricted its civil rights protests in order to support the war
effort, and it also suffered a decline in active membership because of the
departure of those who enlisted in the military. Some, such as Smiley
Rincon, who had headed El Congreso's Youth Committee, lost their
lives. I and others joined the armed forces after Pearl Harbor.

Some effort was made to revive El Congreso after the war, but the
advent of McCarthyism and the Cold War prevented this, particularly
because of the political persecution of a number of Mexican labor and
political activists associated with El Congreso. Both Luisa Moreno and
Josefina Fierro, for example, exiled themselves in order to avoid further
political persecution. Despite El Congreso's short-lived history, however, it spearheaded many struggles in southern California and inspired
a generation of Mexican-American community leaders.

Luisa Moreno

Luisa Moreno was one of the most dedicated, well-organized, and
competent labor organizers I have ever known. Besides her capacity for
hard work, Luisa was a brilliant individual. She was a graduate of the
College of the Holy Names in Oakland, which at the time was a
prestigious Catholic college for women.

---

moving Mexico toward atheism. The Sinarquistas in particular attacked communism and proclaimed themselves the true Mexican nationalists. In the United States,
the Sinarquistas established a number of regional and municipal centers, primarily
in the Southwest. The actual numbers and composition of the Sinarquista groups
in the United States are difficult to determine, but they claimed strength, as they did
in Mexico, among farmworkers and lower-middle-class Catholics.

Luisa was not Mexican. She had been born in Guatemala to fairly well-to-do parents but had come to the U.S. as a young girl. I really know little about much of her early life. However, after graduating from college, she went to New York, where she became a community and labor organizer among the Spanish-speaking population.

Luisa once told me about an incident that motivated her to work on behalf of unifying the Spanish-speaking communities. A Hollywood film called *Under a Texas Moon* opened in New York. Because the film was anti-Mexican, a group of Latinos led by a man by the name of Gonzálo González picketed the theater where the film was showing. The police came down on their horses and attacked the picketers with clubs. They fractured González's skull, and he subsequently died of this injury. To condemn this murder, a huge protest was organized, involving Puerto Ricans as well as Central and South Americans, and Luisa was part of it.

After working among Latino workers in New York in the early 1930s, she went on to work with Dr. Ernesto Galarza, who became a leading Mexican-American labor organizer and intellectual, at the Pan-American Union in Washington, D.C. In the mid-1930s, she met Donald Henderson, who was forming the United Cannery, Agricultural, Packing and Allied Workers of America. Henderson hired Luisa as an organizer.

Luisa organized tobacco workers in Florida, cane workers in Louisiana, cotton pickers in Texas, and sugar beet workers in Colorado. She traveled all over the U.S. and later advanced to the position of national vice-president of UCAPAWA. And, of course, beginning in 1938, she put together El Congreso.

She did all of this at great personal sacrifice, but with great courage during difficult times. She had a little girl, whom she supported. But she never flagged in her dedication to the labor movement and to the cause of the advancement of the Spanish-speaking. When I first met her at the time of the congress, Luisa already had stellar credentials as an organizer.

Luisa possessed a variety of skills and qualities that served her well in her work. She was a formidable and charismatic speaker in both English and Spanish. She wrote very well, and bilingually; she turned out the best written leaflets I've ever seen. She was a small woman, under five feet, but she had a very powerful gift for persuasion. She could convince others by the weight of her logic, her ease of words, and her speaking abilities.

Moreover, she possessed a great deal of courage. I remember her being involved in strikes where there was much violence by company goons and by the police. But Luisa was never afraid. She was once jailed in South Texas while leading a strike of Mexican cotton pickers. The authorities tried to get her to leave the county by promising to release her if she signed a statement vowing never to return. She refused, and so she remained in jail. To further intimidate her, if not to get rid of her altogether, the authorities put a mentally deranged woman in her cell, gave the woman a knife, and urged her to kill Luisa. But Luisa was fearless and survived this ordeal.

Luisa also demonstrated an ability to grasp a situation and to organize in the most effective way. She was a masterful tactician and proved to be a highly successful labor organizer. For example, she played a leading role in unionizing the canneries of California, including such giants as Calpak, Hunt's, Del Monte, Campbell's, and Libby's. At one time in the 1940s, some ninety thousand workers in the California canneries were being organized.

Politically, Luisa Moreno could be considered a radical, in the best tradition of the term. In addition to her work with labor, she was a staunch supporter of progressive causes throughout the world, including the struggle of the Republic of Spain against its fascist foes. She advocated nonintervention in Mexico and Central America and self-determination for the weaker and poorer nations. Later, when she exiled herself because of McCarthyite persecution in the U.S., she returned to Guatemala and supported the democratic government of Jacobo Arbenz until it was overthrown by the CIA. She later went to Cuba after the revolution of 1959 and worked for a time in the new revolutionary educational system. She never was afraid to express her views.

Like so many radicals and militants in the postwar period, Luisa Moreno suffered political persecution. At the height of McCarthyism and the passage of anti-immigrant legislation such as the McCarran Act, Luisa was ordered to present herself for deportation hearings. Although she had lived in this country for many years, Luisa had never become a U.S. citizen and consequently was vulnerable to deportation, based on the new immigration laws that barred from the country any aliens who were associated with the Communist Party.

It is not clear whether Luisa was in fact a member of the Communist Party, but even if she had been, membership in the CP was not in reality a subversive act. Luisa, along with other militants, whether party members or not, played a leading role in achieving greater rights for workers. This was hardly subversive! It was, however, subversive to those who felt threatened by these gains and who wished to deprive the working class of the greater rewards of their labor.

Luisa would have fought the effort to deport her if she had sensed that it would have been a collective struggle rather than just an individual one. Unfortunately, the efforts by the left—specifically, the Communist Party—to defend labor leaders in similar situations extended only to those of European descent and not to Latinos. That same lack of effort also characterized the reaction of the CIO. The efforts of the American Committee for the Protection of the Foreign-Born, when it did attempt to mount a defense, were too little and too late.

Consequently, Latino labor and community leaders such as Luisa, Josefina Fierro, Refugio Martínez, Humberto Sílex, Armando Davila, Frank Martínez, Frank Corona, Tony Salgado, and Fred Chávez, to name a few, found themselves isolated and defenseless. This lack of support by the left is reprehensible and something to be condemned. Luisa was a Latina and a labor leader who had helped build the CIO, but she didn't get the support she should have gotten to put up a fight. If that defense had been there, she would have fought the government tooth and nail.

During this time, I was living in northern California. I heard about Luisa's plight from Alfredo Montoya, the head of the Asociación Nacional México-Americana, which was making some effort to protest these deportations. But ANMA couldn't evoke any interest on the part of the unions; they were all busy defending Anglo leaders.

I myself went to see officials of the Longshoremen's Union, who expressed concern about Luisa and the other Latinos being persecuted but felt they already had their hands full defending Australian-born Harry Bridges, who was also being threatened with deportation. I was told to organize a defense committee and then perhaps the union could do something. But I couldn't get enough of a response from other union leaders to form such a committee. Both labor and the left were in a state of complete disarray. People were busy defending either themselves or their close friends, and these didn't happen to be Mexicans. That's the way the ball bounced.

Consequently, Luisa "deported" herself around 1949, believing that a fight that lacked a base for defense would be futile. Josefina Fierro and others did likewise. Many of these Latinos became very bitter over this experience and the lack of support from the left. I'm not sure how Luisa felt about this, but I do know it was a disappointing and trying experience for her. After many years of living in Mexico, Luisa returned to Guatemala, where she died in 1992.

Josefina Fierro

I came to know Josefina Fierro while working with El Congreso. She was very young—in her early twenties—very flamboyant, and very beautiful. She was married at the time to a Hollywood screenwriter named John Bright. Her mother was related to the Amador family, who owned restaurants in Los Angeles. Josefina was involved with theatrical people. Her cousin Bobby Ramos had a famous band that played at the Cocoanut Grove and at the Saint Francis Hotel in San Francisco and the Stevens Hotel in Chicago.

Josefina was born on the U.S.–Mexican border between Mexicali and Calexico. Her mother was from a Sonoran family, the Borboas, and was a supporter of Ricardo Flores Magón during the Mexican Revolution. When Josefina was an infant, her mother would transport munitions from Calexico to Mexicali hidden in Josefina's stroller.

When the family moved to Los Angeles, Josefina's mother opened a restaurant, which lasted for only a short time. Subsequently, she worked as a *bordera* in the farm labor camps of California. A *bordera* was a person who prepared food for the agricultural camps and assisted the farmworkers in writing letters and forwarding mail to the workers who left for other camps. She also washed their clothes, looked after their valuables, and operated as a banker. If the workers ran into problems with the law, a *bordera* helped them.

As a young teenager, Josefina traveled to the camps with her mother and assisted her by informing the workers of their rights. She told them not to allow the contractors to cheat them out of their wages and explained how they could go about seeking redress if they were cheated. This only got Josefina into hot water with the growers and the field managers.

Josefina was very bright and graduated from high school in Madera.

Her mother sent her to UCLA. While she was back in Los Angeles, Josefina met a young man whom she married but soon divorced. Soon thereafter she met John Bright. Bright was a close friend of Orson Welles; they had been roommates at Harvard. As a result of her marriage to Bright, Josefina, a radical in her own right, became involved with the Hollywood left community, composed of actors, writers, producers, and directors.

Through her work with the Hollywood Committee to Aid Farmworkers, which included Orson Welles, John Steinbeck, Humphrey Bogart, and Spencer Tracy, Josefina came into contact with Luisa Moreno, who was impressed with this dynamic and brash young woman. Josefina was a very charismatic speaker. Her Spanish was not the best Spanish; she had learned much of it in the farm camps. But, like Moreno, she was an excellent organizer with boundless courage.

Josefina became the key leader of El Congreso, as its executive secretary. Besides her own personal qualities, Josefina was an excellent leader for El Congreso because of her wide contacts in the Los Angeles community, especially with the Hollywood crowd, who donated money to El Congreso. Josefina was not shy in representing the interests of El Congreso; actually, she was very gutsy. She could go up to the mayor or the governor and start talking to them about issues affecting *mexicanos*. While Luisa Moreno started El Congreso, Josefina Fierro saw to it that it survived.

As a woman, Josefina encountered much sexism and machismo among men, both in and out of El Congreso. Some men thought that she dressed in too sexy and outlandish a style. I felt that she dressed in very good taste, considering how the Hollywood crowd dressed in those times; in fact, Josefina dressed far more conservatively than many actresses. But her attire was still unacceptable to many Mexicans, both men and women. Because she associated with theater people, some of the men believed that she was very loose, unrefined. Their opinions were shaped by the way she spoke, using the very rough Spanish of the Mexican immigrants, her conversation often filled with *"hijos de la chingada"* [sons of bitches].

Despite these erroneous impressions, Josefina weathered these negative reactions with much courage and even humor. A guy named Slim Connelly, a huge fat man who was secretary-treasurer of the California CIO, once criticized Josefina for her dress. This was when the CIO, with Congreso help, was organizing the steel plants in Los Angeles. Josefina was helping organize *mexicano* workers while dressed in her Hollywood clothes.

This irritated Slim, who told me, "You tell that Josefina that I don't want her to come here in those tight-fitting dresses with half of her tits sticking out, sashaying around here showing her ass to all these workers; this is not that kind of organization."

I was absolutely flabbergasted that this guy would tell me this. "Are you sure you want me to tell her that, Slim?" I asked.

"Yes, tell her that for me, would you?" he responded.

So I went and told Josefina, and she exploded. "Why, that big, fat son of a bitch, you know he's so huge and fat, but he's got a peter that big"—she indicated less than an inch with her fingers—"and what he does have, he can't get it into a woman 'cause his gut sticks out in front of him. You go tell him that for me!"

I did, which shocked Slim. He exclaimed: "Why in the hell did you tell her that? Now she's going to spread this lie about me all over!"

"Well, you told me to tell her," I said.

But Josefina showed up the next day as if nothing had happened or else she didn't give a damn. She was tough-skinned.

Although some Mexican women also frowned upon her because of the way she dressed, in fact many more women, in and out of El Congreso, respected and admired Josefina. To this day, I still run into women who remember her and think the world of her. Josefina was very supportive of other women; she was a woman's woman. Although Josefina and, for that matter, Luisa were not self-conscious feminists in the contemporary sense, they always struggled for women's rights, including equal jobs and equal pay. But Josefina also recognized that, based on class and ethnic interests, both working men and women, especially among the Spanish-speaking, had to struggle together to achieve their rights.

I would say that Josefina was a radical in attempting to achieve short-range solutions through popular action and a socialist in the long run, believing that only through socialism could poor people in the capitalist countries and in the poor countries in the Third World overcome their poverty. She and I talked from time to time about such matters.

We came to these conclusions not only as a result of our own particular political circumstances but also because of the political culture of the times. This was the period in which various radical and leftist movements were quite influential. We lived in a period when many people openly discussed socialism and communism. Many were for something other than capitalism, given the disaster of the depression.

Although Josefina was a radical and supported socialist solutions, I don't believe that she was ever a member of the Communist Party. She never told me that she was a member, and I never heard anyone I knew within the party refer to her as one. Josefina knew many members of the CP. But in these years of the Popular Front, during the late 1930s, activists in the CIO, especially those who were minorities, all worked together and shared similar commitments toward progressive social change.* People could be sympathetic to certain CP causes without necessarily joining the party. The CP led in organizing some of these movements, but in other cases they trailed.

I knew many members of the Communist Party, and some of them who were *mexicanos* attended Congreso meetings. But Congreso members knew that these people were CP members and welcomed them as long as they were loyal to El Congreso. One Mexican CP member by the name of Bill Taylor—his mother was a Mexican—often came to our meetings. He was a big guy with a powerful voice. He had been in the labor movement since the early 1920s, but when he spoke, he used typical CP rhetoric. Everyone knew Bill was a Communist Party member, but he was a good guy, a hell of a fighter. But I don't think that he ever recruited anybody.

Josefina's husband, John Bright, was supposed to have been in the CP, along with some of the other Hollywood writers, but I don't believe Johnny was actually a member. Unfortunately, people were accused

---

*The Popular Front in the United States was a strategic effort by the Communist Party to organize a broad anti-fascist movement, beginning in 1935. With the rise of Hitler and other fascist leaders in Europe, the CP shifted from a position of attacking the New Deal to critical support of it. Fascism was seen as a greater threat than bourgeois democracy. Popular Front groups included Communists and non-Communists in CIO unions, for example, as well as in African-American and Mexican-American organizations. Among labor, minorities, intellectuals, and the unemployed, the Popular Front strategy proved to be quite successful in advancing democratic demands, although it was dealt a setback in 1939, when the Soviet Union signed a nonaggression pact with Nazi Germany.

then, and of course later during the McCarthy period, of being Communists simply because they supported the same causes as the party. But some of those causes, such as support for Republican Spain, opposition to fascism, and support for the CIO, had broad support among many Americans who were not party members.

Josefina, like Luisa Moreno, was accused by the federal government of being a subversive alien, a Communist Party member, or affiliated in some way with the party. Like Luisa, she found herself isolated and with little defense or support outside of certain Mexican-American groups. Consequently, Josefina decided to leave the country in the late 1940s rather than take the chance of possibly incriminating anyone if she was forced to appear before the House Un-American Activities Committee. Since then, she has resided in Mexico.

Eduardo Quevedo

Another key figure in El Congreso and in Mexican-American community politics at the time was Eduardo Quevedo. Before the formation of El Congreso, Quevedo had been very active in organizing Mexicans in Los Angeles. He had formed the Arizona/New Mexico Club, which ostensibly was a social club for Mexicans who arrived from either Arizona or New Mexico, but which also participated in political activities such as voter registration drives, local elections, and various community issues.

Quevedo was likewise well established within the CIO movement. He and his brother were active in Local 300 of the Laborers Union. Along with leaders like Tony Salgado, they had mobilized these workers into a huge union of twenty-five thousand members.

Quevedo was born in Santa Rita, New Mexico. His family had been miners in Chihuahua and active in the Revolution of 1910. Later they had worked in the copper, lead, and zinc mines of southern New Mexico, in Grants County around Hurley, in Silver City, and Bayard. As a boy, Eduardo was exposed to union drives among the Mexican miners. When the family moved to California, it struggled to reestablish itself and to integrate into the L.A. community of Mexicans. Some of the Quevedo children joined the Catholic church as nuns or priests. The whole family, including Eduardo, was staunchly Catholic.

Because of his church contacts, plus the fact that the Quevedos had been a prominent family in Chihuahua, Eduardo soon developed a wide network of connections within the Mexican community. When El Congreso was being formed, its organizers perceived Quevedo as a key leader to cultivate. Luisa and Josefina drew Quevedo into El Congreso, and he served as its first president.

Together, Luisa, Josefina, and Eduardo made a wonderful team. Josefina always spoke highly of Eduardo and how competent he was in organizing. Quevedo's role in El Congreso was an important one: He bridged the gap between the Mexican activists of the 1920s and early 1930s and the new activists of the late 1930s.

Also attractive about Quevedo was his great speaking ability, especially in Spanish. He was a polished orator. Complementing this was his wonderful sense of humor. He could tell all kinds of jokes for hours on end. He had a fabulous memory and remembered many of the risqué jokes and sayings told by *los de abajo* [the Mexican working class] as well as those told in the famous Mexican *carpas* [traveling tent circuses].

While Quevedo may have had some differences with both Moreno and Fierro, by and large he seemed politically and ideologically compatible with them, despite his strong Catholicism. Quevedo acknowledged that activists such as himself, Luisa, and Josefina were considered Communists because they wanted change. But, at the same time, he argued, they had to show their critics that they were good law-abiding citizens who believed in heaven and hell, advocating only the things that *mexicanos* rightfully deserved. Ed cautioned that they should also be leery of being used by those who openly called themselves Communists.

His approach was to deal with people from both the left and the right if it advanced the cause of El Congreso and the Mexican community. He believed it was good to have conservative friends whom you could trust, who would say a good word for you, and who would agree to be on your advisory committee, in order to present a broad front to the public. This was his concept of a popular front. If he could find a conservative to do a task, he preferred to get that person involved rather than a well-known radical. He used to say, "We don't have to convert the radicals; let's go out and convert our enemies and the people who are not yet convinced of our cause." He presented an enigma to those who were used to sizing up people from a dogmatic or sectarian perspective. Quevedo liked to play the role of middle-of-the-roader.

The Communist Party

Although I myself never joined the Communist Party, it is important to understand that a strong relationship existed between Mexican-American activists and the Communist Party in the 1930s. It's hard to know just how many Mexican-Americans or Latinos in Los Angeles belonged to the CP. I remember talking to Rose Chernin, a longtime CP activist, about this question years later.

Rose told me that from time to time the party would throw a big reception with music, food, and drinks and invite many from the Spanish-speaking community, including many non-Communists. She recalled Josefina Fierro being present at one of these functions. Josefina inquired of Rose as to how many Mexicans belonged to the party. Rose, who was quite involved in the Mexican community, responded that as of that day the party had four hundred thirty-five Mexican members. Neither Josefina nor anyone else batted an eye about that number, because in fact the CP was very active in the barrios during the depression.

I also remember that in 1936 leaders of the CP who were attempting to organize Mexican field workers in Orange County were beaten and jailed. Since the CP had targeted the organizing of farmworkers, packing-shed workers, and cannery workers, it was natural that a number of Mexicans in these industries, of which there were many, would be friendly toward the party even if they did not become members.

The party was active not only in organizing workers but also in community issues: working for school desegregation, opposing segregation in public facilities such as swimming pools and housing, protesting police abuse, obtaining relief aid, and preventing the deportation of Mexicans during the 1930s. If you read the *Daily People's World*, the CP newspaper on the West Coast, and its predecessor the *Western Worker* for this period, you can get an idea of the party's involvement with the Mexican community. It was their unwavering dedication to ameliorating the terrible conditions under which poor people such as Mexicans were forced to live that earned CP activists the friendship and support of many Mexicans.

I was never aware that the party organized clubs or committees specifically for Mexicans. Indeed, those Mexicans who worked with the party, either as members or as supporters of particular causes, operated within broader movements such as the CIO efforts, the Workers Alliance, or political causes such as support for Republican Spain.

Because this activism was channeled through such groups rather than directly through the party, it was difficult for me to know exactly which Mexicans were party members. I suspect that the number of active party members was actually quite small but that those who subscribed to the *Daily People's World* were counted as belonging to the party. Some, such as Bill Taylor and Smiley Rincon of El Congreso, were open about their party affiliation. But at that time there were not, as there would be later, Mexicans who operated openly as party functionaries.

During the Spanish Civil War, in the mid-1930s, I didn't know of any Mexican-Americans who joined the Abraham Lincoln Brigade to fight in Spain for the Republic and against the fascists, although the brigade contained many CP members. I did know one Mexican-American— Nick Ramírez—who went to Spain via Mexico, where Mexicans had formed the Benito Juárez Brigade on behalf of the Republicans.

Nick, whose radical father had actually named him Nicolas Lenin Ramírez, was a Communist. He was married to a Jewish schoolteacher named Mary. We were very good friends. Nick was also on very friendly terms with older radicals such as Ethel Duffy-Turner, Alma Reed, David Alfaro Siqueiros, and earlier adherents of the cause of Ricardo Flores Magón. Before going to Spain, Nick had been active in labor struggles in southern California. When he returned from Spain, he was a very sick person. He tried to work on the docks, but his illness prevented him from doing so. He later died in northern California.

Although I never joined the party, I was always being asked to do so. I would be invited to recruiting meetings sponsored by the party, especially those focused on union issues. Sometimes a CP member would directly ask me: "People like you, and we think you could make a contribution. Why don't you join us?"

Another approach would be to get you to subscribe to the *Daily People's World* or to buy Marxist literature and to attend forums on political issues such as what was going on in Russia and in other parts of the world. The party, for example, supported the independence of India, and no one had better information about what was going on in

India than the party did. The same was true concerning Mexico and Latin America.

Still another avenue of recruitment was simply recognizing that some of the key CIO leaders in various locals were CP members. They presented themselves to me as party members and suggested that if I wanted to emulate them, I should consider joining the party, where they had learned many of their organizing and leadership skills.

Many of those who approached me to join the party were actually friends of mine, so it was difficult to resist their efforts. However, I never saw myself as playing a role within the party. I recalled the problems faced by those Mexican workers who were heavily red-baited back in El Paso. But, beyond that, despite many good people in the CP and their good positions on many issues, I was somewhat aware that contradictions existed in the party in regard to sharing power with non-Communists. I believed it was best for me to continue to work directly with the CIO and with Mexican-American groups such as El Congreso.

My overall view of the CP was that it contained many dedicated people. I came to know many members, particularly white ones, who proved their dedication in various labor struggles or in other political fights. Many of these people were not solely interested in promoting the party but were committed to advancing the cause of working and poor people to help obtain such concessions as Social Security and pension bills in California.

This dedication and hard work were what ultimately impressed me, rather than the fact that they were CP members. Once you knew them and respected them, their affiliation didn't mean much. I didn't neces-sarily agree with the party on all issues, and there were some bad and stupid people in the party, but as an organization the CP played a positive role in trying to build a democratic trade union movement that would be controlled by the rank and file. This was very important to me, given my involvement with the CIO.

On the question of war and peace, on colonialism, as well as on a variety of national issues, the party advanced positions that broad sections of Americans supported. The party in the 1930s was not just concerned about theoretical positions. It was a concrete political force to be contended with, and it helped advance the cause of working people such as Mexicans in Los Angeles and throughout the Southwest.

I grew politically because of my relationship to the party, to certain of its members—especially those involved in the labor unions—and to the political culture it promoted. I read the *Daily People's World*, which was then a much better paper. It featured some outstanding writers such as John Howard Lawson, Dalton Trumbo, Howard Fast, Dashiell Hammett, Bishop Harry F. Ward, Herbert Biberman, and Paul Jarrico. There wasn't a labor strike that the paper didn't cover. It would also provide coverage of internal union struggles that you didn't get in the traditional papers.

While I had a relationship with members of the CP, I regarded myself as more of a socialist than a Communist. I read a variety of Marxist literature—not necessarily *Das Kapital*, but various other tracts—and I of course attended many political forums that presented Marxist speakers. But I was more in agreement with that socialist movement out of California characterized by such people as Upton Sinclair, Lincoln Steffens, Jack London, and Thorsten Veblen.

When I was involved with MAM, we had a member by the name of Frank Guzmán, who was attending L.A. City College. Along with Félix Gutiérrez, he used to conduct discussions about socialism and communism. But Frank and Félix, like myself, were really more influenced by the progressive reformers of the early twentieth century, along with muckraking socialists such as Upton Sinclair and Lincoln Steffens.

I have always been more comfortable using the term "progressive" to describe myself and the political movements I've been associated with. By "progressive," I mean not just those movements that adhere to socialist ideas but also those that in a broad way bring people together to struggle for social advancement without necessarily being socialist in orientation. I accept myself as a socialist, or a progressive, but I also see the need not to be sectarian and dogmatic. I believe in united and popular fronts with as many people as possible who can coalesce around issues related to justice, equality, and progress for all peoples.

Blanche Taff

Despite my involvement with both the labor movement and El Congreso, I did find some time for family life, although the two were often intertwined. I got married in 1941, to Blanche Taff. I had met Blanche earlier that year while I was assisting the United Auto Workers in a union drive at the big aviation companies such as North American Aviation.

Blanche and her sister belonged to the Democratic Youth Federation, which in Los Angeles was led by young, militant Jewish-American high school and college students. The federation was composed of youth clubs, and the ones in West Los Angeles—Santa Monica, Westwood, and the Fairfax district—were all assisting in the North American Aviation strike. The clubs sponsored informational and fund-raising parties and dances. It was at one of these events that I met Blanche, who was on the federation committee that raised funds for the strike.

We got acquainted and would often picket together in front of the plant. North American was located where the L.A. airport is today, but at that time the area was mostly bean fields, with a strip for planes to take off and land. It was a particularly difficult organizing drive. The company was run by a former U.S. Army general, and he stubbornly refused to sign a contract. Consequently, the workers went out on strike. Unfortunately, President Roosevelt, citing national defense, approved the use of federal troops to help break the strike.

The troops surrounded the plant when Blanche and I were on the picket line. We were drawn very close together by experiencing the trauma of facing soldiers with bayonets who attempted to clear a path through the picket line to allow strikebreakers to enter the plant. We had about ten or fifteen thousand people on the line. The army at first failed to get through, but they teargassed us and eventually broke through the line with brute force. In the end, however, a contract was signed.

Blanche was then working for an accounting firm, doing clerical work. She had graduated from L.A. High School and had attended L.A. City College. Her parents were Polish Jews from a little town outside Warsaw, in that part of Poland that had earlier been absorbed by Russia. They spoke Russian and also Polish, Yiddish, English, and some German.

Her father had been educated to be a rabbi, but instead he became a watchmaker and later a diamond dealer in this country. Blanche's mother came from a large and poor family. In Central Europe, Jews were prohibited from owning land or engaging in certain kinds of work. As young adults, her parents both joined the Bund, which had been organized in Germany by socialists. It functioned in Poland during the first two decades of this century. Many Jews joined it because it supported their right to equal employment opportunities and their right to live in freedom.

With the coming of World War I, many Polish Jews refused to serve in the czar's army and emigrated to England, Canada, or the United States. Blanche's father, along with his younger brother, was able to get out and come to New York. Blanche's mother soon also arrived. Her parents were married in New York, and the family first lived there when Blanche was born. Around 1920, they moved to California, where Mr. Taff became quite successful in the diamond business. They lived in West Los Angeles.

During the time that I was dating Blanche, I got along very well with her family. They were very liberated people; they were not orthodox Jews and certainly not Zionists. Both parents were always very friendly toward me, even though they were somewhat concerned about the differences in cultural background between Blanche and myself. I learned later that Blanche's mother didn't want her to marry me because I wasn't Jewish, but it didn't bother me. Her parents certainly would have preferred that she marry a nice Jewish boy. But they never pressured her to do anything she didn't want to.

Even when Blanche and I decided to elope, they took it very well. We walked into their house and said, "We just eloped." Blanche's father got up and responded: "Let's have a drink to a new son-in-law!"

We had eloped to Yuma, Arizona, where they had these one-day marriage chapels, whereas in California you had to wait three days to get married. We got married on August 2, 1941. Rather than spending a honeymoon in Yuma, we drove right back to L.A. The CIO was just starting another organizing drive, so we didn't actually have a honeymoon until I went into the service the following year.

The fact that I married a non-Mexican rather than a Mexican woman is hard to explain unless you understand the times. In the labor and radical circles I was a part of, there was a good deal of interaction, both political and social, among people of different racial and ethnic backgrounds. Our common commitments and struggles brought us together. Racism or ethnic conflict was not a part, or at least not a significant part, of these interactions. In the 1930s, young people of all races were drawn together in the unions and in the Popular Front struggles of the period. It was an interracial and interethnic movement with lofty ideals. In addition, my family in El Paso had participated in interethnic relationships. Both my grandmother and my mother had been educated by Anglo-Americans, and we had Anglo and Jewish acquaintances in El Paso.

While Blanche's parents had no problems with our elopement, the same was not true of my family. My mother took my marriage to Blanche all right, but not my grandmother. My mother was still living in El Paso, and my grandmother was splitting her time between L.A. and El Paso. When we eloped, my grandmother was in El Paso. But when she returned to L.A., she went to where we were living and confronted Blanche. Blanche couldn't understand much Spanish, but she definitely knew that my grandmother wasn't happy. My grandmother was upset because she and my mother hadn't been notified of our marriage and because they couldn't attend the wedding. But my grandmother soon got over it and came to like Blanche very much.

The two families got along well, even though there weren't many occasions when everyone got together. My mother, of course, spoke English well and could carry on a relationship with Blanche's family. My sister, Aurora, often did things with Blanche and me and with Blanche's family after she and my mother moved to L.A. Only my grandmother, although she liked Blanche, chose not to participate in joint family affairs because of her unwillingness to speak English. She knew English, but her attitude toward English was very nationalistic, and she spoke it only when she absolutely had to.

In general, my grandmother was anti-Anglo, believing that her two brothers had been killed as a result of the American intervention in Mexico during the time of the Apache and Comanche wars in northern Mexico between 1860 and 1890. She was of that generation of Mexicans from the period before the 1910 Revolution who did not trust the U.S. or English-speaking people. She felt that Americans were inferior people and that their culture was inferior to that of Mexico. To her, Anglo-Americans wanted only money, and they were ruthless in their pursuit of it. Her experiences with Americans had not been good ones. So her relationship with anyone who spoke English was limited from the start. But if she really came to like them, she would speak English with them.

Another factor that prevented a closer relationship between my family and Blanche's was the distance between residences. My mother, grandmother, and sister, once they all moved to the L.A. area, lived further east, first in Alhambra and later in Chino.

When I got married, I think I still held pretty traditional views toward marriage, in that I wanted to raise a family. On the other hand, I had no problem with Blanche continuing to work, because in my family the women had worked for a living. Most of the people in the union movement had very advanced ideas about women working and about the equality of women. Nevertheless, I'm sure I still possessed certain patriarchal attitudes. Blanche still reminds me that even though I was in the union movement and spoke a good line about women's equality, I wasn't in fact implementing it. One area in which I definitely had a traditional view concerned open marriages, which I didn't accept, even though it was in vogue among some of the bohemian left.

Although I don't recall whether I wanted children right away, I do remember wanting them after the war started. I learned of friends being killed, and I began to think we should have children, just in case something happened to me.

When we first got married, I saw myself as head of the household and responsible for most of the decisions. But that changed over time, although not without some tensions. Certainly when I went into the service, I couldn't any longer make major family decisions; Blanche now had to do that. I think that in time we grew to have a more equal relationship with respect to family matters.

After our marriage, Blanche and I lived in the Silver Lake district of Los Angeles, in an apartment on Rowena. This area was just being developed at the time. We lived there until the internment of the Japanese began. Some of our Anglo neighbors were very antagonistic to the Japanese, many of whom lived in our neighborhood, and this whole experience left a very bad taste in our mouths. So even though many labor and left movement people resided in the area, we decided to move out to West Boulevard in the mid-city area, where many Jews were moving from Boyle Heights and other areas of East Los Angeles. West Boulevard was bounded by Pico and West Adams. They were building block after block of apartments there.

Unfortunately, we ran into more trouble when our landlord complained about our having black union members over for visits. As we organized the drug industry, we included various stores with black employees who joined the union. Some blacks were elected to union leadership positions. I invited some of them over, both for strategy sessions and for socializing. The manager of our apartment building became quite upset over this and complained that we were attempting to integrate the neighborhood. He even got together a petition signed by some of the other tenants to have us evicted.

We ignored it at first and instead threw a big party attended by many of our black friends. As the issue became uglier, we responded by talking to our neighbors and passing out leaflets attacking such racism. We organized a party for our neighbors and invited our congressman, Will Rogers, Jr. He wasn't able to come but instead sent his wife, Martha Fall Rogers, who, it turned out, had been a schoolmate of mine at El Paso High School. She was very gracious and helped us convince our neighbors to drop the idea of a petition.

Ironically, it turned out that the owner of the apartments had actually been an old socialist. When he learned of the incident, he decided he couldn't let the manager evict someone for having invited blacks to their home. We lived in that apartment until I went into the service and Blanche moved back with her parents.

CHAPTER SEVEN

The War Years

Several months after Pearl Harbor, I volunteered for the Army Air Corps and was accepted. I was very interested in flying. The Air Corps was also being promoted as a fast entry into combat action; I was told that in the Air Corps one could be readied for combat in six to eight months. However, since they didn't have camps available for all the volunteers immediately, we were sent to schools in our local communities, where we might pick up some useful instruction in such fields as celestial navigation and celestial trigonometry.

The problem was that not many high schools, community colleges, or adult schools taught such classes. I signed up at Manual Arts High School for a class that taught drafting. It was a course on how to measure curves and conical surfaces, which would be useful in navigation. I also enrolled in a course on celestial navigation, but it was taught by someone who had taken it up only as a hobby. I went to school at night once or twice a week.

Basic Training

Because of my enlistment, I resigned my position in the union. We were on twenty-four-hour call in the Air Corps, and I knew I would be called up any day. In the meantime, I did part-time work as a casual laborer on the waterfront.

Finally, in February 1943, I was called to active duty. I first went to Buckley Field outside Denver for an initial six-week training. I arrived by train with a unit of several hundred men. Although most were from southern California, many were men from other states who had enlisted in southern California. All of us wanted to be officers in the Air Corps.

At Buckley, we were put through a whole series of both physical and mental tests. These tests were supposed to determine which of us were capable of proceeding to actual flight training. On the intelligence tests, a mathematics professor from UCLA by the name of Abrams received a perfect score of 164. Another guy scored 163. I received the third highest score in my regiment, 161. Because I received very high grades in most of the tests, it was difficult for them to wash me out. But other *mexicanos* who were there were not as fortunate.

This series of tests revealed much racism on the part of the Anglo instructors and introduced me to prejudice in the military. Many Latinos and Jews—there weren't many blacks at Buckley—who didn't score quite as high on these intelligence tests were weeded out by the Anglo sergeants who administered the tests, although these men scored high enough to have qualified for further air training. The physical tests were used in the same way; the instructors would grade down Latinos and Jews on the tests of certain physical skills.

When I first arrived at Buckley, I saw many Latino faces, but when we got done with the tests, only two of us were left. I scored high enough on the intelligence test and was in good enough physical shape to survive. Those who didn't make it were sent to the regular army to become flatfoot soldiers.

From Buckley Field, we were sent in early March to Cedar City, Utah, for additional training. We were there about two months. We received training in geography, navigation, trigonometry, solid geometry, and astronomy. There was no radar then, so you had to learn how to navigate by fixed points or by using a compass. You could also use the moon and the stars. We were taught aircraft recognition. You got to the point where you could identify the picture of a particular plane, even if it was flashed before you at a speed of a hundredth of a second. We likewise were taught some military history and, of course, received physical training and flying lessons.

Cedar City, Utah, was itself an interesting experience. It was practically an all-Mormon town; there were only about five Mexican and fifteen Indian families. We ran into heavy prejudice against those who were not Mormons. We were housed and trained at Southern Utah State College, located in Cedar City; we literally took over the campus. But when we got there, the whole town—including many merchants— resented our presence. Initially, we had a hell of a time just shopping; we had to be taken in groups to buy toiletries in some of the stores. But then those merchants that we didn't patronize became upset. So other groups were taken to other stores.

To overcome these difficulties and this resistance on the part of the townspeople, the commanding officer ordered that the boundary of the post be extended from the campus to include all of the town. In this way, the town and its officials came under military command. The Mormons liked this even less. They didn't want us there because their boys had gone off to war and weren't as favored as those of us who were being trained for elite officer positions. They resented us further because those young men who had stayed at the college were kicked out when we took over the campus.

But the tension between us and the townspeople also had to do with the fears of the mothers concerning their daughters. This concern and many others finally were openly confronted at a big town meeting that was attended by about two hundred fifty townspeople, along with some of our officers. As the oldest cadet, at age twenty-five or twenty-six, I was asked to attend and represent the cadets.

Our captain opened up the meeting by stating the purpose of the training camp, discussing why we were in the war, and explaining that in no way did we want to deal unfairly with the town. We were then asked all kinds of questions. The older women, who were staunch Mormons, were particularly upset. I'll never forget the first question, which was asked by the mayor's wife.

"Captain, we are very concerned about our young girls," she got up and said. "You have six hundred men, and we have lost eight or nine hundred of our young men to the service. What we want to know is, if these young men are turned loose in our community and they go out with our girls—since you would like to have normal soldier-civilian relationships—how far are your boys going to go with our girls?"

The captain answered, "Well, you know our boys will go as far with your girls as you have trained your girls to allow boys to go. Any more questions along these lines?" There were none.

The meeting quieted the fears of many of the townspeople, and it led to an open town. We were allowed to go anywhere we wanted and to patronize all the stores, which pleased the merchants. Many good relationships were formed. Eventually, a number of marriages occurred—as did a number of out-of-wedlock pregnancies, including the daughter of the mayor.

I enjoyed my stay at Cedar City and successfully graduated to the next part of my training. From Cedar City, some of us were sent in early May back to southern California, to the Santa Ana Army Air Base. It was a huge camp, with about thirty thousand air cadets from all over the country. Here we were to receive further training and testing, including some flight training. If we successfully passed, we would receive our officer's commission.

I was in a wing of about ten thousand cadets under a Colonel Dunsworth, who had been principal of Lincoln High School in the Lincoln Heights area of Los Angeles. As a principal, he had the reputation of being anti-Mexican. My immediate superior officer was a Colonel Honeyman, who was related to one of the big plantation families in Hawaii. While I had my troubles with Dunsworth, I got along very well with Honeyman, and he treated me exceptionally well. I received perfect scores from him in my training.

Colonel Honeyman promoted me to wing adjutant, and I was responsible for a variety of paperwork: pay, classwork, attendance, sick leave, demerits, requests for leave, and so on. I received all of these reports from the squadrons and maintained the files. I worked a sixteen-hour day, eight hours of actual training and eight hours of clerical work. But I handled the work. I had had plenty of experience, both in the drug industry and in the union.

Red-Baiting

Even though I did well in my training at Santa Ana, I unfortunately experienced what would become persistent discrimination toward me because of my earlier CIO work. At Santa Ana, it began when I was called to undergo a psychiatric examination.

These exams were routine and were intended to identify homosexuals and "deviants." I had taken a similar test previously, in which they asked questions such as, "Do you have nightmares? How do you sleep? Do you masturbate? How often? Do you get an erection when you see somebody's bare ass?" Some of these were ridiculous questions, and the guys just used to laugh. But this exam at Santa Ana, at least for me, turned out to be very different.

The psychiatrist asked me questions about politics and about my work with the unions. I think, given my past experiences, that he had been instructed to delve into the possibility that I lacked patriotism. Besides looking for sexual deviants, the camp also looked for political deviants. They were particularly concerned if you had been a member of the Communist Party or if you had been a member of a Popular Front group.

The CP very early on had taken anti-fascist positions and had attacked Hitler and Mussolini before others had. So if the military identified you as a CP member, you were given the label "premature anti-fascist" in your record. If they couldn't prove that you were a CP member but could show that you had belonged to a group such as the Workers Alliance, then you might be labeled a "potential subversive." Another label they used was "probably patriotic."

Some CIO unionists, including members of the Longshoremen's Union, had initially been discriminated against in the service for their participation in some of the big strikes of the 1930s. They were listed as "potential subversives." To counter these actions, Harry Bridges complained all the way up to General George C. Marshall himself, the head of all U.S. military operations.

Bridges told Marshall that a contradiction existed: The longshoremen had fully committed themselves to winning the war, had agreed to a no-strike policy, were volunteering for the service, and yet were being treated as subversives. General Marshall agreed with Bridges and ordered those cases cleared for men who had faced discrimination in the military because of their involvement in the early CIO strikes. As a result, many members of the CP were allowed to go overseas and see action. Many died, and many were decorated.

But my case was not part of this clearance. As a result of that "psychiatric exam," I was described in my record as "probably patriotic," since they had already eliminated the categories "potential subversive" and "premature anti-fascist" as a result of General Marshall's intervention.

The term "probably patriotic," as far as I know, was used somewhat selectively. It was most often applied to individuals from minority groups whose patriotism was considered questionable because of past grievances against the United States. This applied to Mexicans, Indians, blacks, Asians, and Puerto Ricans. Filipinos, for example, could be considered anti-U.S. because of the American conquest of the Philippines. Japanese-Americans, of course, felt the full brunt of having their patriotism questioned, including facing internment. Indians who had lost their lands and were living on reservations also qualified for being questioned about their true loyalty.

The only other case that I knew about of a Mexican-American being classified as "probably patriotic" involved a Chicano who, like myself, was from El Paso. I believe his name was Mendoza. He had joined the paratroopers, as did a lot of Mexicans, along with blacks and Puerto Ricans. The paratroopers were considered to be a real man's type of outfit. Mendoza's case, however, was different from mine in that he had not participated in political or labor causes. He was blacklisted because of out-and-out racism.

Mendoza had excelled in his training at Fort Benning, Georgia. He had gotten high grades for his pre-jump training and was in perfect physical shape. He could do seven hundred sit-ups, run ten miles before breakfast, and successfully run the obstacle course blindfolded. He was a very good boxer and a natural athlete. Because of his skills, he was made an instructor and a sergeant.

When it was discovered that he had had some boxing experience, some of the Anglo officer trainees under him tried to take him on, away from everyone. These guys jumped him, and he decked both of them. They made a big stink about it because he had struck an officer. But the colonel who was running the camp refused to do anything to Mendoza.

Other officers resented him, however. When Mendoza applied to Officers' Training School, he was not accepted, even though he was highly qualified and had passed all the tests. Based on the recommendations of his superior officers, the review board concluded that Mexicans like Mendoza wouldn't make good officer material because they might harbor and manifest anti-U.S. and anti-Anglo feelings. They believed that Mexicans like Mendoza couldn't be trusted behind enemy lines. Disgruntled, Mendoza transferred out of the paratroopers. I didn't know Mendoza, but I heard about him later when I also was at Fort Benning.

Shortly after my psychiatric exam, I was called in to be questioned by a committee of officers. It was a very stiff and cold meeting. They pursued the same line of political questioning as the psychiatrist had, except in more detail. They wanted to know, for example, if I had ever seen Harry Bridges at a meeting of the Communist Party. Did I know whether he was a member of the CP? What did I think about Marxism? How did it connect with the unions?

I told them that our union policies were determined in a democratic fashion by the national conventions and that these policies had very little to do with ideology, but everything to do with concrete issues. I told them that no question had ever been raised at our union meetings because it had been approved or disapproved by the Communist Party and that anyone who tried to do so would be laughed out of the meeting.

They then asked me what I thought about the book *Mission to Moscow,* which had been written by Joseph Davies, a former U.S. ambassador to the Soviet Union, and which had favorably portrayed the USSR.* I told them that I had read the book and thought it excellent. Why? they asked. Because, I responded, it made the point that we needed to be strongly allied with the Soviet Union in order to win the war. And, after all, wasn't the Soviet Union our ally? They became upset at my response.

They then proceeded to ask me if I had also read *One World* by Wendell Wilkie, which likewise advocated an internationalist view. Wilkie had run as the Republican nominee against FDR in the 1940 presidential election. Following his defeat, Wilkie turned around and supported Roosevelt's policy of assisting Great Britain and the other European countries that were under attack by Hitler. Because of his views, Wilkie, like Roosevelt, was attacked by the "America First" group led by William Randolph Hearst, who feared such alliances, especially with the Soviet Union.

I guess if I had said that I thought *Mission to Moscow* was a mistake, *One World* was an aberration, and Vice-President Henry Wallace, who was also under attack by the U.S. right wing, was a fellow traveler of the Communists, this committee of officers might have thought I was a swell guy. This questioning went on for two or three hours. As if this were not enough, I was called for still another similar investigation soon thereafter, this one even longer.

I was never told anything after these meetings, but I saw the writing

*See Joseph Davies, *Mission to Moscow* (New York: Simon & Schuster, 1941).

on the wall, especially since I was aware of the label "probably patriotic" that had been attached to my record. Finally, an order came through removing me from my squadron and eliminating me from the Air Corps. I was just getting ready to go on furlough, preparatory to being shipped out for flight training.

The order came as no surprise; I was expecting it. I had talked about this possibility to my wife and friends. My brother-in-law, who was with the adjutant general's office as an army lawyer, warned me that there was little I could do. Because I was not yet up for a commission and was still in training, they could wash me out without any real explanation.

I did go and see Colonel Honeyman and my squadron commander, a man named Henshaw. Both of them, even though they came from wealthy families, knew about the CIO unions and didn't swallow the idea that Bridges was a Communist and that union activities were a Communist plot. But they also felt that their hands were tied. They thought the whole thing was a goddamn shame. They were willing to write letters of support but felt it wouldn't do much good.*

---

*According to a Military Intelligence Division report on Corona, obtained through the Freedom of Information Act, Corona underwent careful scrutiny by military intelligence officers while he was stationed at Santa Ana. These intelligence agents interviewed several of Corona's fellow cadets, and his mail was examined. They also investigated information concerning Corona's past history, including the environment in which he had grown up in El Paso and the student groups he had belonged to in high school. They heard good accounts of Corona's performance in his military training, including the following description of him: "Well-liked; good mixer; eager beaver, above average in military characteristics; intelligent; high type Mexican; Good soldier."

Nevertheless, military intelligence considered Corona suspect because of his labor union background. Although Corona recalls seeing or hearing about the term "probably patriotic" attached to his army record, the Military Intelligence Division report on Corona contains the term "potentially subversive." According to the report: "The investigation conducted at this station indicates that subject is an excellent soldier, a hard worker, and vitally interested in his aircrew training, and does not indicate any adverse information whatsoever. However, in view of subject's past associations, activities and membership in organizations which are either actually Communist, or sponsored or controlled by the Communist Party, it is the conclusion of this officer that subject is potentially subversive and should not be considered for appointment as a commissioned officer." The report noted that further investigation would be conducted to determine whether Corona was a member of the Communist Party. See War Department, Military Intelligence Division, File II–4319–258, June 17, 1943; contained in Corona's FBI file 363P–92.

The Zoot Suit Riots

During the time I was stationed in Santa Ana, the so-called Zoot Suit riots broke out, in early June of 1943.* For almost a week, hundreds of soldiers and sailors in Los Angeles vented their various frustrations by attacking Mexicans who were wearing zoot suits. Much of this tension went back to the Sleepy Lagoon case from 1942, when seventeen young Mexicans had been accused of murdering another Chicano. At the time, the trial became an occasion for all kinds of anti-Mexican sentiments.

The worst came from the Hearst press, which in Los Angeles was represented by the *L.A. Herald* and the *L.A. Examiner*. These papers consistently attacked Mexican *pachucos* and zoot suiters and implied that Mexicans in general were prone to crime and delinquency. This campaign was abetted by racist remarks from Captain Duran Ayres of the L.A. Sheriff's Department, who commented that Mexicans were a violent people because of their bloodthirsty Aztec ancestors. All of this created much tension and friction in L.A., and it affected the relationship between the thousands of servicemen stationed in southern California and the large Mexican community.

Fortunately, when the riots broke out, members of El Congreso and other Mexican-American community leaders sprang into action. They mobilized a defense committee on behalf of the youngsters who were being arrested and detained even though they were the victims of the servicemen. Being in close proximity, I was somewhat involved with this activity.

But I also recall the tensions at our base at the time. In fact, we had some similar incidents in which some of our Anglo servicemen beat up on local Chicanos. It caused much concern among the fairly large number of Mexican-American soldiers in our camp and in surrounding camps also. After one incident involving the beating of some young Chicanos, hundreds of Chicano kids from the nearby communities advanced on our base and waited for servicemen in the areas where the buses took us into town. That weekend, almost no servicemen ventured out to take the bus.

*For more information about the Zoot Suit riots, see Mauricio Mazón, *The Zoot-Suit Riots: The Psychology of Symbolic Annihilation* (Austin: University of Texas Press, 1984).

More serious trouble was avoided because of the quick reaction from our public information officer, the morale officer, and their staffs, who began a campaign of cooling off the situation and explaining the riots in sociological rather than racist terms. They also issued strong orders that such altercations would not be tolerated.

They were trying to avoid problems not only because of the large surrounding Mexican communities and the Chicano servicemen but also because the base functioned largely with the labor of many Mexicans, who performed service jobs such as working in the PX and in the laundries. For all of these reasons, our base was relatively quiet at a time of racial rioting in L.A. and racial, anti-Mexican disturbances at other southern California bases.

Palm Springs

After I was washed out of the Air Corps, I was sent to Torney Army General Hospital in Palm Springs. It was a big military hospital in the desert. I was first assigned to the mailroom, but when my record with the "probably patriotic" label caught up with me, the G2 officer, who was in charge of intelligence, decided that it would be too risky for me to be handling mail. So I was transferred to the surgical unit as a surgery assistant in eye, ear, nose, throat, and brain surgery.

Although I was disappointed at what had happened to me, I tried to overcome this feeling by keeping active. I became involved in organizing a soldiers' forum, where issues about the war, including social problems at home, could be discussed. Our meetings were held every Friday night at the Palm Springs estate of Joseph Schenk, a movie producer, in association with Eloise Hirt, a former drama teacher in Hollywood who ran the USO activities.

Our forums became quite a success. We held discussions on racism, religious discrimination, red-baiting, and so on. I'll never forget one particular forum about religious bigotry. The chief chaplain, a general for the Third Army, came to check us out. During a lively discussion about the need to eliminate attacks on Jews for being Jews and on Catholics for being Catholics, some people pointed out that much of this bigotry in the U.S. had come from Anglo Protestants.

Now, these were mostly whites who were saying these things at our forums; there were very few minority soldiers stationed around Palm

Springs. These white soldiers related to the issues we were promoting. They would say, "Yeah, I had a buddy who was Jewish, and I took him home once, and the people in our church didn't like it too well because his name was Rosenfeld."

This Anglo chaplain couldn't stand such comments. He got up and declared: "Well, I want to say one thing. I've been a Protestant minister all my life, and my father was a Protestant minister. All I've heard here today may sound all very well and good, but I thank God that America was founded by good, solid Protestant folks. I think that it's been very good that we have had differences of religion, because if you eliminate these differences, you haven't got anything left to be proud of."

Some soldier then stood up and told the chaplain, "I don't take to religion very well. Look what religion has cost in loss of lives in all wars—the crusades that killed millions of people, and all the wars against the Jews and Catholics. What the hell do we want this goddamn religion for?"

This was the way GIs talked. These soldiers were thinking: "Here we are in the army, and we're fighting a war, and this son of a bitch chaplain is giving us all this hypocritical nonsense about being proud of religious differences, when these differences have been responsible for all kinds of hatreds and suffering."

While at Palm Springs, I also became friends with the first sergeant and his assistant, who were in charge of personnel records in the adjutant's office. I talked to them about what had happened to me in Santa Ana. They looked up my records and concluded that the whole thing was preposterous. They got quite mad, and on their own— although they told me about it later—they destroyed that part of my record questioning my patriotism. This way, they hoped, I would be able to transfer out to a combat unit and see action overseas.

It worked for a time. I was able to transfer out to the Forty-Second Infantry Division—the Rainbow Division—in Oklahoma to receive six to eight weeks of combat training. But I quickly discovered that the Forty-Second was not well regarded and that it was considered a goof-off division. Many (though not all) of the soldiers seemed to have no interest in training, and many flunked the tests on purpose. I found out that the only way I could get out and get into a good combat unit would be to get accepted into a training program to become an officer or a highly trained technician or else to be transferred to the paratroopers.

I chose the paratroopers and was lucky to get accepted. I later discovered that the Forty-Second Infantry Division finally did get sent into battle, in Austria, and that bunch of goofballs made quite a good reputation for themselves.

Fort Benning

Having been accepted into the paratroopers, I was transferred to Fort Benning, Georgia, the chief paratroop training base in the country. Everything at first went well in my training as a demolition specialist, although I did have a close call in one of my training jumps.

Every paratrooper had to have at least one jump per month. I had already made three or four jumps with very heavy packs. As a demolitionist, you had to jump with heavy demolition equipment like land mines and learn how not to blow yourself up. All this time, we were waiting to be shipped out, either to the Pacific or to Europe.

One week, we were notified that we had to do a night jump. It was a hurry-up jump, called with only three or four days' notice. However, they didn't check the weather very closely, and there were quite a number of clouds the night we were scheduled to jump. The clouds would blot out the moon, which made it difficult to see—in fact, it got pitch dark.

Usually when you jump at night, as soon as you're out of the plane and the parachute opens, you pull your parachute risers in the direction you want to go, and you go very fast. You look down below and, if the moon is out, you direct yourself so that you don't land in trees. The other problem that night was the wind; there was a heavy breeze. Beyond so many miles per hour of wind, you're not supposed to jump, because your parachute sways. The wind was blowing at almost that rate that evening.

After I parachuted, I saw a field near a farmhouse, and I pulled my risers to go into it. I was holding on tight and going down very fast. Just about when I hit tree level, I felt my chute jiggle, which means you're losing the tight control you need. I looked up and saw that another paratrooper had fallen on top of my chute. This sometimes happened when you jumped in large numbers. That night, a thousand men jumped.

But at the same time, it became quite dark, and I couldn't see the trees. I didn't know what to do, whether to let go or not, when all of a sudden my chute collapsed. All I remember then was that my feet, my chin, and my elbows all hit the ground at the same time. I had a lot of equipment. I was knocked out. When I came to, I saw two or three guys on stretchers, all broken up.

What had happened was that the wind had moved the planes beyond our target, and heavy clouds had obscured our vision. We suffered numerous casualties. The trooper who had fallen on my chute had tried to run off it, in the hope that he could again pull his chute open, because it had collapsed. He couldn't do this, and he fell maybe eighty feet, landed on his head, and broke his neck.

My chute had also collapsed, and I fell with all the weight of my equipment. But I landed on my ass and on top of my equipment. This saved my life because it cushioned my fall. I suffered broken arches and torn ligaments in my knees, which caused me problems later.

After I recovered and was still preparing to be sent overseas, my record, with its blacklisting, once again caught up with me. Although the Santa Ana record had been destroyed or altered, there is always a backup somewhere. This time, unlike the other times, the record was not used openly against me. Instead, a trick was pulled on me to ensure that I would either get kicked out of the paratroopers or miss the opportunity to go with my division to see combat.

The setup occurred when I requested a pass to go into Atlanta for a weekend. It was okayed by the commanding officer and the first sergeant who issued the passes. When I received the pass, it was folded, and I just put it in my pocket and forgot about it.

But when I got off the train in Atlanta, I hadn't walked more than a hundred feet when two MPs approached me and said, "Let's see your pass, soldier." They didn't ask anybody else.

I took the pass out very confidently. They examined it and said, "Come with us."

"What do you mean?" I replied. "I have a pass." They then told me that my pass was for Columbus, Georgia, right adjacent to the camp. I had been set up.

I protested, but they arrested me and took me in. At their headquarters, I asked to contact my commanding officer by phone. I told them that my unit was leaving for overseas and that this was my last pass prior to being shipped out.

"Yeah, yeah," they said, "but you can't call your commanding officer. Write him a letter, or better still, let the sergeant here notify your commanding officer." The sergeant made out like he was writing all this down, and he claimed that my commanding officer would be notified the next day. In the meantime, they locked me up in the federal prison at Fort McDonald in downtown Atlanta, alongside murderers and gangsters. They were playing with me.

For a month, I couldn't get any word out to my unit or to anyone. They wouldn't let me get near a phone. They wouldn't let me send out mail either. I tried to get some of the prisoners who were being released to take mail out for me, but apparently they never mailed my letters, which were addressed to Blanche, my commanding officer, and Harry Bridges. All this time, I was put to work digging out pine tree stumps in the woods or working in downtown parks.

Finally, I got friendly enough with an office guard who happened to have been in a union in Chicago. I told him my whole story. "Jesus Christ!" he said. "Listen, on Fridays, everyone in the office leaves early, and you can come in and place a call to Fort Benning." At that point, I was not being held in a cell, but instead was in a dormitory where I could move about relatively freely within certain restricted areas.

That Friday, the office personnel took off about three-thirty in the afternoon, and I came by on the excuse that I needed to use the toilet. I dialed my unit at Fort Benning. The company cook answered.

"This is Corona," I said.

"Where in the hell have you been?" he replied. "You're AWOL, you son of a bitch."

"No, I'm not AWOL," I answered back. "I'm in Fort McDonald prison." I told him the whole story and asked him to get word to the company commander so that I could get released.

"He's gone!" the cook shot back. "The whole unit shipped out two weeks ago. But I'll get word to the new company commander."

But nothing happened. In the meantime, I got to talking with some of the other men in prison and told them about my case. Some of them were in for getting drunk or for some other disturbance. One or two guys, however, had cases similar to mine, in which they had been tricked on their passes. Still others were conscientious objectors; the army didn't believe them and put them in jail for a year. The real hoods were put in another part of the prison.

I made it a point to get to know the conscientious objectors and other prisoners who had suffered mistreatment. Some of them were being released and given dishonorable discharges. Before they left, I gave them letters addressed to Blanche, to the new company commander, to the company clerk, to Local 26 in Los Angeles, and to Harry Bridges in San Francisco. These letters did get out. My wife and the union wrote letters to Fort Benning, and at last a telegram arrived that led to my release, after about forty-five days of detention.

When I got back to Fort Benning, I told the new company commander the story. "Son of a bitch!" he exclaimed. "They really hung one on you!" He advised me to go to battalion headquarters and try to get the AWOL off my record. When I got there and explained the situation, they looked up my record and, sure enough, I was in the right: I had requested a pass to Atlanta but instead had been given one to Columbus. I was not AWOL, and they changed my record.

Later, however, when I was getting out of the army, the AWOL still haunted me. At first, I was told I would receive no pay for the forty-five days I was AWOL. Not until I protested and they checked with Fort Benning did they acknowledge that I had not been AWOL. But they still didn't pay me. They said these represented nonservice days, which didn't entitle me to pay. So the sons of bitches didn't pay me.

Having missed being shipped out with my unit, I wondered how I was ever going to get into combat. My colonel was not too encouraging.

"Bert," he said, "before they'll ever ship you overseas—unless the war takes a turn for the worse—your record is always going to catch up with you. Even if it doesn't happen before you embark, by the time you get over there, your service record will have caught up with you. Once you're there, with this record, your commanding officer can still send you back. It's a terrible thing that's happened to you. It should never have happened, but some people's brains are twisted."

This colonel's father had been a right-winger, but the colonel was all right. He gave me the run of the post. But I was pretty discouraged and disillusioned. I thought: "How in the hell can a person get out and fight? My God, they're likely to hold me back even if the Nazis invade the country!" It was even more distressing because I had to remain at Fort Benning with all kinds of misfits and unstable guys who had been weeded out and left behind.

I went back to the colonel and said, "Look, what can I do to get out of here?" He finally suggested that I might get transferred to another combat unit if I got discharged from the paratroopers for physical reasons. He checked my record and noticed that I had broken arches and inflammation of the knees as a result of my jump accident. He sent me to the base hospital for a physical exam.

The doctor who examined my feet said my condition wasn't bad enough for a discharge. After I told him my story, he suggested that he could get me off jump status and see about putting me with the supply depots doing kitchen duty or clerk's duty. That way, at least I could get to Europe, even if it wasn't in the front lines. But this wasn't what I wanted. He thought I was nuts.

However, since I still had to participate in practice jumps, I later reinjured my arches and knees. I went back to the same doctor, who this time agreed that I qualified for a transfer out of the paratroopers.

I went back to the colonel and informed him of the doctor's decision. He told me that he had just received a directive requesting people for the Signal Corps, to handle the U.S. secret code. Not enough code operators were available in the Pacific, so rush courses of six weeks were being organized in Neosho, Missouri. "You'll go overseas with a combat unit because they need signal operators."

I was sent to Camp Crowder in Neosho. It appears that when the colonel submitted my application for the Signal Corps, he either deleted from my service record the intelligence information listing me as "probably patriotic" or held back that part of it. In any event, I was accepted. At Neosho, I passed all the tests with high grades and had only two weeks to go before completing the course when bad luck struck again.

I ran into Jaime Del Amo, the former Spanish consul in L.A., who was also at Camp Crowder. Del Amo was a U.S. citizen who was drafted into the service but who was being kept out of combat because of his previous ties to the fascist Franco regime. Del Amo knew who I was. He apparently went and told my captain that I was some kind of subversive because of my involvement with the National Congress of Spanish-Speaking Peoples.

The captain came to my barracks one day, looking for me. I wasn't there but was at the PX having a beer. When he showed up there, he asked me to go outside with him.

Somewhat embarrassed, he said, "You know, I got orders to ship you out to the processing center in California."

"Does that mean I'm finally going overseas?"

"No, it means that you've been busted out of the Signal Corps."

"What?"

"Yeah. You can't be in the Signal Corps."

"But why?"

"Because you've got a bad record for loyalty."

So I got booted out of the Signal Corps. I was one week away from completing all of my training; in another week or so, I would have been on my way to the Pacific. Instead, I was sent to the processing center at Camp McClellan, north of Yuba City, and stayed there until the end of the war. I entered the service as a buck private, and I left as one. I paid the price of having been involved in progressive causes and was one of those stigmatized and red-baited because of my involvement.

Orlando, Horacio, and Aurora

Unlike me, my two younger brothers did see action during the war. Orlando volunteered for the army and was sent to the Pacific right after Pearl Harbor. He was in the Thirty-Second Red Arrow division as an infantryman and a machine gunner. He participated in the invasions of Guam, the Solomon Islands, and New Guinea and went through some rough combat. Besides being wounded three or four times, he also contracted malaria. Although he might have received an officer's commission, Orlando was not too interested in rank and came out a sergeant. Upon returning to the States, he got married and raised a family.

My other brother, Horacio, went into the Air Force about the same time I joined the Air Corps. He also trained at Santa Ana. Unfortunately, he felt the effects of the red-baiting that I experienced. I suspect that Colonel Dunsworth inserted something in Horacio's own record to indicate that he was my brother. In any event, instead of receiving his commission as a navigator when he got out of flight school, he instead was made only a warrant officer, which is between a noncommissioned officer and a commissioned one.

Still, Horacio saw a lot of action. He flew about twenty-five bombing missions from southern Italy into Austria. In a thousand-plane raid over Vienna, his plane was struck by anti-aircraft fire at forty thousand feet, and the plane exploded.

My mother received a postcard with a very cryptic message, saying that Horacio's plane had been shot down but that no information existed as to whether or not he had been killed. We all believed that he had been killed. However, three or four months later, my mother received another postcard, telling her that the copilot of my brother's plane had survived and that they were still investigating to see if there were other survivors.

Finally, a year later, she got a postcard from Horacio, who was in a Catholic hospital in Vienna. The card had been smuggled out of Austria by an Italian soldier who had been in the hospital, but the card was signed by Horacio. He wrote that he had been shot down but that he was okay.

From Vienna, my brother was sent to a German prison camp near the Baltic Sea. Once there, he was able to send my mother a letter, so we knew his whereabouts. He suffered very much in that camp. It was cold, and the Germans were starving them. When the Russian army moved toward Berlin, my brother and other prisoners were freed by the Russians. He was in the hands of the Russians for a few weeks until transferred to American hands. He was sent to a hospital in Paris, where he convalesced for three or four weeks.

He was brought back home, but then shortly thereafter he was shipped to the Pacific, where in the last part of the war he flew a few more missions over Japan as well as over the China/Burma theater. He didn't come home until the damn war was over. Even though he had a wife and he had completed all the missions required to get released, he was still sent to the Pacific—a fact that I attribute to what might have been put on his record linking him with my problems. He was finally made a second lieutenant, after being decorated following his downing in Austria. Yet even this smacked of discrimination. Guys who had done only half of what he did in the service came out captains and above.

Horacio never fully recovered from his war experiences, especially the explosion of his plane. He never quite knew how he had survived, but apparently he and the copilot were blown out of the plane. Although they were dazed, they had enough presence of mind to pull the ripcords on their parachutes. They were the only survivors. After the war, Horacio still suffered anxieties and nervousness. Later he had other health problems, which might have been related to his war experience. He died a few years ago of a massive brain hemorrhage.

My sister, Aurora, also contributed to the war effort, although she didn't go into the service. In El Paso, she got a job with army intelligence as a censor. The El Paso office censored all mail going into Mexico and Latin America. If one mailed a letter from Los Angeles addressed to Tijuana, it had to go first to El Paso, where someone from a team of forty or fifty bilingual censors, including my sister, would read it to see if it contained any possible military secrets.

Interestingly enough, right under the nose of this intelligence operation was the principal German spy ring into Mexico, which operated in El Paso. This ring involved a Dr. Ebell, who worked out of his medical office. He had a string of German and Mexican spies all through the border area and Mexico who fed information to the Nazis. He was later caught and prosecuted.

Both my sister and my mother remained in El Paso during the war. At the end of the conflict, they decided to move to the L.A. area permanently. My sister had met a young soldier, Herman Mirkin, in El Paso, and they later married in L.A. He went to medical school and received his M.D. After their marriage, he opened up a medical clinic in Chino.

Family Reunion

One positive result from all of my problems with the army was that at least I was able to see and be with Blanche on and off during this time. When I was at Cedar City, Blanche was able to come and live with me during my training. We rented a room with a very lovely family, which led to a good friendship. They were Mormons but not dogmatic ones. They were what were called "Jack Mormons"—they did not observe, for example, the strict laws against drinking Coca-Cola, coffee, and liquor. They pointed out that these laws came from the new generation of Mormons and that older Mormons, including Brigham Young himself, had been known to take a drink now and then.

When I was in Santa Ana, Blanche returned to live with her parents in L.A., but I was close enough to see her very frequently. In Palm Springs, we lived together and, in fact, our first child, Margo, was born while I was stationed there. I had to leave them in California when I went to Oklahoma and Georgia, but at Fort Benning and then in Neosho, Blanche and our little baby came and visited me. They were then living with Blanche's parents.

Blanche worked for some of this time as a secretary and as a book-keeper. She also did volunteer work with El Congreso. She assisted El Congreso in building support for the war effort among Mexicans in Los Angeles. This was also done to offset the anti-war efforts of the Sinar-quistas. Working with Josefina Fierro and Eduardo Quevedo, Blanche and others organized the huge rally at the Embassy Auditorium in support of the war.

Blanche also helped in El Congreso's successful efforts to get Mexicans registered to be eligible to work in the new war industries. This process was critical because, with the anti-Mexican attitudes manifested in the Sleepy Lagoon case in 1942 and the Zoot Suit riots of 1943, the mistaken notion was circulating that Mexicans, especially the youth, were all delinquents, didn't work, and were unpatriotic.

This of course was not true. During the entire period of the war, the number of draft dodgers among Chicanos was almost zero. Moreover, Mexicans proved themselves in all areas of combat. Mexican of all ages worked in a variety of nonwar industries; the problem was discrimination against Mexicans in war-related industries.

The Congreso registration drive was aimed to show the great interest of *mexicanos* in such employment. Over fifty thousand people were registered not only in L.A. but also in Pacoima, San Fernando, Oxnard, and the San Gabriel Valley. As a result of these efforts, the Committee on Fair Employment Practice was forced to hold hearings in L.A., which led to more Mexicans being hired in war industries.

When I was finally returned to California to the processing center at Camp McClellan, it was easy for me to come down to L.A. and visit my family. By the end of the war in 1945, I was fully reunited with them in Los Angeles. My ordeal with the military had come to an end.

CHAPTER EIGHT

Coming Home

When I returned to L.A. after my discharge from the military, we decided to live in East Los Angeles. I was attracted to the idea of living once again with mostly other Mexicans, and I was also becoming quite involved in the housing crisis that affected Mexicans in L.A. I had retained a soft spot in my heart for the housing projects that went up during the war, because before I left for the service I had worked in the fight to establish several of these large housing projects in East L.A.—Ramona Gardens, Aliso Village, and Pico Gardens. We moved into Ramona Gardens.

Housing Struggles

Although these projects had been constructed in the barrios, many Mexicans had a difficult time moving into them because priority was given to servicemen, families of servicemen, or those working in the war industries. But now the war had ended, and the projects had many openings as people moved out into newer suburban developments.

Mexicans who had lived in more congested areas wanted to move into the projects. Some families outside the projects had been doubling and even tripling up with other families because of a housing shortage and high rents. Housing was particularly critical for the returning Chicano veterans as well as for many *mexicano* workers who were being laid off, especially from war industries. If you didn't have a job, you weren't eligible to live in the projects. For all those reasons, housing was a major issue for the Mexican communities in L.A.

I worked with community leaders and returning *veteranos* to see about opening up the projects for more Mexicans and improving the quality of the projects. We organized with people such as the Reverend Kendrick Watson and Bill Taylor, who had been a crony of mine with the Longshoremen's Union and who also lived in Ramona Gardens. We formed the Mexican-American Committee for Justice in Housing. Bill and myself plus a couple of other families organized the tenants in Ramona Gardens, while the Reverend Watson worked in Pico Gardens. Other former ILWU union organizers such as Elliot and Libby Wax, who lived in Aliso Village, organized the tenants there.

We took on the county housing authority. When the top directors refused to meet separately with our committee, we organized community meetings at one of the nearby schools and insisted that they meet with the community. The authorities agreed to attend, since they were skeptical about how much support we had. The meetings were packed with people. Even though the housing directors were ostensibly holding the meetings, the residents of the projects very quickly took over the proceedings and voiced their needs and grievances.

In time, the housing authority understood that our committee spoke for the people. The new director, Frank Wilkinson, had been involved in the early fights of minorities for good housing, prior to World War II.* The housing authority agreed to negotiate with us, which led to certain changes and improvements in the various projects, including making them more accessible to other *mexicanos*. All these changes resulted from the level of effective organization we had put together.

On the Waterfront

During this time, I also tried to resume my work with the CIO and, in particular, as president of my old local, Local 26 of the Longshoremen's Union. But I ran into problems. While I and other former union officials

*Frank Wilkinson was the executive director of the Los Angeles City Housing Authority. He achieved national attention when he refused to testify before HUAC during the McCarthy period. He later headed the National Committee Against Repressive Legislation as well as the First Amendment Foundation.

were in the service, new officers had been appointed or elected to our old positions, and these men obviously did not want to vacate their posts. Moreover, it was suggested to me that Lou Sherman, the president of the local, who had replaced me, might have difficulty getting another job if he stepped down, because of his earlier CP connections. I thought about all of this. I didn't relish the idea of bumping a fella who was an officer. In a quandary and just biding my time, I decided to go to the waterfront and find work on the docks.

But here I also ran into difficulty. During the war, the union had been forced to sign an agreement with the Coast Guard that anyone working on the docks had to have a security clearance. Unfortunately, this requirement was retained after the war. Given my experience in the service, I had my doubts about securing work under these circumstances, but I went ahead and submitted my application for a clearance. I told them that I had been in the service and what units I had served in. I never heard from the Coast Guard, and I finally decided that they had simply not given me a clearance after checking my service record. Others like me had the same problems finding work as a result of similar security clauses.

Diamond Salesman

I received offers to work with other unions, but I wanted to stay with the Longshoremen's Union. If I couldn't, then I preferred to go into something else. And I didn't want to leave California.

My father-in-law at that time needed a salesman in San Francisco and the northern territory that he covered for his wholesale diamond business. He talked to me one day: "Bert, you know there's this job, and we can't find a suitable salesman. If you're interested, let me know." I thought about it for a couple of months and finally accepted his offer.

The fact was that I was running out of savings and needed a job. With this job, I could now support my family and maybe do my father-in-law some good. He was very gracious and helped me relocate. He bought me a car and gave us the money to buy a house in northern California. This was about 1947.

We first lived in Mill Valley. I found a house that had been built as a war project in an area called Strawberry Point. It was just a stop on the main freeway heading further north. I bought the house for about six or seven thousand dollars, ridiculously low. It was very convenient, being next to the freeway; I could be in San Francisco in a few minutes.

The house was also large enough for our growing family. Shortly after we moved north, my first son, David, was born. A little later, my second son, Frank, was born. Margo, my daughter, had been born during the war.

Besides helping us to get settled, my father-in-law taught me the business of selling diamonds. I came to know all about them and about other precious stones. I had an office in San Francisco and traveled around the Bay Area trying to interest buyers in my father-in-law's diamonds.

On my trips, I carried around with me very valuable merchandise, close to a hundred thousand dollars' worth of loose and mounted diamonds, which I showed to the retailers or chain store operators. They inspected the diamonds and selected those they wanted, which I would later deliver. Some wanted to pay me with gold, but I never accepted it, since one was never sure of the quality of the gold or the source.

I enjoyed the work. It was interesting but dangerous; you had to watch yourself. You couldn't leave the merchandise alone at any time. A hundred thousand dollars at that time was like a million dollars today.

After we moved north, my side of the family decided to join us. My brother Orlando, who had been working as a manufacturing jeweler after he got out of the army, bought a house across the freeway from us, and he invited my mother and my grandmother to move in with him. They had been living in Alhambra. But they didn't like the move north. My grandmother fell down in that new house and broke her hip. She recovered well, but my brother sold the house, and they all returned to Alhambra.

McCarthyism

Although I was now in the diamond business, I remained very interested in the union movement and in the politics of the Mexican-American communities. Unfortunately, the period of the late 1940s and early 1950s was shadowed by the rise of McCarthyism and right-wing assaults. Even before Winston Churchill's 1946 "Iron Curtain" speech at Fulton, Missouri, which is often seen as signaling the start of the Cold War, efforts in this country were already under way to crush dissent, especially when it came from the unions and from the left. This was being done by painting dissenters as "reds and terrorists."

At the beginning, much of the left seemed undisturbed, believing that these attacks would not amount to much. But very soon all kinds of right-wing groups began to crop up all over the country and to intimidate governmental bodies such as school boards, city councils, and boards of supervisors. This gathered momentum, and it disconcerted the left. To confront this attack, the left took steps to expose the reactionary nature of this movement in the press as well as to public and private groups.

But the left wasn't equal to organizing the kinds of campaigns it had waged before the war. It was strange. The left had suffered losses during the war—leaders killed and wounded—and, coming home, there was much disorientation and disorganization. Before you knew it, the right wing and the red-baiters got the upper hand.

Investigations and propaganda campaigns commenced, with the press as allies of the right wing. McCarthyism took its toll. It became difficult to get progressive groups together; many individuals went underground. Many turned their back on the movement. They had never faced anything like this, and they were not prepared.

In California, civil wars raged inside many of the CIO unions, and many succumbed to the pressure of McCarthyism. Progressive labor leaders were attacked and called Communists. If they had been appointed to their posts, they were fired; if they had been elected, they were denigrated. They were dragged through the mud, and all kinds of lies were printed about them. Efforts were made to dislodge them by filing charges against them and by finding candidates to run against them. This was particularly true in L.A. In northern California, the labor movement proved to be somewhat more resilient. The unions were bigger and stronger, as were civil rights groups such as the American Civil Liberties Union.

All this had a profound effect. Some of the unions most vulnerable to the right-wing assault were the United Auto Workers, the Oil, Chemical, and Atomic Workers Union, the Furniture Workers Union, and the United Steel Workers. The ILWU proved to be less susceptible to the intense red-baiting. Some of it went on, but ideologically the rank and file had been pretty much prepared to resist. The leadership had made it very clear that red-baiting was a false tactic, undemocratic, and not an honest measure by which to judge a person.

While some of the progressive unions such as the ILWU, the United Electrical Workers, and the Mine, Mill and Smelter Workers hung on, many others couldn't withstand the pressures and were taken over by more conservative factions. All of this, of course, was abetted by federal, state, and local governments, which themselves sponsored red-baiting and anti-labor laws such as the Taft-Hartley law and the loyalty oaths.*

As part of its red-scare tactics, the FBI harassed people at home and at work. Of course, those who were in the CP or had been close to the party were subjected to harassment, including having the FBI approach their employers. I remember a fellow named Ralph Dawson, who was a painter with a good job in San Francisco. He had been a great organizer for the CIO in southern California in the days before World War II. The FBI went right to his employers and said, "Do you know who you have working for you? Ralph Dawson is one of the most dangerous Communist organizers in southern California. This is his record. We felt that you should know." The next day, Ralph was fired. There were many cases of this kind.

---

*Taft-Hartley represented the major anti-union federal legislation of the initial Cold War years. Passed as the Labor Management Act of 1947, this bill contained provisions making it difficult for unions to organize or carry on militant activities. Its most significant provision was Section 9(h), which denied a union the right to use the National Labor Relations Board unless each officer of the union filed an affidavit swearing that he or she (1) was not a member of the Communist Party, (2) was not affiliated with the CP, and (3) did not believe in and was not a member or supporter of any organization that believed in or taught the overthrow of the U.S. government "by force or by any illegal or unconstitutional methods." No union with an elected or appointed Communist officer could now use the NLRB to gain certification, even if a majority of the workers voted for the union; and any union that did not comply with Taft-Hartley could now be decertified. Passed over President Truman's veto, Taft-Hartley hampered the union movement and caused major internal tensions within the CIO between those who opposed the legislation and those who opportunistically wished to accommodate themselves to it. The loyalty oath provisions of Taft-Hartley and subsequent similar legislation were finally declared unconstitutional by the Supreme Court in 1961. See Dan Georgakas's entry on Taft-Hartley in *Encyclopedia of the American Left*, ed. Mari Jo Buhle, Paul Buhle, and Dan Georgakas (Urbana: University of Illinois Press, 1992), pp. 767–770.

The Independent Progressive Party

One of the first political activities I became involved with in the Bay Area was the effort to build the Independent Progressive Party, the IPP. This was the party behind the 1948 presidential campaign of former Vice-President Henry Wallace.

Discouraged with the more conservative turn taken by the Democratic Party under Truman, especially its support of the Cold War abroad and red-scare tactics at home, I was attracted to Wallace because of his more liberal positions. He did not buy the line of Churchill and Truman that the socialist countries were as bad as the fascists had been. He had a better policy toward Latin America. And he had better positions on combatting racism in this country. For these and other reasons, Wallace was attractive to those like myself who had been involved in progressive politics before the war. This earlier group of progressives, including militant members of the CIO, proved to be the main organizers and supporters of the IPP.

In northern California, we built the campaign not only for Wallace but also for state and local IPP candidates. We supported candidates who were running inside the Democratic Party but were sympathetic to Wallace as well as those who were running on the IPP ticket. We carried the campaign into the Mexican-American and African-American communities, where the response was quite good.

Many Spanish-speaking people were already acquainted with Wallace's efforts in FDR's administration to influence a more cooperative policy toward Mexico and to build on the Good Neighbor Policy.* During the war, Wallace had strongly supported the Committee on Fair Employment Practice. He had spoken at rallies sponsored by the National Congress of Spanish-Speaking Peoples and other Mexican-American organizations. He had a base with Mexican-Americans similar to the one John Kennedy would later develop.

Mexican-Americans could identify with Wallace, and he had the charisma, as Kennedy would have, to attract them. I was surprised at how many Mexican-Americans sympathized with the IPP. It was, however, the only party speaking out against racism, for integrated housing,

---

*President Franklin Roosevelt's policy toward Latin America in the 1930s was known as the Good Neighbor Policy. It stressed using diplomatic means to resolve political crises in Latin America rather than relying on the previous policy of military intervention by the United States.

for better education, and for many other issues vital to minority communities. The Democrats were being very cautious in opposing the growing right-wing reaction. But not the IPP. It faced the right wing head on.

But by supporting progressive issues, the IPP of course also faced much red-baiting. This did affect how many people, including Mexican-Americans, reacted to the party. It was charged, of course, that the IPP was controlled by the Communists. I didn't believe this. The CP didn't have much strength after the war. It had an influence on the IPP, but it didn't dominate it. Still, the IPP was stigmatized by the media and by others as being Communist.

I remember one time we wanted to have a rally on the San Francisco peninsula, but we couldn't find a place to meet. We tried the Club Cervantes and the Ateneo Español in Mountain View, but these groups wouldn't rent their halls to us because they thought the IPP was Communist. We finally managed to arrange to have the rally on the Stanford campus through the efforts of some professors who were IPP supporters.

We invited Maurice Travis, the head of the Mine, Mill and Smelter Workers, to be the key speaker at the rally. He gave an excellent speech and a very brave one. Maurice at the time was under attack because he opposed the loyalty oath for union leaders as being a violation of constitutional rights. He was being heavily red-baited. The local press announced his speech by referring to him as the "confirmed red leader of the Miners Union."

In his speech, he informed the audience: "You know, not far from where we're standing, Captain José Carrasco, a Mexican in the service of Spain, stumbled onto the world's richest mercury mine at Almaden, which made it possible and profitable for the Spaniards to extract the mercury needed to separate gold from other metals. This opened up the exploitation of mining in California as well as other places in the world. This campus, with institutions such as the Hoover Library, is a testimony to those Americans such as Mark Hanna and Leland Stanford who later benefited from the exploitation of mining and in particular from the exploitation of those workers of different races and nationalities who worked the mines and related industries." The speech tied in history with the present very well. It was a great rally.

Of course, some—mainly liberals in the Democratic Party—criticized the IPP for dividing the Democratic vote and hence making it easier for the Republicans to win. This did not happen, and Truman narrowly won. Moreover, liberal Democrats then and later, such as Adlai Stevenson, actually turned out to be fairly conservative. I encountered some Mexican-Americans during the 1948 campaign who thought the IPP was divisive, but most of the people who voiced these fears were what I call "hothouse Anglo liberals." In fact, they were really fearful of criticizing the Cold War atmosphere and of declaring themselves against McCarthyism. They thought that by playing it safe and staying within the traditional two-party system, they would be protecting themselves and their jobs.

Wallace and the IPP didn't win, but it was an exhilarating experience; and it helped to further politicize many minorities, including Mexican-Americans, who sympathized with Wallace.* I met Wallace on several occasions during the campaign. He struck me as an honest man, in the tradition of midwestern progressives such as Robert LaFollette. Later on, I found out that he and his wife were socially very conservative in their tastes. But in his political thinking, Wallace was very much a full-fledged progressive.

The Community Service Organization

Following my involvement with the IPP, I became active with the Community Service Organization. This group had been organized around 1947 in southern California, but it soon had chapters in the Bay Area as well. CSO was made up predominantly of Mexican-Americans—many of them veterans and their wives—and focused on various community issues, especially voter registration and getting Mexicans to become politically involved. CSO scored its greatest success in 1949 when it spearheaded the movement that elected Edward Roybal to the Los Angeles City Council—the first Mexican-American elected to the council since the nineteenth century.

The key to CSO was its connection to the Industrial Areas Founda-

---

*As a result of Truman's and the Democratic Party's rearticulation of a populist platform as well as the red-baiting that was directed against the IPP, the IPP failed to do well in the election, including in California. Although the IPP continued to run candidates in some states such as California into the early 1950s, it remained a minor third-party movement.

tion in Chicago, led by Saul Alinsky. It was Alinsky who had perfected various techniques for successfully organizing minority and unrepresented working-class communities. Alinsky's method of organizing focused on social issues pertinent at that moment. It involved the use of dramatic tactics, such as mass demonstrations and picketing, that embarrassed the culprits and forced them to deal with you. These tactics were always peaceful. The issues chosen were meant to correct malformations in the system, not to demand a change in the system itself. Still, they were issues aimed at obtaining social justice, better opportunities, better education, and better services.

It was Alinsky who hired organizers such as Fred Ross and a young César Chávez to form CSO, and it was Alinsky who obtained the grants that subsidized it. Because of its grassroots emphasis, many Mexican-American radicals from the 1930s movements joined CSO, along with a new breed of activists who came out of the war as veterans. These younger participants included people such as Tony Rios and young university students such as Herman Gallegos and Dolores Huerta. Roybal, who had been working with the California health and tuberculosis campaign, helped to publicize CSO greatly through his campaign in 1949. The Catholic church also supported CSO. But the key to the organization was its ties to Alinsky and its access to paid organizers such as Ross and Chávez.

I joined and helped organize CSO in northern California because I thought it had a good program of defending the rights of the Spanish-speaking, of advocating redress of their grievances, and of seeking to bring them into the mainstream of American life, especially through voting. One thing I didn't like, however, was that one of its stated reasons for organizing was to keep the "reds" from establishing a base in the communities. I knew that when they referred to "reds," they meant those Mexicans who were either working with the CP or involved with ANMA, the Asociación Nacional México-Americana.

"We're not a Communist organization," Alinsky often stated. "We know all about the commies, and we're not in agreement with them. They don't fool us a bit. We're out here to organize the Spanish-speaking in conjunction with the Catholic church. Don't for one minute think that we sympathize with the reds in any way, shape, or form. We're accused of being reds, but we're not. We're against the reds." He would make pronouncements like this all the time. Nevertheless, I joined CSO and was actually surprised to find very little red-baiting.

I worked on voter registration and on getting out the vote for those campaigns in which CSO indirectly supported particular liberal candidates, such as Byron Rumford, a black man whom we helped get elected to the state assembly from Berkeley. We supported blacks such as Lionel Wilson for municipal judgeships and *mexicano* candidates in San Jose along with Latino ones in San Francisco.* CSO never officially endorsed candidates, but through its voter registration and mobilization, it certainly aided particular ones.

Concentrating on communities in San Francisco, Oakland, and Decato (now Union City), CSO raised issues related to police brutality. We were also very active on the issues of low-cost housing, of improving older neighborhoods in West and East Oakland, and in reconstructing the big wartime housing projects in East Oakland. We participated in health service issues and neighborhood service issues in San Francisco and elsewhere. I also helped to organize political retreats, which were held at Quaker houses or at a ranch owned by the Duvenek family, where Mexican-American leaders came together to discuss issues and how to organize. In some of these activities, I and others worked as members of both CSO and ANMA.

Although Fred Ross was one of the major figures in CSO, I didn't have a close relationship with him. For one thing, he worked primarily in southern California, while I was based in the northern part of the state. However, my impressions were for the most part favorable. A rather quiet, serious, and intensely applied person, he focused on organizing *mexicanos* along the patterns of the Industrial Areas Foundation.

I felt that he understood the suffering of the Mexican people in California, that he recognized the injustices, and that he was concerned about righting the wrongs that *mexicanos* had suffered. I respected him and still do. Fred Ross was a solid organizer; he followed through and was very resourceful. With these kinds of qualities, even though he was not a *mexicano* and not from California, he could go into any town and quickly organize groups of disadvantaged and exploited people. He had those qualities I most admire: commitment, consistency, dedication, and resourcefulness.

At the same time, Fred was also very dependent on those *mexicanos* whom he and Alinsky had identified as key CSO organizers, including

*Lionel Wilson served as mayor of Oakland in the 1970s.

Chávez, Roybal, Tony Rios, Herman Gallegos, Dolores Huerta, Ursula Gutiérrez, and Ignacio López, the publisher of *El Espectador* in Pomona. Many women were active in CSO, as officers, organizers, and door-to-door voter registrars. The women, like the men, were from working-class families or lower-middle-class ones. Ross served as a catalyst to bring these people together in developing a community organization.

The only thing that I objected to concerning Fred—and it was the same objection I had to the Alinsky organization—was that he and Alinsky were used by the Hearst press and other red-baiting media to put the fear of God in the Mexican-American communities. Ross did this by suggesting that unless *mexicanos* organized with CSO, the reds would get them. While I never heard Fred red-bait anyone personally, he was quoted extensively in the Hearst press, such as the *L.A. Herald Examiner*. It's possible, however, that he might have been misquoted or simply used.

While Ross and Alinsky were anti-Communist, they gave you the impression that, more than anything else, they used their red-baiting to scare funders into giving them money—in other words, they used red-baiting as a fund-raising gimmick: "Give us the money, or else the reds are very capable of organizing these people, and then the establishment will have problems with the *mexicanos*. If they're totally abandoned by the churches and social organizations, then it's logical that they will turn to the Communists." I didn't, of course, believe that. I didn't see it happening, nor did I think it could happen.

One of the key leaders of CSO was the young César Chávez. When CSO started and I was in northern California, word came through that there was a hell of an organizer by the name of César Chávez from a barrio in San Jose called Sal Si Puedes (Get Out If You Can). His fame preceded him. Those in the Catholic church, the Quakers, and other religious groups involved with developing leadership and organization in the Chicano communities spoke very highly of this dark, short, very serious, and very committed *mexicano*.

I think I first met César in the late 1940s or early 1950s at a conference sponsored by CSO chapters in the Bay Area. He was invited to speak. I was impressed because he was very direct and honest. He had a very down-to-earth approach. He spoke with a lot of confidence, especially concerning the ability of *mexicanos* to successfully organize to redress their grievances and to obtain a greater measure of justice.

When I first heard about César, he was organizing CSO chapters in the San Jose area around issues such as adequate and affordable housing, sanitation, and police brutality. Later I was aware of his key work among farm communities in the Imperial Valley and the San Joaquin Valley. He was organizing not only farmworkers but also *mexicanos* who lived in the *colonias* and barrios of agricultural towns.

He was successful in getting cooperatives and credit unions started and in participating in early efforts to unionize farmworkers. He believed then, and of course later, that only through a union could farmworkers successfully bargain with growers over wages and working conditions. César had a lot of faith in himself. He believed that he would be successful—that it could be done. It was just a matter of being tenacious, persistent, and patient.

I was not very close to César because I hardly ever saw him. When I began to organize for ANMA, he was organizing for CSO elsewhere. But when we ran into each other, he was always very friendly, warm, and willing to exchange ideas and news.

Two other key people in CSO were Edward Roybal and Ignacio López.* I had little direct contact with Roybal because he worked primarily in southern California after his election to the L.A. City Council. Some of my relatives were quite active in that first campaign. They weren't members of CSO but were in other political clubs whose formation had been stimulated by Ed's campaign.

Later in the 1950s, when Ed ran for lieutenant governor, I was very active in that campaign as a member of both CSO and ANMA, along with other people such as Jimmy Delgadillo and Herman Gallegos. I always thought that Ed was very friendly and open. He was a strong and honest liberal. His commitment to fair representation of the Mexican people was unquestioned. He did not make deals with conservatives in the Democratic Party.

I knew Nacho López much better. His father, the Reverend López, had married my parents in El Paso, and so our families knew each other very well. Nacho was a bit older than the rest of us and had been

*For further information about Ignacio López, see Mario T. García, *Mexican Americans: Leadership, Ideology, and Identity, 1930–1960* (New Haven: Yale University Press, 1989), pp. 84–112.

publishing an influential community newspaper, *El Espectador,* in the Inland Empire area—Pomona, Upland, and that area—since the 1930s. He had also been a strong community leader and had spearheaded the formation of the Unity Leagues after the war. Composed predominantly of veterans, these groups had helped elect some of the first Mexican-Americans to local offices in that area. López then aided in the activity of CSO in southern California.

Nacho was educated; he had a college degree. He was well read, a very sharp person, very witty, an excellent writer, a good political strategist, a marvelous speaker, and had a good sense of humor. He was very up front about his feelings. He was successful as a community organizer and later helped us build MAPA, the Mexican American Political Association. Above all, Nacho was very bold about taking on tough issues, especially when it involved confronting racists. He never showed any fear or trepidation.

CSO proved to be a successful movement, especially in its initial years, although it was very different from the National Congress of Spanish-Speaking Peoples of the prewar years. Unlike CSO, which organized a number of chapters, El Congreso never had the chance to expand very much. Moreover, unlike CSO, which received outside funding from Alinsky's Industrial Areas Foundation, El Congreso received very little, if any, money outside of its own fund-raising. And unlike CSO, which had its own professionally paid organizers, El Congreso relied totally on volunteers.

Although both El Congreso and CSO struggled against racism and against injustice, I believe El Congreso had a more thorough commitment to grassroots control and organization. While CSO had a commitment to grassroots democracy, much of the control rested primarily in the hands of the paid organizers such as César and Fred Ross. The real inheritor of El Congreso's more militant and left tradition was not CSO, but ANMA, the Asociación Nacional México-Americana.

CHAPTER NINE

The Active Fifties

While I worked with CSO in the early 1950s, my more serious commitment was to the Asociación Nacional México-Americana, which I saw as being more akin to El Congreso. I was not one of the founders of ANMA when it was organized in 1949, but I was particularly attracted to the group because its major supporters were the independent progressive unions that I had been involved with: the Longshoremen's Union, the Mine, Mill and Smelter Workers, the Furniture Workers, and UCAPAWA.

Its membership consisted of miners and smelter workers, longshoremen, ship scalers, and furniture workers, along with representatives from other trade unions who believed in tackling issues directly and without any opportunism. ANMA's members were *mexicanos* who were very deeply committed to their communities and to achieving full rights and better conditions for the Spanish-speaking, primarily workers.

Organizing ANMA

Although different unions supported ANMA, its chief patron was the Mine, Mill and Smelter Workers (which was usually referred to as Mine-Mill). The idea of forming a progressive Mexican-American organization in the Southwest to defend the civil rights and culture of *mexicanos* came from Mexican-American members of Mine-Mill who served as leaders of their locals in El Paso, Denver, Pueblo, the southern New Mexico mines, Arizona, and California. These *mexicanos* took the idea of such an organization to one of Mine-Mill's national conventions, where it was approved. From there, a founding convention was held in Phoenix in 1949.

Soon various locals of ANMA sprang up, initially paralleling Mine-Mill locals in the Southwest. It was not just a coincidence that for a time ANMA's main office was in Denver, where the union's international office was also located. While I don't believe that Mine-Mill completely dominated ANMA, its support was crucial. Besides financial donations, the union provided release time for some of its Mexican-American members so that they could participate in helping to organize ANMA. I believe that an organization like ANMA would have been created anyway, without Mine-Mill, but it might not have been so strongly oriented toward *mexicano* workers and toward helping to stimulate trade unionism among them.

If Mine-Mill was critical in ANMA's formation, the role of the Communist Party is less clear. In my opinion, the role of the CP was negligible. It shouldn't be forgotten that the 1950s, when ANMA was active, were the years when the CP went underground because of McCarthyite persecution. The party was under tremendous attack by the FBI and by the Immigration Service. I saw little evidence of very strong CP influence either in ANMA or in the Mexican communities in the 1950s. This, of course, was quite different from the 1930s.

I first heard about ANMA in the late forties or early fifties through Lucio Bernabe from San Jose, whom I had met at a CSO meeting. Lucio, who still lives in San Jose, had been a farmworker and later an organizer for the Longshoremen's Union when it attempted to organize farmworkers around Stockton and Sacramento. He then settled in San Jose and organized for the Longshoremen's Union in the canning and dried-fruit industries. He became a union leader among Mexican workers in northern California.

At this CSO meeting where I met Lucio, I gave a speech about housing discrimination and described a case in which developers had refused to sell a house to a Japanese family, a case that had been taken up by CSO. After the meeting, Lucio introduced himself and invited me to his home. He told me about ANMA, what it was trying to do, and what he, as a member of ANMA, was attempting to accomplish in San Jose. At that time, ANMA was supporting labor strikes by Mexican *braceros,* who had been brought to northern California as part of a contract-labor system. This system had been arranged by the U.S. and Mexico during World War II and then extended in the postwar period through Public Law 78. Lucio had formed an ANMA chapter in San Jose, and it was through Lucio that I became involved with ANMA.

After I joined ANMA, I became its chief organizer for northern California. The first ANMA local that I organized involved *mexicano* members of Mine-Mill who were working in the American Smelting and Refining facility in Tormey, in the Bay Area. These workers had taken on the company, gone out on strike, and won some of their battles. They were a militant lot. When strikes broke out against American Smelting and Refining in Mexico and Latin America, the Mexican-American workers expressed their support by engaging in sympathy strikes of their own. The company tried to fire many of these union workers, but with little success.

I went out to see the workers and to meet them. I introduced myself and told them that I was organizing an ANMA chapter in Tormey and that it was workers like themselves that ANMA was looking toward in building an effective civil rights organization. I explained the general principles of ANMA, and several workers stepped forward and joined. They and, in time, others liked the idea of an organization for Mexican-American workers where they could discuss their problems on the job along with problems connected to their housing and the schools their kids attended. We formed an ANMA chapter around the refinery workers at Tormey.

The Tormey workers had friends who worked in the refineries and the shipyards in Richmond. Soon they too wanted to build an ANMA chapter—they had similar problems with their bosses, with the police, with landlords, and so forth. So we formed a chapter in Richmond. We followed this up with another chapter in Oakland. It went just like that.

In San Francisco, we organized still another chapter, with the help of community leaders such as Aurora Santana de Dawson, Elvira Romo, a woman who was a veteran of military action during the Mexican Revolution of 1910, and Abigail Alvarez. We attracted quite a variety of members in San Francisco: people from Mexico, immigrants from Central America, as well as *braceros* who had left the fields, skipped out on their contracts, and moved into the urban barrios as undocumented workers. We built quite a chapter in San Francisco, organizing between three hundred and four hundred families.

We met at the Mexico Soccer Ball Team Center on Mission Street every Sunday. We also met at times in some of the church social halls, and, as we got bigger, we reserved some of the larger union halls. We put together additional chapters in Vallejo, Watsonville, Salinas, Sacramento, and Stockton.

Organizing around families was a key characteristic of ANMA. In Oakland, for example, we had about one hundred fifty families. In San Jose, about four hundred families joined ANMA. Organizing around a family concept was easier because it was difficult for the husbands or wives to leave their families alone, especially on a Sunday, when the general meetings were held. It was simpler for the entire family, including children, to come to our meetings. People couldn't afford to leave their kids at home; they didn't have babysitters. And if the husband came alone, the wife wouldn't like that very much. So we invited both men and women and their children to participate.

The only requirements to join ANMA were to fill out an application, to pay annual dues of about fifteen dollars, and to attend the meetings and participate in ANMA's activities. The usual practice was to have a regular meeting once a month. In between, various committees met, including the executive board.

The general meeting usually was on Sunday and sometimes lasted all afternoon and evening. The meeting started at two o'clock, and we conducted official business until six o'clock. Then we would have a big dinner or barbecue until about eight that evening. After dinner, a band came in, and dancing went on until midnight. Entertainment was always included after the business session. If the general meeting coincided with a fiesta day such as Cinco de Mayo,* the activities would go on all day. We used to have very large attendance at the general meetings; it was a family affair on these Sundays.

The business portions of the meetings were rather formalistic. They were run like trade union meetings. Minutes of the last meeting were read and approved, and officers' reports were given. We'd have old

*The celebration of Cinco de Mayo (May 5) commemorates the Mexican victory over an invading French army at Puebla in 1862.

business and new business, during which we'd discuss any pressing issues. The meetings were conducted in Spanish.

Our membership varied in each of our chapters. Some chapters included many Mexican-Americans who had been born and raised in the U.S. Many of the Mexican-American men were trade unionists who belonged either to Mine-Mill or to some of the other progressive unions such as the ILWU. Many other members, however, were people from Mexico, some with documents but many without documents.

We developed very strong ANMA chapters in northern California. ANMA was also quite active in southern California as well as in other parts of the Southwest. When the second national convention of ANMA was held in El Paso in 1952, we took between fifteen and twenty delegates from northern California. I believe there were between twenty and thirty delegates from southern California.

That was an exciting conference. We drove all the way from the Bay Area to El Paso and back. Outside El Paso, at Lordsburg, New Mexico, we were red-baited and harassed by the local sheriff. I guess he had heard about the conference and identified us as participants. We were refused service in some cafes. The sheriff wanted to know our business in his town. We told him all we wanted to do was get a meal. He directed us to a Mexican cafe, where we ate and then quickly left.

The convention itself was peaceful, although we did encounter much red-baiting by the El Paso newspapers and by the El Paso sheriff, Chris P. Fox, who had been red-baiting Mexicans and progressive labor since the 1930s. During the convention, he made wild statements about how the "reds"—meaning us—wanted to separate New Mexico and West Texas from the rest of the United States and return them to Mexico. The sheriff also accused us "reds" of being violence-prone. In an interview, he further stated: "But we're ready for them; they're not going to get away with anything here." All this was simply propaganda.

We held our convention in the Mine-Mill hall in downtown El Paso. We had delegates from California, New Mexico, Colorado, Arizona, Utah, Texas, Wyoming, Montana, Nevada, Washington, Alabama, and Chicago. All were *mexicanos* with the exception of one or two blacks and Puerto Ricans. Delegates from the Miners Union in Mexico also attended.

The convention passed excellent resolutions on various civil rights and labor positions. Of particular concern was a strike going on in southern New Mexico among Mine-Mill members—what came to be known as the Salt of the Earth strike. In this strike, which was carried out by *mexicanos* and which lasted for more than a year, the wives and children of strikers took up duty on the picket lines after the courts ordered union members to cease picketing.

The strike was immortalized by the classic film *Salt of the Earth*. In fact, Mike Wilson, who was writing the script for the film, approached me in El Paso and gave me a copy of the script to read. He wanted to know if I had any suggestions about the film, including who might play in it. I didn't have any ideas along those lines, but I liked the script very much.*

Mexican Workers and Unionization

As regional director for ANMA in northern California, I worked on a number of issues in which ANMA became involved. First and foremost was to promote and encourage unionization among Mexican workers. We believed that this was basic in protecting the rights and advancing the interests of the large Mexican working class in the United States. We assisted in organizing drives; we helped the unions in meetings with Mexican workers; and we'd go to the plant gates to leaflet and talk to the workers. We made strong alliances with many unions and actively participated in Labor Day parades as well as joining workers on the picket line. In this way, we earned acceptance from the trade union movement, which saw us as a friendly organization.

Through our work with the unions, we achieved some success in unionizing Mexican workers in the Southwest in industries such as meatpacking, mining, smelting, steel, manufacturing, canning, and agriculture. In the Los Angeles area, for example, ANMA participated in

---

*For information on the Salt of the Earth strike and the film, see Herbert Biberman, *Salt of the Earth: The Story of a Film* (Boston: Beacon Press, 1965); and Jack Cargill, "Empire and Opposition: The 'Salt of the Earth' Strike," in *Labor in New Mexico: Union, Strikes, and Social History Since 1881,* ed. Robert Kern (Albuquerque: University of New Mexico Press, 1983), pp. 183–267. The Salt of the Earth strike lasted fifteen months, from October 1950 to January 1952. After a local judge issued an injunction prohibiting the workers from picketing the mines, members of the women's auxiliary of the union, who were not covered by the injunction, took over the picketing. Some of the women were beaten and arrested. The strike eventually ended after the union won minor concessions.

the Furniture Workers local. It was built as one of the first Mexican-led unions in Los Angeles.

In progressive unions where Mexicans were represented, they proved to be the most loyal and dedicated members. In spite of all the red-baiting and government attacks on these unions in the 1950s, the *mexicanos* held their own. The United Electrical Workers lost many of their Anglo members but retained most of the Mexicans. Mine-Mill lost control of many plants outside the Southwest after raids by the United Steel Workers, which had now become conservative. But in the Southwest, Mine-Mill held on to its locals, owing to the loyalty and courage of its Mexican membership. The same occurred with the Longshoremen's Union and the Laborers Union.

In our activities with the Mexican workers and the unions, we paid particular attention to varied forms of labor discrimination against Mexicans. I remember that management in some of the steel plants and shipyards tried to get rid of Mexicans, especially those active in unionization. Within the steel plants, Mexicans were relegated to the least skilled jobs, such as the open-hearth gang, who worked in the hardest, hottest, and most undesirable department in a steel mill. Mexicans were not being promoted to the better and cleaner jobs. If they wanted a job, they had to start in the oven gang, and that's about where they stayed. We raised complaints and filed charges of discrimination against the plants. Some of these cases took years to process through the federal government or through the courts, but eventually a number of them were won.

As ANMA members, we supported the Salt of the Earth strike in southern New Mexico during the early fifties, as I mentioned earlier. This strike captured the attention not only of the progressive labor movement but also of the Mexican community, since most of the workers on strike and their families were Mexican.

The strike was of historical importance because it focused on the whole pattern of job and wage discrimination against Mexican workers in the Southwest—the so-called "Mexican jobs" and "Mexican wages," which restricted the advancement of Mexican workers. The Salt of the Earth strike aimed to eliminate the "southwestern differential" in wages paid to Anglos and Mexicans. Mexicans received lower wages for doing the same work as Anglos—something that many of us had tried to end through the trade union movement. Another issue was that Mexican workers and their families had little choice but to live in inferior company housing.

Because of its importance, the strike was a very inspiring one. We supported it in ANMA by collecting food and money, which we sent to the strikers in Silver City and Santa Rita, New Mexico, which were the centers of the strike against the copper companies. When we went to the ANMA convention in El Paso, we met with many of the strikers.

But it was a very hard struggle. The strikers were constantly harassed by the local police. When the Hollywood people—many of whom were politically progressive, such as the writer Mike Wilson and the producer Herbert Biberman—arrived in New Mexico, the FBI and the Immigration Service red-baited them and applied increased pressure to both the filmmakers and the strikers. The Immigration Service arrested Rosaura Revueltas, the Mexican actress who had been brought in to play the lead female role. Revueltas was from a prominent artistic family in Mexico. Immigration claimed that her visa had expired, and they incarcerated her in El Paso. Fortunately, the film was almost finished, and the filmmakers were able to shoot around her.

Diego Rivera and Frida Kahlo

I became even more involved in the Salt of the Earth strike later in 1951, when I was asked by Mine-Mill to represent the union at an international conference of mineworkers in Mexico City. Mine-Mill needed support for the strike and was asking the unions in Mexico for help. The Mexican Miners Union, in particular, was assisting Mine-Mill by discouraging strikebreakers from leaving Mexico and going to Santa Rita and Silver City.

Maurice Travis, the head of Mine-Mill, urged me to go to Mexico. He felt it was important that a *mexicano* from the U.S. attend the congress and raise some of the issues faced by Mexican workers in this country. I was specifically delegated to request additional support for the strike—and in particular for Rosaura Revueltas, who was still being held in jail.

I went to Mexico City, where I met mineworkers from all over Latin America—from Chile, Peru, Bolivia, Venezuela, and of course from Mexico. There were representatives from Europe as well. The delegates were especially moved when I discussed the strike and the role of the

U.S. Immigration Service in trying not only to break the strike but also to stop the film by imprisoning Revueltas.

The delegates identified with the Salt of the Earth strike because they recognized that the American corporations who were exploiting Mexican-American workers were the same ones who owned the mines in their own countries and against whom they were struggling—corporations such as American Smelting, Phelps Dodge, Kennecott, Anaconda, and others. So the delegates from Latin America showed a lot of interest and solidarity.

Besides the mineworkers themselves, the congress also drew a number of Mexican artists who sympathized with the Salt of the Earth struggle, especially because of the persecution of Rosaura Revueltas. These included Diego Rivera, Frida Kahlo, David Alfaro Siqueiros, José Chávez Morado, Leopoldo Méndez, Mariana Yampolski, José Berdecio, José Revueltas, and Efraín Huerta, all of whom were either prominent writers or artists in the muralist and popular arts movement in Mexico.* Other supportive artists were those involved in the Taller de Artes Gráficas Popular, who did beautiful woodcuts and linoleum cuts similar to the ones the great Mexican artist José Guadalupe Posada had done in the period of the Mexican Revolution.

All of these artists were interested and moved to hear what was happening to the strike and to Rosaura. To protest her arrest, Diego Rivera and the writer José Revueltas, Rosaura's brother, appealed to university students and to the working class in Mexico City to picket the U.S. embassy. They organized a huge picket line of five or six thousand people. The day after the protest, the Immigration Service in El Paso released Revueltas, largely because of the mounting anger in Mexico over her detention.

I got to know these committed artists better when Diego Rivera and Frida Kahlo invited me to stay at their home in Coyoacán for a few days. Rivera was at that time painting the famous mural on the history of the theater at the Insurgentes Theater.

---

*Diego Rivera and David Alfaro Siqueiros were among the most prominent of Mexican artists, with international reputations. Both had been leaders in the muralist movement following the Mexican Revolution. Frida Kahlo, who was married to Rivera, was part of a younger generation of Mexican artists. Although Kahlo died at a relatively young age, she has since achieved similar international acclaim and has also become somewhat of an icon.

Staying at Diego's house was an interesting experience because, among other things, it was being watched by the FBI. These American agents had rented the house across the street and had cameras in the window, photographing anyone who visited Rivera, especially those who looked American. Diego was aware of this, and, when we arrived at his house, he had his driver speed up and quickly drive into his courtyard in order to prevent my being photographed. This process was repeated every day that I spent in Diego's home.

I had a very favorable impression of Rivera and Frida Kahlo. The side of Rivera that I got to know was an individual who was involved with global issues, especially concerning world peace. He was extremely troubled about the U.S. effort to expand and maintain its hegemony over Third World countries such as those in Latin America and in Asia—countries which the U.S. regarded as fiefdoms. We discussed such issues over dinner.

Rivera expressed much interest in the movement by Mexicans within the U.S. for obtaining full civil rights and for equal justice under the law. He had earlier lived in San Francisco, Detroit, Chicago, and New York, where he had painted murals and where he had come to know the United States. He was very pleased to hear that Mexicans and other Spanish-speaking people were getting organized and were willing to resist American racist policies. During my visit, Rivera wrote an appeal to all democratic and humanitarian forces to support the Salt of the Earth strike.

I got to know Frida Kahlo less well. At that time, her health was already fairly broken down, although she was still able to walk. She struck me as being quite influential with Rivera, with her own very strong personality and ideas. But, like Rivera, she was extremely kind and warm. On the walls in her bedroom, she had hung several photographs of Diego as a child. Rivera prized these pictures of himself. Frida thought that in many ways Diego remained very childlike. Everyone who visited their home while I was there loved and cherished both of them.

Frida was particularly concerned at this time with the fact that Rivera was being given the cold shoulder by the Mexican Communist Party. He had been ousted from the party some years earlier and now wanted to rejoin. But the party had made him wait two years and still had not reinstated him. Frida knew that he did not want to continue living outside the party—it meant that much to him.

She herself had never left the CP. She had always kept her ties, despite her differences with many other members. She had engaged in intense polemical battles with party leaders on many issues. Still, she remained a faithful but critical member, unlike Diego, who had been ousted. She raised this issue of Rivera and the CP several times during my visit.

During my visit to Mexico, I also had the opportunity to meet with Siqueiros. Diego had asked me if I knew Siqueiros. Upon learning that I didn't, he arranged a meeting with the other great Mexican muralist. Rivera and Siqueiros were no great friends, but Diego thought that I could get a message of support for the Salt of the Earth strike from Siqueiros. Siqueiros was very cordial to me and introduced me to his wife and daughter. He expressed support for Latino workers in the United States. He showed me some of his drawings and told me where to go in Mexico City to see some of his murals.

When I asked him for a statement of support for the strike, he very graciously went and got a sketch he had done. On it, he wrote out in ink a testimonial to the workers. I thanked him and told him that Rivera had also done a similar thing but had written his message in crayon pastel. I mentioned that I needed to go to a shop and get it sprayed so that it wouldn't run. Siqueiros insisted that he would do it for me and that I could pick up Diego's sketch later. So I left Diego's sketch with Siqueiros, who, unfortunately, never got it back to me. I tried to reach him several times before leaving but with no luck. My guess is that the rivalry between Siqueiros and Rivera was so great that Siqueiros didn't want Rivera's message to get to the strikers. That was regrettable.

Bracero Strikes

ANMA also participated in the efforts of Mexican braceros to do something about the exploitive conditions under which they worked. During the 1950s, braceros continued to be brought in large numbers to the California fields, under the renewed contract-labor system between the U.S. and Mexico. Faced with oppressive work situations and awful living conditions, the braceros at times took matters into their own hands and went on strike.

I recall one such strike in the Almaden vineyards near Hollister. The braceros were preparing to strike to protest the almost uneatable food the growers provided and to protest that they were being cheated out of their promised wages. They called ANMA in San Jose for assistance. We went out there one night and met with them secretly, outside the vineyards. They wanted to go right out on strike immediately.

But we advised them to first form an organization that would make it easier for us to work with them. So they went ahead and formed their own ANMA chapter in Hollister. It was composed entirely of *braceros*. Soon thereafter they called a strike because they couldn't stand their conditions anymore.

We assisted them by helping to organize the workers. They had us put together a dance for them, just outside the labor camp, in a hall called the Club Cervantes, which was owned by some Spaniards. We hired and brought a band that included ANMA member Abigail Alvarez, who was a professional singer. About fifteen hundred *braceros* attended the dance. Not much dancing took place, however, since there were very few women in the camp; almost all *braceros* were single or came to the U.S. without their wives. The dance was actually a subterfuge to bring the workers together to lay plans for a strike. This was a Saturday night, and the workers agreed to call the strike for four A.M. Monday morning.

I returned to San Jose on Sunday but went back to Hollister the following day. By then, the strike had started. The sheriff's police blockaded the roads leading into Hollister to prevent us or other supporters of the *braceros* from reaching the workers. The police stopped us and wanted to know who we were and what our business in Hollister was. They were clearly there to serve the interests of the growers. I and the other ANMA members in the car acted real dumb, and they finally let us through.

Although we got into Hollister, we couldn't reach the vineyards because those roads were completely closed. The *braceros* had halted all operations. They stuck it out, and we made a lot of friends there. You began to see the *braceros* at ANMA meetings in San Jose, in Hayward, and in San Francisco.

The growers attempted to break the strike by requesting more *braceros,* but they had a hard time getting them. They couldn't get U.S. workers either, because they wouldn't pay them a decent wage. U.S. workers didn't want to come and work for a few pennies an hour as the *braceros* had done; they wanted at least the minimum wage.

When the *braceros* were not rehired by the growers, many of them skipped out on their contracts and became undocumented workers in the cities. Still, my opinion was that they had won their strike because they brought the growers to a standstill and forced them to upgrade conditions for other workers later on.

Besides the Hollister strike, ANMA also supported similar *bracero* efforts in Santa Rosa, Napa, Stockton, and Watsonville. We took food, clothing, and shoes to the strikers and found places for them to live temporarily. We organized dances and used the proceeds to support the strike. Above all, we gave them moral support, which they very much appreciated—a sense that they were not alone, that others cared about them.

One result of these *bracero* strikes was that many of the growers found it more difficult to obtain and exploit such workers. The word would spread: "Don't go to that camp." And there would be no sign-ups. Workers also avoided going to some of the camps because of the violence associated with certain strikes. Some camps were burned; kitchens were particular targets because the food was so atrocious. All of this forced some of the growers to improve conditions.

"Operation Wetback"

The 1950s also saw increased pressure on the Mexican communities from the Immigration Service and the Border Patrol. This was especially visible in southern California, but it affected the Bay Area as well. Like a number of Mexican labor and community leaders who were not U.S. citizens but who had been living in the U.S. for long periods, such as Luisa Moreno and Josefina Fierro, some members of the northern leadership of ANMA were also threatened with deportation.

Lucio Bernabe, for example, was charged by the Immigration Service with all kinds of things—illegal entry, being a felon or a convict, and so on. Because ANMA was just forming when Moreno, Fierro, and others I've mentioned were facing possible deportation, the organization couldn't do much to defend them. But by 1952 and 1953, ANMA was better able to mount a defense for Lucio and others in the Bay Area who were being persecuted. We had access to attorneys, and, in the case of Lucio, we were able to prevent his deportation. But his case took many years; not until the 1970s did he finally get his permanent residency.

Since many of the *mexicanos* who were being politically persecuted and threatened with deportation were union leaders, as Lucio was, we in ANMA worked closely with the unions on this issue. We were able to get unions such as the ILWU to come up with funds for the defense attorneys. We also organized fund-raisers to meet legal fees.

Also of some importance was that we developed a very good relationship with the Mexican consulate in San Francisco—and with some of the Central American consulates as well, since some of those facing political deportation were of Central American background. A number of Mexican consuls were *cardenistas* from the 1934 to 1940 era who were very sympathetic to ANMA and to the labor movement. Many liberals and radicals also served in the Guatemalan consulate after the election of Jacobo Arbenz and before his overthrow by the CIA in 1954, and they too assisted in our efforts to prevent these deportations. Some of these consuls even came to our meetings and encouraged people to organize to defend their rights.

Of course, the deportation drives in the 1950s went beyond those Mexicans and Latinos who had been active in labor or radical circles. They affected thousands of people who were working in the U.S. without documented status. These were the so-called "wetbacks," a pejorative term suggesting aliens who were in this country sponging off its riches. Instead—and more to the truth of the matter—these people were what we would later and more accurately refer to as undocumented workers, who were working productively, some of them for many years. Faced with the lack of jobs in Mexico and unable to obtain the proper papers or to be accepted into the *bracero* program, they had crossed the border seeking work.

Rather than freeloading or cheating other Americans, these people were hard workers who contributed significantly to the wealth of the United States, whether in the fields or in urban industries. But, totally unsympathetic to the contributions or the plight of these people, the Immigration Service and the Border Patrol began in 1954 to organize what was called "Operation Wetback," a military-style program to round up and deport undocumented workers.

What was particularly disturbing about Operation Wetback was the initial subterfuge engaged in by the Immigration and Naturalization Service. One year before the implementation of Operation Wetback, the INS had launched a "friendly" public-relations effort in the Spanish-speaking communities in the Bay Area. Immigration officials contacted community organizations such as CSO, ANMA, and LULAC, among others, and tried to present themselves as having a new policy toward undocumented *mexicanos* that involved helping them to achieve legal status. With no quotas on the number of Mexicans who could enter the U.S., the officials claimed that these undocumented Mexicans could begin the process of legalizing their status if they could show that they would not be a public charge—for example, by presenting letters from employers or potential employers.

As a result of these friendly overtures on the part of the INS, thousands of *mexicanos* went and registered with the INS for what was called "extended voluntary departure." They signed papers agreeing to leave the U.S. at one point or another, but in the meantime they were given a *permiso*, a permit, to stay and work in the country. Some organizations, such as CSO, bought this INS policy at face value and helped the undocumented to register with the INS.

But we in ANMA did not do this. We were skeptical that the INS, which had persecuted so many of our people in the past and which had deported many of them, had actually changed its stripes. We took the position that all this was a trick—that the INS was doing this as a way of identifying potential deportees and that once it obtained more funds to hire additional agents, it would launch another round of massive deportations and repatriations of *mexicano* workers, as had occurred in the 1930s.

Unfortunately, this is precisely what happened. Once Operation Wetback got under way in 1954, the INS sent out letters to everyone who had been given a *permiso*, telling them to come in to the INS office. It was just like turning themselves in. They came in and were presented with "baggage letters" informing them that they and their families had to return in thirty days, with their baggage, in order to be deported. This was the beginning of Operation Wetback.

In the Bay Area, the INS didn't conduct as many raids into plants or neighborhoods as they did elsewhere, because they already had all these leads as to whom they could deport. Some, of course, were picked up by raids, given the opportunity to call their relatives to bring their baggage, and immediately deported. All told, well over a million *mexicanos* from throughout the U.S. were deported in 1954.

To protest these injustices and the actions of the INS, we staged demonstrations and rallies in churches, theaters, and in front of the INS office in San Francisco. An additional part of our role in this major tragedy was to inform people—in some cases successfully—that they in fact possessed certain rights, even though they were not U.S. citizens and did not have legal residence status. For example, they could refuse to give the INS information which could be used to deport them. They could not be deported if they didn't give the INS information about what country they were from, when they had entered the U.S., how they had come in, and through which port of entry. It was up to the INS to come up with this evidence in court. In this way, cases were left pending, and the people could be released.

We were able to prevent some from being deported by providing this information about their rights as well as legal assistance, but, unfortunately, we simply could not reach or convince the great majority. For some of those we did help, their cases lingered for many years and eventually were simply dropped or forgotten, as the INS did not prove their case for deportation.

It appeared to be a contradiction that, on the one hand, the INS was deporting so-called "wetbacks" while, on the other hand, thousands of *braceros* were being allowed to enter and work in the U.S. But as we analyzed what was happening, we in ANMA concluded that, in fact, there was no contradiction at all—Operation Wetback in reality was in support of the *bracero* program. What was concerning the INS, in league with the agricultural industry and other employers of *braceros,* was that *braceros* were protesting their poor working and living conditions and that numbers of them were skipping out on their contracts and moving into the cities to find work without documents. Hence, Operation Wetback was really a response to the weakening of the contract-labor system that regularized the pool of cheap labor, especially for agribusiness. It was meant to scare the *braceros* into remaining in their camps and accepting their conditions and, in this way, to preserve the revolving door of reserve surplus labor from Mexico.

But despite the terror sown by the INS and the Border Patrol, Operation Wetback failed in its purposes. It did not stem the flow of undocumented workers—although it limited their numbers for a few months—and it did not prevent *braceros* from leaving their camps. Consequently, a population of tremendous proportions, clandestine and undocumented, was built up. It would be an issue that I would return to later in my life.

ANMA took forthright positions on the conditions faced by the undocumented and the *braceros*. We strongly opposed the *bracero* program on the grounds that the contracts were fraudulent, that the working conditions—including substandard wages—were inhuman, and that it represented a horrid exploitation of human beings. We argued that the only way to make the *bracero* program more acceptable would be to have the contracts enforced not by the growers or the federal government but by the unions in both countries—and, more specifically, by a union of farmworkers. Our position on the undocumented was that they were workers who had to be helped.

Here we differed even with the Communist Party, whose position was closer to that of middle-class Mexican-American organizations such as LULAC. They viewed the "wetbacks" as strikebreakers or as "scroungers," as people taking jobs away from U.S. workers. We differed with this view. We saw the undocumented as workers who were forced to work cheaper because of the unfair and unjust immigration laws that made it impossible for them to stand up and defend themselves. Consequently, they needed organization more than anyone else. Many undocumented workers recognized that and in fact participated in efforts to unionize.

Police Violence

ANMA also protested against the victimization of *mexicanos* in the urban areas. Perhaps the most celebrated case involved some *braceros* who had skipped out on their contracts and moved into San Jose. One night at the Tico Tico, a Mexican restaurant where they were having dinner, they requested that the band play a particular tune. For some reason, the attending waiter got into an argument with the *braceros* over this request. He called the club bouncer over to throw the men out.

In the ensuing scuffle, the guard shot the men. He killed one and wounded two others. The police arrived, but instead of arresting the guard, they arrested the *braceros*. They took them to the police station, without attending to their wounds, and then turned them over to the Immigration Service. The men were taken to the Santa Rita detention camp for "illegal aliens," outside of Salinas.

The *mexicano* community became aroused over the treatment of the *braceros*. Various community people who had witnessed the affair went on the air at the radio stations to denounce what had happened. I heard about it over the radio in Oakland, and I called Lucio Bernabe in San Jose, who said, "Yes, it's true. I've had relatives and friends of the *mexicanos* who were arrested calling me up for help." As representatives of ANMA, Lucio and I went on the air to denounce the police and the owners of the Tico Tico.

The police and the INS denied that they were detaining the men, but we got an anonymous call informing us of their detention at the Santa Rita camp. We drove down to Salinas and walked right into the camp. Sure enough, we found the men, still all splattered with dried blood. They had not yet received medical attention. One had been shot in the leg and one in the side of the stomach. They were being held for deportation.

We immediately lodged a complaint with INS officials and forced them to take the men to a hospital. Unfortunately, they were still deported. But in the *mexicano* community, this case became a cause célèbre because it typified the kind of treatment that Mexican immigrants were receiving not only from authorities but also, regrettably, from those Mexican-Americans who abused them.

International Solidarity

Because we worked with Latino groups in the Bay Area besides *mexicanos* and because ANMA had an internationalist perspective, we participated in a number of efforts to support popular struggles in Latin America. The Guatemalan consul appointed by Arbenz spoke at ANMA meetings and told us how the U.S. was attempting to overthrow his government—not unlike U.S. efforts to do the same in Nicaragua in the 1980s. Delegations of refugees who had fled Franco's repressive regime in Spain also attended our meetings and asked us to support their efforts to obtain amnesty for political prisoners who had been condemned to be shot in Spain. We passed resolutions to support them as well as other resolutions supporting labor struggles in countries such as Chile, Bolivia, and Peru.

We also participated in demonstrations supporting these causes. One demonstration, in support of the Cuban liberation movement headed by Fidel Castro, was organized by Camilo Cienfuegos, one of the later leaders and martyrs of the Cuban Revolution, who was in San

Francisco in the mid-fifties. After the overthrow of the popular Arbenz government in Guatemala by the CIA, we joined in demonstrations denouncing these actions. I spoke at some of these rallies, including those held around September 15 and 16 each year, dates celebrating the independence of several of the Latin American countries.

The fifties, of course, marked the beginning of the Cold War, with the threat of still another major world war and nuclear annihilation. ANMA was against the U.S. intervention in Korea and a possible confrontation with China. We opposed the Cold War and took strong positions against nuclear war between the U.S. and the Soviet Union. We participated in the peace movement by supporting various peace initiatives such as the Stockholm peace initiative, and we gathered signatures for the petition calling for an end to the Cold War.

Women in ANMA

Several ANMA chapters had strong women leaders. In San Jose, for example, Dora Sánchez, who had been born in Colorado, was the heart and soul of ANMA. The INS tried to deport her husband, who was also in ANMA, but we were able to prevent it. In San Francisco, key women leaders were Aurora Santana de Dawson, Elvira Romo, and Abigail Alvarez.

Abigail Alvarez, who was a professional singer, was a fascinating woman. She was a *cantora* from Michoacán. The *cantoras* are part of a rich musical tradition in Michoacán, where it is sometimes customary for an entire family—father, mother, sons, and daughters—to be tremendously proficient in singing and playing string instruments. They perform at church festivals and birthday parties, they serenade, and they compose songs for special occasions. Abigail was from that tradition. Her father had been a supporter of Lázaro Cárdenas and served as the librarian of his town. Abigail grew up as a young *cardenista*.

When she came to San Francisco, she fell in love with Hugh Bryson, who was the secretary of the Marine Cooks and Stewards Union. This was a very militant CIO union. It was always being raided by other unions, but the membership held tight. Bryson was later tried under the Taft-Hartley Act for refusing to sign a non-Communist affidavit. He later signed it, but he was then accused of having lied, because he was charged with being a Communist.

In San Francisco, Abigail got a job at the Sinaloa Club as a *cantora*. She dressed in typical costume and sang songs that she amusingly made up about the members of the audience. She was one of those singers who go to bars and restaurants and can come up with songs off the top of their head. Abigail became a big hit. She was also an actress, having performed in some films and in theater in Mexico. At one point, she was seriously considered for the lead female role in the *Salt of the Earth* film. She was recruited into ANMA by Aurora Santana de Dawson, who was also a singer. In addition to her other activities in ANMA, Abigail contributed immensely through her singing and performances at our meetings.

There was little conflict between men and women in ANMA, as far as I can recall. When we attended the El Paso convention, I was surprised to see how many women were there. Since many of the women in ANMA didn't have wage-paying jobs, they actually did a great deal of the organizing work, especially in planning meetings and rallies. The women would organize and prepare fiestas for several hundred people. They would start making tamales the night before, and by two o'clock on Sunday they would have made enough to feed an army. Selling tamales raised funds for ANMA. But the women did many other things as well, such as leafleting churches. They talked with the priests and often won them over to our issues.

ANMA's official position on women's rights was a very progressive one. It supported equal pay for equal work and declared that women were entitled to all the same rights as men.

Alfredo Montoya

Although we had our own strong leaders in ANMA in the Bay Area, we also relied on the leadership of Alfredo Montoya, who was the chief organizer in the Southwest for ANMA. Montoya was from New Mexico and had graduated from the University of New Mexico before working for Mine-Mill and then with ANMA. He was a very self-sacrificing individual, with an almost priestlike dedication to his work. He never complained. Alfredo received very little in the form of a salary from either ANMA or Mine-Mill, and his wife had to become the chief breadwinner for them and their children.

Alfredo was a good leader. He was not necessarily a very demanding or action-bent person; rather, he was more of an intellectual who thought things out and tried to understand problems instead of trying to change them without fully comprehending all the ramifications. Although he was based in Los Angeles and later in Denver, Alfredo visited us regularly and attended our regional conferences and the meetings of our executive boards.

I don't believe Alfredo was a member of the Communist Party. In fact, in our conversations—and I got to know him quite well—he would at times express puzzlement about contradictions affecting the policy and behavior of CP groups. He especially believed that the CP did not really understand the issues *mexicanos* were facing. He observed that even while the CP fought for the attainment of full rights for Mexicans, some of the party leaders manifested a chauvinism against *mexicanos* and displayed a certain amount of discrimination and even racism when it came to accepting *mexicano* leadership within the party. He was very sensitive about that. If Alfredo was a party member, he must have been a very critical one.

Dissent, Decline, and Evolution

As had been the case with El Congreso and CSO, there did exist some tensions and differences within ANMA, although never to the point of causing a serious split. But, as in the earlier Mexican-American organizations, some ANMA members believed that ANMA was too confrontational and that its focus on Mexican-American issues might be interpreted as being separatist. This faction believed that ANMA should instead be less political and more cultural and social in its orientation. They also believed that a more political program, such as the one ANMA was pursuing, would open up the organization for persecution and would result once again in forced deportations of the leadership and members. I disagreed with this position. I strongly believed that if ANMA didn't raise these critical issues affecting Mexicans in the U.S., no one else would.

ANMA eventually declined because the FBI intimidated its members and destroyed the organization. Moreover, as a result of McCarthyism and the Cold War atmosphere of the 1950s, it became even more difficult for progressive unions to help support ANMA. But the FBI infiltration and harassment certainly took its toll on ANMA throughout the Southwest.

I didn't escape such tactics. Around 1953 or thereabouts, the FBI tried to intimidate me and Blanche. Rather than coming to see me in my office in San Francisco, where I handled my father-in-law's diamond business, the FBI agents instead tried to scare Blanche and me by visiting my home while I was away. They told Blanche, "We're from the Department of Justice, and we'd like to talk to your husband."

Blanche told them that I wouldn't be back until around six that evening and that they could come back around that time. Blanche knew what was going on and refused to be intimidated. When they returned, I was back home.

I let them in and asked them to sit down. After beating around the bush for a while, I finally asked just what they wanted.

"Well," one of them responded, "we know very well that you are or have been a member of the Communist Party, and we want to see if you would cooperate with us to ferret out the Communists in ANMA. We want you to let us know about some of these unions which you know Communists are in." And they provided me with a whole list of unions.

I responded by asking them to give me questions regarding this list. "Well," they shot back, "is Lucio Bernabe a Communist? What about Montoya?"

I simply told them the truth: "I don't know."

"Well, you aren't helping very much!" they cried out in anger.

So I noted for them that the biggest threat to American security in California during the war had been the work of German spies and of right-wing fanatics such as the Sinarquistas. I suggested that they should go after these right-wing fanatics, who represented the real enemy. "If I knew some of those names," I told them, "I would quickly turn them over to you."

They looked at each other in disbelief and replied, "We sure would appreciate it if you would think about what we said. We'll be back."

They called me back a few times later on. I would say, "Look, I've got nothing to say to you. You're the FBI, and you're looking for people that you can do in. I'm sure not going to help you in any way, so don't bother me. If you want to talk to me, call my lawyer." They called two or three more times, but after that they never bothered me again. Once they know that you're wise to them, they generally avoid you.*

*In an FBI document dated August 26, 1953, the FBI reported that Corona had cooperated in an interview during which he had admitted membership in the Communist Party from 1940 to 1943, when he entered the military. The report further noted that Corona had resigned from the CP over disagreements with the

FBI tactics and pressures took their toll in ANMA, and by 1954 many local chapters had folded. But we in the Bay Area survived and even grew stronger. I think the reason why we didn't fold was that we worked in close relationship to the very strong and still very viable progressive union movement. By contrast, the union movement was not as strong in southern California, at least not during the mid-fifties.

ANMA in the Bay Area never collapsed as it did elsewhere. Instead, it evolved into a much broader popular organization. Devoid of a national ANMA organization after 1954, we worked through CSO, for example, or through some of the old Mexican mutual-benefit societies that still functioned. While we recognized that we had been able to reach a good number of *mexicanos* in the labor movement, we also realized that we had not had as much success with *mexicanos* in the churches and in other sectors. The way that we could reach them would be through communitywide civic activities such as Cinco de Mayo festivities or the 16th of September celebrations* or through working with athletic clubs such as the soccer teams.

So, beginning in 1957, we voluntarily abandoned ANMA and in Oakland formed the Organización Mexicana, which was composed of ex-ANMA members, CSO, church groups, soccer clubs, and various other groupings. All of us got together to form one umbrella organization so that we could speak with one voice on matters that affected us—bad schools, the need for jobs, scholarships, defense of our language, defense of our heritage.

For example, we did not want to have to celebrate the 16th of September in some dingy little hall in the barrio—we wanted to celebrate it in the main civic arenas. After we formed the Organización Mexicana, we rented the Shrine Auditorium in San Francisco for the next *dieciséis de septiembre*. Across the bay, we reserved the Oakland Arena Auditorium, which seated twelve thousand. Some people laughed and said, "These guys are gonna fall flat on their faces."

But we didn't. We had tremendous success. These large ceremonies increased the social awareness of the community. *Mexicanos* and Lati-

---

party. The report added that a Max Silver, in testimony before HUAC on January 24, 1952, had identified Corona as having been a CP member before World War II. Corona denies that he cooperated with the FBI and challenges the truthfulness of this report concerning membership in the CP. See FBI document SF 100–32214 in Corona's FBI file 100–201342.

*September 16 marks Mexico's Independence Day.

nos began to realize that they were a sizeable group—that they were somebody. We invited the governor to attend these fiestas. Once, Governor Goodwin Knight came, and later Governor Pat Brown. The mayors also attended. We used these fiestas to raise funds and to register voters.

We felt that it had served a purpose to move from a narrower dimension of work in ANMA, which had been focused more on work related to trade unions, to one that involved larger sectors of the community. We were able to recruit Latino students from UC Berkeley as well as new activists.

But times were also changing. As we perceived the need to become more directly involved in electoral politics as well as in national politics by 1960, I and others looked forward to still another organizational vehicle. We had survived the fifties, despite the worst aspects of McCarthyism and the Cold War. We now moved to position ourselves as we entered what would be a turbulent decade: the 1960s.

Noe Corona, Bert Corona's father. Ciudad Juárez, 1916.

Margarita Escápite
Salayandía, Bert Corona's
mother. Ciudad Juárez, 1912.

Ynes Salayandía de Escápite,
Bert Corona's grandmother.
Chihuahua, 1907.

Bert Corona at the age of one year. El Paso, Texas, 1919.

Left to right: Orlando Corona, Aurora Corona, Horacio Corona, and Humberto (Bert) Corona. El Paso, Texas, 1924.

Bert Corona, *left;* and his cousin Kiko Fonseca. Los Angeles, 1937.

Members of the Mexican American Movement (MAM). *Left to right:* Bert Corona, David Morales, Charlie Peña, *unidentified,* and Chief Carrasco. Los Angeles, 1939.

Members of the International Longshoremen's and Warehousemen's Union, Local 26. Bert Corona, *second from the left, back row;* Lloyd Seeliger, *fourth from the left, back row.* Los Angeles, 1940.

Bert Corona as a member of the Longshoremen's Local 26 basketball team. Los Angeles, 1939.

Luisa Moreno,
circa 1940.

Josefina Fierro,
circa 1940.

Blanche Taff Corona and Bert Corona, wedding picture. Los Angeles, 1941.

Bert Corona. Los
Angeles, 1942.

Bert Corona and
his mother. Los
Angeles, 1943.

Bert Corona with Margo and David. Orinda, California, 1950.

Blanche Corona with David, Frank, and Margo.
Orinda, California, 1953.

Left to right: José Gordillo, Frida Kahlo, Bert Corona, and Diego Rivera. Mexico City, 1951. The message displayed in Spanish is from Diego Rivera and Frida Kahlo. Its text may be translated as follows: Greetings to my Mexican brothers in the U.S. who are fighting for the preservation of our national consciousness, our rights to complete equality with Anglo workers, to equal pay for our work, and for the preservation of our pride in being Mexican and friends of peace. And a special greeting to the heroic and militant wives of the miners of Bayard and to our brothers the Negro workers, and others in the Mexican community who are fighting for freedom and peace. Warm greetings. Diego Rivera and Frida Kahlo.

Officers of the Organización Mexicana. *Left to right:* Miguel Camberos, J. P. Fernández, and Bert Corona. San Francisco, 1957.

MAPA rally at San Francisco State College with Senator Robert F. Kennedy, *middle of photo; from Kennedy's left to the right of the photo:* Eduardo Quevedo, Bert Corona, Herman Gallegos, and Lino López. San Francisco, December 1967.

Bert Corona and César Chávez. 1968.

Soledad "Chole" Alatorre, Hermandad Mexicana Nacional/ CASA. Los Angeles, early 1970s.

Bert Corona, Cuauhtémoc Cárdenas, and Blanche Corona at an Americans for Democratic Action banquet. Santa Monica, California, May 1990. The son of Lázaro Cárdenas, Mexico's most progressive president since the Mexican Revolution, Cuauhtémoc Cárdenas is one of the leaders of the opposition to the PRI (Partido Revolucionario Institucional), Mexico's dominant political party which has governed Mexico since the late 1920s.

Bert Corona, Josefina Fierro, and Blanche Corona. Los Angeles, 1991.

Left to right: Bert Corona, Chole Alatorre, Josefina Fierro, and Mario T. García. Los Angeles, 1991.

Bert Corona and Mario T. García conducting an interview in Corona's home. Los Angeles, July 1989.

Bert Corona speaking at a testimonial dinner in honor of retiring Representative Edward Roybal. Los Angeles, December 16, 1992.

CHAPTER TEN

New Frontiers

I lived in the San Francisco Bay Area for twenty-two years, from 1947 to 1969. We lived in Orinda for about eleven years, until we moved to Oakland in the early 1960s.

These were difficult times for me financially. I folded up the diamond business around 1961 or 1962. I wasn't making any money, and I couldn't make a living with the business because of my political commitments—especially by the early 1960s, with the formation of MAPA, the Mexican American Political Association. Despite my business failure, my father-in-law never complained. He understood that my first interest was to build an organization among the Mexican people, and he never ceased to support me.

After I closed my business, I didn't work for about a year and a half. Fortunately, Blanche had already started to work four years before my business went under. She worked as a secretary, first in private law firms and then later for the Alameda County Civil Service Commission. During most of the 1960s, she was the primary breadwinner.

Beginning in about 1964, I worked as a political consultant, as a labor organizer, as a campaign director. I had income for part of the year, but not for all of the year. I drew on unemployment. I went on like that until 1969, when I went to work full time as an organizer for the National Maritime Union. The sixties were very hard years for us economically.

My Family

Raising a family while being heavily involved in community organizing and trying to sustain a business was, of course, very difficult. Still, both Blanche and I worked hard to provide a strong family environment for our three children. There's no question, however, that Blanche carried the load in this.

I worked at trying to convey a bilingual and bicultural Mexican-American tradition to my children, but it was not easy. My main regret is that I was on the road so much, both making a living and organizing first ANMA and then MAPA, that I was not able to dedicate as much time to my children as I would have liked. I did expose them to their Mexican legacy, and all three grew up to be very comfortable with being Mexican and appreciating their Mexican heritage. My oldest child, Margo, in particular, has been interested in her Mexican roots. At a very tender age, seven or eight, she belonged to a Mexican folkloric dance group.

We always took our children to Mexican fiestas, and my mother and my grandmother used to take care of them for a week or so during summer vacation times. At their grandmother's and great-grandmother's, they grew to appreciate Mexican food and other Mexican traditions. As they grew older, they came to know some of the problems faced by Mexican people here in California and elsewhere, since it was a constant topic at home. There was always a stream of Mexican people coming through our house, and so they got to know many of my political colleagues: workers, members of ANMA, artists, writers, and musicians.

My children felt very comfortable with my friends. I would often take my kids to some of our political and community meetings. We also traveled to Mexico quite a lot. Consequently, I don't think they ever faced the problem of cultural clash, at least regarding their Mexican backgrounds. They always felt at home with the idea that they were bicultural. In fact, if anything, they suffered from not knowing enough about their Russian-Polish Jewish background. They felt more at home with Mexican culture because it's more alive here in California. They could be exposed to it more readily here.

My children almost always attended public schools. The only exception was when we moved back to Los Angeles in 1969. We put our youngest son, Frank, into Salesian Boys School, a Catholic high school in East Los Angeles. We weren't Catholics, but Frank, who had at first started at Roosevelt High School, had some coordinative problems in speech and thinking as a result of some brain damage suffered as a child. He was beginning to outgrow these problems, but they still necessitated a special program. No such program existed at Roosevelt, so we enrolled him at Salesian, where a program was available. Margo and David went only to public schools.

The sixties also saw the death of both my grandmother and my mother. My grandmother died in 1961 and my mother in 1968, the same year Bobby Kennedy was assassinated. Both women, as I've described, were tremendous influences in my life, especially since I had barely known my father.

The Origins of MAPA

During the early 1960s, my principal involvement was with the Mexican American Political Association. MAPA was formed as a reaction to the unwillingness of the Democratic Party to support in any real sense the needs and interests of Mexicans and other Spanish-speaking people in California and the Southwest.

For example, when Edward Roybal ran for lieutenant governor of California in 1954, he received only token support from the Democratic Party. Even though Ed had been overwhelmingly nominated at the Democratic convention, the party provided very little funding for the campaign. What money he obtained he had to go out and personally solicit from friends in the Spanish-speaking community.

The party instead put its money and effort into trying to unseat Goodwin Knight, the Republican incumbent governor, although this effort proved unsuccessful. In the election, we even discovered that some Anglo Democrats who voted for a Democratic gubernatorial candidate refused to do the same for Roybal for lieutenant governor. Roybal's name was on the ticket, but the party made no real effort to get out the vote.

Despite these obstacles, the Spanish-speaking community fully supported Roybal, and he wound up getting more votes than the Democratic candidate for governor, Richard Graves. The large vote for Roybal was the result of his own organizing efforts. Earlier, when Ed had worked for the state health department on an anti-tuberculosis campaign, he had visited dozens of little and medium-sized towns all over California, working with the Spanish-speaking, with black communities, and with poor whites—all of whom, as poor people, were most susceptible to tuberculosis. He made many friends in this way. Thus when he ran for statewide office, he in a sense already had a built-in organization, composed of poor people of all races.*

Four years later, in 1958, we ran into the same problem with the Democratic Party when Henry (Hank) López ran for state treasurer. Despite opposition from the party war-horses such as Pat Brown and Jess Unruh,† who felt that a Mexican was not electable statewide, Hank had a lot of grassroots support and easily won the nomination at the state convention. But, like Roybal, López received almost no support and very little money for the campaign from the Democratic bigwigs.

Hank's campaign, like Ed's, had to be based on what he personally could raise and what the Mexican community could raise. It was sad. He went up and down the state, with no money, in a broken-down old car. He couldn't afford public-relations agents, billboards, speaking halls, literature—not to mention expensive radio and TV spots. To his credit and that of his supporters, Hank ran a very close, though unsuccessful, race.

The campaigns of Roybal and López affected the Mexican-American political community in two ways. On the one hand, they embittered many of us toward the Democratic Party and discouraged us from believing that the party would ever seriously support Mexican-American candidates for statewide offices or that it would really champion the struggles and issues of the Spanish-speaking. On the other hand, both campaigns generated large turnouts of Mexican-American voters, which encouraged us to believe that a Mexican-American political organization could effectively deliver a sizeable vote. And not just the Mexican vote, but a broad spectrum of poor and working people from different races, if the campaign addressed their day-to-day needs.

---

*Subsequently, in 1962, Edward Roybal was elected to the U.S. Congress from the Los Angeles area and served until his retirement in 1992.

†Edmund G. "Pat" Brown was governor of California from 1958 to 1966. Jess Unruh was chair of the California Democratic Party during the 1960s and early 1970s. He later was elected and served several terms as state treasurer of California.

Following the López campaign, we felt that the only answer was to form our own Mexican-American political organization in order to mobilize broad sections of the Mexican community to register to vote, to participate in political campaigns, and to encourage those Mexicans who were not citizens to become citizens in order to vote. We felt that the time had come to organize an independent electoral organization that could take up questions pertinent to the Mexican communities without having to compromise itself with other groups inside the Democratic Party. It would be an organization based on the needs of the community and not on the electoral needs of the Democratic Party. This was a significant step forward in the political thinking of the Spanish-speaking in California and the Southwest.

We conceptualized and discussed such a political organization in 1958. At first, we hoped to create not just a California group but a southwestern one. We met with groups in other states. In Texas, we met with PASSO, the Political Association of Spanish-Speaking Organizations, and with key figures such as Commissioner Albert Peña of San Antonio and Henry B. González, who then represented San Antonio in the state legislature. We met with state politicians in New Mexico and with Senator Dennis Chávez, who since the 1930s had represented New Mexico in the U.S. Senate. We also had contacts in Arizona, Colorado, Illinois, Iowa, and Indiana.

Representatives from these different states met in 1958 to try to form an organization. But we failed to do so, largely—and foolishly—because we couldn't agree on a name for the group. The Texans wanted "Latin American," the New Mexicans wanted "Spanish-speaking," the Arizonans wanted "Hispanic" or "Latin American," the Coloradans wanted "Hispanic," and we in California wanted "Mexican." All this, of course, smacked of provincialism.

While everyone parted friends from that 1958 meeting, it had still proven to be a failure. Those of us in California who had initiated the whole thing now resolved to go ahead and built separately in California and then, once established, expand to other states.

The Fresno Convention

Those of us who had been involved in both the Roybal and López campaigns, including some who had been active in groups such as

ANMA and CSO, organized MAPA in April of 1960 at Fresno. Around one hundred fifty-five delegates assembled at the founding convention. We had earlier built for the meeting by contacting key people in Los Angeles, San Jose, San Diego, Oakland, San Francisco, Fresno, Stockton, and elsewhere. People such as Frank Paz, Julio Castelan, Herman Gallegos, Fred Castro, Ed Quevedo, Nacho López, and Lucio Bernabe represented links with earlier groups such as the National Congress of Spanish-Speaking Peoples and ANMA. Ed Roybal and others from CSO furthered that continuity from the 1950s. We represented, on the whole, a GI generation from World War II and Korea, at least for the men.

Many women also attended the Fresno convention. Many of them had been active in Democratic Party politics, but they felt that the party had not responded to the needs of *mexicanas* or to the needs of the community. Some of these women went on to become key MAPA organizers, such as Mary Soto, who is still active in East Los Angeles, and Hortencia Solis from Bakersfield.

The majority of the men and women at the convention were either middle-class professionals working for state or local government or professionals in the private sector, such as lawyers and engineers. Others were trade unionists. Most delegates to the convention attended as individuals who were interested in building a political organization rather than as representatives of particular groups. Most of the delegates were in their thirties.

As we had in 1958, we unfortunately faced the problem of terminology and of what to call ourselves. Some, who turned out to be in the minority, called for using the term "Latin American," "Hispanic," or "Spanish-speaking." My own feeling, which proved to be that of the majority, was to be uncomfortable with such terms. I had never, for example, accepted the term "Latin American." I always felt that it was an attempt to obscure our true identity as *Mexicans*. I didn't object to "Spanish-speaking"—after all, El Congreso in the 1930s had used that term—but I felt that it was more appropriate for a national organization composed not just of Mexicans but also of other Spanish-speaking groups, such as Puerto Ricans and Cubans.

Because this new group was going to be initially and predominantly an organization by and for Mexicans, I felt that the best term was "Mexican-American." The name "Mexican" *had* to be included. It was important for the Mexican community to recognize itself. If we didn't recognize ourselves and instead shied away from using our name in order to be more acceptable to Anglos, we would be giving in to all of the discrimination and belittling that had characterized our political experience.

Consequently, I was very strong for using the term "Mexican-American"—with an emphasis on *"Mexican"*—because I really felt that we needed to identify ourselves very clearly and not make any bones about it. Moreover, those of us who had had previous political experience in organizing Mexicans understood that Mexicans would in fact participate politically if they identified with our name. After some discussion, we adopted the Mexican American Political Association as our name.

Reflecting the continued bilingual and bicultural character of *mexicanos* in the United States, the delegates at the Fresno convention spoke in both English and Spanish. In fact, some of the dyed-in-the-wool *mexicano* cultural nationalists absolutely refused to speak in English. Julio Castelan, for example, who was an engineer from Daly City, could speak English, but he didn't do so at the convention because he always wanted to remind us that "we were *mexicanos* and that this was our country before the Anglos came in 1848." He spoke in Spanish, and it was effective. The nationalists did have some effect.

We visualized MAPA then as an organization whose main membership and constituents were to be Mexican-Americans. This was not because we wanted to exclude; rather, we simply recognized that by concentrating on California and eventually on other parts of the Southwest, our main concerns would be with Mexicans and not with other Spanish-speaking groups. Some argued that other Latino groups, such as those from Guatemala, Cuba, and Puerto Rico, were just as persecuted and discriminated against as Mexicans were. We sympathized with that position, but a stronger argument was that we had to organize ourselves. If we couldn't do that, how could we offer strength and support to other groups? At the same time, while we agreed on the term "Mexican-American" and agreed that our focus should be on Mexicans, we certainly weren't going to turn down anyone who wanted to work for the same goals, whether they were other Spanish-speaking persons, blacks, or Anglos.

Indeed, some of us fought for a plank that would have committed

MAPA to establishing coalitions with other nonwhite minorities such as African-Americans, Asian-Americans, and Native Americans. This generated much discussion. Although some delegates were willing to use the term "Mexican," they were not prepared to come out front and state that we considered ourselves nonwhite. This question of whether Mexicans are whites or people of color has been a thorny issue for years, both in Mexico and in this country. Because it proved to be rather controversial, we withdrew the resolution, especially since the organization was just getting started. Two years later, however, the coalition position was adopted, and we went on through the sixties to engage in many joint struggles with other racial minorities, particularly blacks.

Perhaps the key debate at the Fresno convention was over the actual nature of MAPA. What kind of organization was it supposed to be? We all agreed that it would be a vehicle to involve Mexican-Americans in electoral politics, but the issue was whether MAPA would represent a specific interest group working within the Democratic Party or whether it would be a completely independent group without ties to the party. Another issue regarding the nature of MAPA was whether we would involve ourselves only in electoral politics or whether we would engage in broader civil rights struggles similar to those engaged in by earlier groups such as El Congreso, ANMA, and CSO.

Those who argued that MAPA should be an interest group within the Democratic Party were mostly those Mexican-Americans who were in public office as a result of appointments by the party. They worked for Governor Pat Brown and other Democratic elected officials and wanted to protect their jobs and obtain support for their Anglo patrons. These types were very cautious and were unwilling to support a fully independent political organization.

My own position, and that of many others, was that we had been rejected by the Democratic Party in previous electoral efforts. We needed therefore to build an independent electoral machine, one that could engage in progressive politics without having to compromise with the Democrats—or with the Republicans, for that matter. I also believed that MAPA should not remain strictly an electoral organization but that it should involve itself in the various issues affecting the Mexican communities.

In the end, we all compromised in order to ensure that we came out of Fresno with an organization. Those who were Democratic appointees accepted an independent political association. In practice, they worked after Fresno to tie particular chapters to the Democratic Party. This was an issue that MAPA couldn't escape.

For our part, those of us who supported an independent position recognized that we had to deal with the Democrats, who, despite their arrogant treatment of Mexican-Americans, still constituted a more liberal party. The Republican Party was not a real alternative, and no group like the Progressive Party of the late 1940s existed. Consequently, although we declared our independence, we recognized that we would have to work within the Democratic Party for the time being. There was no sentiment for a third-party position. We also compromised in forming MAPA essentially as an electoral political organization and not a civil rights organization.

I would like to have seen a more progressive and independent position come out of the Fresno convention, but I also recognized that it was more important to further the concept of unifying Mexican-Americans and to establish a vehicle for political involvement. These aims were more important than engaging in a free-for-all and possibly winding up with no agreement because different people were stubborn about what they wanted. The crucial thing was to build an organization as we entered the 1960s.

As far as I and other more progressive delegates were concerned, the direction of MAPA would be decided by those of us who had experience organizing in the communities. We believed that we would be able to steer MAPA in progressive directions, even beyond electoral politics—for example, taking a position on the threat of nuclear war or participating along with blacks in the growing civil rights struggles.

Because of its initial focus on electoral politics and on a broad political consensus, MAPA was not, at least in the beginning, as progressive or as militant as El Congreso or ANMA. Unlike El Congreso and ANMA, which were more grassroots organizations based on the labor movement, MAPA came out of the struggles inside the Democratic Party. The purpose behind MAPA was not to build a party with an economic ideology but rather to build a party or association that would encourage the fullest participation of Mexicans in political life. Mexican-Americans had not had that opportunity in the Democratic Party, but MAPA represented an effort to rectify that condition. MAPA was seen primarily as an electoral vehicle and as a protest movement against the policies of the Democratic Party.

I was comfortable enough with this situation at first because I did believe that Mexican-Americans needed to move more systematically into the political arena. We had been doing that since World War II. ANMA, for example, sponsored or supported particular electoral campaigns, as had CSO. But these had been more localized efforts. By the early 1960s, we felt that it was important for Mexican-Americans to play a larger role—at first in state politics, especially in California, but in time also at the national level. As Mexican-Americans increased in number, this had to be translated into political power. MAPA was seen as the beginning of this new political effort.

The MAPA convention at Fresno was a success because it launched a new attempt to politically organize the *mexicano* communities. In this sense, it built on other, previous efforts. Yet some discontent lingered over the nature and composition of the association. Perhaps the harshest critic was Nacho López, the publisher of *El Espectador* in Pomona. A longtime activist and an uncompromising one, Nacho considered MAPA to be a "freak"—or at least that's how he categorized it in some stinging editorials in his newspaper.

By "freak," he meant that while MAPA aspired to play an independent political role in California politics, in fact it contained too many who were beholden to Anglo Democratic elected officials. So how could these Mexican-Americans be independent? They were freaks! Here was a group, Nacho complained, which was going to represent the Mexican people and yet was not independent enough to do so; it was really representing Anglo politicians.

I sympathized with Nacho's criticisms but felt that this contradiction could be dealt with in time. My feeling was that his objection could be demolished by us—"us" meaning the more progressive and independent wing of MAPA—going out and organizing the communities. MAPA would be controlled and directed by those who knew how to organize the people.

I knew very well the people in whom Nacho had little confidence. It wasn't that they weren't well-meaning, but, as Nacho noted, often times their efforts to do something for *mexicanos* were contradicted or restrained by their ties and loyalties to the Anglo politicians who gave them jobs and patronage. Mainly Democrats, almost all of these people were appointed officials, including judges who had never been elected. They might speak for the Mexican-American communities, but they had no real following. I understood that they might pose an initial

problem in making MAPA a more progressive group and a more independent one, but I viewed this as a challenge.

Whoever could organize the people would call the shots in MAPA.
In fact, these Democratic appointees didn't know much about organizing. They didn't have any experience; most were young attorneys.
Their main goal was not to organize but to get a job. Their idea of
organizing was to throw a banquet and sell a lot of tickets.

In contrast, some of us had been in the labor movement, where we
had picked up lifelong organizing tactics. We'd gone out and organized
workers. I and others had further experience in the National Congress
of Spanish-Speaking Peoples and in ANMA. Ed Quevedo, who had
been in El Congreso and who would play a key role in MAPA, understood this; he knew we could organize. Others such as Lucio Bernabe
and Herman Gallegos had done a hell of a job organizing CSO in many
parts of the state.

People like this, who were the progressives in MAPA, could go out
and call a meeting in a church, raise the issues that were hot at the time,
and come out with an organization. That's what it would take to build
MAPA. I believed that Nacho's criticism had some validity, but I also
believed that the "freaks" didn't stand much of a chance of dominating
MAPA.

At the Fresno convention, an executive committee was formed to
direct MAPA until the next convention. Ed Roybal was named chairman of the committee. The committee, despite Roybal's efforts, never
functioned very well. The members of the committee, with the exception of Roybal, were not inclined to do the kind of grassroots organizing needed to build an effective organization. If there's no will, there's
not going to be any tenacity or persistence to make the sacrifices that
are necessary. Fortunately, others stepped in and organized chapters.

Defining MAPA

I met with such a group in northern California. It was a heterogeneous
political gathering, but everyone was committed to organizing MAPA.
We first convened people who had participated in past electoral campaigns as well as those who were involved in issues such as fair housing,
employment, police brutality, and immigration. In 1961 I was elected
MAPA organizer in the Bay Area, and so I had a lot to say about the

kinds of people we should be bringing in as we organized the chapter. Since I was of the opinion that MAPA should more closely resemble what El Congreso and ANMA had represented, I favored a diverse membership.

Some of the people we reached out to were working in government—for example, in civil service jobs. Others were professionals, and we welcomed them because we needed their kind of talent and preparation. But many others were just workers or housewives who had taken an interest in our people receiving a fair shake and who wanted to work on civil rights, education, and employment.

We were always looking for people who were willing to get involved and who had a high moral sense of justice. We wanted people who were outraged at the antics of the police in their local areas and at the negligence of school authorities toward the education of *mexicano* children. Of course, much racism was still manifested in the 1960s. So my role and that of others was to organize, as we had with ANMA, a mass membership combining electoral politics with civil rights issues. Above all, we sought to build an organization that would lead to grassroots empowerment so that the people themselves could correct the wrongs they experienced.

Working in this direction, over the next couple of years, we organized chapters throughout northern California: in San Francisco, Oakland, Berkeley, Richmond, Vallejo, Hayward, Union City, Pittsburg, San Jose, Santa Rosa, Napa, Sacramento, Stockton, Salinas, Roseville, Watsonville, and Castroville. Other chapters were formed in southern California: several chapters in Los Angeles as well as single chapters in San Pedro, San Fernando, and San Diego, although I didn't play a role there. We also built chapters in more remote areas such as Modesto, Madera, Barstow, Coachella, El Centro, Brawley, Escondido, National City, Oceanside, and Santa Barbara—places where you wouldn't expect to find a lot of interest, but it was there.

In these chapters, especially in northern California, we pursued a two-pronged but related strategy. Although MAPA was ostensibly a political and an electoral organization, many of us understood that unless MAPA involved itself in key community issues, it would not be able to mobilize politically at election time. Community issues and electoral politics were two sides of the same coin. MAPA could not afford to become engaged only around election time. While elections came around every two years or so, community issues went on all year round. So we built on community concerns such as the schools, police brutality, integration, affirmative action, job-related problems, unionization. Those of us who saw MAPA as an association with a broader civil rights agenda were the ones who set the tone for many of the chapters.

By the 1962 MAPA convention, almost half of the delegates and half of the state officers who were elected represented those members who were committed to working on issues all year long and not just at election time. By 1964, those who had joined MAPA to engage strictly in electoral politics had fallen by the wayside. These types were simply not willing to invest time and energy on civil rights issues.

These were the people who thought MAPA would be just a clean-cut political club, with secretaries and press conferences, and that would be it. They couldn't deal with grassroots participation. They couldn't master the day-to-day task of collecting dues and bringing in new members and explaining what MAPA was all about. Once they knew that it required time and sacrifice and making enemies locally where they lived, they weren't interested anymore. By the 1966 convention, the vast majority of the members and officers were grassroots activists who were committed both to civil rights struggles and to obtaining a greater political voice.

During the first half of the sixties, as MAPA developed, we became involved in a number of community issues. In northern California, we took on the military establishment regarding jobs for Mexican-Americans. We took on the question of poor schooling in the Oakland public schools. In San Francisco, we got involved in obtaining better housing in the predominantly Latino Mission District as well as opposing police brutality in that area.

We took on a lot of job-related or discrimination cases among the auto repair firms and the auto dealers, who paid such low wages and refused to unionize. We took up cases with city councils, especially concerning police brutality against Mexicans in smaller towns such as Mojave, Barstow, Calexico, and National City. We were able to get early releases for some prisoners in cases in which young Chicanos had not been properly defended and had to languish in jail for too long a period. By our involvement, we were able to get them released to their families.

All this led people to want to become part of MAPA. They saw it perform effectively. The word began to spread that if you wanted action, you should join MAPA. That's how we got members. We had no problem getting members. The problem was teaching people how to organize and run the chapters.

While building on community issues, we didn't neglect electoral politics. We sponsored voter registration drives throughout the state. We encouraged noncitizens to acquire citizenship so that they could vote. It was very hard in those days to convince large numbers of Mexican nationals to become U.S. citizens. Historical, cultural, and personal factors all played a role in Mexican nationals refusing to give up their Mexican citizenship. But we succeeded in getting some to become U.S. citizens.

We provided training on how to build permanent precinct organizations. Where we had MAPA chapters, we supported particular candidates, both Mexican-Americans and sympathetic blacks and Anglos at both the local and the state levels and for a variety of offices, including school boards. Some of the candidates we endorsed were MAPA members. The 1960s saw the greatest increase of Mexican-Americans running for offices in California. In many of the small towns, such as Pico Rivera, La Puente, San Gabriel, and Montebello in southern California, we saw Mexican-Americans running for office and getting elected.

Floating Seminars

In organizing MAPA chapters, we used what we called "floating seminars." These were groups of three to four MAPA members who visited the smaller towns where we organized chapters. A lot of the *mexicanos* in these towns were very new to politics, but they were very eager to know all they could, especially about what it takes to run a campaign.

These seminars were conducted by old-timers who had participated in the political campaigns of the 1950s, such as the Roybal and López campaigns. They knew all the mechanics, and they knew a lot about strategy and tactics. To conduct a floating seminar, these political veterans would go to one of these towns, organize a meeting, and answer questions about electoral tactics. This was particularly important where Mexican-American candidates were waging campaigns.

These floating seminars came in handy and in some cases assisted in the election of a Mexican-American to a city council post or a school board. The fact that we achieved some electoral success in the early 1960s, especially at the local levels, helped to promote the floating seminars elsewhere. Once you could show that you could elect *mexicanos*, that was half the battle in those days, because we had not had that success before. Until then, we had not proven that we could elect Mexican-Americans, even in districts where the majority of the population was Mexican. So this was a very important period, from 1960 to 1965. I think that it was carried off with great success, and it established once and for all that *mexicanos* were electable.

By the mid-1960s, when we began organizing MAPA in other states, I had participated in a number of floating seminars both in California and outside the state. I particularly remember one seminar that we conducted in a place called Pasco in Washington state, in the Yakima Valley. The *mexicanos* there were farmworkers in this predominantly agricultural area. We were asked to come in and conduct a seminar in the hope of encouraging *mexicanos* to participate in local elections and to run for office.

The seminar was scheduled for Sunday afternoon. The previous night, there had been a big dance and rally. I was slated to be the keynote speaker at the seminar. What was interesting was that the Anglos in the town, including the local press and police, became quite alarmed and suspicious about Mexicans holding such a meeting. They were not used to this. They had always considered these Mexicans to be politically passive.

So besides the *mexicanos*, a number of Anglos, including the mayor, also came to the seminar. In fact, the front row was full of Anglo reporters, Anglo city council members, and Anglo political honchos who were waiting to see what I was going to say. I guess they expected terrorism or sedition or something like this.

They were very surprised when I spoke about the nuts and bolts of participating in electoral politics. I took the position that what *mexicanos* were doing was within the great American tradition of democratic elections and participatory democracy. I noted that the Mexicans in that area had many complaints and that we were going to use our voting power to remedy these conditions. Afterward, the mayor came up and congratulated me. I guess he and the other Anglos were relieved that we were not promoting some kind of race war. We formed a chapter of MAPA in Pasco, and it operated until the 1970s. Many of those *mexicanos* are still active there on a number of issues, especially around farmworkers' rights.

As we grew in strength and numbers, Anglo and black politicians paid attention to us and solicited our endorsement. These included young and ambitious Democratic politicians such as Willie Brown and Don Edwards.* Republicans also got very interested in MAPA and attended our conventions. Both parties realized that it would serve their purposes to have MAPA's support listed in their campaign literature, particularly in their appeal to Mexican-American voters.

While we participated in a number of campaigns locally and state-wide, our most ambitious engagement in electoral politics involved presidential and national elections.

John F. Kennedy and the 1960 Election

In 1960 MAPA was just being formed and was not in a position to play an active role in the presidential campaign of that year. Still, the 1960 election was important because for the first time at the national level Mexican-Americans participated in an organized fashion in presidential politics.

This took the form of the "Viva Kennedy" group, which formed in support of John F. Kennedy after he received the Democratic nomination. The Viva Kennedy organization in California was composed of people who were later part of MAPA. I participated in the Viva Kennedy campaign in the Bay Area, although I was not one of the leaders in organizing it. I was then primarily interested in working with the Organización Mexicana and in seeking to maintain a grassroots base.

The Viva Kennedy clubs throughout the Southwest succeeded in bringing out a strong Mexican-American vote for Kennedy. In Texas, which proved to be a decisive state for Kennedy, Mexican-Americans were the margin of victory. While Nixon won California, the over-whelming number of Mexican-Americans voted for Kennedy. Conse-

*Willie Brown was first elected to the California State Assembly in the 1960s and has served numerous terms, including as speaker of the assembly. Don Edwards was elected to the California State Assembly in the 1960s and was subsequently elected to the U.S. Congress from the San Jose area.

quently, *mexicanos* had large aspirations and expectations for the new Kennedy administration.

Unfortunately, those hopes were not fulfilled, despite Kennedy's popularity with Mexican-Americans. When Kennedy won, a lot of his people took the position that they had done it all by themselves. They took a very patronizing attitude toward Mexicans, thinking that they could just throw us a crumb and that would be enough.

One of the people who had done a good job in mobilizing Mexican-American support for Kennedy in California was Hank López. Kennedy's people called him to Washington after the election and offered him some two-bit job that was meaningless. The same thing happened to Carlos McCormick, who had headed up the Viva Kennedy effort and who was also offered an insignificant appointment in the administration. Hank López turned down the job offer. He thought it was beneath him to accept that kind of meaningless job when the needs of the Mexican communities were so great.

All this left Mexicans in California and the rest of the Southwest with a bad taste toward the Kennedy administration. Kennedy and his administration didn't understand Mexicans. Kennedy was a Boston political animal, and he didn't know very much about the problems of Mexicans. He had well-intentioned people around him, but they were just totally unfamiliar with Mexican-Americans.

I don't underestimate some of Kennedy's contributions, especially in keeping the country out of war with the Soviet Union and in resisting pressures from the warmongers to bomb Cuba. I think he deserves a lot of credit for that as well as for stressing to some extent the needs of the poor. But unfortunately, when it came down to performance, in the case of Mexican-Americans, his administration rated very low.

Despite Kennedy's poor performance on issues affecting Mexican-Americans, his tragic assassination on November 22, 1963, deeply affected the *mexicano* community. I was in Oakland that day, and a friend came by my office and said, "Did you hear that President Kennedy has been shot?" I hadn't, so I turned on the radio and heard that he had been shot and had been taken to a hospital. Of course, he died, and everybody stayed glued to the radio or TV for the rest of the day.

Mexicanos felt very sad. The first Catholic president to occupy the White House had been killed. Kennedy had been the first president to have been specifically identified with *mexicanos* through the Viva Kennedy campaign. The fact that his wife spoke Spanish and addressed crowds of *mexicanos* in Spanish had endeared the Kennedy's to Mexican-Americans. All this made Jack Kennedy much more *simpatico* than any other president to Mexicans.

The *mexicano* community grieved deeply for Kennedy. I shared those feelings and feared that things might get worse under Vice-President Lyndon Johnson. Johnson was more conservative in foreign policy and in domestic social issues than Kennedy. He was a Texan, and even though he knew more about Mexicans than Kennedy had, his political instincts by nature were much more conservative.

Viva Johnson

My suspicion of Johnson, however, quickly dissipated, as LBJ very rapidly embraced the reform agenda of the Kennedy administration and moved beyond it in civil rights legislation and the whole package of domestic reforms that came under his Great Society programs. As Johnson prepared for the 1964 presidential election, he made direct overtures to the Mexican community.

Some of his people met with us in MAPA and asked us to organize a "Viva Johnson" campaign. MAPA not only endorsed LBJ before the Democratic primary in California, but we also voted to participate in the Viva Johnson movement for the fall election. But we insisted that this effort be different from the Viva Kennedy campaign.

In 1960, the Viva Kennedy clubs had come under the auspices of the state Democratic leadership, and that had limited the independence and initiative of the Mexican-American effort and had also brought out the continued prejudice of white Democrats against Mexicans. In 1964, we insisted on running our own campaign, apart from the regular Democratic state party apparatus, funded separately, and beholden only to the national campaign leadership. Herman Gallegos in particular vehemently insisted upon this form of participation.

Johnson's people were amenable to our proposal, even though the state party leaders objected. The building of a Viva Johnson campaign run directly by Mexican-Americans represented a major breakthrough in national politics, increased MAPA's stature, and provided many of us with national political experience for the first time.

I was named as one of two national campaign coordinators of the

Viva Johnson effort, along with Cris Aldrete from Texas. My name had been proposed by MAPA to the Johnson people. Aldrete represented PASSO in Texas. We built the campaign not only in California and Texas but also in a variety of other states. I traveled throughout the Southwest as well as to Indiana, Illinois, Michigan, Nebraska, Iowa, Kansas, Washington, and Oregon.

Our basic pitch to get Mexican-Americans to organize Viva Johnson efforts in these states was not only to emphasize support for LBJ's reform programs but also to stress that this was a unique opportunity for *mexicanos* to influence national politics and gain national experience. Some people at first found it difficult to accept the idea of building politically outside the main Democratic channels, since they had always been dependent on the Anglos. But we encouraged this independence and told our people that we would provide the funds for them to open their own Viva Johnson headquarters, print their own literature, organize their own precincts, and operate their own get-out-the-vote organizations. In this way, we built a national Viva Johnson movement.

Besides traveling to these other states, I moved to Los Angeles for six months, where we set up national Viva Johnson headquarters. The other national office was headed up by Aldrete in San Antonio. We ran the L.A. campaign out of an office in East Los Angeles. Since this was only a temporary relocation, Blanche and the kids remained in Oakland.

Although our national and statewide offices were in Los Angeles, we didn't concentrate only on that city. We also organized important committees in San Diego, Fresno, Sacramento, San Jose, San Francisco, and Oakland. This was the first time that we as Mexican-Americans had been able to accomplish such a level of electoral organization.

Over the months leading to the November election, we concluded a large voter registration campaign that we had initiated earlier in the year. We set up campaign committees in every congressional district, in every assembly district, and in every local council district where *mexicanos* lived. In all the major barrios, we organized Viva Johnson campaigns. We opened up something like sixty-five headquarters throughout California. With our own budget, we promoted our own political ads on radio, but not too much on television. We published our ads, particularly in the Spanish-language newspapers, and printed and distributed campaign literature in Spanish.

In the six months that I spent in L.A., I couldn't help but notice various political changes in the *mexicano* community since I had last resided there permanently, after the war. For one thing, of course, the population was much larger. There were also a great many more political activists and candidates. And I found a greater political sophistication. Young people as well as middle-aged *mexicanos* were more willing to participate in politics. All this was very different from what it had been in the 1930s and 1940s. In the thirties, the number of political activists was quite small. After the war, especially as the veterans returned, the number of activists grew, but it was still small in comparison to what I found in 1964.

This political change involved not only quantity but also quality. More *mexicanos* were now asking about the issues, demanding answers to the very serious problems affecting Mexicans, such as racism, segregation, poor education, the administration of justice. I felt that our community was now very conscious of what needed to be done.

Many people were willing to be active, and we got a lot of volunteers for the campaign. Some of these were veterans from World War II or Korea, who were now mature adults. But others were young people coming out of the universities and community colleges as well as young workers from the unions. All were keenly interested in obtaining effective political representation.

This was the big issue in the early 1960s—to get *mexicano* political representation for the first time in the state legislature, in city councils, on boards of supervisors, and boards of education. Fortunately, in our efforts, we were spared the dangers of political factionalism. Much more factionalism existed among whites and blacks. We had a lot of unity behind our candidates and behind the Viva Johnson campaign.

At the end of the campaign, we had registered a record number of Mexican-American voters in California. On election day, we coordinated our get-out-the-vote effort by driving people to the polls, calling people to remind them to vote, and mobilizing our volunteers right up to closing time at the polls. Johnson won a smashing victory over Barry Goldwater in California, as he did throughout the country. More Mexican-Americans voted in the 1964 presidential election than ever before. We turned out record numbers of voters in the barrios and recorded overwhelming majorities for LBJ.

Viva Brown

We used our experiences in the 1964 election two years later in the 1966 gubernatorial race in California, which pitted incumbent Governor Pat Brown against movie actor and archconservative Ronald Reagan. This was a major election with important repercussions. It was also complicated because of the topsy-turvy relationship we had had with Brown ever since his first election in 1958.

Brown, for example, was unwilling to overhaul the state Employment Development Department. He was willing to make some token changes, such as appointing minorities to serve as trainees for higher jobs or to serve as outreach consultants to the minority communities, but he resisted our recommendations for parity. Parity would have meant that if we were twelve percent of the population, we should be twelve percent of the employees in the Employment Development Department.

We had similar problems with Brown regarding other state agencies such as the Motor Vehicles Department. We wanted more Spanish-speaking people there, and we wanted bilingual instructional brochures. Brown didn't support us fully here either. He also refused to hear our complaints and advice on the penal system, which discriminated against the poor and minorities and favored laxer penalties for those who had good connections and were wealthy. We had a lot of problems getting him to appoint more Spanish-speaking judges to the bench. He, of course, refused to meet with César Chávez when the farmworkers marched to Sacramento seeking recognition for their right to unionize.

However, despite Brown's limitations, he did begin to come around more during his last couple of years in office. This resulted from a combination of political opportunism on his part and the pressures from the minority communities, especially after the 1965 Watts riots in Los Angeles. He supported some of the big job-training programs that flowed from LBJ's Great Society reforms. He began to understand that you couldn't deal with the Mexican community by offering tokens, but that you had to grapple with the problems facing our community. He began to reach out more to the *mexicano* community.

But if Brown had a mixed record regarding minority issues, we understood that conditions under Reagan would be even worse. So

MAPA endorsed Brown, and we set out to duplicate our 1964 effort
with Johnson. Brown's advisors recommended that he support a similar campaign organization headed by Mexican-Americans.

I was asked to become the director of what we called the "Viva
Brown" clubs, and I accepted. I was also one of three statewide campaign managers for Brown, along with a white and a black. We opened
up our central Viva Brown office in L.A., but, as we had done in 1964,
we sponsored several other campaign headquarters throughout the
state. We developed a good working relationship with Brown during
the campaign.

At first, neither we nor others perceived that this would prove to be
a difficult campaign. At the beginning, everybody underestimated Reagan. When I first saw Reagan campaign, I thought that the people could
detect an actor who used makeup and smiled at everything but who
knew nothing about the issues. Reagan was ignorant of politics, but he
could grin and quip very affably. I thought that people would be able
to see through him, but I guess they couldn't.

As in 1964, we went all out. The Viva Brown campaign utilized spots
on television and on the Spanish-language radio. We held parades. On
election day, we turned out a sizeable vote for Brown. But 1966 was not
1964, and Brown was not LBJ. Reagan proved to be an attractive
candidate, and he put Brown on the defensive. In the end, despite our
efforts, Brown went down to defeat, even though he was unquestion-
ably the superior candidate. There was also no question that the minority communities were clearer than white voters were about the dangers
that Reagan represented. I think Reagan fooled more whites than
blacks or *mexicanos*.

The Black Civil Rights Movement

The early 1960s, of course, saw increased efforts by African-Americans
to achieve full civil rights and equal opportunities. We in MAPA were
clearly influenced and motivated by the black civil rights movement.
That didn't mean that our struggles came only as a reaction to those
of blacks; we had our own history in fighting for civil and human rights.
But the so-called black revolution of the 1960s affected us in many
ways.

In MAPA, we developed close working relations with black civil
rights leaders and organizations such as the NAACP, the Southern

Christian Leadership Conference, SNCC, and CORE and with Black Power activists such as Stokely Carmichael, Rap Brown, and many others.* We also worked closely with black churches in nondenominational coalitions.

In northern California, efforts to work together had always been made. In California as well as in other areas of the Southwest, black leaders understood that they needed broader support than just their own race, and hence they extended their hands to whites, Mexicans, Asian-Americans, and Native Americans to join in a crusade for civil rights for all nonwhite people. MAPA joined in this effort.

As a MAPA officer, I participated in a number of civil rights coordinating councils. I was on a statewide committee that worked to defeat unfair housing propositions. And I was on other statewide campaigns to bring about a broader measure of civil rights for minorities.

Some Mexican-Americans, including some in MAPA, did not agree that we should form coalitions with African-Americans. They felt that we had our own axe to grind and that we would do better by remaining separate from black struggles. This was a form of separatism that really had a racist rather than a political basis to it. But, in MAPA, this proved to be a minority opinion. We had more to gain by working with blacks. Black politicians in California, for example, always supported us. While white officials always were opposed or ambivalent, black leaders could always be counted on to endorse Mexican-American initiatives because it also helped them.

Consequently, during the sixties in California, we joined with African-Americans on a number of fronts. We took on government employment policies in the U.S. Post Office, in military employment, and in the defense industry. We singled out racist employers who were excluding blacks and Mexicans. We demanded more black and Mexican teachers. We took on welfare offices, which were biased against nonwhite people. We protested against state and local employment commissions, which discriminated against blacks and Mexicans by rarely promoting employment in industries and services. Instead, they shuttled minorities into farm labor or unskilled urban jobs.

During the early sixties, some MAPA members also participated in

*The Southern Christian Leadership Conference (SCLC) was led by Dr. Martin Luther King, Jr. The Student Nonviolent Coordinating Committee (SNCC) and the Congress of Racial Equality (CORE) represented, along with the NAACP and SCLC, the key leadership in the black civil rights movement.

the sit-ins and freedom rides in the South. Some went to Alabama and to Mississippi, some as voter registrars and as legal assistants. I myself signed up to go to Mississippi to register voters, but before our group was scheduled to leave, the trip was called off. While I did not attend the historic March on Washington in August of 1963, some of our members did go.

For me, one of the memorable events of the sixties was getting to know Martin Luther King, Jr. Not that I really got to know him, but I was honored to have attended several events at which King met with representatives from MAPA and other Mexican-American groups after he had spoken to large audiences. We talked as part of a group.

I didn't get a chance to talk to him on a more personal level until 1968, when Dr. King invited me, Corky Gonzales from Denver, Reies López Tijerina from New Mexico, and a few other *mexicano* leaders to meet with him in Atlanta. We were there for three days, at his expense, to talk about common issues facing us and about our participation in the March Against Poverty that was coming up. In fact, we left Atlanta the day before King went to Memphis, where he was killed.

His death was a tragic loss. In all our conversations with Dr. King, he always exhibited a sensitivity to the needs of *mexicanos*. He understood our particular historical conditions, but he also stressed that we needed to struggle together to correct common abuses. He was very sympathetic and supportive. Had he lived, such a national coalition might have been possible.

CHAPTER ELEVEN

Expectations and Frustrations

Following the election of Lyndon Johnson, Mexican-Americans had high expectations that LBJ would reciprocate the strong Mexican-American support he had received by endorsing new initiatives to address the problems of *mexicanos*. In May 1966, I and a few other key Mexican-American leaders arranged for a meeting with the president at the White House.

The group included Judge Alfred Hernández of Houston; Ray Elizondo of PASSO; Dr. Hector García from Texas, the founder of the American GI Forum;* Augustín "Teen" Flores from Riverside, California, who was in the American GI Forum; and myself from MAPA. Our main purpose was to lay our agenda before the Johnson administration. Civil rights in general was very high on this list. But we also wanted to stress the special needs of the *mexicano* and other Spanish-speaking communities in the United States.

We felt that there needed to be a recognition that we were no longer a regional minority but were now a national minority, from coast to coast and border to border. Besides the five million or so Mexican-Americans, almost two million Puerto Ricans were living on the East

---

*The American GI Forum was organized by Dr. Hector García in Corpus Christi, Texas, in 1948. Its members were Mexican-American veterans returning from World War II. It has since functioned as a civil rights group for Mexican-Americans.

Coast. A growing number of Latinos were coming into Florida from the Caribbean, including Cuba and the Dominican Republic. In the Midwest, *mexicanos* were working and living in a number of communities.

We felt that we needed to spell out this national dimension to the administration in Washington so that they would stop thinking of the Spanish-speaking only as a southwestern problem. We particularly wanted to press for a federal commission or committee that would devise new and broad programs to deal with the particular problems facing the Spanish-speaking, including racism, job discrimination, poor schooling, lack of higher and professional education, and inferior housing. This commission or committee would represent all of the Spanish-speaking.

A White House Meeting

The meeting at the White House was an interesting one. LBJ was very cordial and amiable. We met in the evening; it was a long meeting that included cocktails, hors d'oeuvres, and dinner. Before we sat down to have our discussion, the president insisted on showing us movies of several of his international trips, trips to different parts of the country, parts of speeches he had made, and films of his family. He then took us on a tour of the White House.

We spent some time in Lincoln's bedroom, which was kept exactly the way it was when Lincoln slept there. Johnson insisted that all of us lie on the bed. "Why don't you try it out?" he asked us. Johnson was sort of a cornball type. He wasn't very sophisticated, but he was shrewd as hell. I and the others lay down on the bed, which was hard as nails. Finally, very late in the evening, we sat down and discussed issues.

Besides the various problems facing Mexican-Americans, we brought up the idea of a specific federal committee to work on these problems. The president's advisors who attended the meeting liked the idea in general but felt we needed to go one step further. Their opinion was that a special White House committee would have only short-range impact. What they wanted—and LBJ concurred—was an interagency, cabinet-level committee that would be more permanent and that could play a more effective role with departments such as Health, Education, and Welfare and the Labor Department. They agreed to establish a working committee, including Mexican-American representatives, to formally propose the idea.

As a result, the meeting broke up on a positive note. None of us had gone to the White House with any illusions about what might come out of the meeting. We knew it would be exploratory, but we were pleased with the concrete results concerning the agency.

As I look back on that meeting with LBJ, I'm impressed by the fact that it took place and that it signaled a new and national political position for Mexican-Americans. But, on the other hand, I was not awed by the realization that here I was—someone from the El Paso barrio, someone who had struggled to organize workers in L.A. in the 1930s, who had been persecuted in the service during the war because of my labor commitments—and here I was in 1966 breaking bread with the president of the United States. I had believed for many years that it wasn't any kind of a feat for a *mexicano* to sit down with the president of the U.S. and talk about problems.

I was perhaps less awed than the others because I had been affiliated with labor leaders such as Harry Bridges who often met with Roosevelt and Truman, and with Mexican-American leaders such as Josefina Fierro, who as a very young woman had met with Vice-President Wallace during the Zoot Suit crisis in Los Angeles. I knew that *mexicanos* could more than hold their own with these leaders once we had put together enough political and organizational strength to bargain effectively. I didn't believe that such meetings should be only symbolic—although of course they had symbolic value—but rather that we should use such occasions to press our issues. And we did that at our meeting with LBJ.

The White House meeting with LBJ marked the beginning of a more concerted lobbying effort in Washington by Mexican-Americans. We had never really done such lobbying before, and we learned by trial and error. I and others returned to Washington during the Johnson administration to press for manpower development programs, for job-training programs, for adult education, for housing programs, for the needs of farmworkers, and for bilingual education.

This was a period when we didn't have professional Mexican-American lobbyists, as we do now. The only *mexicanos* we had in Washington in the mid-sixties were a few who held government jobs, and they were few and far between. We didn't have the resources for MAPA or LULAC to establish offices in Washington. So, besides our visits, we relied on *mexicanos* who held federal jobs in Washington in the Postal Department or in the Education Department, such as Pedro Esquivel, to moonlight as lobbyists for us on a number of issues. We were also able to rely on friends in the labor movement who were based in Washington, such as Henry Santiesteban and Esteban Torres, who used their influence to open doors for us.

All of this was very different from what exists today, when we have two or three dozen Latino organizations with offices in Washington. People now know their way around. They know the legislative labyrinths, the important people, and access is much easier. It's a far cry from what it was more than twenty-five years ago.

The Great Society

Following our meeting with LBJ and the beginning of a more systematic lobbying effort in Washington by MAPA, LULAC, and other Mexican-American groups, the Great Society programs generated by Johnson began to include *mexicanos* and other Spanish-speaking people. The Inter-Agency Committee on Mexican-American Affairs, headed by Vicente T. Ximenes, was established to coordinate a number of programs and federal departments that affected Mexican-American issues. More *mexicanos* were recruited into important positions in the War on Poverty programs and the Equal Employment Opportunity Commission, the EEOC.

Other *mexicanos* began receiving appointments in the departments of Education, Labor, and Justice. Rural assistance programs were expanded to help Mexican migrant farmworkers in states such as Texas. We were able to place *mexicanos* not only in Washington agencies but also at the state and local levels, where Great Society programs operated. Those at the local levels were better able to assess the value of particular programs.

Even before 1966, MAPA had become directly involved in a variety of anti-poverty programs in California. The one we were most engaged in was the Manpower Development Training Program. This program came out of the struggles of farmworkers and the poor to get food and income through better jobs. We recognized that as long as our people were not trained for the better-paying jobs, that lack of training, along with racism, would deprive them of the kind of income they needed to alleviate poverty. The Manpower programs provided training for unemployed workers with limited English proficiency so that they could get jobs. The program extended stipends for those enrolled in it. They received not only job training but also cultural and educational training in order to make them more marketable.

MAPA participated in this program by setting up community-based corporations under the Manpower program, directed by Spanish-speaking administrators in the barrios. Community people sat on the boards of directors and helped to set policy. These became agencies run by *mexicanos*.

We organized Manpower programs throughout California. With the support of Governor Brown, we were able to get a million and a half dollars for a statewide project. At the Napa state hospital, we opened the first training program for teaching Spanish-speaking functional illiterates. We had one hundred trainees for six months, who were paid a stipend of one hundred dollars a week. We started teaching them how to read and write, first in Spanish and then in English. It was an excellent program.

The "Sleeping Giant"

As Mexican-Americans became more involved in national politics during the mid-1960s, the media ironically referred to us as the "sleeping giant," indicating our political potential, if only we were to wake up politically. I rejected this term. I thought it was historically wrong and politically harmful. It was a way of blaming the victims for their fate, claiming that we had supposedly been passive all these years.

But the *mexicanos* in this country had never been asleep. We had always been giants, working like hell to produce to stay alive and to keep the Southwest and other areas going. So how could they call us a "sleeping giant"?

This was a media term that was being handed down to us so that we would not seize upon other slogans more pertinent to our situation. It was an attempt, whether conscious or unconscious, to steer us away from saying things such as "Let's talk about the *mexicanos* who have been dispossessed"; or "Let's talk about the land question," as Reies López Tijerina was raising in New Mexico; or "Let's talk about really sharing the wealth and wiping out all the discriminatory laws, customs, and regulations that private industry and government impose in dealing with *mexicanos*." Raising issues such as these in fact indicated not a sleeping giant but a fighting one. And that's what the power structure in the country didn't want—fighting *mexicanos*.

Frustrations

But by the mid- and late 1960s, the country was seeing fighting *mexicanos*. This was the result of growing frustration with the Johnson administration, despite the anti-poverty programs LBJ had initiated and despite the *mexicano* participation in them.

Two basic issues led to our frustration. For one, although *mexicanos* had been appointed to lower-level positions in the War Against Poverty, we sensed that we were being excluded from more major roles. On top of that, with the increased U.S. military role in Vietnam and the move to a war economy, LBJ's domestic reform programs took a second seat to the war. The budgets for the anti-poverty programs were cut back. At the same time that we had experienced rising expectations, the programs most directly affecting us were being limited, and our role in them was being diminished. All this led to growing frustration, but also a growing militancy, among Mexican-Americans.

I found myself in the middle of this confrontation between rising expectations and increasing frustrations in my official position in MAPA, as vice-president from 1964 to 1966, and as president from 1966 to 1968. I had never believed that the federal government by itself, even under a reform administration, could alleviate many of the social ills facing the country. But I did believe that a reform period would allow minority groups an opportunity to influence policies that would improve conditions for themselves and also help to politicize and organize the communities. I became frustrated, however, when I began to see the ineffectiveness of some of these reform efforts.

In 1965, for example, I was appointed to the California Civil Rights Commission by Governor Brown. These state commissions had been established through provisions of the civil rights laws passed in 1964 and 1965 and were intended to provide recommendations to the federal Civil Rights Commission, among other tasks. I thought that the commission would be a good forum to air the issues facing minorities in California. But I was quickly disappointed, after a meeting in San Francisco where the U.S. Civil Rights Commission chose to ignore our recommendations for better implementation of the newly enacted civil rights laws.

The main obstacle was the head of the federal commission, Father Theodore Hesburgh, who was the president of the University of Notre Dame. Hesburgh was, in my opinion, a racist and a jingoist. A lot of people thought that he was a great person, because he hid behind the cloth of a priest. But I saw him then—and I still do—as an apologist for big business and for the military-industrial complex. He was anti-Mexican and anti–Latin American. He was willing to weep crocodile tears for the poor, but not willing to help them to do something about their victimization.

We on the California commission raised a variety of issues with Hesburgh. We raised questions about the blatant discrimination against racial minorities by the University of California. While we protested the arrests and beatings of minority students at Berkeley who were trying to establish ethnic studies programs, Hesburgh saw them as lawbreakers who deserved what they got. We protested police brutality in Los Angeles, following the Watts riots in 1965. Police were also brutally beating up Chicanos in L.A. A scandal was unfolding in the federal prisons in California concerning the racist treatment of Chicano prisoners. We were likewise requesting an investigation of violations of the one-person/one-vote principle, based on the gerrymandering of Mexican-American districts.

Hesburgh rejected all of these issues and our recommendations. He was not willing to talk about the gross violations against Mexican immigrants by the Immigration and Naturalization Service. What Hesburgh wanted was innocuous position papers and testimonies by so-called academic experts.

I questioned what I was doing on such an ineffective commission. I called a press conference sometime in 1966 and publicly resigned. I criticized Hesburgh and the U.S. Civil Rights Commission. It didn't draw too much attention, but at least it left some impact on people who knew me, who then began to think, "What's with the Civil Rights Commission?" Other pressures that came to bear on the Hesburgh Commission in time forced it to become more sensitive to the issues we had presented, including the civil rights of Mexican-Americans. Still, this experience revealed many of the shortcomings of the Johnson administration, especially in its dealings with *mexicanos.*

The Albuquerque Walkout

What in time became widespread frustration with the Johnson administration was initially and vividly expressed as early as March 1966 at a meeting of the Equal Employment Opportunity Commission in Albuquerque. The commission had scheduled this meeting supposedly to hear complaints and recommendations by Mexican-American community representatives regarding the discriminatory employment practices that our people suffered from both the private sector and the government.

I was late getting to the meeting, but I later heard that the opening remarks by the chairman of the commission were very insensitive and insulting to the *mexicanos* leaders who had come to the meeting. The chairman told them that the commission would not be dictated to. He stated that only very concrete cases of discrimination would be taken up by the commission, instead of looking at the historical and aggregate discrimination against *mexicanos* in industries and government. These statements offended even the more conservative Mexican-Americans who, of course, were interested in opening up job opportunities.

As I arrived at the meeting, I encountered the delegates coming out. They were walking out of the meeting in protest, and they were mad as hell. One group was hurrying to hold a press conference to denounce the meeting, and another was setting up picket lines to boycott the rest of the meeting. Others simply left Albuquerque, determined to come up with new strategies to deal with the insensitivity of the Johnson administration.

That night at the hotel, I met with numerous other *mexicanos* who expressed their frustrations. In a way, I thought the commission people had done us a favor by turning their backs on us, since many Mexican-American professional people and educators who had never before displayed their anger and disgust with the government were now coming out to protest. I had never seen some of these people from LULAC and the American GI Forum speak so militantly.

I was not surprised by the insensitivity of the EEOC representatives, because I was already beginning to see the end of the reform phase of the Johnson administration. Johnson had initially surprised many of us, but he was still essentially a conservative. He was a supporter of the military-industrial complex and was not particularly pro-labor. His Great Society program was not a revolutionary or radical program; it was not anything like the New Deal. It was not something that released the force and strength of the great body of poor and working people, nor was it a new Declaration of the Rights of Man. If you want to wipe out poverty, you have to go to the causes, and you have to provide poor people with the means to work themselves out of poverty. I didn't see that in Johnson.

The Albuquerque meeting was significant because it signaled the beginning of a new militancy among Mexican-Americans, both young and old. Before we left Albuquerque, those of us there agreed to raise new demands and to begin to mobilize independent of the Johnson administration. This led to the historic confrontation between the administration and *mexicanos* one year later in El Paso.

El Paso and La Raza Unida

We had been pressing the administration for a White House conference on the Spanish-speaking as a way of bringing attention to our frustrations and our agenda. Johnson didn't agree to this, but he did agree instead to put together a conference on Mexican-American issues in El Paso for October 1967. This was scheduled at the same time LBJ was to come to El Paso and finalize the Chamizal Treaty with President Díaz Ordaz of Mexico. The treaty transferred a parcel of U.S. land back to Mexico.

This was not the meeting that we wanted, but we didn't oppose it. Indeed, those of us in MAPA—in consultation with LULAC, the GI Forum, and other groups—planned to use the El Paso conference as a forum to express our grievances. The list of demands that we brought to El Paso and raised at the conference included support for the farm-workers' struggle led by César Chávez, better job opportunities, better educational opportunities, better housing, an end to police brutality in our communities and in the prisons, and, in general, more funds to recharge and expand the anti-poverty programs.

The conference was held at the University of Texas at El Paso. LBJ didn't attend the conference, but some of his cabinet heads came, along with Vice-President Hubert Humphrey. Inside the hall, the atmosphere was one of confrontation. The Johnson people were saying, "You people have to be patient, and we'll take care of your problems."

But the people there didn't see it this way. They wanted some changes then and now. I along with others spoke out several times during the initial session. I didn't speak for myself, but as president of MAPA I interpreted MAPA's position.

We believed that the Johnson administration had let us down. We had participated in Johnson's election in 1964 and had helped carry the southwestern states for him. Johnson had reciprocated by including Mexican-Americans in the initial phase of the anti-poverty programs, but then, once the Vietnam war became his obsession, he quickly cut back and put the needs of *mexicanos* and other minorities on the back burner. The bottom line was a scaled-back budget. We believed that the problems of the Spanish-speaking were so great that they would require forceful action, not band-aids. We were expecting an elephant to be born, and instead we got a flea.

We raised our demands, and when it was clear that our agenda was not going to be listened to, we walked out of the conference and formed informational picket lines outside the hall. The large majority of the delegates agreed with us and supported our walkout. We had a large picket line on the second day, when Vice-President Humphrey arrived to address the conference.

All of these demonstrations, of course, embarrassed the administration. But we wanted to do more than protest and boycott the conference; we wanted to organize among ourselves. We needed to discuss what should now be done. We all agreed that we could not let the administration get away with such a namby-pamby program in the face of such great needs.

We met at the Hotel Paso del Norte in downtown El Paso. We got a big ballroom and held our initial meeting. We invited all the delegates, and four to five hundred attended the meeting, from every state in the union. We agreed that instead of just meeting in the hotel we should go to El Segundo Barrio—the core Mexican barrio in South El Paso, where the poor people lived. The next day, we met at the Sagrado Corazón Church, the Sacred Heart Church, in the barrio. We met there for another two or three days. We also went across the border and met with poor people in Juárez.

At the meetings in the barrio, the assembled delegates discussed a range of issues and possible strategies to pursue. Above all, we did not want to hear the administration's side of the issues—we wanted instead to hear what the delegates and the poor people had to say. Very high on the agenda was the feeling that the Johnson administration had really gone back on its word after promising to push for a significant attack on poverty among the Spanish-speaking—and not only had gone back on its word but also had cut the programs, making them insignificant. We wanted an all-out program and plentiful money to do a significant job on all the issues: health, jobs, education, housing, and so forth.

People also raised a series of demands at the barrio meetings that recognized the need for enhancing the political power of the Spanish-speaking. We believed that the Democratic Party in particular had to be taken to task for not playing a role in the political empowerment of Spanish-speaking people. We stressed the need to build political organization among our people and to help our communities organize. We discussed the importance of supporting the farmworkers, of organizing our youth, and of dealing with the needs of women.

While issues particular to women were not in the forefront of the discussions, they were indeed raised. Many women were at the barrio meetings, and they participated actively. Nuns who were supporting the farmworkers were in attendance. Polly Baca, who would later become very prominent in Colorado political circles, was at El Paso, having just returned from the Caribbean, where she had been doing union work. And women attended from the various MAPA chapters.

At the barrio conference, the term "Raza Unida" was used for the first time. Later, these barrio meetings came to be referred to as the Raza Unida conference. Although the words *"raza unida"* literally mean "united race," they were used in El Paso more to mean "a united people" and less to indicate a racial connotation. This term was introduced, I believe, by Dr. Ernesto Galarza. The term "Raza Unida," however, didn't play as prominent a role as some later suggested. It certainly was not used in El Paso to call for an independent Chicano political party, along the lines that would later develop. "Raza Unida" at El Paso was used to stress the great need for political organization. It was used to encourage the delegates to return to their communities and to organize for political empowerment. We needed to put our people on the school boards, into city councils, and into state assemblies.

Ernesto Galarza

To understand the use of the term "Raza Unida" and what came out of the El Paso barrio conference, you have to understand the role played by Ernie Galarza. After he had finished writing his marvelous book *Merchants of Labor,* exposing the exploitation of Mexican workers in the *bracero* program, Galarza, who had for years worked to organize farmworkers, became active with both MAPA and CSO, especially in northern and central California.* His major concern was how to make organizations like these more effective and more committed to grass-roots needs.

Beginning around 1965, Ernie met regularly with Herman Gallegos, Jimmy Delgadillo, Hector Abeytia, Nacho López, Ed Quevedo, and myself—all involved in MAPA and CSO—about how we could expand the political organization of the Spanish-speaking. We would rent a hotel room and spend a day or two talking about what had to be done. Ernie argued with us that it was not enough just to elect a Spanish surname; we had to elect a Spanish surname who would carry out a program on issues that affected the people. We also all agreed that we needed an organization that could make those we elected to office remain accountable to us and the people. Just as we had helped to get them elected, we could help to get them defeated if they compromised or equivocated.

We were all impressed with what the farmworkers and César Chávez were doing, and we looked to the farmworkers' union as a model. Galarza really tied into Chávez's idea about reaching out to the grassroots people, to the poor, and helping them to organize themselves on issues that affected them. In the fields, this organization would take the form of a union. In the barrios, it would involve a strong barrio organization.

But Galarza believed that the urban organization would have to go beyond MAPA and CSO. It would have to be an organization that would go into every nook and cranny of the barrios. His idea was to establish *concilios,* or councils, everywhere—around the churches, the Boy Scouts, the teachers, and existing organizations. These *concilios* would meet regularly to discuss common problems and to plan strategy for combatting the establishment. In Galarza's mind, this *concilio* movement would spread throughout the Southwest.

Out of these discussions, and primarily as a result of Galarza's

*See Ernesto Galarza, *Merchants of Labor: The Mexican Bracero Story* (Santa Barbara: McNally & Loftin, 1964).

efforts, we had organized a group called the Mexican-American Unity Council in 1966, patterned after Ernie's concept. It was predicated on building from the bottom up and had similarities to the ideas of Paulo Freire and liberation theology, especially the idea of *comunidades de base,* base communities. It was an understanding that we could not achieve real political power without the participation of the people who were suffering from the ills of society.

When we met in El Paso, some of us, particularly Galarza, already had in mind which political direction we should go in. It was in this context that I believe Galarza raised the cry of "Raza Unida," and this was why he played such a prominent role in El Paso.

Out of the El Paso conference, Galarza moved on to form the Southwest Council of La Raza. This was meant to supersede the earlier Mexican-American Unity Council and to provide the vehicle for putting Ernie's ideas into action. Unfortunately, especially for Ernie, it didn't work out that way.

Following the El Paso conference, Galarza was able to sell the *concilio* concept to the Ford Foundation, which put up the money to establish what was called the Southwest Council of La Raza (later called the National Council of La Raza). But the problem here was that despite all the talk about grassroots organizing, the Southwest Council in fact represented organization from the top. Worst of all, despite the good intentions of Galaraza and others such as Maclovio Barraza, who was appointed executive director, they in the end were beholden to the Ford Foundation. This limited the effectiveness and autonomy of the group and steered it toward more of an establishment perspective. Within six months, Galarza was thoroughly disappointed and eventually became less active in the Southwest Council.

The Julian Nava Campaign

Fortunately, some of us released our frustrations in other directions. One way was our involvement in the 1967 campaign by Julian Nava for a position on the Los Angeles school board. Although it did not involve a major elective office, the Nava campaign electrified the Mexican-American community. No *mexicano* had served on the L.A. school board in this century.

MAPA endorsed and supported the campaign. I came down from the

Bay Area and spent a month working with the different MAPA chapters in the greater L.A. area to mobilize and turn out the *mexicano* vote for Nava. Before I arrived, an effective voter registration job had already been concluded.

What we also had going for us was an attractive candidate. Julian Nava had received a Ph.D. in Latin American history from Harvard and was teaching at San Fernando Valley State College (later to be California State University at Northridge). He was a member of a very prominent and activist family in East Los Angeles. I knew the family and had known Julian since he was a small boy.

We promoted Nava as a highly qualified person—one who had been raised from early childhood in the East L.A. community, who was an educator, who understood the problems that students, teachers, and parents faced in trying to obtain a better and more significant education for Spanish-speaking children. It was easy to sell Nava to the people. To a large extent, the Nava campaign was an ethnic one, but his qualifications ensured that it went beyond that and appealed to all people concerned about the state of the public schools in Los Angeles.

Besides promoting Nava as an attractive and qualified candidate, we of course also addressed specific issues. One was the high dropout rate among Mexican-American children. At that time, it was around thirty-five or forty percent; it's even worse now. We still had a lot of segregation in the schools. The worst-equipped schools were still in the barrios.

We also discussed the need to improve parent-teacher relations. This was a particularly burning issue—many parents complained bitterly about the poor attitudes of teachers and their lack of concern about the needs of Spanish-speaking children. This cultural clash took place every day in the schools. Teachers scolded and punished students for speaking Spanish and told them to forget their *mexicano* traditions, to Americanize themselves and forget that they were *mexicanos*. The Nava campaign addressed all of these racist practices.

The combination of Nava's qualifications plus the issues involved inspired the *mexicano* community. The excitement was comparable to the Roybal campaign for city council in 1949. Many people registered to vote and formed barrio clubs for Nava. Although the school board elections then were by city and not by district, the Mexican-American vote provided Nava with an electoral base.

My job was to bring out the voters, walk precincts, organize precinct headquarters, and make sure that we had everything mobilized for election day. We made a massive effort at grassroots mobilization. The election was close but definitive in Nava's favor. It was a great victory!*

*Besides serving on the Los Angeles school board for several years, Nava served as ambassador to Mexico during the last year of the Carter administration.

CHAPTER TWELVE

¡Viva Kennedy!

The year 1968 proved to be a tumultuous one in the history of the country. For me, 1968 meant, above everything else, my deep involvement with Robert Kennedy's campaign for the presidency. I had not been a particularly devout supporter of John Kennedy and was critical of his failure to support Mexican-American issues. But his brother Bobby was different. He proved to be intensely interested in *mexicanos* and supportive of our goals, in a nonpatronizing fashion. I and others believed that a successful run for the presidency by Bobby would accelerate our efforts to assist the *mexicano* communities. Much more than JFK had done, Bobby touched our souls, and in him we saw a grand opportunity.

Robert Kennedy

I and other *mapistas* first became politically involved with Bobby Kennedy in 1966 during the farmworkers' strike against California grape growers and the subsequent boycott of grapes. As U.S. senator from New York, Bobby was part of a Senate subcommittee on labor, which held hearings concerning the condition of farmworkers. One of his aides approached us, asking where to hold hearings in California so that people suffering ill treatment in the fields could testify. Kennedy believed that such hearings could put political pressure on the growers by exposing some of the terrible working and living conditions facing farmworkers and their families.

Herman Gallegos of MAPA recommended Delano, of course, the site where the farmworkers' struggle had begun and where César Chávez and the United Farm Workers union had their headquarters. We also recommended places such as Stockton, Sacramento, and the Imperial Valley. Kennedy at the same time invited the Mexican-American urban leadership to participate in the hearings; he wanted to hear from MAPA, CSO, the American GI Forum, the Mexican-American Unity Council, and others.

When the hearings began in Delano, a group of us went there and testified about our knowledge of the farmworker's plight. After the session, Bobby came over to where I was standing with others of our delegation and said to me, "Bert, would you like to accompany me to the airport? I've got to catch a plane." Al Piñón, who was then the president of CSO, Herman Gallegos, and I went with Bobby in his car to the airport.

On the way, he thanked us for testifying and said, "I want to work with your people. Anything that I can do for MAPA and CSO, I want to do." I believe that he was already thinking of challenging LBJ for the presidency. It appeared to me that what he was really saying was, if you guys work with me, I'll work with you.

But he was sharper than that. He didn't put it in such a cold-blooded way. He did say, "Look, your people need political strength here in California because the growers are so powerful and your people have a lot of problems. So use my committee, my office, my influence as your friend. I'd like to see you build your organization, and whatever I can do, I'll be more than happy to do."

I asked him if he would be interested in coming to either San Francisco or Los Angeles to speak at a public meeting we would sponsor. He said yes, he would be happy to do so. And, sure enough, just a few months later, he came to San Francisco to speak at San Francisco State to a meeting that Herman Gallegos had arranged. He spoke to a packed auditorium.

Hubert Humphrey at Stanford

As we began to work more with Kennedy, before he announced that he would run for the presidency, we received overtures and even pressure from the Johnson administration to stay loyal to LBJ for the 1968 election. I'll never forget a particular event that illustrated the

Johnson administration's paranoia over the possible Kennedy challenge.

I got a call one day from California Congressman Phil Burton's office. I received it in Delano, where I was working on behalf of the farmworkers. Burton told me, "You know, the vice-president is looking for you and Herman Gallegos. He wants to talk to you, and he's sending a plane to Delano to bring you to San Francisco, where he'll be tomorrow."

Herman and I caught the plane, and we were scheduled to meet with Vice-President Hubert Humphrey that morning at the Hilton Inn by the San Francisco airport. But Humphrey didn't arrive from Washington on time, and so we waited and waited.

In the meantime, Herman and I figured out just what Humphrey wanted from us. At the time, MAPA and other Mexican-American groups were picketing post offices to bring attention to the discriminatory hiring practices of the U.S. Postal Service toward *mexicanos* and other minorities. This was embarrassing the Johnson administration. While we waited for Humphrey, Herman and I drew up a list of demands we could present to Humphrey before we could agree to end the picketing, including, for example, administration support for the farmworkers' strike.

Finally, as we waited in Humphrey's suite, we received word that of course he would be late and that he wanted us to accompany him by car to Stanford University, where he was to deliver a speech. We had no choice but to agree to this type of meeting.

On the way to Stanford, Humphrey asked us to lift the picket lines. In return, he would arrange a meeting for us with the Postmaster General and members of the House Post Office Committee. We told him that we weren't authorized or empowered to make that decision and that we would have to check back with other MAPA leaders. Humphrey responded that he didn't see how he could arrange those meetings until we stopped the picketing.

I thought this was pure blackmail and told Humphrey: "That's like holding a gun to us. We're not that strong, but you've got a little fly in the ointment. And I don't know that the people are going to want to let go of this."

The other thing Humphrey wanted was more or less a commitment that we would support Johnson in 1968. I said that it was too early to make such a commitment, even though I had been one of LBJ's national campaign directors in 1964. It was obvious that the Johnson people were feeling the pressure of a possible Kennedy challenge, especially in California, where Bobby was becoming active with the *mexicanos.*

Humphrey then bluntly asked "what it would take" for us to support LBJ. I said, "Well, one of the things is support for the farmworkers' strike."

He replied, "We can't do that."

I questioned that and pointed out to him that the strike was more than just a labor dispute. It represented the aspirations of the entire *mexicano* population for justice, just as the coal miners' strikes of the 1930s had symbolized the same for white ethnics. Humphrey, however, refused to commit himself, saying only that the administration was friendly toward labor.

We didn't come to any agreement as we approached Stanford. What happened next served only to impress Herman and me about the tenuous condition of the Johnson administration, as a result of its ill-fated policies in Vietnam.

As we drove into the campus, we were met with the biggest goddamn demonstration of students—this was even bigger than the earlier ones at Berkeley. People had come from all over the Bay Area to demonstrate against Humphrey and the war. It took what appeared to be several hundred motorcycle police to clear a path for Humphrey's car. I particularly remember seeing David Harris, one of the key anti-war leaders at Stanford and the husband of singer Joan Baez. I knew Harris, and when he saw me inside Humphrey's car, he called out, "Bert Corona, get outta that goddamn scab car!" Jesus Christ, I was embarrassed!

Of course, I was personally against the war, but neither MAPA nor the other Mexican-American groups had actually taken an official position on it. But here we were, faced with this huge demonstration—and Herman and I are stuck in Humphrey's car. The car moved forward as slowly as a funeral procession.

When we finally got to the auditorium, Humphrey asked us to go with him onto the stage. Herman and I said, "Mister Vice-President, we just can't." We stayed behind the stage with his aides. We never showed our faces to the crowd.

The people, of course, were not there to hear Humphrey speak; they were there to shout him down. I had never seen anything like it. They

booed him for ten or fifteen minutes solid. He just stood there and
finally said, "Well, I've only got five minutes left. Do you want to hear
our position, or should I just pack it up, leave, and bid you farewell?"

Finally, Harris and others quieted things down. Humphrey tried to
speak, but he spoke only about five minutes before the people booed
and drowned him out. He just packed up his notebook and stomped
down and out of the place. We followed him and got in the car, since
he was supposed to return us to the airport. On the way out, students
threw themselves in front of the car, while others threw tomatoes at the
car windows and spat all over it.

On the way back, Humphrey was trembling. He could hardly calm
himself. He didn't say a word to us. We finally got back to the freeway.
All this time, he kept repeating, "Goddamn Communists."

However, he finally agreed to set up those meetings for us in Washington, even though we were still picketing the post offices. We had the
meetings and won major concessions on the hiring of Mexican-Americans, including positions as postmasters. All of this, of course, was
affected by the upcoming presidential campaign of 1968.

Leaning Toward Kennedy

Despite the pressure from the Johnson administration, we continued to
gravitate more toward Kennedy. This move was helped along by our
contacts with the United Auto Workers, whose president, Walter
Reuther, was backing Kennedy. The UAW provided strong support to
the farmworkers, dispatching Henry Santiesteban to be their key liaison
with the farmworkers and with the Mexican-American community in
California. Another key person was Paul Schrade, regional director of
the UAW.

Both Santiesteban and Schrade spearheaded the push to elicit support for Kennedy if he chose to run. They assured him that the farmworkers, along with MAPA and other groups, would support him.
They were particularly impressed with our organization's work. For
example, we put together a large "Tribute to Labor" fund-raiser for the
farmworkers at the Palladium in Los Angeles. Besides César Chávez,
Walter Ruether and other bigwig labor leaders attended. We drew
about six thousand people to the event. This only increased Santiesteban's efforts to line up MAPA support for Kennedy. He impressed upon

us how crucial California was and in particular how crucial the Mexican-American vote would be for Kennedy in the primary.

One day, Henry returned from a trip to Washington and called me and several others to his office. He told us, "Bobby Kennedy is going to run for sure. We're going to have a lot of problems, but there will also be a lot of opportunities for groups such as yours." He acknowledged MAPA's effective organization and the fact that, outside California, we had chapters in Arizona, New Mexico, Washington state, Oregon, Illinois, Iowa, Nebraska, Michigan, and Indiana. Some of these were crucial primary states, and Kennedy needed our help. He was prepared to launch a national Mexican-American campaign in support of his candidacy.

Henry informed us that Kennedy had asked him to recommend someone to head up such an effort, the "Viva Bobby Kennedy" campaign. "I recommended Bert Corona," Henry said. "I recommended you, Bert." He told us that Kennedy had been excited about my possible involvement in the campaign, that he knew me and respected me.

I was flattered but told Santiesteban that I would have to think about it. Following the New Hampshire primary early in 1968, when Senator Eugene McCarthy came very close to defeating LBJ, Kennedy announced his candidacy. Shortly after that, I accepted his offer to sign on as head of the Viva Kennedy effort.

The Campaign

The first thing I moved on was securing MAPA's support for Kennedy. This was not an easy matter, since many of the board directors representing large chapters in East Los Angeles were already working for Senator McCarthy. They were doing so even before our board had endorsed anyone. At a heated meeting of the board, we clashed over whom to endorse. We knew by then that we didn't want LBJ or Vice-President Humphrey. So it was between Kennedy and McCarthy.

I argued that Kennedy had already displayed his commitment to Mexican-Americans by his endorsement of the farmworkers' struggle. He had held hearings on this issue in Delano. He had spoken at MAPA-sponsored rallies. I concluded that supporting Kennedy was the natural thing to do and in the best interest of MAPA.

As far as McCarthy was concerned, I observed that he had not committed himself to the farmworkers' cause and, in fact, saw it strictly as a labor issue rather than a social one. He was from Minnesota, and he didn't have a feeling or understanding for Mexican-Americans. His support came largely from young whites who were against the Vietnam war but who didn't relate well to minorities such as blacks and Mexican-Americans.

The pro-McCarthy faction in MAPA countered that, unlike Kennedy, McCarthy had for some time opposed the war that was killing and maiming Chicanos and denying resources to our communities. McCarthy, they claimed, didn't possess some of the dirty linen of the Kennedys. Many of the pro-McCarthy people in MAPA were younger activists, and they simply saw Bobby Kennedy as part of the old Democratic establishment. I saw Kennedy differently and felt that he, unlike his brother John, represented something new that would benefit *mexicanos*.

After a full discussion, the board voted, and two-thirds of the representatives endorsed Kennedy for the primary. This was not an official endorsement; under our bylaws, MAPA couldn't endorse in the primaries, only in the general elections. Still, the unofficial vote reflected MAPA's off-the-record endorsement. Some bad feelings remained after the meeting, but the majority of *mapistas* committed themselves to work for Kennedy.

I then set out to widen Mexican-American support for Kennedy in preparation for the upcoming primaries. We established the national Viva Kennedy campaign office in Los Angeles, but we also opened offices and initiated campaign efforts throughout California, the Southwest, the Pacific Northwest, and the Midwest. It was a national effort because our job was to assist in all the states where good numbers of Mexican-Americans resided. In California alone, we opened up over a hundred headquarters.

Besides our MAPA membership, we secured the support of other activists, such as those who had helped elect Julian Nava to the Los Angeles school board. Kennedy also inspired a whole new group of young people to become politically active. We did have a problem with organized labor because the AFL-CIO was supporting Humphrey after LBJ pulled out of the race. Still, large numbers of Mexican-American rank-and-file union members joined the Kennedy campaign. Although César Chávez did not endorse Kennedy as soon as we did, he finally did so, and both he and Dolores Huerta, vice-president of the union, did a hell of a job.

One other problem we had in California concerned the reluctance of Jess Unruh, Kennedy's campaign manager in the state, to allow us to run our own independent campaign. He wanted to control everything, including us. He wouldn't, for example, give us the money that was coming to us. We had to go to Bobby and tell him what was happening.

He called Unruh and said, "Jess, it's not working with Corona and the Mexican-American campaign. I'd appreciate it if you'd cooperate with them and support their campaign." Unruh, who was called "Big Daddy Unruh," tried to pretend that no problem existed and that he would take care of whatever questions we had. He was some bull-shitter.

Finally, Bobby just got real mad and told Unruh, "Look, Jess, you're the campaign manager in California, but I'm the candidate. I'm telling you, I'm running the campaign. You help Corona, and if I hear about any more of these shenanigans, I'm going to have to take the time to straighten you out." We still faced problems, and often we didn't know how we could afford to keep our campaign going, but toward the end of the campaign things did improve with Unruh.

From the campaign, several events stand out in my mind. Perhaps the most memorable experience involved the parade we organized for Bobby that went from the Long Beach airport all the way to La Placita on Olvera Street, in downtown Los Angeles. The parade took several hours as it wound its way through numerous towns and barrios—Compton, Maywood, Lynwood, Bell, City of Commerce. Finally it came into East Los Angeles, through Brooklyn Avenue, and then down onto Whittier Boulevard until we swung down on First Street. It was a massive sea of people all the way. I have never again seen as many *mexicanos* come out to anything.

Once we arrived at La Placita and got out of the cars, swarms of people descended on Bobby. He lost his cuff links, his tie, and one of his shoes. I lost my coat. The people just grabbed on to anything that involved Bobby. But Bobby enjoyed it all.

During the parade, he had gotten quite upset when the police used their motorcycles to get the people out of the path of the cars. He got so damn mad that he yelled to one of his aides, Jimmy Bruno: "Jimmy, get those motherfuckin' cops out of the way! We don't want them here." Bobby was mad because the police were hurting people. Bobby had hoped to say a few words at La Placita, but the press of the crowd wouldn't allow it. The people would hang onto his hand and wouldn't let him go. It was fantastic.

On another occasion, we again staged a rally for Bobby at La Placita. This time, we tried to have enough of our people line the path to where he was to speak, in order to keep the crowd back. We couldn't stop them. He was crushed, but we finally got him to the stand.

I think it was Chole Alatorre, a marvelous female labor organizer, who actually led Kennedy up to the stage. She stood right by him while he made his speech. When he finished, the people crushed in on him again, and Chole dragged him, while pushing people aside, all the way back to the car. Bobby always remembered this incident and Chole's help. Later, at a rally at the Greek Theater, he inquired, "Where is that woman, that 'Chalie' who saved my life?"

Another incident I'll never forget occurred when I campaigned with Bobby in Indiana. Jack Ortega from MAPA was our advance man in that state, and he singlehandedly organized a huge rally of *mexicano* steelworkers in Nicosia. There must have been close to twenty thousand people inside and outside a big basketball arena. Generally, the campaign staff would come up with two or three hundred staffers to provide security. But because Jack hadn't really cleared the rally with the main Kennedy campaign staff, we weren't able to get adequate security for such a big rally.

Jack tried to get some of the *mexicano* steelworkers to help out, but he didn't know any of the local people. When I arrived in Nicosia that morning for the rally, Jack said to me, "Bert, there's going to be all kinds of shit hitting the fan tonight because I don't have security. I don't know what's going to happen. You're supposed to be at the platform with the mayor and the bishop." According to Jack, Kennedy would arrive in the back of the auditorium and be brought to the portable stage.

Kennedy was quite late in arriving, which wasn't unusual for him during the campaign. The people began to chant and stomp impatiently. All of a sudden, we heard a big roar, and about half of the people in the back of the auditorium rushed out the back door, because Kennedy was coming in through the front rather than the back. We had forgotten to tell Bobby to come in through the back.

In their rush to get to Bobby, the crowd broke down the doors, broke down windows, and carried Bobby on their shoulders. They flattened out every folding chair. When they came up against the platform, they pushed it back with their bodies. I was on the platform, and they pushed it all the way back to the wall. It took us about fifteen minutes to clear the people from the platform so that the speeches could begin.

I looked around, and, my God, all I saw were *mexicanos*. There were hardly any Anglos. And the crowd is hollering, yelling, and stomping. Bobby turned to me and asked, "What are they saying? What's going on, Bert?" I said they were just happy to see him.

Finally, Bobby got to deliver his speech. We had forgotten to get a translator, so I had to translate for Bobby in Spanish. But it was so chaotic and the crowd was so enthusiastic that I finally dropped the translation, which was too difficult to do. Instead, every time Bobby paused for me, I just simply delivered my own speech. I ad-libbed the whole thing, and the crowd clapped at everything I said. Whatever Bobby was saying, I was saying something completely different. Bobby never caught on.

Later, when we all returned to Los Angeles, he asked Henry Santiesteban, who had been with us, why the reaction in Indiana had been so strong. Henry told him, "Bobby, Bert Corona was making up his own speech as you went along." From then on, Bobby had a lot of respect for my speech-making ability.

The California Primary and Tragedy

Coming into primary day in California in early June, we felt good about our chances against both Humphrey and McCarthy. We had one hundred five headquarters all over the state, zeroing in on the heavy Mexican precincts. We at first didn't know how we would get enough volunteers to canvas all of these precincts, but we did.

In San Diego, for example, the Hermandad Mexicana Nacional [Mexican National Brotherhood], which provided services for permanent residents and undocumented immigrants and which also doubled as a MAPA chapter there, performed yeoman work. Many of the members, such as Phil Usquiano, were members of the Central Labor Council, which was supporting Humphrey. But that didn't intimidate Phil and the others, who took on the Labor Council and organized many of the *mexicano* workers for Kennedy. When we got through organizing San Diego, we had over a thousand volunteers working the precincts. I had never seen anything like it in San Diego. Phil's daughter, Julia, and his son, Albert, led the campaign in National City. Julia started out with about five people and ended up with about three hundred precinct workers. We had, of course, put on a massive voter registration drive as part of our effort throughout the state.

On primary day, I just tried to put out fires and get resources to our people as fast as I could. We needed extra cars to transport voters to the polls because they were turning out in such great numbers. Many of our people didn't have cars, so they called for assistance. We even rented trucks that day to get people out to vote.

The other problem was getting enough food during the day to feed our army of volunteers. We had underestimated the number of volunteers who turned out that day. So I telegraphed for money up and down the state. Fortunately, one good thing about a Kennedy campaign was that they brought in cash from all over. I'd call up the main headquarters at the Ambassador Hotel in L.A., tell them that I needed so much money, and ask if they could meet me right away at Western Union. They would say, "Sure, Bert."

In the end, the voter turnout was very heavy. We had certain key precincts—in San Jose, in the Mission district in San Francisco, and in East L.A.—that we hoped would give us an early reading on the results. Early returns showed a massive turnout. In some East L.A. precincts, about ninety-seven percent of the registered voters came to the polls, and about ninety-six percent voted for Kennedy. Without question, the Chicano vote was a big factor in Kennedy's victory. The black community split more between Bobby and Humphrey.

That evening, I and my co-workers on the Viva Kennedy campaign heard the returns in our headquarters' cottage in the Ambassador Hotel. Of course, we were overjoyed at the results. Everyone was streaming into the ballroom, waiting for Bobby to come down and proclaim victory. I hadn't seen Bobby that day. We waited for him for a long time.

Meanwhile, I left the ballroom because I had been told that a group of Brown Berets and farmworkers had arrived, and they wanted to come in.* I went to the entrance, and there was David Sánchez, the head

*The Brown Berets were a group of militant Chicano community youth in Los Angeles and elsewhere in California. The group was organized in 1967 and func-

of the Berets. I didn't know which side the Berets had been on in the election, but they wanted to come in. A couple of hundred farmworkers were also there.

I had arranged for all of them to enter when someone came up to me and said, "Bert, they're calling your name from the podium. They want you up there." I reentered the hall, and as I made my way up through the huge crowd, Bobby was thanking various people, including Dolores Huerta from the United Farm Workers. He then turned and left the podium.

Since it was too late for me to be introduced, I turned back and began to leave the hall. I decided to return to our headquarters in the hotel, where a number of our volunteers were gathered, including my niece and two sons. On my way out of the hotel, I faintly heard what sounded like gunshots. Then someone rushed up to the mike and said, "Please, please, please be quiet. Bobby Kennedy has been shot. Bobby Kennedy has been hurt."

The place broke apart. I rushed back to our headquarters, and our kids were in tears. They had heard that Bobby had been shot. I went up to Bobby's suite in the hotel, where I ran into Henry Santiesteban. He said, "Bert, Bobby's been taken to the hospital, let's go there." We drove over in Henry's car, following the ambulance carrying Bobby.

We stayed outside the emergency room with others from the campaign staff until they finally told us that Bobby was dead. It was like they had blown the bottom out of the boat. Winning California wasn't a guarantee that we would have won the nomination and the election, but we felt that with this victory we couldn't be stopped. All of a sudden, we didn't have a campaign. It's a horrible feeling—here you've worked so hard and so well. What are you going to tell all of the people?

Remembering Bobby

The only thing that we thought would matter was to try and bring people together to continue working on some of the issues important

___

tioned until about 1972. Characterized by their semi-military uniforms, including brown berets, these activists emphasized the right to self-defense and self-determination for Chicanos. See Chapters Thirteen and Fourteen.

to us. The one thing that stood out in our minds was the farmworkers' struggle. And so, the next day or so, I talked to César, and he suggested that some of us in MAPA join him in the Coachella Valley, where he was preparing a new strike. We agreed and mobilized some of our people. We took a lot of people to the Coachella strike. I couldn't bear to go to Bobby's funeral. Instead, I went on strike. It was good therapy.

If we felt bad after the assassination of Bobby, so too did people in our communities. For several days, it was quite gloomy in the barrios. We saw more grief than when John Kennedy was assassinated. When Jack Kennedy died, a lot of people felt it throughout the nation, but we as *mexicanos* didn't feel it as pointedly as we did when Bobby was killed. The guy had been out there, with us, in the fields and in the barrios.

I'll never forget once in Oxnard when we had a parade through La Colonia, the main barrio, and we passed a little church. Bobby stopped the car, got out among the people, and went into the church to pray. All of this, of course, was symbolic, but the important thing is that Bobby was sensitive to the symbolism of the *mexicanos,* and he cared enough to show his interest in our communities. He did things like that in other places as well.

Bobby had come around a lot more than John Kennedy. He had shorn himself of some of his brother's Cold War attitudes. I recall Bobby saying several times that there was no point in our policy toward Cuba, no point in isolating it and trying to overthrow Castro. He thought we should instead try to influence Castro by working with his government.

What was also important about Bobby Kennedy and the campaign in 1968 is that it elevated Mexican-Americans as national political players for the first time. We and our issues were seen as part of Bobby's national agenda. Other, earlier campaigns such as the 1960 Viva Kennedy clubs and the 1964 Viva Johnson campaign had still seen Mexican-Americans in sectional or regional terms, not as a national minority. Bobby did see our issues on a national scale and in so doing helped to change perceptions about Mexican-Americans. If Bobby had been elected president, Mexican-American issues would have received much more attention. Some of us would have had a lot to say about policies and resources.

Despite the tragedy of Bobby's assassination, the campaign in 1968 changed certain things for us. His campaign gave us political experience at the national level. It taught us that, as Mexican-Americans, we could function politically on a national level with other groups. It was a campaign that I'll never forget.

CHAPTER THIRTEEN

Chicano Power

The 1960s also saw the rise of what came to be known as the Chicano movement. This movement, *el movimiento,* was very much a part of the larger and militant temper of the sixties, which witnessed numerous social upheavals including opposition to the Vietnam war, the black civil rights movement, the rise of Black Power, the women's movement, and the hippie counterculture. I couldn't help but relate to the radicalism of the time, but certainly I felt the effects of the Chicano movement most closely.

The movement had different manifestations. One of these was in many respects a much older struggle, but in the sixties it motivated younger activists, who then went on to be involved in other areas. This inspiration came from the farmworkers' struggle, led by César Chávez.

César Chávez and the Farmworkers' Struggle

In the early sixties, in my efforts to build MAPA, I had often visited with César, who was laying the groundwork for a national farmworker organization. We in MAPA shared his vision. By the mid-sixties, César's views had further evolved, and he began to feel that a labor union, not just an interest-group organization, was needed to deal with the plight of farmworkers. We also agreed.

By then, we were already involved in helping Filipino farmworkers in the Coachella Valley. These workers had gone out on strike, led by the Agricultural Workers Organizing Committee (AWOC) of the AFL-CIO, which was headed by Larry Itliong. Hector Abeytia and Ernesto Galarza strongly supported this effort. When the strike spread to the San Joaquin Valley, AWOC led the way, organizing not only Filipinos but Mexicans as well.*

We provided support right off the bat. We talked to the workers at the big DiGiorgio farm, and they told us they were all for the strike, the *huelga*. César was not totally sold on whether the workers really wanted to strike, whether they were serious. We kept telling him, "Yes, César, the people are serious. They want to strike."

His position was, "Well, we've got to be sure. Let's not pull them out on a wild goose chase." He finally was reassured, and in September of 1965, everybody went out on strike at DiGiorgio. As the strike spread to vineyards and farms throughout the Delano area, it became the largest and most solid strike in U.S. agricultural history, focusing on the grape industry.†

Through MAPA, we helped the farmworkers in various ways. We collected food for the strikers. We sent some of our people—such as Jimmy Delgadillo, Herman Gallegos, and myself—to Delano, the main center of the strike, as organizers. Many of the MAPA chapters throughout the state worked on the picket lines when the national boycott of grapes began. We also raised money for the union, and we put pressure on politicians such as Governor Brown to support the farmworkers.

---

*When AWOC members went out on strike protesting low pay in the San Joaquin fields in September 1965, they were joined by the National Farm Workers Association, an organization started by Chávez, who had left CSO in 1962. The following year, the NFWA merged with AWOC to form the United Farm Workers Organizing Committee, AFL-CIO.

†The Delano strike lasted from 1965 to 1970. It involved thousands of farmworkers and thousands of urban supporters who participated in boycotting grapes and picketing supermarkets. The key issue in the strike was having the union recognized as a collective bargaining agent for farmworkers. The strike succeeded in achieving union recognition with various growers and in improving wages and working conditions. Into the 1970s, however, as a result of fierce competition from the Teamsters Union as well as renewed recalcitrance on the part of growers, the union (now the United Farm Workers of America) began to lose contracts and members. Nevertheless, despite setbacks, Chávez and the union had accomplished what had never before been achieved: collective bargaining and improved labor conditions for farmworkers.

Ed Quevedo and I personally spoke at various support rallies. Like other speakers at these events, we focused on the injustices that the farmworkers had suffered for so many years and the need for new policies and programs to rectify these problems. The most immediate issue was the boycott. MAPA unconditionally endorsed the farmworkers' cause. It inspired and energized us.

We were particularly inspired by the leadership of César Chávez. The César I came to know in the 1960s, unlike the young César I had known in the 1950s, was a much more experienced man, a much better leader, much more resourceful, and more knowledgeable. He saw the farmworkers' struggle not in regional terms but in national ones. He understood that it would have to be national in order to win, because the growers were tied in to multinational companies all over the world. César still exhibited some of the earlier Alinsky influence, and some of his key advisors, such as Fred Ross, were Alinsky disciples. But César by now also had a firm hold on his own ideas, what he wanted to do, and how he wanted to do it.

The farmworkers' struggle in the sixties had a dual character, which César artfully shaped. It was a labor battle, but it also had the dimensions of a mass community involvement. The labor conflict was combined with the characteristics of a nationalist ethnic movement on the part of *mexicanos*. The strikes were something that *mexicanos* had to do and were doing themselves. *Mexicanos* stood to gain in this struggle, and therefore it was singled out as part of a history of *mexicano* struggles.

At the same time, however, the *huelga* reached out and moved a lot of Anglos and people of all races. Numerous people supported the strike and the boycott because they understood the contradiction involved when the workers who harvest the food of the country don't have enough money to enjoy the fruits of their own harvest.

César understood these different dimensions of the strike and politically capitalized on them as a way of drawing support from a variety of people who saw in the struggle something pertinent to them. He always reminded us that there was a lot of support out there and that we just had to learn how to get it. He believed that people would react very honestly and fervently if only we would take our message out to them. César was very competent and resourceful in being able to do that. That's why he fasted and did all these things that some people thought were crazy. He wanted to attract attention to the issue and keep it before the public.

Although efforts to organize farmworkers had been made as early as the 1930s, the organizing drive in the 1960s proved to be more successful, and it attracted national and international attention. For one thing, it was tied to the whole question of justice in America, which was so much a part of the social movements in that period—whether related to blacks, women, or young people fighting against the war in Vietnam. All of these movements, including the farmworkers', seemed to come together and to reinforce one another. A second factor was the nationalism of the farmworkers' movement, which was centered around the rights and demands of *mexicanos*. This complemented the stress on ethnic nationalism and ethnic revival in the sixties.

What was important about the farmworkers' ethnic nationalism was that it was not sectarian. As nationalism, it recognized the suffering of a particular ethnic group and demanded that we had to be true to the needs of that ethnic group. Hence it employed all the trappings of a *mexicano* national movement: the symbols of the Virgin of Guadalupe, the Mexican flag, Emiliano Zapata and Pancho Villa, the songs, the colors, the eagle—all that became a movement. Yet César also understood that this nationalism had to be guarded and that he had to reach out to many other groups in order to sustain the struggle. It was ethnic nationalism, but it was interpreted through César's earlier experiences and consciousness, which reflected a broader and more class-based approach.

I never had any major differences with César's leadership during the early years of the farmworkers' struggle. I thought he was doing an excellent job. I considered him very competent, and brilliant in many ways. He had a lot of insight and was not afraid to stand up against so-called better and more experienced advisors who were always trying to tell him what to do.

While I didn't have any problems with César, I did have some with the people around him, who were rather proprietary. Some of his advisors came from the outside, from other organizations. They knew that César had a lot of influence, a lot of power; and they wanted to share in that by sealing him off from others. We in MAPA didn't see ourselves as trying to hog or capture any of that power. We felt that the farmworkers had earned the right to determine the course of their own struggle. I was happy to see farmworkers looked upon as strong rather than weak for once in their lives.

Later in the 1960s, when I began to organize undocumented immigrants full-time in the Hermandad Mexicana Nacional, I did have an important difference with César. This involved his, and the union's, position on the need to apprehend and deport undocumented Mexican immigrants who were being used as scabs by the growers. We differed. The Hermandad believed that organizing undocumented farmworkers was auxiliary to the union's efforts to organize the fields. We supported an open immigration policy, as far as Mexico was concerned, that did not victimize *mexicanos* because they did not have documents. We did not support deportation of people.

At the same time, we understood César's frustration at the collusion between the growers and the Immigration Service that permitted undocumented workers to enter the U.S. as strikebreakers and then allowed them to be exploited by the growers. We always condemned that relationship, even though some of César's staff people didn't appreciate our position.

Some of these people had simplistic answers. They would say, "Well, these people are scabs. They should be kicked out, and no more allowed to enter." What they didn't understand was that many of the undocumented could and should have been organized into the union. Many of the immigrants didn't want to scab. I thought, "Who in the hell are these Anglo advisors to say who is to come in and who isn't?" Some of these young Anglo radicals took the position that Mexicans should not be permitted to come in because Mexican workers would scab and would increase the labor force, thereby lowering wages. They proposed all kinds of economic mistheories about the undocumented.

I sympathized with César, even though I disagreed with him and the union. He had to go along with the AFL-CIO, which was supporting repressive policies against undocumented Mexican immigrants.

Despite our differences with the United Farm Workers, we never had a major confrontation, even though on our side some people on the extreme left tried to provoke it. The Hermandad always supported César and the union. Later, of course, during the 1970s, he came around and supported efforts to pressure the Immigration Service to be more humane in how they treated the undocumented. The union also supported the more positive measures of immigration reform. In turn, the

Hermandad has joined the farmworkers in opposing the importation of contract farm labor from Mexico. In the main, we have agreed on ninety percent of what the farmworkers have done or advocated. The battle, of course, goes on.

Dolores Huerta

Besides César, Dolores Huerta is one of the key leaders of the farmworkers' movement. I've always considered her to be an excellent labor leader. She's very strong, brave, and honest. She is an extremely competent and hard-working organizer. I've seen her lobby tirelessly in both Sacramento and Washington.

Dolores had been a schoolteacher. Then, like César, she became involved with CSO in the 1950s around the Stockton area. During these years, I only vaguely remember Dolores at conferences and conventions. Our paths didn't cross when she was beginning to organize farmworkers, before the union drive in the mid-sixties. Later, she came to some of our MAPA conventions, where she spoke and even criticized us, which we certainly merited at times. Yet she always supported our work and collaborated with us in some of the political campaigns.

Dolores Huerta is certainly part of a line of key female labor organizers, many of whom I have worked with over the years. I think particularly of Luisa Moreno. Yet Dolores and Luisa are also very different types. Dolores is a very active, hands-on organizer. She gets deeply involved in all aspects of organizing—forming picket lines, developing networks, confronting the growers and public officials. She possesses a very solid view of the needs of people and of their struggles. Her style, however, can at times be an abrasive one. She attracts people because she is strong, but she scares away others who see her as abrasive. Of course, Josefina Fierro could also be abrasive and direct, though only when she was confronted in an aggressive or antagonistic manner.

Dolores Huerta is more a pragmatic organizer than an ideologue or strategist. Luisa Moreno, on the other hand, was very ideologically sophisticated. She was a brilliant writer and planner, who was trained as a strategist. Luisa's style was one of persuading people, of being diplomatic. Rather than arguing her ideas as the dominant ones, she got people to think on their own.

Although there are differences between some of the great female organizers I've worked with or known, I think that they all have one common characteristic: They believe in humankind and in the need for people to progress and to have the right to a decent existence. Stemming from that philosophy, these women have always struggled for those in need. That quality distinguishes them from ordinary persons.

Luis Valdez and El Teatro Campesino

Another important figure in the farmworkers' struggle was the young Luis Valdez, who organized the famous El Teatro Campesino, initially as an adjunct of the union. He was an actor, an artist. He was very expressive, articulate, and theatrical. He had quite a flair and did things for their theatrical impact, which was very effective.

As a labor organizer, Luis was less effective. He lacked patience and was always seeking confrontation. He was too young to have developed the skills César had. Although he was from a farmworker's family and had suffered their plight, he hadn't been out there laboring in the vineyards, organizing people and holding them together for weeks, months, and years.

His real contribution to the union was his ability to dramatize the farmworkers' plight—both to the farmworkers themselves and to the larger public. I saw many of the skits El Teatro Campesino performed in the fields. Besides educating and entertaining the workers and their families, the Teatro proved to be an effective weapon in the fight against the growers.

The relationship between Luis and César was pretty close. But, like many theatrical people, Luis developed an egocentric view of the Teatro. At one point, Luis and the Teatro thought that they were leading the union rather than the union leading them. This caused some tension, and the Teatro finally decided to go off on its own. But Luis and the others remained friendly with the union and raised money for the cause. Yet they wanted to be independent; they didn't want to be captive to the union. I respected their desire, because when you're an artist, it's hard to be captive to anybody.*

*El Teatro Campesino used one-act plays (*actos*) to publicize the struggle of the farmworkers. The group toured throughout the United States as well as abroad and received critical artistic acclaim both nationally and internationally. After leaving the union, El Teatro Campesino diversified its productions, which became more

Reies López Tijerina and the Land-Grant Movement

The development of the Chicano movement in the sixties was also strongly influenced by Reies López Tijerina and the land-grant movement in New Mexico. In this struggle, the Hispanos of northern New Mexico, led by ex-preacher Tijerina, were attempting to reclaim communal lands lost years earlier when U.S. commercial interests, supported by the federal government, had penetrated New Mexico to exploit its mining, ranching, and timber resources.

Tijerina's militant movement called attention to this historical injury to Hispanos. Members of this movement, the Alianza, made citizens' arrests of local officials, engaged in violent confrontations, and took over national parks. All this stunned New Mexico, attracted national media coverage, and strongly inspired the urban Chicano community.

MAPA supported Tijerina and the land-grant movement. As crazy as Tijerina appeared in some things, we thought that he was pretty sound in his claim that the U.S. government had not dealt fairly with Hispanos in their land claims. Much of that land was and still is being leased out to oil, uranium, and gas companies, even though it rightfully belongs to the Hispanos and the Native Americans. Neither group, however, has had the political clout to get their lands back.

The unfortunate thing about Tijerina was that, given his earlier Pentecostal training, he seemed to believe that he was a messiah. Consequently, he did a lot of unrealistic things, although he did many positive ones as well. He motivated people, and he called attention to their conditions. But he retained a very narrow religious semi-fanaticism, and I think it hurt him. It created an extremely sectarian leadership.

But we supported him. MAPA sponsored fund-raising tours for Tijerina in California. One statewide tour raised twenty thousand dollars for him. I also went to New Mexico several times to express MAPA's support. We spoke together on several occasions. Tijerina even stayed at my home once during a California trip.

I liked him as an individual. He was a strong, virile, healthy guy. He was from a poor family, and most of his education had been within the

---

elaborate and included more mystical and pre-Columbian themes. While Luis Valdez has remained the director of the Teatro, he has also diversified his work through writing and directing stage productions such as *Zoot Suit* and the popular film *La Bamba*.

fold of the Assembly of God church. He had very little public education. He was a poor man, who had a hard time keeping his family
together financially. Yet he was thrust into the political arena as a result
of his leadership of the land-grant movement, the *mercedes* movement.
He was not really prepared to deal with all these responsibilities and
this attention. He lacked the sophistication of César Chávez or Corky
Gonzales. But I thought Tijerina was an honest man; he didn't mislead
people.

When we talked in my home—and this was when I was still living
in the Bay Area—uppermost in his mind were the lawsuits the Alianza
had filed against the federal government and, of course, the whole fight
to regain the lands. He spoke of the people's right to use the land to
pasture their sheep and cattle, to cut wood, and to farm rather than the
government keeping the land in reserves and then leasing it to private
corporations. He talked to me about his own legal difficulties—he had
been arrested after a 1967 shoot-out at the courthouse in Tierra Amarilla, when the Alianza had made a citizens' arrest of the local sheriff.
I wound up taking Tijerina to San Francisco, where I arranged for
Beverly Axelrod, a liberal activist lawyer, to take his case.

Having been trained as a preacher, Tijerina was quite articulate. He
spoke at various universities, churches, and community settings when
he visited California. He spoke to anybody who would hear him.
People reacted very well to him and to his cause.

One time, I took him on a tour of garage meetings. We organized a
lot of meetings in garages in poorer neighborhoods when we couldn't
rent a hall. We simply asked the people to find a large garage. Tijerina
spoke in one of these garages. He was great with small groups of twenty
or thirty people. He spoke very loudly and with much force and pas-
sion. The *mexicanos* loved it. They might not necessarily have all
agreed with him, but they all contributed money to this ex-preacher.

I always regarded Tijerina as a serious political actor. I think what
happened to this man was that events he helped to ignite got the better
of him—he lost control of what he started. He was persecuted, threatened, and harassed. His every move was watched, and his family was
watched. He couldn't make a decent living. He had to deal with spies
in his group. He was indicted, sentenced, and sent to jail.*

---

*Tijerina was tried in 1968 for the Tierra Amarilla raid. He defended himself
and was found not guilty. However, based on his participation in a 1966 occupation

When he came out of jail, he was a broken man. He went back to the only thing he knew: He started holding revival meetings. He no longer advocated taking the land and instead developed a "Love Thy Neighbor" program. I've lost touch with him over the years, but I understand he's once again trying to resurrect the land-grant movement.

Like Chávez, Tijerina can be categorized as a nationalist. But he was more of an extreme nationalist than César. Tijerina's theory was that "we are a new race—the *mestizo*." This race was formed in 1492, when Columbus encountered the natives of the Americas. Tijerina would say that when the first Spaniard mated with the first Indian maiden, a new race was born, joining the children of the sun with the fathers of Spain. He was very race-oriented.

Tijerina never used the term "cosmic race," which had been coined by the Mexican philosopher José Vasconcelos following the Mexican Revolution to describe the people of Latin America, but both views are similar. I never understood exactly what the "cosmic race" implied. In my opinion, however, it was close to the kind of German racial superiority theory associated with Hitler. In fact, Vasconcelos himself became a fascist. Many Chicanos later considered Vasconcelos and his views of the "cosmic race" as an inspiration. But I recall Vasconcelos as a fascist.

I myself never became reconciled to the idea of a "cosmic race." Are we a superior race? The concept certainly seems to imply that we as Latinos, *mexicanos,* or Chicanos are superior to everyone else. Tijerina seemed to be saying all of this without using the term "cosmic race." He had a definite race theory. He believed that most Anglos were devils, that they had come to the Southwest as thieves in the night, stolen the house, the farm, and the horse of the *mexicano.*

I couldn't accept all this. We're not a superior race. No race is superior to another, despite the exploitation involved. Tijerina had no concept of class; it was all vengeance on his part. It's like the fanatical Israelis and the fanatical Palestinian groups, who believe the only solution is to eliminate each other.

---

of a portion of the Kit Carson National Forest in New Mexico, Tijerina was tried and convicted of two counts of assault in 1967. He lost an appeal of the conviction and served two years in prison.

The Chicano Student Movement

Motivated and inspired by the farmworkers' struggle and by Tijerina's rebellion in New Mexico, Chicano youth, particularly students, in the urban areas commenced their own militant movements in the mid-sixties. I welcomed this youth revival. I thought it was wonderful. But I also knew that it didn't occur out of thin air. Besides being influenced by the farmworkers and Tijerina, the Chicano youth movement, like the general student movement of the 1960s, was built on earlier student ferment that began in the 1950s.

I recall that in the late fifties, when the House Un-American Activities Committee held one of its witch-hunting sessions in San Francisco, the thousands of union workers who protested against the committee were joined by large numbers of students from Berkeley, Stanford, and other Bay Area schools. These students were predominantly Anglos, since few Chicanos attended colleges at that time. But the Anglo student movement was already visible by then.

The students protested against McCarthyite repression on the campuses where certain radical professors were being fired. They advocated freedom of ideas, of association, and of speech. Out of this would later develop the Free Speech Movement at Berkeley. During the Kennedy administration, as the efforts to depose Castro in Cuba accelerated, student groups formed to protest such attacks on the new revolutionary government in Cuba. Of course, the civil rights movement also activated much enthusiasm and support on the campuses. The beginning of the U.S. intervention in Vietnam saw even larger numbers of students organize in protest.

But, as I recall, it was around the issue of U.S. intervention in Latin America during the early 1960s that some Chicano/Latino students on the campuses emerged as protest leaders. These students were very strongly against interference in the internal affairs of Cuba or of Central and South American countries. I remember Froben Lozada at Merritt College in Oakland, along with Peter Camejo—both of whom would later become Trotskyite leaders—becoming active in the student movement. They sometimes appeared on TV, where they focused on Latin American issues.

Some of these early student activists also addressed Spanish-language audiences. They printed Spanish-language leaflets and distributed them throughout the Bay Area. They were later joined by other Chicano/Latino students, as more minority students entered the universities as a result of the protests of the period and through affirmative action programs.

As more Chicanos appeared on campuses, a definite student movement surfaced through new Chicano student organizations such as MECHA, El Movimiento Estudiantil Chicano de Aztlán. This new leadership pushed for further changes, including additional recruitment of Chicano students and faculty as well as Chicano Studies programs and research centers. They worked on community-related issues: police abuse, the problem of high-school dropouts, jobs, and health care.

Gradually, what happened was a fusion between the university students and the young people in the barrios. You saw the formation of groups like the Brown Berets, who were mostly students but worked on barrio issues. By the time of the farmworkers' strike in the latter half of the sixties, this Chicano student/youth movement had developed into the center of what was being generally referred to as the Chicano movement—the rebellion of youth; a new generation that was becoming very nationalistic, wanting to speak Spanish, wanting to recover its roots; and the birth of bilingual newspapers, presses, graphic arts, and all the other characteristics of a cultural nationalistic movement, propelled largely by youth.

This was the generation who resurrected the term "Chicano" as a term of self-identification and ethnic pride. The word "Chicano" was not new; I first heard it in El Paso in the 1920s. It was used by the *gente del barrio,* the people in the barrios, as a term of endearment and as a way of identifying the community and our people. I used it, and you heard it at all social levels; I don't recall my grandmother or my mother objecting to it. Although I early on preferred to simply use the word *"mexicano,"* I did at times say "Chicano," and I can recall the term being used on into the thirties, forties, and fifties.

Its revival in the sixties didn't surprise me, and I thought it was foolish that some Mexican-Americans objected to its use. The fact was that "Chicano" was being used all the time by both activists and nonactivists. On the other hand, I thought it was also foolish when Chicano activists insisted that it was the only appropriate term. It was one of many terms of ethnic identification for Mexicans in the United States, and one had to be sensitive to this diversity.

In looking back to my own youth, I see some fundamental differences between the Chicano youth movement and what could have passed as a youth movement in my day—in the 1930s, for example. The youth movement of the 1930s, both Chicano and non-Chicano, was essentially motivated by the workers' movement to form unions and militant organizations. Chicano youth supported their working-class parents, who were joining the CIO unions and striking for better wages and conditions.

This was not the case in the 1960s. The sixties saw a joining together of college-age youth of all races, seeking a new lifestyle and at the same time combatting some of the atrocities of the time. But unlike the youth of the thirties, who worked with and within the militant CIO unions, the youth of the sixties joined a movement that was largely campus-based. Students worked with civil rights and other community groups, but not with the unions, which the students of the sixties saw and confronted as part of the establishment. The farmworkers' union, of course, was an exception.

Another difference lies in what we mean by being "radical." Certainly the youth of the sixties used much more radical rhetoric to challenge the system. But I'm not convinced that this was in reality more radical than the thirties generation. The difference is that we as youth in the 1930s helped build a powerful workers' movement, which challenged the power structure in a way that the sixties generation did not. Certainly the Chicano youth of the 1960s provided support for César Chávez and the farmworkers, but they did not participate directly in the building of unions as we did.

Labor in the thirties was a very vibrant and militant movement that took on the real power in America, which was found in General Motors, U.S. Steel, and other corporate giants. When we talk of a movement in the thirties—and it involved many young people like myself—we are talking about confronting the very sources of power. The movement of the sixties, on the other hand, was instead confronting the authoritative agencies of the government—the university administrators, the police, the politicians, the FBI, and so forth—that the real corporate powers had put in place. It's one thing to challenge the holders of power, as we did, and another to try to change the government that they control.

In battling the real economic powers in the country, we in the thirties had to contend with the vast resources that the giant corporations threw against us: government, army troops, the national guard, and private armies plus the whole range of media. We had our picket lines broken by a division of thirteen thousand soldiers with bared bayonets when we struck against the aviation industry in Los Angeles. I didn't see that during the sixties.

I saw kids getting beaten up, but there was no focus or organized movement against corporate power in the 1960s. The challenge was to the system in general, but mainly to the manifestations of the system. A lot of the ideologues of the Chicano youth movement of the sixties talked as if they were more militant than the so-called Old Left, but were they really? They talked as if they were the only ones who were for change. But what did they mean by change? To wear a different hairstyle?

The sixties generation had a new religion. They were very nationalistic and adopted the religious tenets of the Aztecs, and they were very anti-gringo. But, in the end, their rebellion was a personal rebellion; they built a movement around those personal likes and dislikes. They didn't understand where the power was. They thought the power was in the cop on the street; they thought the power was in the president of the college.

What was the Chicano anti-war movement about? It was about the draft quotas, which meant that, proportionally, more Mexicans than Anglos were going to Vietnam. But suppose that the government had stopped drafting Mexicans all of a sudden. Where would that anti-war movement have gone? You simply didn't have an organized, ongoing fight against the central elements that controlled society.

This isn't to say that the youth groups of the sixties didn't do some good. I think that they did. The Chicano movement was essentially a movement to rectify the inequities that had characterized Chicano life in the U.S. for years. Chicano nationalism was a product of the efforts to redress basic grievances. Chicanos awakened other youth to become involved in the fight for justice against the schools, the police, and other repressive agencies. But they were not building a movement to change the relationship of forces. Or at least I never heard it expressed in this way.

As long as you don't recognize that the real forces are General Motors and the other big corporations, you can engage in all sorts of things. They don't care. You can fight the police; you can fight for integrated swimming pools and schools. As long as you don't say *this* is the enemy, the corporate powers, and we're going to organize an army of workers to take them head on, then you can do all kinds of things.

Generation Gap

There was definitely a generation gap in the 1960s. The sixties generation, unlike that of the thirties, never understood that they needed to have a strong connection to a base community such as the workers. Part of the problem was that the Chicano generation didn't know its past, especially the past of the Mexican working class. For that matter, they didn't know very much about the working-class history of the United States.

In the thirties, some of us knew that history by working in the unions. We read about the Wobblies, and we heard from those still living about the Pullman strike, the Molly Maguires, the minority struggles. In reading those histories, you weren't just going through pictorial books. You were also going through economic, philosophical, and political evaluations. In learning about the history of early workers' movements, we understood the real struggle before us and what we had to do.

By contrast, when I started to teach Chicano Studies courses in the late 1960s and early 1970s, my students were very unaware of such history. I asked them to read books such as *The Robber Barons* and *Who Rules America?* and *North From Mexico.** In teaching such books, I asked my students, "What's your feeling about what should be done to rectify the imbalance between the robber barons and the people of America?" I got back mostly philosophical answers about the role of the working class. These were for the most part idealistic responses, rooted in a Christian outlook concerning right and wrong.

You might have heard some similar responses in the 1930s, but then

*See Matthew Josephson, *The Robber Barons: The Great American Capitalists, 1861–1901* (New York: Harcourt, Brace, 1934); William G. Domhoff, *Who Rules America?* (Englewoods Cliffs, N.J.: Prentice-Hall, 1967); Carey McWilliams, *North from Mexico: The Spanish-Speaking People of the United States* (Philadelphia: Lippincott, 1948).

you also got many more reactions expressing the understanding that class conflict was at the root of American history. You heard that corporations and the rich had built the economic order so that they could exploit it to the detriment of the workers—and these responses were accompanied by a great deal of outrage. That wasn't necessarily the case in the 1960s. I guess the generation of the sixties was a generation fed and raised on more idealistic principles than mine of the thirties.

What we have to understand is that the generation of the sixties did not go through the crisis of the thirties. Consequently, the kids of the sixties still had a lot of hope. They thought things were going to change in America. They didn't know exactly how, but they figured that they were on the right side and that their views were just. It reminded me of very typical Christian approaches. I think their more idealistic reaction came from the fact that these kids weren't really forced to get out there and dig and scrounge, as their parents had been forced to do. The Chicano students who were in college in the sixties were exceptionally fortunate. Even the kids who were not in college in the sixties were at least working.

But the generation of the thirties went through a different experience. The Mexicans of this period saw starvation. Their parents were uprooted, many deported. They knew what it was to have to share one tomato with others or to have only a loaf of bread for a week. These sufferings made their generation much more materialistic, realistic, and more ready to accept the theory of the struggle of classes. In the 1960s, the class struggle was diffused. The battles were less class-oriented. Some were over how you combed your hair, what clothes you wore, or other more culturally oriented concerns—and not about how one could stay alive.

I remember discussing this very question with Ernesto Galarza, and I'll never forget what he said: "Well, I love the way all the young people are turning on to all these things that we thought they'd never do. But I think that what has happened is that they've missed one very important thing—and that is an understanding of what it takes to really make a living and how to sustain themselves in their country. It's so hard. It has been hard for our people."

Because of such differences, a generation gap did exist in the 1960s. This led to a lot of misunderstandings and tensions between the older leadership in groups such as MAPA and the new student leaders. I remember attending a meeting against the Vietnam war at Belvedere Junior High School. It was sponsored by Professor Ralph Guzmán, who at the time taught at Cal State, Los Angeles. It was a packed audience, and I got up and spoke against the war. One Chicano student also got up and attacked me by asking, "What have you done to resist the war in Vietnam?"

"Well, I'm no longer of draft age, but my son was the first one to burn his draft card in northern California, and I'm sort of proud of that," I replied. But this Chicano youngster wasn't satisfied. He was rebelling against the older leadership.

I recall another incident that this time pitted Chicano students, led by one of their Chicano administrators, against César Chávez and the farmworkers' union. The union was holding a retreat concerning the grape boycott at the Santa Barbara mission. A group of students from the University of California at Santa Barbara attended some of the meetings. The retreat was really a training session for the workers on how to organize picket lines in front of stores and how to develop a support network.

The students sat very quietly. When the session was over, the young Chicano administrator stood up and told the audience that the students wanted to know why César and the union had not consulted with them on organizing the boycott.

"We provide the support at the colleges. We provide the troops. We're asked to join picket lines. We're asked to raise money. But we're never consulted on strategy," this administrator went on. "We're very let down that the union didn't consult with the students and professors."

César got up and responded: "Well, first of all, my feeling is that it's very difficult for us to have that kind of dialogue. We can have a dialogue on how to implement policy after the farmworkers have decided what that policy is going to be—because we're the ones who are working in the fields and suffering bad wages. When we have decided what we want, then we can discuss with other groups whether they want to help us or not. If they want to help us, we can come together. But I don't see how we can bring in outsiders who don't have a stake in the outcome."

The administrator and the students didn't like this, and they attacked César and the rest of us there. They said, "The trouble with you people is that you're old-timers. You can't lead anymore."

Finally César got up and put the students in their place. "We can agree on a number of things," he stated, "but it seems that we can't agree on one thing—and that is that we as farmworkers have the major responsibility for our organization. We're going to have to pay the piper. You guys won't. Maybe you'll go to jail, but you won't pay the piper whether we win or lose. If we take on a grower and we lose, we have to suffer for three or four years before we can take them on again.

"You've already made it. You've already decided that you don't want to be a farmworker. But that's not a choice we have. You want to become something else, and that's good. But that makes you incapable or unfit to come in and vote with us and have an equal voice in deciding what it is we need and want."

Although these kinds of tensions existed, on the whole we in MAPA worked well with the new student and youth activists. We had good relationships with the Brown Berets. We helped them whenever we could.

When the students in East Los Angeles schools walked out in the so-called "blowouts" in the spring of 1968 to protest inferior conditions, we supported the action.* When the county sheriffs started arresting some of the students, a group of us staged a sit-in in the sheriff's office. We sat in all day and into the night. Finally they let the kids go.

I thought that the blowouts dramatically emphasized the issue of inferior education and that the young people had shown good sense and timing. Unfortunately, it didn't last long. We had the blowouts, and then within three or four months the issues were supposedly settled. No permanent level of organization flowed from this conflict. It was, however, a good example of what can happen when people get together and decide to take on the power structure.

---

*The "blowouts" occurred in March 1968. Thousands of junior and senior high school students in East Los Angeles walked out of their schools to protest the unequal education being provided to Mexican-Americans. Some students and supporters were arrested; some were later indicted for conspiracy. The blowouts forced the school board to initiate some improvements, although schooling remained inadequate. The blowouts signaled the commencement of militant actions by a new generation of Chicanos in Los Angeles. See Carlos Muñoz, Jr., *Youth, Identity, Power: The Chicano Movement* (London: Verso, 1989).

Corky Gonzales and the Crusade for Justice

Of all the new leaders who sprang out of the Chicano movement, clearly the one person most closely associated with students and young people was Rodolfo "Corky" Gonzales. Corky headed the Crusade for Justice, which was based in Denver. The Crusade was oriented toward creating a new sense of militant Chicanismo among youth and steering young people toward political action. Although he was somewhat older than the contemporary youth, Corky still personified the new leadership and style of the Chicano movement.

I had a favorable opinion of Corky. I thought that he was able to motivate and inspire young people. He was essentially a youth leader. He had been a boxer, and his whole style, appearance, and approach exuded youth. I think that Corky came to have a pretty good philosophical understanding of what was happening in the country. I came to know him as well as you can know someone without living in the same town. I saw him at many conferences and conventions. He was always very supportive of MAPA and of my later work with immigrants.

I'll never forget the time, during the height of the movement, when I went to Denver because of the problems that were occurring with immigration officials stopping cars on the freeway and arresting Mexicans who didn't have their green cards. At the conference I attended, Corky got up and made a great speech attacking the Immigration Service.

"We're not an organization of immigrants," Corky said of the Crusade. "We deal with people already here, the youth who were born and raised here. But we have to support the immigrants from Mexico because that's where Chicanos came from. That's the source of our race."

He made a hell of a good speech. This was especially impressive because in Colorado and New Mexico many of the local people think that the issue of immigration doesn't affect them. But Corky reminded them that it did. Corky was not provincial; he understood the larger issues.

At the same time, Corky was a strong Chicano nationalist. He was concerned about those who wanted to use the Chicano movement for their own opportunistic ends. He believed that some were exploiting the new Chicano nationalism, using its symbols and culture when they didn't really believe in them. These opportunists would sell their people out when it was convenient and would use nationalism only to accommodate themselves, in colleges and universities and in government and industry. He was very adamant about this; in almost every conversation I had with Corky, he complained about Chicanos who had been with him but who now had good jobs in Washington or in Denver.

Corky was like Tijerina in some ways, but he was more educated and modern than Tijerina. Tijerina's views on social justice came primarily from the Old Testament. He could be sort of anachronistic and even contradictory. Corky, on the other hand, was more consistent in his views and in his strategies. I think that Corky, besides being a nationalist, understood the class struggle. Tijerina did not.

Corky was a militant nationalist, but he wasn't sectarian. He supported the struggles of other racial and ethnic minorities and of the poor; he didn't fight only for Mexicans. Corky was what I would call a modern nationalist. He had a sense that the true nationalist also had to be a universalist. Just because one nation or a group of people, such as Chicanos, is being oppressed, this does not mean that they are the only ones facing such conditions. Chicanos cannot win their freedom until other oppressed peoples and nations are also free.

At his first youth conference in 1969, Corky supported the concept of Aztlán, the mythical nation of the Aztecs in the Southwest, which now had to be recaptured by Chicanos. Aztlán was to be the Chicano nation-state. Corky sponsored the concept of Aztlán, and the Plan de Aztlán that flowed from it,* although I don't know how much stock he actually placed in this belief. I heard him talk about the desirability of regaining Aztlán. But I didn't get the impression that he firmly believed that this would come in his lifetime.

Despite the rhetoric of Aztlán, Corky was a pragmatist and a community organizer. He formed a variety of youth programs, including a

---

*The Plan de Aztlán (El Plan Espiritual de Aztlán, the Spiritual Plan of Aztlán) was drafted at the first National Chicano Youth Liberation Conference, which was held in Denver in March 1969 and which was sponsored by Corky Gonzales and the Crusade for Justice. The Plan was a compilation of resolutions passed by the delegates. The Plan stressed ethnic renewal and pride for Chicanos as well as raising a demand for self-determination for Aztlán—the Chicano homeland. The Plan de Aztlán became a rallying cry for the Chicano movement.

school for children. Many times he would say, "You know, we have to start with children as early as possible in order to build their ethnic and cultural pride as Chicanos, because it's going to be a long struggle. The gringos aren't going to let go easily."

Aztlán and Chicano Nationalism

I understood the nationalist origins for the concept of Aztlán, the need for ethnic self-pride. It reinforces our historical right and presence in the Southwest. Aztlán does for us what the Old Testament does for the Jews. The Jews claim to be the pioneers of both Judaism and Christianity, to be the people of the Book—and, of course, they claim that this supports their right to Palestine. Aztlán, in a way, provides the same sense of historical origins and presence. It reinforces people's confidence in themselves.

As a political strategy, however, I don't think it's a good one. It's not realistic. I think you have to deal with what is. Aztlán suggests a colonized relationship. The theme of colonialism, or internal colonialism, caught the fancy of many Chicano militants. But while a colonial analogy might pertain to an earlier period, such as after the U.S.–Mexican War, the Southwest is no longer a colony in that sense. We can't say, for example, that Los Angeles is a colonial entity. It's very much a part of the main socioeconomic, political, and cultural life of the nation. The same is true of other cities and areas of the Southwest.

If the goal is the reconquest of the Southwest by Mexicans, it can't be the result of an anti-colonial struggle. I don't think that's possible, because those conditions aren't present. A colonial situation is one in which the dominant country, the outsider, controls a large native population with military and economic might but with a small number of colonizers. These are the key characteristics, but they certainly don't apply to the Southwest today, nor did they in the 1960s. That's why an anti-colonial strategy doesn't work for Chicanos. It doesn't take into account the complexity of changed conditions in the Southwest.

I see myself as a Chicano nationalist, but not a total one. I think we can talk about two types of nationalists: the one who says, "We come first, and to hell with the rest"; and the other, like myself, who feels that other national groups are also oppressed throughout the world. They're oppressed by an economic order that is capitalist and imperialist. Consequently, every oppressed national group has to support every other. There is no superior race or national group. I believe in that. I'm that kind of nationalist—not the kind who believes that Mexicans are the best people on earth and that we're superior to blacks, Jews, Native Americans, or other groups. I don't believe in supremacy.

La Raza Unida Party

The Chicano movement also led to the idea of creating an independent Chicano political party—El Partido de La Raza Unida. The actual building of the Partido was carried out by younger Chicanos after the concept was introduced at the 1969 Denver Youth Conference. But we in MAPA had already been moving toward a more independent position with respect to the two-party system, as we became more and more alienated by the policies of the Johnson administration. We agreed with the younger Chicanos that since at least the 1930s the Democratic Party had taken our votes but had returned very little. The Democratic Party was racist, exclusive, and showed very little serious concern for the needs of Spanish-speaking people. The Republicans, of course, were even worse.

Many of us had conceived of the idea of forming a third party at some point. The concept had been broached vaguely at the so-called Raza Unida barrio conference in El Paso in 1967. Consequently, when El Partido actually came to be organized in the late 1960s and early 1970s in Texas, Colorado, New Mexico, California, and elsewhere, I fully supported it.

However, while I supported the idea of an independent Raza Unida party, I disagreed with and was uncomfortable with some of the electoral strategies pursued by El Partido and by certain factions of the party. My basic disagreement was twofold.

First, I felt that key people such as José Angel Gutiérrez, the most successful organizer of El Partido in Texas, did not understand that the party had to employ different electoral strategies in different areas, given the heterogeneity of the Chicano demographic and political situation. In some areas, such as Crystal City, Texas, Chicanos were in a majority. In Crystal City, Gutiérrez was able to put together very successful campaigns that led to Chicanos taking over the political power in that small town. But in other areas, we were only an important minority, not a majority; and in some areas, we were just a small percentage of the total voting population. Gutiérrez seemed to feel that the case of Crystal City could be replicated elsewhere. But it couldn't, and I thought that he displayed a certain lack of political maturity.

The other disagreement I had with the Partido was about building coalitions—specifically, about supporting certain progressive candidates of the Democratic Party. Some of the Partido leadership believed that unless one fully agreed with El Partido, one was a sell-out. Hence, we couldn't support Democratic candidates unless they in turn supported El Partido. I disagreed with that. I believed that the Chicano community needed to exercise various political options, including supporting candidates in the Democratic Party who were willing to work for the interests of the Chicano community.

I thought El Partido's position was too sectarian. El Partido was nowhere near the point where it could compete on equal terms alongside the two main parties. It still had to win the loyalty of the people. We were a small party that had to prove itself by organizing and by showing that we could elect candidates as well as defeat them.

One of the key figures of El Partido was, as I mentioned, José Angel Gutiérrez. We were friends, and I respected him. He was a hard worker, and he had a lot of commitment. I think that he displayed political brilliance in his organizing of the struggles in Crystal City.

But I think that he made the mistake of equating the rest of the country, or at least the rest of the Chicano communities, with Crystal City. This just missed the mark. In Denver, for example, *mexicanos* are not the majority. So Corky Gonzales, running on a straight Raza Unida ticket, could not hope to get elected mayor of Denver. José Angel felt that the party could win everywhere because it had won in Crystal City and other similar small communities in South Texas. But this wasn't the reality elsewhere. This naive and almost infantile attitude on the part of José Angel alienated more veteran politicians such as Corky, who knew better.

While Corky possessed some mistaken ideas, such as his adamant stand against supporting Democratic candidates even if they were progressive, he still showed more experience, maturity, and insight toward Partido politics. After all, Corky had been around longer, and he had had previous political experiences within the Democratic Party in Colorado. What I liked about Corky was that he didn't close off any avenues to developing coalitions with other progressive groups outside the Democratic Party. He was more open to other grassroots groups and less exclusive, although he was committed to building El Partido. He understood that in a place like Denver, El Partido had to develop a less sectarian electoral strategy that would lead to political coalitions with other groups. There was no other way to achieve electoral victory.

Corky was also more of a political progressive than José Angel Gutiérrez. Corky supported all the anti-establishment forces in Mexico, while José Angel supported the dominant PRI, the Partido Revolucionario Mexicano. Given some of the differences between José Angel and Corky—including both their strategies and their personalities—I was not surprised at the tensions that developed between the two and that affected the development of El Partido.

Seeing El Partido as a political education tool and as a way of motivating more Chicanos to get into politics, I and other MAPA members supported the organization of the party in the Los Angeles area. The Hermandad Mexicana Nacional, which I became more involved with in the early 1970s, provided a lot of troops who did house-to-house work during the first important Raza Unida campaign in 1971. That was when Raul Ruiz, a young professor at Cal State Northridge, ran for a seat in the state assembly. Ruiz later ran again, but the best campaign was the first. The people in the barrios enthusiastically worked for one of their own. I think that many *mexicanos* were very happy with Raul's positions and with his candidacy. He won about eight percent of the vote and certainly scared the Democratic Party.

The highlight of the Raza Unida Party was its national convention, which was held in El Paso in September of 1972. Hundreds of Chicanos from all parts of the country attended the first and only national convention of El Partido. Unfortunately, I was unable to attend because of another commitment, but we did send a rather large contingent from the Hermandad.

While I supported the building of El Partido and supported the national convention, I disagreed with the position adopted at El Paso of not endorsing Democrat George McGovern in the presidential race. The argument, supported vehemently by Corky and less so by José Angel, was that there was no basic difference between McGovern and President Richard Nixon, that they were both bad for Chicanos.

I shared some of these concerns and apprehensions, but I disagreed that McGovern and Nixon had no fundamental difference. There was a difference. McGovern, for one thing, opposed the war in Vietnam. McGovern wavered a bit on policies toward minorities, but he certainly was better and more progressive on the issues than Nixon, who was far to the right. Some of us met with McGovern during the campaign, and although we argued with him on various positions, we recognized that he had much better policies than Nixon. Consequently, I believed that we as Chicanos should have supported McGovern and that El Partido should have endorsed him.

Because of these kinds of unrealistic positions—as well as the sharp personal tensions between Gutiérrez and Gonzales, El Partido's two key leaders—I was not surprised that the party declined after the 1972 convention. I knew that building a third party, especially one primarily dominated by Chicanos and built around Chicano issues, was going to be a rough row to hoe. We had a lot of educating to do and a lot of organizing. I'm not saying that it couldn't be done—and it might still be done some day—but it's not going to be easy.

It takes a lot of work and sacrifice, and I had the impression that the young people in the party were not realistic about what it took to run a political campaign. They also didn't have any experience. It wasn't their fault, but when things didn't succeed immediately, many of them became discouraged. One thing I learned from my days with the CIO and my later political experiences is that any labor, political, or community organization takes time and commitment. There are no shortcuts. The young people in El Partido wanted a shortcut to political power, only to learn the hard way that there's no such thing.

The Tom Bradley Campaign

In contrast to some of the romantic strategies of El Partido, a more realistic electoral effort was the 1969 campaign to elect Tom Bradley as mayor of Los Angeles. Bradley was then a city councilman.

Besides building the Hermandad Mexicana, I was also doing a lot of voter registration work around that time. One day, I received a call from Maury Weiner, who was an executive assistant to Bradley. Weiner wanted to meet with me. When we met in his office, he said, "You know, the campaign committee would like you to help run the Spanish-speaking campaign for Bradley."

I went back to my office and discussed the matter with some of my

Hermandad people as well as with MAPA leaders and those with whom I had worked on the Bobby Kennedy campaign. All of them supported my involvement with Bradley and committed themselves to work with me. So I agreed to be one of Tom's campaign managers.

I was enthusiastic about the Bradley campaign because I thought it was very important to elect a nonwhite as mayor of Los Angeles. Both blacks and Mexicans had been largely excluded from effective political representation, and I believed that the time was right to change this. If we elected a black mayor, it would prepare the way to elect *mexicanos* and Latinos as well. I felt that, as Chicanos, we had a vested interest in electing a nonwhite. The Bradley campaign proved to be a coalition of minorities plus the liberal Jewish community and organized labor.

It was a difficult campaign. The incumbent, Sam Yorty, was very strong. He had doled out patronage to many Mexican-Americans on the east side of L.A., and he had done it very effectively. This was old-time machine politics: You scratch my back, and I'll scratch yours. The Yorty campaign also resorted to racism. In the Mexican districts, Yorty campaigners tried to scare *mexicanos* with the threat that blacks were going to burn down East Los Angeles. They suggested that blacks wanted to oust Mexicans from their homes and that, if Bradley was elected, he would appoint only blacks to office and hire only blacks as police.

We countered by working hard and mobilizing our own people. We resurrected much of the campaign organization we had successfully applied to the 1968 Kennedy effort and modified it for Bradley. We countered the racism and the scare tactics by getting Bradley to campaign very heavily in the Mexican barrios. He supported all of our efforts. He went out to Estrada Courts, Pico Gardens, Aliso Village and other neighborhoods, and he campaigned among the *mexicano* poor. Besides targeting specific neighborhoods, we also had Bradley walk the downtown streets where *mexicanos* congregated and shopped.

We went, for example, to North Broadway around five P.M. and leafleted several blocks while Bradley walked the streets shaking hands with people. He entered barber shops and restaurants and said, "My name is Tom Bradley, and I'm running for mayor. I'd sure appreciate it if you would support me." This was very effective. We also had rallies at which I spoke and introduced Bradley.

We further countered the Yorty campaign's racism by debating

Yorty's people on TV, both on KMEX, the Spanish-language station, and on some of the English-language stations. In some of these debates, I took on Yorty's Mexican-American supporters. We debated questions such as, "How does the Spanish-speaking community view the possibility of a black mayor? Do you view him as a threat?" Despite some Mexican-American support for Yorty, we organized even more support for Bradley. Most of the Chicano movement, including groups such as the Brown Berets and the MECHAs, worked for Bradley.

In the election, Bradley lost by a close margin, but he won strongly in the Mexican districts. Later on, we had some tensions with some liberal Jewish groups who felt that Chicanos hadn't done enough to elect Bradley. But, in fact, while we produced a majority vote for him, the largely Jewish west side was more split. Still, it was an exciting campaign that laid the basis for Bradley's subsequent victory as mayor four years later.

CHAPTER FOURTEEN

¡Raza Sí, Guerra No!

One of the major thrusts of the Chicano movement concerned opposition to the Vietnam war. But, as was true for some other issues, the Chicano anti-war movement didn't occur in a vacuum. It was affected by the general anti-war movement in the country and by a heritage of peace mobilization in the United States.

Living in the Bay Area, I was very cognizant of this rich history of opposition to war. As early as the 1950s, peace groups in northern California had mobilized first against U.S. intervention in Korea and later against U.S. policies toward China. These movements arose in reaction to calls for the overthrow of the Chinese Communist government. For example, we had in California at that time Senator William Knowland, who was known as the senator from Formosa (as Taiwan was often called then) because of his support of Chiang Kai-shek and the reactionary Nationalist forces on Formosa.

In the 1950s, the peace groups also reacted to what already was a growing U.S. involvement in Southeast Asia. No sooner had the Korean war ended than the U.S. built up forces in the Philippines and in Southeast Asia. In return for bases, the U.S. propped up corrupt governments in the region. Astute journalists and observers of Asia in this country, such as Anna Louise Strong and Edgar Snow, warned about a possible new war in Southeast Asia. If you followed events and the playing out of U.S. policy, you saw very quickly that the intent was to encircle China with military might. I never believed that the U.S. policy of military intervention in Asia had ended with the Korean war. On the contrary, it intensified into the late 1950s.

Vietnam and MAPA

Unfortunately, this intervention continued after the election of John Kennedy in 1960. Every month, there seemed to be an increase in the U.S. presence in Vietnam and in Southeast Asia. Anyone who was knowledgeable could see that we were heading right into war. Even before President Johnson openly sent combat troops to Vietnam, following the Gulf of Tonkin Resolution in 1964,* I was convinced that the Johnson administration was pro-war.

I supported the beginning of the anti-Vietnam war movement in Berkeley, as the students began to resist U.S. intervention. They protested against the presence of the ROTC and CIA recruiters on the campus. But the anti-war movement, as it unfolded, was not just the students. It also drew in a variety of community-based peace forces, not necessarily all leftists, with many coming from the churches and the nonviolence movements, including the civil rights movement led by Martin Luther King. This combination of students on the campus and various groups in the community created a very powerful movement in the country, and especially in the Bay Area, with its anti-war history.

The rise and growth of the anti-war movement directly affected MAPA. As the war escalated and the protests grew, MAPA, like the rest of the country, was split between administration supporters and those of us who opposed the war. In 1966, MAPA's state executive board voted to condemn the war. However, those who opposed the resolution rallied the next day and joined members of the conservative American GI Forum in lobbying against the resolution.

*Following an incident in which North Vietnamese gunboats allegedly fired on U.S. ships in the Gulf of Tonkin in August 1964, President Johnson requested and received a joint resolution of the U.S. Congress—the Gulf of Tonkin resolution—authorizing the president to use any measures, including the use of combat forces, to repel North Vietnamese attacks. Johnson had insisted that these gunboat attacks off the coast of North Vietnam had occurred in international waters. Subsequent disclosures, years later, revealed that the American ships had penetrated North Vietnamese waters.

They made impassioned pleas, arguing that as long as the U.S. was involved in Vietnam, we had to support young Chicano men in the military by supporting Johnson's policies. Many of them cried and urged us to be patriotic and not abandon our young men. As a concession to these members, the board voted to put aside the resolution until a policy could be adopted that would not in any way show disdain for the need to support Mexican-Americans in the armed forces.

Still, MAPA in the next couple of years saw a growing anti-war sentiment. Many of us supported those young people, including my own son David, who refused the draft and burned their draft cards. At our 1967 convention, the Brown Berets and other community groups who were against the war picketed us on the war issue. A resolution condemning the war was introduced, but it failed by one vote. By the same token, a resolution supporting the war also failed.

All this didn't necessarily mean that a majority or even a strong minority of MAPA members endorsed the war. But it did mean that many were reluctant to condemn the war because of the argument that we couldn't abandon our boys. Yet one year later, in 1968, an anti-war resolution was finally adopted. The reason for this change had to do with the increasing casualties from the war. More and more Chicanos were coming back in body bags.

One tragic case involved the body of a young man named Ricardo Vásquez. No one knew whether there was a family to claim the body; he was just a body with the name Ricardo Vásquez. All they knew was that he had enlisted or been drafted from the Stockton area. It was a very sad situation. They finally found a brother-in-law, who came to San Francisco to claim the body. He asked some of us in MAPA to accompany him. We did, and we learned that Ricardo Vásquez had been the son of a farmworker. He had been born in a tomato field and had never had a decent education. His mother had died when he was about four years old. This tragic story only served to emphasize the number of young Chicanos who were dying. By the time of our next convention, in 1968, there was no question that we would succeed in condemning the war.

In northern California, most MAPA chapters participated in anti-war activities, with the exception of the San Jose chapter, which was controlled largely by members who also belonged to the GI Forum. The chapters in San Francisco, Oakland, Richmond, Hayward, Vallejo, and

Napa—and also chapters in southern California—joined demonstrations and picketed draft boards and induction centers. I personally spoke at many anti-war rallies on campuses such as UCLA, Berkeley, Stanford, the University of San Francisco, and San Francisco State.

I also spoke at one of the huge national moratoriums in Washington, D.C. This was an incredible experience. I was one of sixty-six speakers. The rally went from two in the afternoon to seven in the evening. There was no violence. You could see a solid mass of people all the way from the Capitol to the Washington Monument. Every hotel in town was occupied; you couldn't find a room.

At these anti-war rallies, I emphasized that the Vietnam war was just one more step in carrying out a U.S. imperialist policy in Asia, going back to the conquest of the Philippines in 1898. Since then, the U.S., like England and France, had treated the Asian countries as colonial subjects. But from 1967 on, I, like many others, began to address more and more the human costs of the war. Casualties mounted. Every day in the newspaper you read the names of young Chicanos killed in action. By 1967, the war was without question a major issue for the Chicano community. More and more Chicanos complained about the war.

Of course, as we spoke out against the war, more conservative Mexican-Americans, including some in MAPA, warned that our participation in the anti-poverty programs would be jeopardized if we attacked Johnson's war policies. But that didn't distract most of us. The truth was that many of us were already protesting the cutbacks in the anti-poverty programs and the patronizing way Mexican-Americans were being treated in the running of these programs. I remember Ernesto Galarza clearly warning that Vietnam and the War on Poverty were tied together, that as the U.S. escalated the war in Vietnam it would cut back the War on Poverty. And he was right. Unfortunately, some of the Mexican-American administrators of these poverty programs were timid and never criticized the war, even though it was hurting their efforts.

The National Chicano Anti-War Moratorium

The most significant manifestation of this growing Chicano anti-war movement was the National Chicano Anti-War Moratorium on August 29, 1970, in Los Angeles. Between twenty thousand and thirty thousand people participated in this demonstration, which was brutally suppressed by the police and sheriff's deputies.

Prior to the moratorium, organizers had taken steps to prepare people for the big demonstration. As early as a year before, Chicanos had organized marches and demonstrations in Los Angeles. There was a big march against police brutality through the barrios of East Los Angeles. At these early demonstrations, in which I participated, a lot of people in the barrio cheered us, and many joined the marches.

About three or four months before the national moratorium, organizers staged a type of mini-moratorium in preparation for August 29. All of this was put together by a coalition of Chicano groups under the auspices of the Mexican-American Unity Council. Church people belonged to it, along with the MECHA students, MAPA, and several other groups.

In this mini-moratorium, we distributed thousands of leaflets that focused on some very startling statistics. While Chicanos represented about eight to twelve percent of the population of the Southwest, we were twenty-two percent of the war casualties from the region. We were also about sixteen to eighteen percent of the armed forces. A clear and unfair discrepancy existed between our representation in the population and how we were being used as cannon fodder. Together with blacks, Native Americans, and Asian-Americans, Chicanos and other people of color in the country were damn near half of the casualties and half of the armies.

Publicizing these statistics had a very strong effect in the communities. They helped us to draw a lot of people to this demonstration— maybe five to seven thousand. It was a remarkable demonstration because instead of marching through the main streets of L.A., we went through the internal heart of the East L.A. barrio. The streets were lined with people. Various speakers addressed the rally at Third Street Park, including Professor Juan Gómez-Quiñones from UCLA and MECHA speakers. Abe Tapia and I spoke on behalf of MAPA.

Of course, the police kept tabs on us. Besides the police, there were also FBI agents working through COINTELPRO, a side program of the FBI, which was directed against anti-war people much of the time.*

---

*COINTELPRO, a counterintelligence program secretly run by the FBI, was first established in 1956 as part of the FBI's anti-left and anti-union activities. It

They were there in plainclothes, photographing us with their long lenses. We identified them. But no violence occurred at this demonstration.

The key organizer of the whole moratorium process was a very brilliant young man, Rosalio Muñoz. He had just graduated from UCLA, where he had served as student body president. He was a very good organizer, very bright, extremely enthusiastic, ingenious, and resourceful. I respected him very much. He was not a great speaker, but he definitely was a great organizer. He didn't chair the moratorium working committee, because he was smart enough as an organizer to defer such a position to more prominent community figures. But, in fact, Rosalio was a key figure behind the moratorium.

To build up for the main demonstration on August 29, Rosalio and the moratorium committee sent representatives to different areas of the country to encourage participation. People were sent to El Paso, Albuquerque, Denver, New York, Chicago, and, of course, throughout California. Chicanos and others responded very enthusiastically. We knew it was going to be a big demonstration. We just didn't know how big.

Rubén Salazar

Besides sensing that this might turn into a huge demonstration, we were also very concerned about the possibility of police violence against the moratorium. We felt very uneasy about this. We believed that there was evidence indicating that we should expect provocation from the police.

Our suspicions increased a few days before the moratorium when I got a phone call from Rubén Salazar, the most prominent Mexican-American journalist in the country. He was working for both the *Los Angeles Times* and KMEX, the Spanish-language TV station in L.A. Rubén had been writing and broadcasting strong criticisms of police treatment of *mexicanos*.

---

later was used to destroy civil rights and anti-war groups during the 1960s and early 1970s, employing methods that included harassment of individuals, disruption of organizations, illegal spying, provocation, and violence. Citizen as well as congressional complaints and investigations in the mid-1970s led to exposure of COINTELPRO's illegal activities and to the closing of its operations, at least as a fixed group within the FBI.

Rubén asked to see me at the station. So Chole Alatorre, who was working with me, and I went to KMEX. Rubén wanted to talk to us, but he said, "We have to get out of here." So we left the office and went to a nearby restaurant.

He told us that he had been having some discussions with Chief Ed Davis of the L.A. Police Department, with some of Davis's men, and with people from the county sheriff's office. He also felt disturbed about the presence of the FBI around the moratorium preparations. Although we had assurances from the different police forces that they would allow the demonstration to take place peacefully, Rubén was not convinced. He feared that the police would break up the march and rally.

Rubén was also uneasy about his situation at KMEX. He told us, "I don't feel quite assured that the station officials are really leveling with me and with the moratorium committee when they say they support our aims for a peaceful, nonviolent demonstration. I have some trepidation."

"What is it?" I asked him.

He didn't specifically respond, but said only that he was keeping records of his conversations with the police and his supervisors. Because he thought that his desk at the station was not secure and that he had evidence of someone going through it, he was keeping these files in his car. He didn't feel the same insecurity about the *Times*. "The *Times* has given me carte blanche," he said, "and they have not interfered with my investigations."

Rubén again asked to see us the night before the moratorium. We met at the Century Plaza Hotel, along with attorney Hank López, who had just returned from teaching at Harvard, and Tom Martínez, who at the time was the West Coast director of organization for the National Maritime Union, which was supporting the moratorium.

Rubén came right out and told us that he really feared there was going to be police action against us. He had reason to believe that agent provocateurs had infiltrated both the moratorium committee and the Brown Berets and that we had better be on alert. He believed that the provocateurs would cause incidents to "justify" police repression of the moratorium.

Rubén also said that he knew from some of his sources that top officials in Washington, including President Nixon, were quite concerned about the moratorium, since it would be the first large minority-sponsored demonstration against the war. These officials were very sensitive to this; because minorities were carrying the brunt of fighting the war, the government couldn't afford to lose the support of minority communities. According to Rubén, the word out of Washington was, "What the hell is going on in Los Angeles? Why have officials there allowed things to reach this point?"

Rubén wanted to warn us and to discuss how we might prevent provocations. We informed him that we would have a number of monitors from the MECHA groups as well as from the supporting trade unions. Representatives from the United Auto Workers, headed by Esteban Torres, would be out there helping us. Rubén encouraged us to utilize many of the priests and ministers as monitors, and he suggested that they should be very evident in the crowd, in the hope that their presence might prevent an incident. We discussed all the other possibilities to prevent police action.

Before we left, Rubén told us that he and his TV crew were getting lots of heat from their supervisors about publicizing the moratorium. Rubén just couldn't understand why their own station was making these efforts to intimidate them. "We're out there risking our lives, and they should support us, Bert," he told me. Rubén concluded by telling us that he had all his evidence, including tapes, in his car. "And when this is all over, when it's history, I'll be able to share it with you guys." I next saw Rubén at the moratorium, shortly before the police killed him.

Requiem 29

The next morning as I went to the assembly point at Belvedere Park in East Los Angeles, I noticed thousands of Chicanos gathering for the march. Many from outside L.A. had arrived two days before; others had arrived the night before, and some were still arriving that morning. I was with the MAPA contingent and with the contingent from the Hermandad Mexicana, which we had just formed in Los Angeles to protect undocumented workers.

We assembled at Belvedere Park and marched on Whittier Boulevard all the way to Laguna Park, which is now named Rubén Salazar Park. Along the way, we noticed the strong presence of the police, specifically the county sheriffs. We saw, off the main street, that they had brought in anti-riot water-cannon tanks.

But the mood of the thousands of demonstrators was very upbeat, with a lot of singing. People were there with their families, with their children. Many older people were in evidence. If the demonstrators had planned violence, as would later be alleged, then they had certainly picked a strange place, with so many families and children in attendance.

As we walked into Laguna Park, our contingent went to the east side of the park, across the way from the platform where the entertainment and speeches were to take place. As we settled in, and while thousands were still marching in, I picked up on my transistor radio that the police were beating up on some kids at a liquor store close to the park.

Soon we saw a force of police coming into the park, chasing some of the kids, and beating them. Before the police could move completely into the park, many of the Chicanos began to pelt them with sticks and rocks, defending themselves against this invasion.

I and some of the older people, including Salazar, Professor Rudy Acuña, and Father Antonio Casso, attempted to get between the police and the kids in order to stop the advance of the police and their beating of the young people. We told the kids not to run, not to throw things, and not to answer back to the police. We pleaded with the police to stop beating the kids. The police listened to us and agreed to retreat.

But then, within three or four minutes, they turned around and started moving in to beat more Chicanos. There must have been around fifty or sixty sheriff's deputies, all well-armed with guns and clubs. Outside the park must have been some two or three hundred more cops.

There was no question but that the police had been instructed to break up the rally. We later found out that the sheriffs had an operation post where they were instructing their officers about how and where to proceed. Some of the officers were in battle fatigues, with helmets and gas masks. They were prepared to do battle.

Soon after the police moved in to break up the rally, they shot tear-gas canisters into the crowd. Some of the kids picked up the hot canisters with their bare hands and lobbed them back. But the tear gas got bad, and it drove the people out of the park. Some of us had hoped that we might still be able to salvage the rally by talking to the police and convincing them to back off. But when they began to use tear gas, we knew it was hopeless.

All we could tell the people was, "File out this way, and go out into the street. If you're hurt, knock on people's doors." A lot of people in the crowd were actually given safe haven in nearby homes.

The police kept beating up people and arresting large numbers of them. Patrol cars were everywhere. We learned later that they were even stopping cars that drove off the freeways and appeared to be heading toward Laguna Park and were arresting Chicanos this way. Corky Gonzales and some of the Crusade for Justice people, for example, were arrested in their cars several blocks from the rally.

The whole barrio became a war zone. The use of force by the police was incredible. I saw one Chicano literally get hit on the head with one of the tear-gas canisters. The police arrested Chicanos well into the evening. The use of such force was later justified on the basis that it was the Chicanos who were perpetuating the violence. But that was nonsense. I have no question but that the police deliberately planned to destroy the moratorium.

During the rest of the afternoon, I and others from the moratorium committee spent the time helping those who had been arrested or those who needed medical assistance. We set up an emergency legal aid center to help those arrested. We got some attorneys and law students to bail people out. We directed many to a local medical clinic where we knew the doctor in charge. He was also treating some of the cops who had been hurt. Although later reports described looting on Whittier Boulevard, I never saw any looting, nor did I see any broken windows.

The most tragic personal consequence of that day was the killing of Rubén Salazar. I had seen him at the rally, and we had talked briefly about what to do at the point when the police moved in and started to beat the kids. All this time, Rubén's TV crew had been filming what was going on. At the time, I could have sworn that the cops were deliberately shooting the tear-gas canisters at Rubén's crew as a way of forcing them to stop filming. To this day, I don't believe anyone has ever seen the film that Rubén's crew shot that day. I have no idea what happened to it.

I lost sight of Rubén as we all streamed out of the park. I later heard that, some time afterward, he and his men went to get a beer at the Silver Dollar Cafe on Whittier Boulevard.

I was at one of the neighborhood centers helping the kids who were hurt when someone told me that Danny Villanueva, the manager of

KMEX, was on the phone trying to reach me. When I picked up the phone, I heard Danny weeping.

"Bert, I can't bring myself to tell you, but do you know that Rubén has been shot? And we don't know if he's still alive." This was late afternoon. It wasn't until about midnight that Rosalio Muñoz came and told me that Rubén's body had been found inside the Silver Dollar some hours after a sheriff had shot a tear-gas projectile into the cafe at point-blank range. The missile struck Rubén in the head; he must have died instantly. But the police refused to allow anyone, including themselves, to enter the cafe until sometime later. Rubén's death ended what was a horrible and tragic day. A documentary film later made about the events of August 29, 1970, was appropriately titled *Requiem 29.**

Who Killed Rubén Salazar?

In the days following the moratorium and the killing of Rubén Salazar, the Mexican community in L.A. was aroused and angered. People were particularly upset over Rubén's death and how he had died. What business did that policeman have firing that kind of projectile at that level into a bar? It didn't make sense to anyone. From all the evidence gathered, there was no brawl or disturbance inside the cafe that might have even remotely justified the use of such firepower. It was just senseless, all of this, and the inability of the police to reasonably justify their actions angered the community.

A lot of pressure came to bear on the city, county, and federal authorities to do something. And so a public inquest was held to determine who shot Rubén Salazar and why. People around the moratorium, including myself, organized a committee to coordinate witnesses for the inquest and to alert the community to the inquest's deliberations.

Unfortunately, the inquest degenerated into an attempt by the presiding officer to indict the moratorium as some kind of Communist

---

Requiem 29, a documentary on the August 29th National Chicano Anti-War Moratorium in Los Angeles and the ensuing inquest conducted to investigate the death of Rubén Salazar, was produced in 1970 by Moctesuma Esparza and directed by David García. It won a Bronze Medal at the Atlanta International Film festival in 1971. It is available through the UCLA Media Center.

plot. Rather than probing the actions of the police in breaking up the moratorium, the anger of the police toward Salazar over what they considered his anti-police editorials, and their attack on the Silver Dollar Cafe, the inquest instead largely exonerated the police and condemned the moratorium for perpetuating violence.

It was an utter sham. Equally as bad was the collusion of the media with the police. Despite all our efforts to get the media to report our side of the story, including the role of police provocateurs in these events, the L.A. media ignored us and supported the police side. It was all a whitewash.

Was Rubén Salazar deliberately murdered? He was killed, but how his death came about is open to question. If I were asked whether the officer actually knew of Rubén's presence in the cafe and whether he aimed directly at Rubén, I couldn't say. The curtain through which he shot could have been blown aside by the wind, and then he could have seen who was inside, and he could have known Rubén was there. All of this is conjecture, however. What is clear is that the officer made a premeditated move to shoot into a crowded cafe full of Mexicans. So he intended to kill people who were in there. He knew, as a trained officer, the damage that could be caused by shooting a tear-gas projectile directly into a group of people at close range. And yet he chose to fire.

Was the officer guilty? Yes, he was guilty. When you shoot directly into a group of four or five people or into a building where you know there are people, you're guilty of killing whomever you hit. What's the difference between shooting blindly into a crowded room and shooting into a crowd out in the open daylight?

I believe that in the eyes of the L.A. police force, Rubén Salazar had become a dangerous target. I believe they knew that he had information about police infiltration of our organizations. I believe that the police received orders or advice from the FBI in Washington that led them to plan to break up the moratorium with force and violence. President Nixon at the time was quoted as saying that he recognized that the U.S. intervention in Vietnam no longer had public support in this country when even the Mexicans, who were never known to publicly protest, were out by the thousands protesting the war.

In fact, two weeks after the moratorium, Frank Martínez, who was the vice-president of the Brown Berets, contacted me at the Hermandad office. He said, "I'm in hiding. Where can I see you guys?" I told him to come over to our office. He came and told us, "You guys have to hide me. I was working for the police during the moratorium. I was a paid inside man for them, and I was paid to climb up on one of the poles at the park and raise a gun so that they could photograph it. But they're after me now, and I need your help."

Martínez explained what the police had wanted. They wanted to justify their actions by pointing to the fact that Chicanos at the rally were armed, and they used Martínez for that purpose. But the people didn't have guns, and no police were ever shot. We hid Martínez for about six weeks, and he told us more information about his role as a police informant. We gave the whole story to Tom Brokaw, who was then working at KNBC in Los Angeles, but he failed to use it, or perhaps he was told not to use it.

My belief is that the L.A. Police Department, the sheriff's department, the Secret Service, the FBI, and who knows who else were involved in efforts to put an end to the Chicano moratorium. It was too threatening to U.S. policy in Vietnam and too threatening to the local power structure, which was afraid of the growing militance in the Chicano community. The moratorium had to be destroyed. And it was.

The moratorium was destroyed, but the Chicano anti-war movement was not. Chicanos continued to protest the injustice of the Vietnam war in smaller Chicano-sponsored moratoriums and in the other local, regional, and national demonstrations put on by a broad coalition of forces. Into the early 1970s, until the victory of the Vietnamese insurgents in 1975, I participated in anti-war activities through our newly formed Hermandad Mexicana. The Hermandad was organized to help undocumented Mexican immigrants by providing various legal and social services for them. But we also organized them in protest against the war.

The undocumented immigrants themselves saw the war as an injustice on the part of the U.S. government. Seeing the injustice of U.S. immigration laws and how they themselves were being victimized by the government, the undocumented drew a parallel between their oppression and the oppression of the Vietnamese people as a result of U.S. policies. Moreover, the undocumented immigrants also lived in the same Chicano communities where families were losing their sons to the war, and the immigrants sympathized with the sorrow of these families. They drew another parallel here, between their own oppression as exploited immigrant workers and the oppression of Chicanos who were being used as cannon fodder in the war while most whites escaped the fighting. With this understanding, many immigrants came out and participated in anti-war demonstrations.

CHAPTER FIFTEEN

¡Raza Sí, Migra No!

Although I supported and participated in the Chicano movement, my main interest and involvement at the end of the 1960s continued to be basic community organization—and, in particular, organizing the thousands of undocumented workers from Mexico who were entering the United States. It is a commitment that I'm still involved with into the 1990s.

I moved from the electoral political work I was doing with MAPA to working with the undocumented as a result of my experience in trying to help César Chávez build the farm labor union. Following the assassination of Bobby Kennedy in 1968, I and several others from MAPA went to the Coachella Valley to help César with the strike that he had called to pressure the growers there to accept farm labor unionization.

The strike was a difficult and bitter one. The main problem that the union faced was the growers' ability to recruit undocumented workers from the Mexican side of the border and use them as strikebreakers. This practice was aided and abetted by the Immigration and Naturalization Service. The INS, along with the Border Patrol, looked the other way when these workers were brought across by the growers. Rather than apprehending the undocumented who were here as strikebreakers, these agencies instead harassed undocumented Mexicans who were members of the union. It was a hypocritical policy. But it worked, and it prevented a successful union drive in the valley.

It was understandable, then, why César and other union officials such as Dolores Huerta and Jim Drake developed a very harsh attitude toward all undocumented workers. The union advocated closing the border to keep these people out of the labor force on this side of the border.

We understood César's dilemma but rejected his strategy. We believed that these undocumented farmworkers who were being used to break strikes also had to be organized. Unless we directed ourselves to educate them politically and to organize them, they would always be at the disposal of the growers.

Return to L.A.

Unfortunately, we couldn't win César and the union to our position. But this experience stressed to me that any successful mobilization of Mexican workers, whether in the fields or in the cities, would have to include the thousands of undocumented *mexicanos,* as well as those from Central America, who were flocking into California and other parts of the United States. Some of us who had gone to help César and who had experience with the unions returned to Los Angeles later in 1968, determined to build an organization of immigrant families.

As part of my decision to organize the undocumented, I removed myself from MAPA. It had grown considerably over the 1960s, from nothing to one hundred five chapters. It had fulfilled some of my expectations, but not all—especially with respect to bringing in large blocs of working people, including immigrants. I was also disturbed that, increasingly, middle-class lawyers were coming to be the driving forces inside the chapters.

Here we had a people who were ninety-five percent workers being led by the five percent of lawyers and other professional people. It just didn't make sense. I could see that MAPA was not going to become a mass organization, which I believed it had to become. This was especially critical because of the increasing numbers of Mexican and other Latino immigrants entering the country. MAPA was not fulfilling its great potential.

In order to organize undocumented workers full-time, I decided to relocate my family to Los Angeles from the Bay Area. This wasn't such a major step, because Blanche and I were from L.A. to begin with. In addition, since my involvement with the 1964 Viva Johnson campaign,

I had spent considerable time in southern California. Blanche, who had been working with civil service in Oakland, was able to find work in L.A.

We first rented an apartment on Echandia Street in Boyle Heights. A few years later, around 1972, we bought a home in the Atwater–Silver Lake area. My oldest son, David, enrolled at San Fernando Valley State College (now Cal State University, Northridge). Frank attended Roosevelt High School in East Los Angeles until we enrolled him in Salesian Boys' High School, the Catholic school in Boyle Heights. My daughter, Margo, had married in the early 1960s and was finishing a Ph.D. at the University of Illinois in Urbana.

Undocumented Immigrants

While the issue of undocumented workers in California agriculture had become an important one by the end of the 1960s, it was magnified in cities such as Los Angeles, where the great majority of the undocumented arrived to look for work. They found jobs, ones that were poorly paid and highly exploited, and they also found much hostility and oppression.

By 1969, immigration policy toward Mexicans had become punitive, as the media sensationalized the issue, claiming that the U.S. had lost control of its border and that "hordes" of Mexican "illegal aliens" were crossing, with little to stop them. Consequently, the Immigration Service and the Border Patrol—both referred to as *la migra* by immigrants—stiffened their policies and accelerated the rate of apprehensions and deportations, as they had during the 1930s and during Operation Wetback in 1954.

The INS conducted mass raids in downtown L.A. and in industries suspected of hiring undocumented workers. INS officers would seal off the entrances of a factory or a big apartment complex and force everyone to prove their citizenship or status. Those unable to do so were herded onto buses and taken down to the border, detained in Border Patrol jails, and eventually deported. The INS raided bus stops in the mornings and afternoons when people were going to and coming back from work. In some cases, INS officers broke into homes and, without warrants, arrested people who turned out to be U.S. citizens, sometimes taking them as far south as El Centro in preparation for deportation.

INS and Border Patrol officers claimed, as they still do, that they could detect "illegals" by merely looking at them, by the way they walked, dressed, and talked. There was in fact a near breakdown of civil rights and civil liberties for Spanish-speaking people and for those who looked Spanish-speaking, such as dark-skinned Jews, Native Americans, Italians, and Middle Easterners. All of this was blatantly racist. But it took place all over southern California.

This big movement of undocumented Mexicans resulted from the unequal economic relationship between Mexico and the United States, which was nothing new. This relationship had caused mass migrations of Mexicans to the U.S. since at least the turn of the century. In the late 1960s and into the 1970s, Mexicans crossed the border because the Mexican economy failed to provide adequate employment. The Mexican government claimed that the country had only twelve percent unemployment, which was certainly high. But in reality, almost half of the adult work force was unemployed. The government was counting as employed workers every paper boy, every person who sold chewing gum in the streets, and every man or woman who scrounged for food in the dumps.

All of this was made worse by serious crop failures at the time. Prices fell, and many parts of Mexico went bankrupt. Most of their production was for export to the U.S. and included nonfood items. People couldn't eat the unsold coffee, cotton, and other fibers that were being mass-produced and that had replaced corn and beans.

Although Mexico had increased investments in luxury tourist facilities, these did little to produce the jobs needed for an expanding population. Mexico was not industrializing rapidly enough. Even its historically important mining industry was still backward. Mexico is one of the world's largest producers of copper, but even today it still ships ingots in ninety-eight percent pure form to U.S. smelters and refineries such as those in El Paso and Douglas, Arizona. This hurts Mexico financially, since the price for nonrefined copper is much lower than the price for copper that has been refined. All this created an economic crisis that literally forced *mexicanos* out of their own country.

On the other side, of course, various industries of the Southwest and elsewhere, including agriculture, had always been attracted to cheap Mexican labor. In Los Angeles, the big need for Mexican labor was in small and middle-sized industries, which relied on cheap labor in order to compete nationally and even internationally. These included the garment industry, for example, which traditionally has been characterized by sweatshop conditions. This industry in particular attracted lots of young women workers.

The food service industry in L.A., of course, couldn't operate without access to undocumented Mexican workers. I don't think there's a restaurant in L.A.—even Chinese restaurants—where the cooks, busboys, workers, and dishwashers are not Mexicans. The service industry that maintains and cleans buildings is totally dependent on the undocumented. In the hotels and hospitals, all of the nonskilled service is performed by undocumented workers. This includes old-age homes and convalescent hospitals.

Industrial manufacturers in L.A., such as the plastics and chemical industries, also employed large numbers of the undocumented by the 1970s. Once white and U.S.–born workers learned about the dangers of handling plastics and chemicals, they didn't want any part of this. But the immigrants, not knowing about these dangers, readily accepted these jobs. In fact, one of our organizers, Sara Mariscal, later died of a form of liver cancer that has been linked to polyvinyl chloride, a compound used openly in plastics manufacture. In the various foundries in the L.A. area, employers also hired many *mexicanos*. Foundries that make wheels for American and Japanese automobiles today employ a work force that is about ninety percent Mexicans.

All of these are low-paying jobs—the so-called dirty jobs. What transpired in the 1970s was a speedup of the Hispanicization of poverty in America. A greater percentage of the permanently poor are Mexican or Hispanic, and the growing permanent underclass—or a lower working class that has few, if any, opportunities for advancement—is increasingly composed of Hispanics, along with other racial minorities. This transformation began in the late sixties and early seventies with the significant increase in immigration from poor Third World countries to the United States.

La Hermandad Mexicana Nacional

When some of us decided to organize the undocumented in L.A., we were fortunate that we didn't have to reinvent the wheel. We had the advantage of knowing a group out of the San Diego area who had been attempting to do precisely this since the early 1950s. This was La

Hermandad Mexicana Nacional, the Mexican National Brotherhood, led by Phil and Albert Usquiano, two trade union leaders in San Diego. The Hermandad was an organization of Mexican workers who were essentially Spanish-speaking immigrants. The group had chapters in San Diego, National City, Oceanside, and Escondido. The members were, for the most part, members of the Carpenters Union or the Laborers Union.

The Hermandad had been formed in response to efforts by the INS after World War II to cancel the work visas of many Mexicans who were working in the San Diego area but living in Tijuana. In fact, these workers had acquired the right to live in the U.S. as permanent residents, but they had been forced to raise their families on the other side of the border because of housing shortages during and after the war years. The INS threatened not only their jobs but also their hopes of eventually residing in the U.S.

The Hermandad was formed around 1951 to protect their rights, and it succeeded in many cases. During the sixties, the Hermandad in these towns formed strong chapters of MAPA. We knew of the organization and respected its work. Consequently, when I moved back to L.A. to work with the undocumented, we simply extended the Hermandad Mexicana to this area, beginning in 1968. Besides myself as the L.A. area organizer of the Hermandad, other key people who put together the initial base of the organization were Soledad "Chole" Alatorre, who had been organizing Mexican workers in L.A. since the fifties; Juan Mariscal and Estella García, who organized for the United Electrical Workers; and Francisco Amaro and Andy Aguilar.

In Los Angeles, we opened up our first Hermandad office on West Pico near Vermont, which was largely an immigrant area. Our most immediate task was to provide some assistance and protection to the undocumented in the face of the deportation pressures being exerted by the INS and the Border Patrol. We passed out cards and leaflets informing people that we were there to counsel them at no charge regarding their status and offering information about how to protect their rights in the detention and deportation process. People showed a lot of interest. They were not aware that they had rights under the Bill of Rights of the U.S. Constitution. These rights offered protection from arrests without warrants and from arrests for merely looking like a class of people whom the INS and the Border Patrol defined as "illegal."

We informed people that they were protected by the Fifth Amendment and thus did not have to incriminate themselves. We also taught them that, according to the law, they did not have to give any information other than their name and address to the INS or the Border Patrol if they were apprehended. That was it. They didn't have to give any information which could be used to deport them. They had the right to call an attorney and to be released on bail.

The INS, needless to say, became quite upset over our counseling of immigrants. Officials felt that we were impeding their ability to enforce the law and to do their job properly. Up to this time, the policy of the INS had been that people could be deported merely if it was determined that they had entered without an inspection by INS officials. This determination could be made by the apprehending officer or by obtaining an admission from people that they were here without proper inspection. Those who were arrested were given what was called "voluntary departure." In effect, they were not given access to their constitutional rights.

Instead, they were pressured to admit their status. Then they were taken to the border and released to return to Mexico without a hearing or a trial. Out of some seven hundred thousand recorded voluntary departures during the late 1960s and early 1970s, only about one hundred people had been given the right to legal counsel. The rest had been unjustly induced to sign voluntary departures. This is how the INS covered its tracks.

But the methods the INS used to obtain such departures ranged from verbal intimidation to physical threats and actual beatings. They would round up people and put them on a bus to a detention center. On the way, an INS officer would say, "Look, the easiest thing for all of you is not to hire a lawyer or put up bail, but to sign a voluntary departure. Tomorrow morning, you'll be in Tijuana and back here the next day."

With this kind of questionable law enforcement, the INS built up a big record of arrests and voluntary departures. But in very few cases were there valid efforts to determine whether a person had a right to be in the U.S. or not. Voluntary departures and actual deportations caught up people who were U.S. citizens but who had lost their birth certificates, people born in the U.S. but raised in Mexico, those who spoke no English but were legally in the country, and permanent residents who had been legally admitted but who had no papers on them.

To counter these illegal and unjust acts of the INS and the Border

Patrol, we took the federal government to court. We counseled immigrants to request a hearing, in which they were entitled to a lawyer. We requested that copies of appropriate records, such as birth certificates, be given to those people who claimed they had been born here. We won a number of these cases. We appealed any case that we lost, and we usually won, based on facts revealing that people had been improperly or falsely arrested with no proof that they were deportable. Many persons who had been here for years, with immediate family relations who were permanent residents or citizens, found that they could appeal their deportations. We also aided immigrants in processing their applications to normalize their status and to obtain permanent residency.

We felt that we were playing a legitimate adversarial role with regard to the INS, in representing the right of people to stay here or to be given the right to prove that they merited staying here. Our position was that the INS had developed an illegal policy, based on its unproven premise that most of the Spanish-speaking people who walked the streets were deportable and therefore had no rights to constitutional appeals or defenses. We disagreed, and our position was reinforced by countless court cases, including earlier U.S. Supreme Court rulings.

The Supreme Court had ruled that *every* person in the U.S., regardless of citizenship status, is covered and protected by the U.S. Constitution, no matter how they entered the country. Once they're here, they're covered by the Constitution, including the Bill of Rights—especially the Fourth and Fifth amendments, which involve the right to an attorney and the right to a reasonable bail. With the help of our attorneys, we established that the policy of the INS was unconstitutional and a violation of American standards of justice. Unfortunately, this did not halt continued violations and deportations.

As a result of our efforts and our partial success in helping people stave off deportation, the Hermandad grew rapidly. By 1971, we had developed a very large membership in the West Pico area, later known as the Pico-Union area. We attracted people from all over Los Angeles County as well as Orange County. We held meetings every night to inform people of their rights. Our meetings began to overflow, and we had to find larger halls.

By 1972, we had several thousand members and were servicing about sixty thousand immigrants. Besides opening up additional chapters in the greater L.A. area, such as in the San Fernando Valley and East Los

Angeles, we also expanded nationally. One year later, we opened new offices in San Diego, Oakland, San Antonio, Chicago, New York, and Seattle.

The Hermandad was staffed largely by volunteers, many of them members of immigrant families, both men and women. A number of young Chicano students, members of the MECHA groups on campuses, also helped. Other volunteers included social workers, law students, nuns, priests, and pastors. We had no real paid staff. Members of the Hermandad paid fifteen dollars a year, but this came nowhere close to covering the costs of the legal and other services we provided. For this, we counted on volunteer work. If we had money, we divided it to provide for some of our volunteer family assistance, which could range from ten to fifty dollars a week.

The Hermandad was very similar to the earlier Mexican mutual-benefit societies, which were also characteristic of other immigrant groups. Some of the current immigrants had relatives who had arrived earlier, and they knew that such societies had existed to assist immigrants. In these mutual-aid societies, immigrants paid a small fee every week or every pay day. If they suffered any calamity, such as their house burning down or a death in the family, they could secure assistance through their contribution to the society. The societies functioned like insurance companies. They likewise defended immigrants who were unjustly accused of crimes such as murder or theft. These *logias,* or *sociedades de beneficencia mutua,* were often the only means immigrants had to defend themselves and to acquire help. Even though they represented an adaptation to life in the U.S., the societies were not unknown in Mexico; in many small villages, some forms of mutual assistance existed.

We applied this concept of the mutual-benefit society to the Hermandad. We needed and wanted the participation of our members. We needed voluntary services in maintaining our headquarters, gathering food and clothing, and in our public demonstrations against the INS and the Border Patrol. We were an extended family, which looked after the needs of all of its members. All of this kind of assistance we got from our members.

As had been the case in ANMA, our general meetings in the Hermandad were family-based; all family members attended and participated. These were educational meetings where we talked about how the immigration laws were affecting our people, about the policies of the local police agencies, and about housing, schools, and other relevant matters. Our general meetings in each chapter were once a month, on either Saturday night or Sunday afternoon. We also sponsored picnics and potlucks. This social activity was very important because social life for immigrants, outside of the family, was very restricted.

Assistance for Immigrants

Besides assisting immigrants in combatting deportation and in obtaining permanent residency, we helped them in other ways as well. One of their common needs was housing. In addition to the general lack of affordable housing, Mexican immigrants faced a lot of discrimination in finding decent places to live. We discovered that in many areas Mexicans could not rent houses. This led to ghettoization.

Barrios were formed and continue to be formed in this country because of racism in the rental or sale of houses. It's no accident that barrios are formed in the way they are. Mexican people are segregated because they are not able to rent decent housing in better neighborhoods. They are able to rent or buy only where owners have decided that they will cater to the Mexican market. That's how barrios are formed; Mexicans don't form barrios by themselves.

Housing was critical as a result of the heavy influx of immigrants in the late 1960s and early 1970s, not only men but also women and children. Whole families arrived. Widows or women who had been abandoned by their husbands came with their kids. There were few places for them to live. The churches had no facilities.

Consequently, we housed some of them. From housing a few, we went on to offer shelter to more and more. Finally, we rented a big, two-story building to house immigrants. Officially, we had a permit to house forty people, but sometimes we had as many as a hundred. We also provided food, clothing, medical attention, and, of course, help with finding jobs. The number of Mexican immigrants who are homeless is often overlooked in the current concern over homelessness in America.

When people finally did secure housing, we at times had to defend them against eviction. Owners often refused to maintain rental homes in lawful sanitary conditions—they refused to repair leaks in the roofs, broken windows, and leaks in toilets or to get rid of rats and cock-roaches. When tenants came and complained to us, we organized them to withhold their rent until these conditions were improved. The owners then tried to evict the immigrants. But, through legal assistance, we were able to prevent many evictions. To this day, we still aid thousands of people in withholding rent from such landlords.

The Hermandad also assisted immigrant workers by organizing them into unions. We did this because many of the AFL-CIO unions refused to organize undocumented workers. The few exceptions were unions such as the Teamsters, the United Auto Workers, the Long-shoremen's Union, the United Electrical Workers, and the Hotel Employees and Restaurant Employees Union. But the unions in the building trades and the metal trades, as well as the big service unions, would have nothing to do with the undocumented. Their organizers told me that they weren't interested in organizing plants with mostly undocumented workers; they believed that these workers were not organizable, because the INS could come in and threaten them with deportation, and the people would run like quail.

This attitude didn't begin to change until we proved during the 1970s that immigrant workers could organize and win contracts. I think that one of the most important contributions the Hermandad has made has been to prove to the world, to employers, and to unions that immigrant workers are among the most organizable, most militant, and most pro-union members of the work force.

Because some of the unions didn't have enough Spanish-speaking organizers, they couldn't communicate with the workers or write leaflets in Spanish. Unfortunately, this was sometimes true of some of the U.S.–born Latino union people, who couldn't speak Spanish at all, much less the Spanish of the immigrants. But many of our people could. So we talked to the workers outside the plants in the mornings and in the afternoons. We also had Hermandad members who worked inside some of these plants, and they organized internally. The fact was that most of the workers trusted us rather than the regular union organizers.

We were particularly successful in electrical, plastics, and auto parts plants. In this way we helped unions such as the Teamsters, the National Maritime Union, the UAW, and the Longshoremen's Union. Besides asking us for help, these unions put us on the payroll as organizers. Chole Alatorre, for example, worked for several years with the

Teamsters, the UAW, and the Maritime Union. I worked for the UAW and the Maritime Union on and off, but not nearly as long as Chole did.

Some of our unionizing drives led to strikes by the workers. We had some bitter strikes in the plastics industry and in the auto parts plants. We tried to negotiate contracts, but the companies refused. We had no choice but to go on strike. The employers initially thought that they could break the strikes because most of the workers were undocumented. But they found out different.

The threat of the INS coming in didn't scare our people once they were united. Because of the conviction and courage of many undocumented workers, some of these plants were unionized. Besides their trust in us, the workers knew our record of defending immigrants against deportation. They were willing to organize and to go out on strike because they knew that if the employers brought in the INS, the Hermandad would defend them. We gained many new members in the Hermandad as a result of our work with the unions.

CASA

As we grew organizationally, with branches in different parts of the country, we decided to establish separate centers that would be responsible on a day-to-day basis for the legal and social services we provided to immigrants, especially to those who were still trying to regularize their status. These centers would also concentrate on trying to affect immigration policies. The centers became known as CASAs, using an acronym that stood for Centros de Acción Social Autónomo [Centers for Autonomous Social Action].

The Hermandades remained as broad immigrant organizations that continued to build political community among immigrants, but the specific services were directed out of the CASAs. Both the Hermandades and the CASAs had their own separate boards of directors, although some directors sat on both boards; I, for example, served as executive director of both groups. In some communities where CASAs were not formed, the Hermandades provided the various services. There were linkages, but it represented an effort to systemize our large operations.

The CASAs also gave us an opportunity to include many more nonimmigrant volunteers. While the Hermandades were composed predominantly of recent immigrants, including many of the staff volunteers, the CASAs—especially their staffs—were composed of young Chicano professionals, social workers, priests, pastors, nuns, and students. But one could be a member of the Hermandad and CASA at the same time. We established a number of CASAs in southern California as well as in other parts of the country.

Chole Alatorre

In all of these initial activities of the Hermandad, one of the truly indispensable people of our group was Soledad Alatorre, or "Chole," as she is called. Chole comes from an interesting background. She had been born into a large family, mostly women, in the north central Mexican state of San Luis Potosí. Her father was an officer in the Railroad Workers Union, in which he had been active for many years. He was a very strong union man, and he imbued his children with a sense that unions were important for working people.

In the early 1950s, Chole and her husband came to Los Angeles and worked in the garment industry, where employees were traditionally paid low wages, often at piece rates. At one of these plants, which made Rosemary Reid swimsuits for women, Chole became both a supervisor and a model. By coincidence, she was the perfect size required for the models who tried on the suits that came off the assembly lines. Her bosses discovered that they could use Chole as one of their testing models without having to hire an experienced professional model. While this was exploitative, it also gave Chole the ability to move around the plant since she wasn't tied down to a machine. She was also assigned to be a supervisor, which gave her even more leeway in the plant. When the workers, who were all women, began to have problems, Chole talked to them about forming a union. Before they could start a union, however, the company was either sold or moved elsewhere.

Chole then moved on to a pharmaceutical plant being organized by the Teamsters. She became very active in the union and was named a steward and a member of the contract negotiating committee. This gave her direct experience in how unions work in this country, including participating in a strike over the contract negotiations. Later, when this plant also closed down, Chole went on to a nonunion plant, which she soon helped organize for the United Electrical Workers. She continued union work into the 1980s.

I first met Chole when she joined us in supporting César Chávez's organizing work in the fields. She expressed an interest in organizing MAPA chapters, but she was not able to do so because of her union activity.

In 1968 or 1969, a plant that she had organized was struck by the workers, and they stayed out on strike until they won a new contract. In the meantime, the owner called the INS and had thirty-three of the strikers arrested, all of them Mexican women. Chole came to those of us who were organizing the Hermandad and asked us to help her with the apprehended workers, which we did. From this contact, Chole joined the organizing committee of the Hermandad, and she's been active ever since.

Both in the Hermandad and in her continuing work with unions such as the ILWU and the UAW, Chole has been a very successful organizer—possibly one of the best organizers that I have ever known, male or female. She has organized not only women workers but men as well. Chole is brilliant at immediately sizing up a situation and determining what has to be done, whether it involves leading a strike or solving a problem with a worker.

When she organized workers into the union, she also organized them into the Hermandad. She brought into the Hermandad many immigrants who had particular problems that the unions were not well prepared to handle. She traveled to other parts of the country, including New York, to organize chapters of the Hermandad. On several occasions, Chole has attended conferences and meetings of immigrant workers in Europe. She's been an organizer, officer, member of our executive committee, and national codirector of the Hermandad.

What has made Chole an effective organizer has been her ability to relate to workers and to make them feel comfortable with her. She's very friendly and amiable, and she inspires confidence. People believe in her and in her ability to represent them properly. She still gets calls from workers she helped back in the sixties and seventies who no longer are in the unions but who still have some problem they would like Chole to help with. Her main strength has been this very personal contact with the rank and file, as opposed to the union hierarchies.

Another factor has been her total dedication to organizing. She and her husband separated in the 1950s, and they had no children, which meant that domestic obligations did not pose obstacles to her work or limit the time she chose to devote to it. Chole lived with some of her sisters who had migrated from San Luis Potosí, and they helped organize both in the unions and in the Hermandad. Having been originally inspired by their pro-union father, Chole and her sisters together were a ready-made staff and a very effective one.

Because of the leadership of Chole and other women organizers among both women and men, we didn't have any particular problems in the Hermandad over the role of women. We were a service and defense organization, and people were interested in getting those services and in being defended from jail or deportation, regardless of whether this assistance came from men or women.

But there were problems from within the unions. Complaints about Chole and other women were often raised by those male union leaders, both Mexican and Anglo, who wanted to retain their leadership positions and did not want to share them with women. Many of those union leaders were very ineffective in organizing workers. The unions were full of inept men who had inherited their positions rather than really earning them. Many of them had never led a strike or organized workers, so they resented strong leaders, especially women, such as Chole.

But this wasn't the sentiment of the rank-and-file *mexicanos*. They knew that a person as experienced and effective as Chole was better than almost any man. Chole and the other women who worked with the unions and with the Hermandad didn't pay attention to the complaints of some of these union leaders; they just went ahead and organized the workers.

Legislative Battles

One of the major efforts that has involved the Hermandad since the early 1970s has been combatting anti-immigrant legislation, which portrays undocumented immigrants as economic and social threats to American society. Our first battle in the legislative arena came when the California state legislature passed the Dixon Arnett bill in 1971.

Named after a conservative state senator from northern California, the Dixon Arnett bill focused on employer sanctions to deter the hiring of "illegal aliens." Employers who knowingly hired undocumented workers would be subject to fines. One of the problems with this legislation was that now, rather than the state determining whether or not a worker was legally in the U.S., the employer would make that determination. It made employers into immigration officials, which was absurd. If that wasn't bad enough, this piece of state legislation also invaded an area—immigration control—that was the authority of the federal government.

Yet above everything else, from our point of view, what was essentially wrong with Dixon Arnett—and with other, later legislation—was that it was based on the false premise that undocumented Mexican immigrants represent a liability to the U.S. rather than an asset. Instead of understanding the important economic contributions of these hard-working people, this legislation in effect maliciously dismissed them as "scrounges" and "parasites."

You have to see this situation as also emanating from the revisions of U.S. immigration laws that had been made in 1965 and later in the 1970s. These revisions for the first time in history placed a quota on immigration from Mexico and Latin America. Whereas before Mexicans could easily migrate across the border, as they had been doing since the nineteenth century, now immigration from Mexico was restricted to twenty thousand people annually. But this was a ridiculous figure, given the previous levels of Mexican immigration; there was no way that this quota could be enforced.

Given the proximity of Mexico and the long border between the two countries, Mexicans who couldn't fit into the quota began to cross over without documents. This increased the outcry and protests not only from those who perceived this migration as an economic threat to domestic workers but also from others who, in certain cases, represented racist elements who frankly felt that the country shouldn't absorb so many people of color. These people and others conveniently used the undocumented as scapegoats for all the ills of American society, from unemployment to the welfare system to the schools.

Besides these almost neo-Nazi types, there were, unfortunately, many in the labor movement who also supported legislation like the Dixon Arnett bill. These people—including the United Farm Workers union—were not necessarily racist, but they believed that such legislation could combat what they considered unfair labor competition and could force employers to stop discriminating against U.S. workers and undercutting unionization. Consequently, the forces behind Dixon Arnett proved to be strange bedfellows.

Yet Dixon Arnett, rather than actually doing anything about this issue, instead created chaos and confusion. Fearful employers, even before the legislation was enacted, dismissed or refused to hire Mexicans and Latinos if there was any uncertainty about their legal status. This caused discrimination against Mexican and Latino workers, both U.S. citizens and noncitizens. In other cases, unscrupulous employers or foremen used the legislation to blackmail their workers and to exploit them even more by threatening to expose them to authorities.

Our principal reaction to Dixon Arnett was to mobilize popular protests. We organized several marches against the proposed legislation in Los Angeles and other key California cities. We took hundreds of people, including many undocumented workers, to protest in Sacramento. We continued this even after the law was enacted. We also initiated letter-writing campaigns to legislators and to the media, and we met with many legislators. We tried to meet with Senator Dixon Arnett, but he refused. So we distributed literature noting that he was proposing legislation that would affect thousands of people and he wasn't even willing to meet with some of them.

Through the intervention of some priests who were supporting us, we finally met with Arnett. Besides some priests and nuns, we took to the meeting a good sampling of undocumented workers, along with their children. Dixon Arnett became particularly upset when he saw these little children, some of them crawling and some crying. He had never realized the human dimension that he was touching. So he made all kinds of apologies, but he still refused to change his mind on the legislation.

After the Dixon Arnett bill passed, our attorney, Frank Pestana, filed suit in the state courts, charging that the bill was unconstitutional. But even before the courts considered it, the bill was causing a lot of confusion. The bottom line was that the state couldn't enforce the legislation. It simply didn't have the personnel to enforce it. All Governor Ronald Reagan did was issue a notice to employers that they would be fined if they hired "illegal aliens," although this in itself caused much damage. Fortunately, very soon after the bill was enacted, the state Supreme Court ruled it unconstitutional because the enactment and enforcement of immigration laws were reserved for the federal government and not for the states.

What I found to be surprising and disturbing surrounding the Dixon Arnett debate was the level of hysteria and hype this issue generated. It got out of hand and became almost comical and ridiculous. On some radio talk shows, the host and the people who called in blamed every problem imaginable on "illegal aliens." I remember a group called the American Association to Protect Taxpayers, who complained that the long gas lines during the Middle East crisis in 1973 were really caused by "illegal aliens" using up all the gas. Others blamed the immigrants for using up the water when we had droughts, and still others charged that "illegal aliens" were responsible for spreading the Asian flu.

Chief Ed Davis of the L.A. police complained that he couldn't protect citizens from crime because so many of his officers were being used to arrest "illegal aliens." We challenged Chief Davis on this, and he couldn't really back it up with actual data. We reminded him that his department lacked jurisdiction in arresting immigrants and that this was reserved for the INS. Chief Davis then issued an order to the LAPD not to ask people for their immigration papers and not to arrest those who didn't have papers. He also established Operación Estafadores [Operation Swindlers] to prosecute those who were abusing undocumented persons. This was the first and only such program in the country.

One guy, a Dr. Cecil Johnson, who called himself a biological demographer, warned on his TV show that "illegal aliens" were threatening to infect the white human strain in the country. On one of these shows, Rudy Acuña, professor of Chicano Studies at Cal State, Northridge, and I debated Johnson. Johnson always invited a live audience, which generally was conservative and sided with him. On this particular program, he brought in a number of senior citizens.

Dr. Johnson started in on the litany of problems and crimes alleged to be caused by undocumented immigrants. Rudy and I countered all of his arguments. We especially stressed to this audience of senior citizens that undocumented immigrants were hard-working people who, together with their employers, were paying something like fourteen percent of their wages into the Social Security system. This amounted to several billion dollars a year. Yet, since they didn't have permanent-resident status, they couldn't draw on that money. So what was happening was that this money was helping to sustain Social Security, which benefited senior citizens. When we finished our remarks, we got a fantastic ovation—which, frankly, surprised us.

When the question-and-answer period started, one conservative guy stood up and asked Dr. Johnson, "These people—they're eating up all the resources, and don't you think, Dr. Johnson, that they should be deported?"

"Absolutely, they should be deported," responded Johnson. "I would round up railroad cars, and I would load them up and send them back to Mexico."

But instead of responding positively, the senior citizens booed. They had been sold on what Rudy and I had said. In fact, the whole show got pretty hot and heavy, and a few fistfights broke out in the audience between the old-timers. One little old man got up and swung at this big guy. He was so upset, and he said, "You don't know what you're talking about! I'm going to fight you wherever I have to fight you! These are good people. We've got to keep them here in this country, you goddamn fool!"

Because anti-immigrant hysteria was also evident in the newspapers, we met with the editorial boards of the key papers. At the *Los Angeles Times,* we convinced publisher Otis Chandler and the editorial board to drop the term "illegal alien" in their reporting. We stressed that such a term fed the hysteria. We told them that we couldn't understand the *Times* saying that it wanted to relate to the Chicano community and that it regretted the death of Rubén Salazar and at the same time using inflammatory terms such as "illegal aliens." The one reporter who continually used this term was Harry Bernstein, the *Times* labor reporter. We asked Chandler to have Bernstein drop the term, and Chandler did.

From then on, the *Times* actually did some good and sensitive reporting on the plight of the undocumented. On the other hand, the Hearst paper, the *Los Angeles Herald,* refused to listen to us and continued to engage in yellow journalism, employing terms such as "invasion" to describe the entrance of immigrants.

Lobbying in Washington

In the early 1970s, we had to contend with federal legislation that was being proposed to deal with the so-called problem of "illegal aliens."

This legislation, which was almost identical to the Dixon Arnett bill and was equally anti-immigrant, was referred to as the Rodino bill because it was sponsored by Congressman Peter Rodino of New Jersey.

As we had done with Dixon Arnett, we opposed the Rodino bill on several fronts. We expanded our network to include not only other Hermandades and CASAs but various church and welfare groups as well. We had contacts all over the country: in Michigan, Kansas, Missouri, Wisconsin, Minnesota, Indiana, Iowa, New York, Massachusetts, Connecticut, New Jersey, and Maryland as well as throughout the Southwest. All these groups pressured their respective congressional representatives to oppose the Rodino bill. This coalition was formalized into the National Coalition for Fair Immigration Laws and Practices.

We organized mass demonstrations and marches in various cities. In Los Angeles, our marches drew up to fifteen thousand people. This was also one of the few ways to get the attention of the media.

But perhaps the most effective tactic we employed against Rodino was taking contingents of undocumented workers to lobby in Washington, D.C. We would take as many as forty or fifty people on a lobbying trip. We sponsored fund-raisers to pay for the travel costs, or we got individuals to donate certain amounts. The undocumented themselves turned out to be the best spokespersons for their cause. Some of us would translate what they said to the members of Congress and the senators. We did the same thing when we organized press conferences, which we often held in congressional caucus rooms. Supporters such as Congressman Ed Roybal or Henry González from San Antonio arranged this for us.

I remember in particular a meeting with Senator Ted Kennedy. Although a liberal, Kennedy seemed to be waffling on opposing Rodino, because of his strong labor ties. His aides agreed to a meeting and wanted to know how many representatives we would have. Since all of our group was dispersed throughout the Capitol building, we thought that only about eight of our people would be available. However, some in our group either ended their meetings early or had their meetings postponed. In any event, when we went to Kennedy's office, we had about twenty-five people instead of eight. His aides were quite upset, but they arranged for a larger room.

When the senator came in, he was astonished to see such a large contingent. He wanted to know who all these people were. So we introduced each one of our group to him, told him who they were, and where in the U.S. they worked. Kennedy was polite, but you could also see that he was getting upset at the length of the meeting and at the number of people in our delegation.

At one point, he broke in and said, "I can't listen to everybody. You're going to have to have a spokesman. I only have ten minutes." We agreed, but we decided to have a spokesperson from Los Angeles, one from San Diego, one from Arizona, and one from New York. Each had only a couple of minutes.

The first fellow, from L.A., got up and introduced himself again. He spoke very openly and frankly, right at Kennedy, using the familiar Spanish form *"tu"* rather than the more formal but subservient *"usted."* He spoke very loudly and clearly in Spanish, which one of us translated for the senator:

"I don't expect you as a politician to understand our problems. I don't think it's possible for you—an Anglo and a senator and a rich man—to understand the problems of the poor like ourselves. The only thing we want to tell you is that we are in this country not to do harm but to work and produce. Yet instead of getting thanks and recognition, we get low pay, injustice, and persecution."

This fellow set the tone for the other speakers. The next one got up and said to Kennedy, "I come from such and such a place, and I work in the fields picking onions and grapes as well as other crops during the summer. In the fall, I go and work in Oakland. I'm always just one step ahead of the *migra* and one step away from going hungry with my kids.

"That's why I'm here today. This is a country of justice. This is a country where they say that everybody is equal. Well, that's why we've come—to get equality and justice. What we want to know is what you're going to do to help us."

The others came on just as strong. After about an hour and a half, instead of the ten minutes Kennedy wanted, the senator was speechless. He was also getting very red in the face. Finally, he caught himself and said, "I have to answer some of these things. First of all, you people don't know who I am or what I've done. My brothers—"

At that point, one of our guys interrupted: "Don't tell us what your brothers did. They're not here. We're talking to you. What are you going to do about this bill?" They nailed him to the cross.

I've never seen Ted Kennedy so frustrated, flustered, and red. He couldn't keep his composure. He wasn't exactly mad, but he never expected that the immigrants would talk to him like this, that they could express themselves so well and with such conviction. He finally recovered toward the end, and to our delight he said, "Well, I must tell you that I'm going to vote against this bill."

Although they were in the halls of great power, the undocumented workers were not intimidated by this power. Their lobbying experiences gave them an opportunity to talk to those they believed were their enemies. They put together materials in English and Spanish, which they distributed and explained to the members of Congress and their aides.

In all of this, we had a variety of experiences, some good and some bad. We had experiences where a representative or an aide would start shouting and threaten to throw us out of the office. But our people, although polite, persisted and pushed the issue.

Of course, we also had pleasant surprises. We sometimes entered the office of a representative or a senator who was a conservative Republican and yet who, after listening to the undocumented, would express sympathy and support. We learned that on this issue it didn't necessarily matter to which party a person belonged. It didn't matter whether someone had the reputation of being a liberal or a conservative; it wasn't so pat. We learned that we had to approach representatives individually as if they knew very little about the Rodino bill and explain to them, as much as we could, the problems with the legislation.

This is how our people worked. Some of them have continued to serve as informal lobbyists over all these years. In their time, despite their backgrounds, these veterans have become experienced lobbyists. Some of the representatives whom they first knew as freshmen in Congress are now big shots, and our people know them personally. It's been a very positive experience.

Contrary to the idea that immigrants are supposed to find it hard to integrate into the mainstream because of lack of knowledge or lack of will, in fact this is not necessarily the case. It is true that they have not had the opportunities to know as much about how the political system works, and there is definitely a language barrier. But despite these obstacles, undocumented immigrants have learned a great deal about influencing the system. They have formed the nucleus of our efforts to influence national immigration policy. Instead of allowing policies to victimize them, they have actively struggled to control their lives and the policies which affect them.

Both women and men have been part of this process. The many women in our lobbying delegations to Washington over the years have been as outspoken and effective as the men. In some ways, as they tell their stories, they have been more effective. I recall undocumented women who walked the halls of Congress day in and day out. By the third day, they had so many blisters and their feet were so swollen that they couldn't walk with shoes.

Some of the women used to get very emotional when they talked to the representatives and senators. Unlike women in the U.S., women in Latin American societies don't find it embarrassing or extraordinary to cry when making a presentation or a speech. So when these women talked about their lives and their families, they started crying. This would really get to the politicians. They'd say, "Well, now, sit down here; we'll bring you some coffee." They weren't used to such sentimental approaches on an issue. They were used to Anglo women lobbyists, who were hard-nosed on the issues. Our women were not professional lobbyists; they were just human beings.

As more women, including younger Chicana activists, participated in support of the rights of the undocumented, feminism became a very positive influence in our organization. It has made it easier to mobilize women and easier for them to make a contribution. Over the years, women have come to predominate in many of our activities, and they could sustain the organization by themselves. Feminism has not been a divisive issue—on the contrary, it's been a unifying one.

The Young Turks

During the early 1970s, one of the significant developments that particularly affected the CASAs involved the entrance of many young and energetic Chicanos. Some of them, especially a few who would emerge as key leaders, first came to my attention as a result of their participation in the National Committee to Free Los Tres [the Three].

In 1973, three young Mexicans were falsely charged in the shooting of an undercover police narcotics officer. Those three young men, who became known as Los Tres del Barrio, had been working to rid the *mexicano* community of illicit drugs and to expose the corrupt involvement of police officers in drug dealing. The three had worked with community-based groups such as Casa Carnalismo [the House of Brotherhood].

The defense committee that quickly organized to help defend them was known as the National Committee to Free Los Tres, or the Los Tres Committee. During and after the trial of the three young men, who were convicted, some of the Los Tres Committee members became involved with CASA. Of these, the most important were the Rodríguez brothers.

The Rodríguez brothers were part of a large family who had left Mexico and come to Los Angeles. They lived in Aliso Village, in the tenements. The older boys were teenagers when they arrived, and they soon became involved in the Chicano movement. Antonio, for example, participated in the struggle to establish a Chicano Studies department at Cal State, Los Angeles. Another brother, Jacobo, worked with the Brown Berets. A younger brother in high school helped to organize Chicano student groups such as MECHA. Antonio and his sister, Isabel, went on to law school at UCLA and later passed the bar. It was the Rodríguezes who organized Casa Carnalismo, a community rights information organization.

Already activists during the early seventies through their involvement with the Los Tres Committee and Casa Carnalismo, the Rodríguezes gravitated toward working with immigrants. They were especially interested in the CASAs, where they could perform legal and other services for the undocumented. They first worked at the CASA on Pico and Vermont. I developed a good relationship with the Rodríguezes and admired the work they were doing in the community.

The Rodríguezes were joined by many other young Chicano activists who also came out of the student movement. These young people were not interested in the Hermandades, which were dominated by recent immigrants, but in the CASAs, which were composed primarily of young Chicano professionals and students—people like themselves. These young activists were interested not just in providing services to the undocumented but in building a political movement. Many of them were somewhat confused; they didn't know whether they wanted to build a political party or a social movement. But they did know that they couldn't become politically active in the way that they wanted to be by working only with immigrants.

Many of them were children of immigrants, but they had lost the characteristics of immigrants. They were now English-speaking, young

Chicano adults. Many were college students, college graduates, and professionals. They were looking for some political vehicle more commensurate with their own characteristics. They found that in the CASAs, which they believed would provide them with a working-class base that they—as more acculturated, educated, and radicalized individuals—would lead.

They decided that they wanted to see if they could use many of the CASAs throughout the country to form their political movement. They approached me and some of our other people and wanted to know if we had any objections to allowing them to build their movement out of the CASAs. We had several meetings with them, and our position was that we didn't have any objection. In fact, we said, "If you guys want to come here and you want to learn what it took to build this, we'll be very happy to turn this operation over to you." This first involved the CASA on Pico. The fact of the matter was that we already had so much to do in working with the different Hermandades that we couldn't fully operate some of the CASAs.

But the stipulation we gave the young activists was that while they might want to use the CASAs to build their "revolutionary" movement, at the same time they had to continue providing services to the undocumented, had to maintain the files, and had to take over the leases to the buildings. They thought about it and finally agreed to accept our offer. Some of them were elected to our CASA board of directors, and Chole and I continued to work with them, especially on the large number of cases concerning undocumented workers who needed services.

Working out of the CASA in L.A., these Young Turks organized a national network of some of our other CASAs. With their network, they then decided to become almost like a political party. It was to be a vanguard party, a Marxist-Leninist party. They published a newspaper called *Sin Fronteras* [Without Borders].

But the problem was that they could never pull it off. It was unnatural for such a party to be formed out of a social service organization. They were well-intentioned, and I tried to help them as much as I could. I spoke at several of their meetings about how you form political parties. But it was all rolling in the wrong direction.*

---

*FBI records indicate that the FBI maintained periodic surveillance of Corona's activities into the 1960s and 1970s, including surveillance of CASA. An FBI report on CASA, dated November 30, 1972, contains the following note: "Bert Corona, Director of CASA, was an active member of the Communist Party, USA from 1940

What was wrong was that they were trying to substitute the vanguard for the working-class base. Rather than having the Hermandades, for example, be the base, they were trying to make the CASAs the center. It was putting the cart before the horse. They called their effort at such ill-founded organization the Hermandad General de Trabajadores [General Brotherhood of Workers], which was distinct from our Hermandad Mexicana. I warned them that this formula wouldn't work, but they insisted on taking a chance. They saw themselves as a vanguard, but it was a vanguard without a "guard"—without a base!

Perhaps the problem wasn't so much the idea of a vanguard, but more that these young people simply lacked the experience of developing a base. They formed a committee on unionism, and I would explain to them how we had organized in the Longshoremen's Union and in other unions. You had to first bring the workers together and develop leadership among them. But the young people wouldn't listen.

There's no question but that there was a fundamental ideological difference between me and the young people on how you organize the community. It was less a political difference than a tactical one. It was a difference of experience. At their age, they were certainly smarter than I had been at the same age. But we did differ on how you build leadership.

It's been my feeling all of my political life that the principal concern in organization is to build a base of workers and members. Once the workers are organized, they will take care of developing educational networks or consumer movements. If they want to develop a vanguard party, then they will do so. But all this comes after the base is secured and not before. The problems we have recently seen in Eastern Europe with the dissolution of the Communist parties there is that these parties were formed without the adherence of a mass base. I know one thing from my experiences with the CIO, and that is that you first form the base—and, even more important, you develop leadership out of that base, not apart from it.

Although the young people spent a considerable amount of time and energy trying to build a political movement and publishing *Sin Fron-*

to 1945. His 'Brown Power' ideology goes back to the 1950's. Corona is a strong guiding force in the Chicano movement in the Los Angeles area." See the report in Corona's FBI file 100–201342.

teras, some of them also serviced their clients in the CASAs. Despite their inexperience, these young activists were highly idealistic and motivated. In the end, however, they just couldn't do everything. They couldn't operate the service centers while at the same time trying to organize a mass movement and build a revolutionary party.

By 1975, they were encountering all sorts of problems. They couldn't, for example, raise the money to maintain the lease on the big CASA operation on Pico. They had to dispose of some of their assets. They were forced to move and find a more modest place in East Los Angeles. They couldn't get enough volunteers to help with the case load.

As they retrenched, they lost momentum and unity. Worst of all, they lost clients and members of the CASAs. If you lose members, you lose money. The whole thing disintegrated. I hated to see this happen. But it was somewhat predictable. They were being pulled in two directions, and they could never reconcile the two in their hope of becoming a vanguard party. Those of us in the Hermandad, however, were too busy with our operations—organizing workers into the unions and, of course, struggling against all of the anti-immigrant legislation—to salvage the CASAs.

There are some who claim that a major split erupted between the Young Turks in CASA, on the one hand, and myself and the older leadership in the Hermandad, on the other. This is simply not true. Certain tensions existed, but no major ideological or political divisions occurred. I was never, for example, forced to resign from the CASA leadership. We voluntarily turned over some of this work to the young people. In fact, we continued to work with them. Chole and I would meet at least once a month with the Rodríguezes and the others. We worked together in the National Coalition for Fair Immigration Laws and Practices.

The idea of an ideological split is also more complicated. A range of ideological commitment existed among the young people themselves. They were not a monolithic group. Toward the end, they became more dogmatic, but when they first worked in the CASAs, they exhibited more ideological diversity. Besides certain differences among key people such as Antonio Rodríguez, Carlos Vásquez, and Magdalena Mora, there were further differences owing to the presence of CASA members who were *mexicanos* from Mexico and who came out of some of the youth movements there. These included people such as Leon de la Selva and Pepe Medina. I saw all of them as a disparate group, from both sides of the border. Some were closer to the position of the Communist Party, while some were very anti-CP. Others, especially those from Mexico, leaned toward different shades of Trotskyism.

One ideological position developed by the Young Turks which I strongly supported was the concept of *sin fronteras,* the idea of no borders between Mexicans in the U.S. and those in Mexico. Historically and culturally, Mexicans on both sides are really one people, and the great majority compose one class of working people. I think this is especially true along the border area. Anybody in their right mind who looks at the border will readily see that it isn't a border. When I visited Europe, I saw there more stringent borders between Spain and France or between France and Germany. In Eastern Europe, for example, until very recently, it was very difficult to go from Czechoslovakia to Hungary.

By contrast, the border between the U.S. and Mexico has been more fluid and porous. It's not a wall. It's not a rigid thing. People and goods travel back and forth. It's impossible to make it an effective border. Instead, it's essentially one economy, one piece of land. Of course there is a political division, but culturally and economically the area is one. Language, for example, filters back and forth. We influence the Spanish of northern Mexico as well as the habits, manners, values, and traditions of those who live there. Conversely, they do the same to us. The closer you get to the border line, the closer *mexicanos* and Chicanos resemble each other culturally.

The tensions that emerged between the young people working in the CASAs and those of us who were older were less ideological and more concerned with tactics. I remember some young people up in the Bay Area who wanted to be able to make decisions on our board of directors as soon as they became involved. Our position was that intent to work was one thing and actual participation was another. It was very easy for some people to say, "Hey, I want to be a leader; name me to this position." They would be named, and they wouldn't function. What we needed were people who were prepared to volunteer their work and services on a sustained basis. We didn't want political gurus and ideologues. We didn't see these demands as hostile, however; we attributed them more to youthful insistence.

There were some exceptions, people who did prove to be more troublesome. We had some guys who came from Mexico and claimed to be part of the left movement there. In fact, they turned out to be members of a right-wing paramilitary group called the Halcones [the Hawks], who were very active in Mexico during the early seventies in suppressing young populist groups. At some of our meetings, they would say, "Well, it's time now for all of the old people to get up and leave. It's time for the young bloods to take over." But they were only a small minority. Few, if any, listened to them. During this time, of course, we were also faced with police and FBI informers. But this was par for the course. It didn't really affect our operations.

By 1978, more or less, the CASAs had ceased to function. *Sin Fronteras* stopped publication. The CASA movement, if we can call it that, died because it didn't continue to organize families as they came for services. It failed to build that base of support. And not having that base, what could the CASAs depend upon to exist? They had only the good will of the few professionals or semi-professionals who were willing to stay and provide services. It became very difficult for a few attorneys, social workers, and students to support the service centers.

Whether one attributes the problems of the CASAs and the differences that existed between the younger people and the older leadership to ideology or not, it all still centered on different experiences, or lack of experiences, and what this dictated as to the correct strategy to employ. The young people, because of their lack of experience, didn't believe they had to actually build the base. They somehow believed that the workers would come on their own and form the base. They thought the people would be attracted by the political line, by the rhetoric, or by the glamour.

They were wrong. There is no substitute for hard work and persistence. You build one step at a time. One individual at a time. One family at a time. This becomes a mass base if you keep on long enough. The problems the young people encountered were a matter of their not having any experience with mass organizing and—unfortunately, I think—of their unwillingness to learn from what they considered the "old left."

The demise of the CASA movement left many of the young people very disappointed, but most of them learned from this experience. Antonio Rodríguez, for example, is very honest and frank about it. He told me, "I don't know what happened. We just couldn't do it!" To their credit, most of them have remained politically active. Some came back and went to work with us in the Hermandad. After the demise of the CASAs, we didn't have the resources to maintain the centers, although we took over as many of the cases as possible.

Renewed Legislative Battles

Throughout the rest of the 1970s and into the 1980s, we continued to battle repressive immigration legislation in the Congress. During the Carter administration, the basis for new legislation was laid through the work of the Hesburgh Commission, chaired by Father Theodore Hesburgh from Notre Dame. The commission heard testimony from countless experts and collected a mountain of documents. I didn't testify, but we did submit documents.

The recommendations of the Hesburgh Commission, which were transformed into the Carter plan on immigration reform, maintained the earlier call for employer sanctions. They also suggested introducing a national ID or work-permit card and strengthening the Border Patrol and the INS. What was new was the suggestion for an amnesty program for some of the undocumented that would facilitate regularizing their status.

Carter's plan was never fully formulated during his administration. It wasn't until the Reagan administration that specific new legislation was proposed. This was the so-called Simpson-Mazzoli bill, named after Senator Alan Simpson, a Republican, and Congressman Romano Mazzoli, a Democrat, the two co-sponsors of the bill. It would later be referred to as the Simpson-Rodino bill, but it was the same legislation.

We consistently opposed Simpson-Mazzoli on several grounds. We opposed employer sanctions for the same reasons as before. It made employers into quasi–immigration officials, arbitrarily deciding who was documented and who was not. We feared that this would lead to many abuses and possibly discriminate against all "foreign-looking people," including Americans of Mexican descent.

We, of course, also objected to the increases in the Border Patrol and the INS, which in our minds furthered the militarization of these two agencies and aimed at mass arrests and deportation of undocumented workers. We, along with civil libertarians, strongly condemned the proposal for a national ID card. This smacked of totalitarianism and violated the constitutional rights of Americans. We rejected the call for a new *bracero* program, since the previous one had led to many injustices for the workers.

What was more difficult for us was the new provision on amnesty. We didn't object to the concept of providing amnesty for the undocumented so that they would no longer be subject to deportation. But we did object to the restricted version of amnesty in the legislation. It would have covered only a certain percentage of the undocumented and would have mostly omitted the thousands who had come in the recent past.

In all, we believed that the Simpson-Mazzoli bill was a band-aid job that was more repressive than progressive. It didn't deal with the substantive issues rooted in the economic problems in Mexico, which were connected to that country's relationship with the United States. It also didn't deal with another major issue: Since the establishment of immigration quotas for Latin America in the 1960s and 1970s, only twenty thousand Mexicans had been able to legally emigrate to the U.S. on an annual basis. This was a ridiculously low figure, given the larger numbers who had come earlier, plus the reality of Mexico's proximity and interconnection with the United States.

The problems with this quota were further exacerbated by other new policies adopted in the seventies that made it more difficult for legally documented immigrants to bring in other close family members. The Eilberg Law of 1976, for example, denied permanent residency to parents of minor U.S.–born children. The lack of a reasonable family reunification policy only led to more undocumented immigration.

For all these reasons, we fought and lobbied against the Simpson-Mazzoli bill. We helped to create a coalition against the legislation, including groups such as the American Civil Liberties Union, various public welfare groups, the National Lawyers Guild, the American Immigrant Lawyers Association, the U.S. Catholic Conference, the National Coalition for Fair Immigration Laws and Practices, the National Council of Churches, and the National Conference of Catholic Bishops. Key Latino groups in the coalition were MAPA, LULAC, and the National Council of La Raza. This coalition was able to successfully defeat Simpson-Mazzoli in 1982 and 1984.

However, by 1986, our coalition had fallen apart. It had been hard to maintain momentum. The critical issue was the liberalization of the amnesty program to include more immigrants. At first, amnesty was to be applied only to those who had come to the U.S. before January 1, 1980. Then it was extended to cover those who had entered without documents before January 1, 1982. This new date still excluded thousands, but some in our coalition, such as the church groups and the National Council of La Raza, believed that this was better than nothing, and they supported the revised legislation, now the Simpson-Rodino bill. We lost by a few votes, and Congress passed the Immigration Reform and Control Act of 1986, which included employer sanctions.

Since the passage of the 1986 law, significant problems have manifested themselves. As we predicted, the bill has not done what it purported to do. It hasn't decreased the flow of people coming from Mexico, and it has further complicated conditions for many on this side of the border. The only positive aspect is that it has better positioned some three million of the undocumented to regularize their status.

Nevertheless, the amnesty program contains major obstacles. To begin with, it does nothing about those who have come since 1982 and who continue to live and work in fear of being deported, all the while contributing to the economy. But even those who qualify for amnesty face complications. The bill also requires them to prove that they will not be a financial burden. The INS has misinterpreted this provision to mean that anyone on welfare or anyone who has applied for welfare is not eligible. Despite the fact that the bill says nothing about being on welfare, this misinterpretation discouraged many from applying.

Other misinterpretations by the INS involved individuals who had initially entered the country legally on business or student visas, but who then remained when their permits expired. The INS claimed that these people were ineligible for amnesty because they had first entered legally and hence were not covered by the new legislation. In fact, the law doesn't exclude them.

In general, many who might have qualified didn't apply for amnesty because they were poorly informed, not only by the INS but also by lawyers or church groups who themselves were confused about the law. To remedy some of these conditions, the Hermandad filed several suits that called on the INS to accept late applications for amnesty when the delay was the result of people being ill informed. Fortunately, the courts responded favorably, but I believe the damage had already been done. We were able to recontact a small portion of the people who had earlier been discouraged, but many others returned to Mexico or continued an underground existence even though they were eligible for amnesty.

Even for those who can prove that they entered the country before January 1, 1982, other problems remain. Once they pass their first test, they are then called on to prove that they are learning English and American civics. They must either pass an exam or prove that they are satisfactorily passing a course of at least forty hours of instruction. But this has confused many and has especially discouraged those who are illiterate. Some just don't have time to attend these classes because their work hours are prohibitive; many of the undocumented often work more than eight hours a day, and many work at two jobs. For mothers, it means having to hire someone to take care of their children while they attend these classes, and some can't afford this expense. And, of course, there are simply not enough of these English and civics classes for all who want them.

Finally, the employer sanctions mandated by the law have not worked. The bill has not served, as its proponents claimed it would, to decrease the employment of undocumented workers; more are now employed than ever before. This is because few if any native-born Americans will take these low-paying and highly exploitative jobs. They might take the jobs if employers paid higher wages and made work conditions better, but not under the present circumstances. If you want to get people to do these dirty, dead-end, and dangerous jobs, pay them ten to twelve dollars an hour.

Instead, sanctions have only aided those employers who are predisposed to discriminate against Latinos and other "foreign-looking" groups. Recent investigations reveal that employer sanctions have led to job discrimination against Mexican-Americans and other Latinos by employers who will not hire *any* of these workers rather than risk being investigated or fined.

The Hermandad and Amnesty for the Undocumented

Since passage of the 1986 immigration law, we in the Hermandad have worked to help those who qualified for amnesty to comply with the other provisions, which they have to complete within five years before their status can be regularized. Essentially, this means completing the language and civics qualifications. This is a big job, since about three million people qualified for amnesty.

We, of course, first conducted large campaigns to assist people in applying for amnesty. Since then, we have helped churches, schools, and community-based organizations to open up English classes for the immigrants. We ourselves opened up classes, and in 1989 we probably taught about forty thousand students. In 1990 we reached about fifty thousand. By 1992 we had taught a total of some one hundred sixty thousand.

In these classes, our concern is that the students not only learn survival English but also achieve work-site literacy so that they can be better prepared to enter the economic mainstream and receive job training. We're also helping some of them, as many as we can, to obtain their high school diplomas and to pass their citizenship test.

In our classes, we employ the methods of the progressive Brazilian educator Paulo Freire, who believes in utilizing the circumstances of the poor as teaching tools. Under Freire's method, teachers are not the only persons who possess all of the knowledge. Instead, the people, the students, also have knowledge and can be teachers themselves. Freire's method accepts the great value of human beings and considers people who can't read or write to be just as important as those who are literate.

Using Freire's method in our classes, we teach civics and U.S. history not as dead questions but as living ones. We stress that history is being continually made by people, by the masses of people who struggle to correct injustices and to improve the quality of life for their families. We don't believe that civics, for example, can or should be learned only from memorizing pamphlets and books. We feel that in order to learn civics, people must be involved in the civics process.

And what is the civics process? It's the people, the body politic, confronting those who make policy and who determine how resources are spent. Consequently, we take our students in large numbers to the state capital in Sacramento and to Washington, D.C., to lobby for more funds for these amnesty classes. The time they spend lobbying is counted as part of their time in class. This is how they really learn civics.

We're also providing citizenship instruction for those who have qualified for amnesty. Under the 1986 immigration law, those who qualify for amnesty don't have to become U.S. citizens, but we feel that in the long run citizenship will provide more security and resources for the immigrants. We're trying to get federal and state resources to establish job retraining for immigrants because many of the unskilled jobs they now fill may no longer exist in the future and, of course, are dead-end jobs anyway.

The past twenty years of working on the issue of providing protection for the undocumented have been gratifying ones for me. It has been wonderful to see the immigrants, despite all of the pressures on them, stand up for themselves and their families. They have responded with great honor and courage to the attacks and abuses heaped on them.

It has likewise been gratifying to see the Hermandad grow. Nationwide we have about thirty thousand members, and we service many more thousands. We have centers in various parts of the country and have opened a new leadership training institute in Washington, D.C.

The Hermandad still continues to provide a variety of services to immigrants. We help those who are having problems with the INS. For those immigrants who are trying to bring the rest of their families from Mexico or Central America, we assist in processing their applications. We help to handle consumer-fraud cases, and we have a lot of dealings with the police concerning their treatment of immigrants.

When people have housing problems, the Hermandad offers assistance. We counsel parents about problems their children are having at school, problems with drugs, with AIDS. We help people with their taxes, and we assist workers in obtaining the Social Security funds owed to them when they return to Mexico. These are just some of the services we continue to provide to people who are in this country contributing to its wealth but in turn receiving very little.

CHAPTER SIXTEEN

Pensamientos

I've lived a long time and have been a part of a good deal of history. But my life is not over yet, and I continue *la lucha,* the struggle. The 1990s and the new century ahead of us hold many challenges for Latinos in the United States. To meet these challenges, we need to think about how far we have come, where we are now, and where we want to go. In this last chapter of my *testimonio,* I want to share some *pensamientos*—some thoughts—concerning the past, the present, and the future. Some of these *pensamientos* are personal to me, and some are more public in nature.

My Family

Although my labor, political, and community involvements over all of these years have obviously affected my family life, I am very proud and appreciative of my family. My wife, Blanche, has always supported my commitments, and she has shared these commitments. She has also worked both inside and outside our home to help sustain us economically.

My daughter, Margo, married young, but she completed a Ph.D. in literature at the University of Illinois under Professor Luis Leal, one of the foremost authorities in Mexican and Chicano literature. My older son, David, attended California State University at Northridge. He is married, and, for the last several years, he has had his own business in San Luis Obispo.

My younger son, Frank, despite the slight brain damage he suffered as a young child, courageously overcame much of this retardation. He completed high school, attended community college, and has been responsible for the building of a house for the last few years. Our kids have never been afraid to work.

Our children have also given us grandchildren. We have one grandson from Margo, Baltie, who lives in Chicago. From David, we have two granddaughters, Liza and Clare.

Although none of my children have fully followed in my footsteps, I am certainly not disappointed. I'm very proud of all of them.

What I've done with my life, I've chosen. My life and career are shaped by the particular circumstances that I encountered. But these are unique to me. My children have had other influences and circumstances to contend with. I never told my children what profession or career to pursue. They have been free to choose their own paths.

Even so, in their own way, they have inherited some of my commitment to better people's lives. Margo, for example, has been involved at the university level and in the community in Chicago in assisting undocumented immigrants. Of my children, she's closest to my community involvement. But my son David also worked for a while with the farmworkers' movement, and more recently he's shown an interest in assisting in the education programs for those undocumented immigrants who have little English proficiency.

One thing that I have not been good about with my children has been relating to them the extent of my life experiences. I regret this, because in my own case I greatly benefited from my grandmother teaching me about our family history and about events in Mexico. My grandmother was a wonderful narrator. I, unfortunately, have not been able to do the same with my own children. Whatever they've come to know about my past, they've picked up indirectly. I've never sat down, like my grandmother used to do with me and my brothers and sister, and told my children about my past. This narrative, I suppose, is to help make up for my neglect. Still, I believe that my children appreciate my life and the causes I've been involved with.

Influences on My Life

As I look back on my life, I can single out some key influences. First of all is the memory of my father, who fought for social justice in the Mexican Revolution of 1910 and died for what he believed in. I never knew my father, but who he was and what he did always served as a model for me. His involvement in the Revolution led me years later to read as much as I could about the Mexican Revolution, especially about those who fought on the side of Pancho Villa, as my father did.

Of course, my grandmother and my mother were obviously major influences on my life. Both encouraged me to pursue an education and to read as much as I could. It was important to be informed, they told us. As a youngster, I was an avid reader, and I notice that my kids are also great readers. If you don't read, you don't become aware of many things.

My grandmother and my mother never pushed us to pursue a particular career, and they never expressed any disappointment over my choice to be a labor and community activist. They were proud of my work. Being from the well-to-do classes in Chihuahua, they weren't hungry for social status, and they were not necessarily obsessed with their children becoming lawyers, doctors, or engineers. It was more important that the children learn to be good people.

They stressed commitment to humanity and to leading a good moral life. They deplored any form of exploitation and believed that people should instead conduct themselves in a humane, honest, and responsible manner. One should be a good citizen. I think that my grandmother and my mother did a good job of child-rearing.

An additional aspect of my grandmother's and my mother's influence concerned the role of Protestantism in their lives and in mine. Both of them were against fanaticism. They had encountered it in their own lives in Mexico, when Protestants were persecuted. We had some relatives who were fanatic and rabid Catholics in Mexico. But my grandmother and my mother followed a moderate Christian credo. They weren't given to believe in fetishes, in saints, in idols, in ritual. They were not superstitious. They believed that one should live a truly Christian life—not by worrying about the hereafter but by uplifting one's fellow human beings in this world.

Outside of my family, I was strongly influenced by my encounter in the 1930s with both the CIO labor movement and those leaders such as Luisa Moreno who worked to organize the Spanish-speaking people. These included people such as Josefina Fierro, Ed Quevedo, Frank López, Refugio Martínez, Lloyd Seeliger, Harry Bridges, Ralph Dawson, Elliot Wax, Kendrick Watson, Frank Wilkinson, and many others. Besides their commitment to justice for working people, these individuals taught me how to organize workers and people in the community to stand up against abuses by employers and those in power.

Many different people have served as role models for me; it would be hard to single out only one. I've tried to pattern my life after people who I believed possessed good qualities—for example, both my mother and my grandmother. My father-in-law was also a very hard-working and generous person whom I admired.

Many with whom I have worked have served as role models: people such as César Chávez, Herman Gallegos, Harry Bridges, and John L. Lewis. Then there were the old Wobblies and those from the Longshoremen's Union. I wanted to do the things that they could do. These individuals were impressive to me because I saw them as being successful in their particular life activity. By success, I don't mean that they achieved status and wealth but rather that they comported themselves as honest and committed human beings who cared about the plight of others.

I've had heroes, but I certainly don't consider my own life as heroic. I've not lived in or experienced what I would consider heroic times— times such as those in wars or revolutions, where people have to put their lives on the line to save themselves, their families, and their communities. By comparison, I think my experiences have been relatively quiet. I don't believe that I've had to be heroic to subsist.

I've been asked, "Is there anything about your life that you regret?" My answer is yes. I wish that I had stayed in college longer—not to get any particular professional degree, but to acquire at least a degree in teaching or political science. I think that a college degree would have helped me at times in various circumstances that I found myself in.

I learned how to be an organizer by doing it and by observing how others did it, but I would like to have studied more about organizing in a formal way. When I started my own business as a diamond salesman, I learned all about it without any training. Perhaps if I had studied something about management, I might have done better. Certain parts of my life might have been easier if I had studied more.

Outside of this desire for more formal education, I have absolutely no regrets about what I've done with my life. I wouldn't change my life in any way.

I've also been asked whether I've ever felt discouraged or felt that the struggles I've been engaged in would never reach fruition. But I've never been discouraged or given up hope for positive and progressive social change. I guess this has been so because at a very early age I sensed that life was evolutionary.

I read all of Darwin when I was about thirteen or fourteen. Later, when I read or heard about political theory, I understood that if physical life was predicated on evolution, so too was political life. If things are this way today, that's not necessarily the way they're going to be tomorrow. For want of a better expression, I came to believe that "change is the only sure thing in life." My reading of Darwin, however, was not opposed to my later reading of Marx and Lenin on political organization; I saw them as complementary. Both Darwinism and Marxism-Leninism posited change.

In Marxist terms, the evolution of society came as the result of class struggle. Society changed, for example, from a primitive state to tribal organizations and eventually to feudal ones. But in all cases, struggles between competing factions, or what could be construed as forms of classes, were involved. So too with the class struggles under feudalism, which eventually produced capitalism.

The socialist revolutions, beginning with the Russian Revolution of 1917, introduced a new phase of social change. It's true that these later socialist societies obviously did not become the ideal ones envisioned, as witnessed by the recent changes in Eastern Europe and the Soviet Union. However, even here I don't believe that what will appear will be a full reversion to capitalism. Renewed class struggles in these societies will lead to new forms of social arrangements. The workers of East Germany, for example, aren't about to give up easily many of the supports they had under socialism, such as low rents and free education for their children.

I believe that social change comes both gradually and, in some cases, in a rapid manner. My sense of constant change has always kept me from feeling discouraged. It has allowed me to retain a positive outlook. I'm driven by my optimism that in spite of how bad things can get, human beings will work and sacrifice to make things better.

All this, at least for me, is not an academic issue. I've seen positive social change in my life. And I can reach further back in history and recall my grandmother telling me how difficult and repressive life was in Mexico during the mid-nineteenth century. She recalled how stifling education had been under the Catholic church until Benito Juárez came to power in the 1860s, after the overthrow of the French intervention. Juárez secularized and liberalized education. My grandmother related to me how positive change had occurred in Mexico, and I of course have also witnessed it in my life. Only a cynic believes that things can't be changed. And I'm not a cynic.

The Decade of the Hispanic

Some proclaimed the 1980s as the "Decade of the Hispanic." I'm afraid that I was never quite sure what that meant or in whose interest this proclamation was being made. I can't accept the idea that a particular decade belongs to a particular group. I have no problem with the idea that Hispanics or Latinos are going to accelerate their struggle for social change. But it can't and shouldn't be done in isolation from other forces that are also struggling for social justice.

The Decade of the Hispanic in fact turned out to be the institutionalization of a number of so-called Hispanic issues, such as education. By this I mean that in the 1980s the more independent and militant movements for educational equity and desegregation came to be channeled through more institutionalized and—by their nature—more conservative public and private agencies.

At the university level, we saw the greater institutionalization of Chicano Studies programs. These programs became more and more removed from the community interests which had given rise to them or in whose name the programs had been started. The social problems of the Chicano community were studied more and more, but with less interest in actually realizing social change.

In the end, the Decade of the Hispanic saw little overall improvement for most Hispanics. In fact, many were worse off at the end of the Reagan years than they had been at the beginning, as a result of Reagan policies that reduced resources for the Hispanic communities. For example, by the end of the Reagan years, California was allocating a lower percentage of funding to education, whereas it used to rank at the very top in terms of allocations for education. We saw reductions in health care, fewer hospitals and clinics than we had before. Although more Latinos are working, more find themselves in low-paying jobs. They're not able to meet the needs of their families.

We are simply not keeping up with the needs of our people—and, at the same time, the numbers of Hispanics are growing dramatically because of high birth rates and increased immigration from Mexico, Central America, and the Caribbean. We have actually lost ground in the eighties. This is a result of the cuts in federal, state, and local resources and the greater privatization of the economy; but perhaps it is also because our own efforts at effectively organizing fell short of what they should have been.

All this doesn't discourage me, but it makes me conclude that we've got to take a harder look at what has worked and what hasn't. Yes, it's true that many more Latino-Hispanic organizations are now working within the system and using the system as much as possible. I have no problem with this as long as it doesn't mean that we give up the struggle to effect changes in those policies that harm our communities. What good is it to have a lot of organizations working within the system if the policies that characterize the system remain racist and discriminatory?

The term "Hispanic" is a new one that was introduced in the 1980s. I know that some prefer it, while others reject it. My own view is that it can be a pragmatic and useful term if it is used correctly—that is, when one is trying to be inclusive and refer to all the different types of Latino groups in the country. I think that it's sectarian to speak in national terms about the problems of education and immigration, for example, and to refer only to Mexicans.

On the other hand, when one is discussing the Southwest and states like Texas, I'm against the homogenizing of the particular history and culture of *mexicanos*. Here we should retain our roots and our cultural characteristics as *mexicanos* as well as our ties to Mexico. We shouldn't ever give up calling ourselves Mexicans or Mexican-Americans.

But when we're referring to the nation as a whole, then we have to be sensitive that it includes two or three million Puerto Ricans and two or three million other Central and South Americans. Here we do need a term like "Hispanic." So if one wants to use the term "Hispanic" or "Latino" in this context, it doesn't necessarily ring a negative note in my mind.

Despite the limitations of the Decade of the Hispanic and the sometimes problematic use of the term "Hispanic," I am optimistic that a basis or foundation is being laid for a political coming-together of the different Latino groups. We look alike; we sound alike. We have a color, a language, and a culture that are very similar, even though we may come from different nationalities. We suffer the racism that is practiced in this country by institutions, by government, by the media, by business, and by education. Understanding this, we know what we have in common.

We're also characterized by the conditions of our existence. Economically, we occupy lower levels than whites as a result of racism. We have economic interests in common. The only way to get out from under the difficulties created by racism, marginalization, and injustice is through political means. We must have the power to force changes. We need political power to change policy and to change its implementation.

Latinos are going to get together because of our common position in American society. I believe that more and more Latinos are becoming aware of this situation. This includes a whole range of people, all the way from recent immigrants to those Latinos who have been here for many generations, such as those in New Mexico. I think we're at a point similar to where we were back in 1939 when the National Congress of Spanish-Speaking Peoples was formed, when an express need to unify the Spanish-speaking people in this country was stressed. The dream of this unification hasn't been realized yet, but we're in a better position now to do so than we were fifty years ago.

Actually, when you think about it, fifty years is not a very long time. It's taken the Jews a lot longer to learn how to work in coalitions, and the same is true for black people. We haven't had that long a history, at least not that long a political history within the United States. In a sense, it hasn't taken us that long. It's been a gradual process, but it's been growing in terms of both the number of people involved and the quality.

This doesn't mean that it's been easy. My own political career is a testimony to the difficulties we have faced. We have to remember that we've been a marginalized group; we've been rejected. Therefore we've had to do all of this organizing by ourselves, with our own resources. The system hasn't helped us. The educational system, rather than being a liberating force, has actually damaged us. The schools don't tell us what our history has been, who we are, and who our forebears were. Instead, the schools lie to us continually.

Given such obstacles, I'm surprised that we've moved as fast as we have, relatively speaking. Even with some of the limitations of the 1980s that I've noted, we have still exhibited certain positive political characteristics that are irreversible and that are indicative of greater changes to come.

Latino Empowerment

One of these characteristics is a growing sense of our political and economic power as Latinos. It's a sense that we don't have to take a back seat to any group. It's a sense that we don't have to remain quiet about injustice any longer. We're determined to be heard. You see more and more Latinos fighting cases of discrimination. We're seeing a whole new feeling on the part of Latinos about getting quality education for themselves and for their children. You see it in New York among Puerto Ricans, where they're moving to take over the school system. The same thing is happening in Chicago and in San Francisco, and it's also coming in Los Angeles. More and more Latinos are pressing for political representation.

What is aiding this new consciousness is that, despite the Reagan-Bush cutbacks that have affected Latinos, these administrations as well as those at the state and local levels are making all kinds of political overtures to us. They may not like us, and they might even fear us, but they can't ignore us anymore. This courting of the Latino vote is in turn giving Latinos a greater sense of their power, or their potential power.

Bush, as conservative as he may be, appointed two Latinos to his cabinet. This would have been unheard of ten or fifteen years ago. It doesn't mean that these two cabinet people, or their counterparts in lesser positions, are of the caliber to make dramatic changes. What is important is that they symbolize the pressure exerted by our communities, pressure that the Anglo power structure is responding to. This pressure is coming not only from native-born Latinos but also from immigrants, who are becoming quite active politically on their own behalf. This awareness on the part of immigrants reminds me of the kind of political activity Latino immigrants engaged in back in the 1930s when we were building the CIO unions and El Congreso.

On the issue of Latino political activity and on the prospects for building a successful Latino political coalition, I've been asked how this can happen when you have sharp class differences between Chicanos, on the one hand, who are largely working class, and Cuban-Americans, on the other, who are mostly middle class. What interests do I have in common with these wealthier Cubans? Well, on the surface, not much. Still, it is interesting that, outside of foreign policy issues—especially with regard to Cuba and communism in Latin America—the Cuban-American leadership displays liberal positions on a range of civil rights and economic issues.

In fact, the pressure they have exerted on certain issues has benefited other Latino groups. For example, the first big breakthrough in getting minority-owned banks among Latinos came as a result of Cuban pressure. Of course, this has helped the Cuban community, but it has also made it possible for banks owned by Mexican-Americans to get started in New Mexico, Texas, and Colorado. This hasn't happened as much in California, however, because it's a much more expensive undertaking to start a bank here.

We may not have many things in common with the Cubans, but we do share common aspirations for new opportunities. Class differences certainly exist among Latinos, but I believe that a pragmatic political coalition can and will develop in spite of these class differences. Only fools would want to turn their backs on this growing Latino political potential.

The fact of the matter is that this Latino political influence is no longer just potential; it's a reality now as we enter the 1990s. We possess a lot of muscle in Congress right now. We have key Latino congressional representatives as chairs of important committees that can affect policy toward Latinos. Ed Roybal, for example, headed the House Committee on Aging until his recent retirement. Kika de la Garza is the chair of the House Agriculture Committee, which affects policy in an area where we still have many Latino workers and small farmers. In the area of finances, Henry González heads the House Banking Committee.

Of course, we also have Latino appointees in various federal agencies. Some of them are just fluff, but many others are dedicated people with a sense of doing something for their communities. The same is true at the state and local levels.

At least from the standpoint of government and what government can implement in terms of services, we're making some progress. East Los Angeles, for example, still has health clinics of all kinds, despite recent cutbacks. It also has many educational and training programs. We didn't have such things before, even in the 1960s. What I see ahead is that as our numbers increase and as our political know-how is sharpened, we'll be going for resources that will bring us improvements and satisfactions as Latinos. That's why I'm encouraged by the kind of political activity that I see developing. Of course, it has its ebbs and flows, and certain contradictions are to be found. But in general, as we go back over the last fifty or sixty years, we have come a long way.

Latino Opportunities in the 1990s

Latinos are going to be presented with some major opportunities in the 1990s. One of these will be increased political representation. At the federal level, we'll elect additional people to the House of Representatives and perhaps elect a senator or two. At the state and local levels, we may win some governorships, and we'll definitely see more Latinos in the statehouses and on city councils, county boards, and school boards.

One thing that will affect political representation is the three million undocumented immigrants who have qualified for amnesty. Most will become U.S. citizens, with voting rights, and their children in time will also become voters. This significant addition of new voters over the next few years, added to the numbers of people who already can vote, will only increase the political influence that Latinos wield. This influence will likewise increase because we are concentrated in many of the growth states, such as California, Texas, and Florida, where population growth will expand the number of congressional districts. In these states, Latinos will be in a good position to contest for these new seats.

Immigration will, of course, continue to be a critical issue. But we may well see a moderating of opinions on this question. There'll still be those who cry that immigration from Mexico and Latin America is undesirable and has a negative economic and cultural effect on the

country. These types of racist claims will continue and may even esca-
late in some places. However, there also will be—and in fact there
already is—a growing and sober recognition that we are going to need
some twelve million new workers over the next decade and that these
workers are largely going to be the result of new immigration. Even the
conservative Heritage Foundation has recently recognized this and
called for a more sensible approach toward immigration policy. We're
going to need these workers; we're simply not reproducing our own
native work force.

This economic recognition will change the terms of the discussion.
Nothing changes the racist feelings of an employer faster than the
realization that he won't be able to hire upstanding young white Americans and instead has to rely on Mexicans. And the competition for
those Mexicans will get even stronger.

The larger number of Latinos will further lessen some of the previous hostilities. It's very easy to be hostile toward a weak minority. It's
very difficult to hold the same attitude toward a big, powerful, and
increasingly important consumer group. Latinos will continue to play
a greater economic role as both producers and consumers. We will
begin to break into new and more skilled jobs, including professional
ones, as we become the fastest growing segment of the labor force. The
same importance will be attached to Latinos as consumers, and more
and more businesses will cater to this market.

Still another area that will grow in importance will be the influence
of Latinos on U.S. foreign policy, especially in regard to Latin America.
It will be a critical, not an apologetic, influence. It was significant that
several of the Latino men and women in Congress opposed the 1989
invasion of Panama by the United States. We will have more to say
about our policies toward Mexico and toward Puerto Rico. The same
will be true of our Central and South American policies.

In the case of Mexico, I think that our Latino representatives can
play a critical part in reassessing our policies toward that country and
especially our policy toward immigrant labor. As Mexican-Americans,
we need to play a role in the consideration and possible implementation
of the proposed North American Free Trade Agreement with Mexico.
This agreement, which is aimed at lowering trade barriers between the
U.S. and Mexico as well as with Canada, will lead to further integration
of Mexico's economy with that of the United States. As Mexican-
Americans, we should be concerned that this agreement not accelerate

the movement of "runaway" industries from the United States to Mexico, which might dislocate thousands of Latino workers even in the historically low-wage Southwest. On the other hand, if Salinas de Gortari's economic policies, which are based on the free trade agreement, fail, we will in all probability see an even greater increase in undocumented immigration from Mexico. Latinos need to participate in these discussions and in the making of these policies that will affect our communities.

Latino Leadership

The opportunities, issues, and challenges that the Chicano/Latino communities will face in the 1990s and beyond have a lot to do with the quality of leadership. I frankly think that we've never before had as many prominent and competent leaders as we have today. This is true not only politically but also in academia, the arts, the media, and business. These men and women can stand on their own achievements, and they are more and more becoming interested in correcting many of the social ills they see around them. We have more lawyers, doctors, and educators than we have ever had in our history.

A distinguishing characteristic of this leadership is that, regardless of political ideology, the people who are part of it are extremely knowledgeable. You can't be a leader—certainly not a national Latino leader—and be unaware of the issues affecting the Latino communities. You've got to have at your fingertips the data about education, poverty, immigration, and so on. You must have this knowledge in order to qualify as a national leader.

After all, who sanctions the national leadership? Who acknowledges it? It's the Anglos as well as the Latinos, but primarily it's the Anglo power elite. And this elite is not ready to confer recognition as a national leader upon some Latino unless he or she knows what the hell is going on and can interpret the issues and conditions of our community. In this sense, our Latino national leaders, such as those in Congress, are and have to be in tune with the grassroots. If they're not, they lose their recognition as leaders. This doesn't mean that these leaders are necessarily effective in changing conditions, but it does mean that they are at least aware of the problems and can articulate those problems.

Much of this leadership is new, coming from the generation of the

1960s and 1970s, and still needs to better define its identity and goals. But that it is the best trained and most knowledgeable generation of leaders goes almost without saying. And yet, even though this new, college-educated leadership is taking center stage, I believe that there is still room for the leadership of the older generation and for the older Mexican-American groups. This may sound self-serving, but I do believe in generational accommodation rather than generational conflict.

I think, for example, that LULAC can still play a very useful role. With the right leadership, LULAC has a tremendous potential for growth. Why? Because the needs are so great at the grassroots level that locally based LULAC chapters can still be very effective. But, to realize this potential, LULAC must resolve the whole question of a stronger national leadership that will measure up to the needs of its membership. If it doesn't, it'll be left behind by other and newer groups.

I also think that Chicano/Latino trade union leaders, such as Alfredo Montoya of the Latin American Council for Labor Advancement, have an important role to play because the majority of our people are still workers, and their numbers continue to grow. While the older Latino trade union leadership is in fact disappearing, it's hopeful to see a new, militant, and grassroots-oriented Latino leadership emerging in the unions. Such grassroots-oriented leadership was exemplified by the late César Chávez. Before his death in 1993, Chávez showed his adaptability, his resiliency, and his creativity by taking one of the concerns of farmworkers—pesticide poisoning—and transforming it into a major national environmental issue.

Although I'm optimistic about the future of our leadership, at the same time I think we should be as critical of our leaders as we feel the need to be. This is especially true for our elected leadership. We have to expect and demand that our leaders who are elected or appointed to office reflect the needs and aspirations of our people and that they work to better our communities. We've got to be very hard on them on this issue of accountability. On the other hand, I don't think we should make the mistake of demanding from them a level of activity and participation that only saints can bear. We have to keep in mind that they're human beings.

And we should never assume that they know all about our problems just because they're Latino. I remember that when we went to lobby in Congress on the immigration issue, someone said, "There's no need to go and talk to the Hispanic Congressional Caucus, because they know all about this issue." Well, as it turned out, they didn't know all about this issue; they had to be informed just like anybody else. I think that we should deal with our Latino elected officials just as we would with any other elected officials. We should expect the same of Latino leaders as we would of anyone else.

The Left in American Politics

Given my own political background, I'm at times asked, especially recently, if there is still a left in American politics. My response is that the left definitely still exists. It is a very broad left, focusing on a variety of issues.

There are still the sectarian left groups that are very small and not very influential, as well as pseudo-left groups that call themselves leftists but in reality aren't. But you also see many people who have abandoned organized left groups such as the Communist Party, but who remain socialists as they work with other groups. Or you see, as you do more recently in other countries, previously self-proclaimed left groups changing their names to appeal to broader interests. This is happening in Eastern Europe, where the communist parties are now calling themselves socialists or some other names.

Despite these changes and the general sense that socialism or communism has faded, I believe that what has happened in Eastern Europe and the Soviet Union in no way makes the principle that people should have some control over private capital any less desirable or less valid. These changes don't make it any less desirable, for example, to provide accessible medical assistance and hospitalization for all—what used to be referred to as "socialized medicine." We need it now more than ever.

We need unions to be strong. We still need what can be called socialization of the workplace. One of the reasons why U.S. production today is not competitive with Japan and Western Europe can be attributed to the lack of strong workers' organizations that provide security and effective participation in the production process. American workers, unlike those in Japan and Western Europe, still feel very separated from the production process and don't have a vested interest in the process because of the job and wage insecurities they face.

If I were to describe the left in the U.S. today, I would begin by saying that it is composed of the original parties of the left such as the Communist Party and the other socialist parties. This is the formal, structural left. That, however, is only a very small part of what I would consider the left. I would include independent activists such as Ramsey Clark, Bill Kunstler, David Dellinger, and Ralph Nader as part of the left. It is also made up of people involved in various movements—those working against U.S. intervention in Central America, people in the peace movement, in environmental groups, in the pro-choice struggle, and in the various movements demanding justice for racial minorities. This also includes many church leaders, educators, human rights advocates, and civil libertarians. This part of the left is not formalized in a political party, but it nevertheless exists as a body politic that raises money, concentrates on issues, and works in the political arena.

As to the future of the Communist Party in the U.S., I'm not sure just where the party stands at present. I don't read their press very much now. On a more general level, I believe that there is still a future for socialist-minded parties, because many of the issues that these parties have raised over the years are still very relevant—greater economic equality, an end to racism and discrimination, and a broader interpretation of American democracy.

It has always seemed to me an anomaly that the CP in this country never advocated a communist economy or even a communist society. It always just called for a more democratic society. In the Soviet Union, they called their system communism, but when you questioned them on this, they would admit that they were still a socialist state and that they had not really entered into a communist phase. They had not really reached a point where each person would be compensated according to his or her needs.

When I visited the Soviet Union in the 1970s, the people I talked to didn't feel that they could fulfill the needs of everyone. They simply didn't have that kind of production capacity. My point is that we in this country have never gone much beyond the nomenclature of socialism and communism to understand what these parties really stand for.

As for new elements in what we might consider the left, such as Jesse Jackson and the Rainbow Coalition, I'm afraid that here I have some problems. Jesse Jackson, to me, is a typical religious leader turned politician. I'm uncomfortable with religious leaders when they come out as political leaders, especially in an electoral context. Perhaps this is the influence of my grandmother's experience in Mexico with the political role of the Catholic church there.

But aside from that, Jesse Jackson doesn't strike me as a workers' person, although he supports workers' causes. It's one thing to be a worker and another thing to be an advocate for workers' causes. My other reservation about Jackson is that he has never belonged to a mass organization that could call him into account. He hasn't had this type of development, outside of his early years with the Southern Christian Leadership Conference. The lack of this contact with a mass organization means that Jackson is essentially an individualist rather than someone steeped in a cooperative mass movement.

Insofar as the Rainbow Coalition is concerned, I find a lot of chaos in the organization. I was actually elected at one time as one of its national co-leaders, but I was never invited to a meeting, and I never saw my name on any piece of literature that would indicate that I had an obligation to the coalition. There is so much disarray in the organization that almost anybody can gather five or ten people and claim that they control something in the coalition. So my experience has been that no one knew who was really speaking for the group or who was the Rainbow Coalition.

The left also used to be represented much more within the Democratic Party, but, unfortunately, this is less the case today. It's not even a question of the left "boring from within" the Democratic Party, because there isn't much to bore into. Unlike the Republican Party, which is a more permanent and institutionalized structure, the Democratic Party doesn't have a disciplined base or structure. It's an organization that changes every two years or every four years at election time. In addition, the Democratic Party has lost much of its soul. It is less committed to social change. Rather than trying to provide a real alternative to the Republicans, the Democrats are trying to act like Republicans and appeal to conservative-minded voters.

I don't see in the Democratic Party a Bobby Kennedy who could revitalize it. I'm sure that there are a lot of well-intentioned candidates within the party, but they're handicapped because the party itself doesn't have a progressive platform. Its platform is so watered down with trying to appeal to what the polls say that the party has certainly lost its character as the party of the working class, of minorities, and of the poor. It's not the party that I knew and responded to in the 1930s.

Then, the left was a main driving force within the party. The Democratic Party today is more a party of entrenched officeholders and not a broader progressive coalition.

I know that it isn't in vogue right now to call oneself a socialist, but I still do. If by socialism we mean someone who believes that the principal means of production should be regulated by government or by the people in the form of coops, then I would call myself a socialist. I still believe that socialism has a future. One of the things we are seeing today, for example, are moves by employees—in the airline industry, for example—to buy out the companies and have them run by the workers. Nobody's calling these people Communists, and I think that we're going to see more of this taking place in other industries.

I still believe that the working class is the vehicle for achieving socialism. It's the workers as a class who can buy up their companies and then advocate laws to benefit employee-owned businesses. I know that the question of who is part of the working class is more blurred now because of the decrease in industrial jobs and the rise in service and information occupations. This gives some wage-earning people a sense that they're not part of the working class but instead are middle class, whatever that means. In fact, they're really working class, although they don't have a consciousness as workers.

However, I think this is going to dramatically change in the next century, when the bulk of our work force will be people of Third World backgrounds, including Latinos. Some of these workers will be coopted, but in general they're going to retain a consciousness as a working class. Racial minority workers in this country, unlike those of European backgrounds, don't have a long history of convincing themselves that they're something other than workers. Racism will play a role in this, too. Even though there will be a greater demand for Third World workers, which will allow some mobility, the persistence of racism will help to maintain sharper class divisions. These tensions, I believe, will at the same time ignite a more open form of class struggle.

I believe in the American dream—or at least in my version of it. I interpret it as a hope and a wish, which has not been completely fulfilled for all Americans such as Latinos and other racial minorities. It's similar to the dream of the Mexican Revolution, which also promised freedom, equality, and democracy. Clearly, that hasn't been fully achieved. In both cases, they're unfulfilled dreams.

My Life and History

It's hard for me to think how I would like to be remembered by history. I never planned my life. It just happened the way it did. I'm proud that I was able at certain times to help organize a plant or a community group and that these organizations helped people struggle to better their lives. Frankly, I've never concerned myself with a place in history. I've been too busy organizing and working with others. If my life has meant anything, I would say that it shows that you can organize workers and poor people if you work hard, are persistent, remain optimistic, and reach out to involve as many people as possible.

One of the most gratifying aspects of being a community organizer is seeing that you're influencing others in such a way that it empowers them. I've seen this when people participate in a strike or in a political campaign. I've felt that I've been able to influence people when they have actually moved and done things. Even when I was teaching at the university level, I felt that I was being more effective when I motivated students to participate in a boycott or in a labor strike or in voter registration.

I think that by getting people to participate in such actions, I've also had some ideological influence on them. By this I mean that when people become involved in social movements, they understand in a very direct way what is important and what isn't. These experiences stick with them and create a sense of unity.

For example, I ran into some black people who cornered me and said, "Hey, don't you remember us?" And I said, "Gee, I don't." But they reminded me: "Well, do you remember we had those sit-ins? We lay down in the passageways of the San Francisco post office, and the postmaster came out and tried to throw us out of there. But, by God, we now have seven minority postmasters in the San Francisco area!"

That's what people remember—what they did! Not so much that they heard a speech. That doesn't mean that a speech or a lecture in a classroom or reading isn't important. But it does mean that when you experience something, like participating in a strike, a boycott, or a sit-in, you learn very vivid lessons that are hard to forget.

If I can pass anything on to younger people, it would be that, based on my experiences, successful community organization depends on establishing as broad a coalition as possible, regardless of personality differences, organizational differences, or political differences. I would also insist that the essentials of strong, effective leadership are consistency and stubbornness in pursuit of one's goals. But to have a goal, you have to develop a philosophy or an ideology that inspires you to accept the need for social change. With that vision, commitment, and tenacity, strong progressive leadership is possible.

I've known too many young people who will tell me, "Mister Corona, I really want to work for my *gente,* my people. I don't want to make a lot of money; I just want to be with my *gente.*" That's a very noble expression, but you still need to know *why* you want to be with your *gente*. To do what? You can't just do something because you think it's cool or glamorous, because pretty soon this will wear off unless you have a broader and deeper understanding of your commitment.

My advice to young people who want to work in the community is that if they can develop those qualities or characteristics I've mentioned, they'll be able to find their niche, where they can get people together to build collective strength. This is how they'll become leaders. It can be done.

Will I ever retire? No. I want to be able to do more things and see more things. I think we're entering into a very exciting epoch in the 1990s. A lot of things will be happening that I'd like to be around to participate in and to see.

Afterword

In thinking about the different ways in which one can interpret Bert Corona's narrative, several important concepts seem pertinent to the text. Here I would like to play the role of critic and, in a sense, provide a partial guide for other critics—both historians and scholars of literary/cultural studies—suggesting how one might consider Corona's narrative.

Testimonio and Autobiographical Representation

When I told colleagues about my project with Bert Corona, they often responded: "Oh! A biography—that sounds wonderful!" Yet, of course, this is not a biography. Rather, it is an oral history that in form and content is closer to a Latin American *testimonio*, involving the collective authorship of scholar and activist, than to a personally written autobiography or biography. Why not a biography? I never intended to produce a biography, although Corona is certainly worthy of one. Instead, I believed that it would be more important and valuable to assemble Corona's memories in testimonial form.

Testimonies and autobiographies have been rare in Chicano history. Although some exist in both formal and oral history forms, this genre is not an especially expansive one. Consequently, the direct voices and narratives of Mexican-Americans over the years have been less audible and available. Few published autobiographies exist, even of prominent individuals. The two works best known in this field are *Barrio Boy*, a coming-of-age autobiography set in the early twentieth century, by Ernesto Galarza, an outstanding intellectual as well as a labor and community leader; and the more recent and controversial *Hunger of Memory* by Richard Rodríguez, also a coming-of-age narrative, which received a great deal of attention because of Rodríguez's attacks on affirmative action and bilingual education. Unfortunately, Galarza, whose life somewhat parallels Corona's, chose not to extend his narrative to include his mature years and thus, in my opinion, limited the oppositional and contestatory character of his autobiography.[1]

This dearth of autobiographical and testimonial narratives convinced me that it would be of greater value to allow Corona to tell his own story. Moreover, I rejected the notion of a biography because of the greater difficulty involved in compiling the additional sources required to trace Corona's life and career in complete detail. Corona some years ago lost his personal collection of papers and documents. He has turned over some materials to Stanford University, but these relate only to his more recent work with undocumented immigrants. Hence, the degree of difficulty and the time required to come up with the full archival materials—assuming they even exist—covering Corona's long and varied career from the 1930s to the 1990s would undoubtedly have added several more years to the project. I judged it more important for Corona to tell his story in his own words with his own interpretation and to produce this narrative while Corona could still enjoy its publication and address the issues that flow from his story.

Any autobiographical text, in comparison to biography, suffers from some lack of authenticating various facts. Although both Corona and I have checked certain facts to be sure that the narrative matches the actual chronology, I have not attempted to prove every point he makes or to authenticate every memory he brings forth. History, as some

---

1. Ernesto Galarza, *Barrio Boy: The Story of a Boy's Acculturation* (Notre Dame: University of Notre Dame Press, 1971); Richard Rodríguez, *Hunger of Memory: The Education of Richard Rodríguez* (Boston: Godine, 1981). For an excellent analysis of both these texts, see Ramón Saldívar, *Chicano Narrative: The Dialectics of Difference* (Madison: University of Wisconsin Press, 1990), pp. 154–170. Also see various articles in *Americas Review* 16 (Fall-Winter 1988), a special issue on Latino autobiography.

suggest, is a selection of memories. What I have helped to assemble here is a collection of memories selected by Corona, or by me as I have prompted his memory. What we get in the end are Corona's views and interpretations of history, reinforced by my own. The facts of these memories are important, but of greater importance is how Corona (and I) have chosen to re-create these memories and the implications of their meanings.

Double Voices

Unlike traditional autobiography, in which there is one sole author, in *testimonios,* or what can also be described as ethnographic history or ethnohistory, we find what Philippe Lejeune calls "collaborative autobiography."[2] This book is a collaborative text. Corona is clearly the subject of the *testimonio,* and he provides both the raw materials and a certain structure to the narrative. I, as his collaborator and the producer of the project, help to assemble the narrative by the very questions that I raise and the organization I give to these questions, in addition to transcribing and writing the narrative itself.

I do not doubt that if Corona had ever had the time to write his own autobiography, he would have written an even more formal political text, focused more on his overt public life. Our collaborative text contains a great deal of Corona's public life, but I have also made an effort to have him talk about his private life: his parents, his grandmother, his siblings, Blanche, his children. Indeed, one afternoon while I was pursuing this line of questioning, Bert suddenly stopped me and asked, "But will anyone be interested in this?" I responded, "Yes, of course, Bert. People want to know about your whole life, not just your public one."

At the same time, I must say that I also respect Corona's privacy, and I entered into the realm of his private life only with some diplomacy. Undoubtedly, there are many other sides to Corona's less public life that I did not approach. Anyone who knows Bert, however, knows that for him his public and private lives are so intertwined that at times it's hard to distinguish one from the other. He himself admits that his

2. Philippe Lejeune, *On Autobiography* (Minneapolis: University of Minnesota Press, 1989).

family life, for example, was strongly affected by his political commitments.

So who is the author? The answer is that we both are. In a sense, a "double voice" is heard in the narrative, although the two sides are in a symbiotic and complementary rather than a conflictive relationship. A double voice appears in the writing and shaping of the narrative, but it is Corona's life story. Like Nell Irvin Painter's *Narrative of Hosea Hudson*, Elisabeth Burgos-Debray's *I, Rigoberta Menchú,* and various other examples of oral histories and *testimonios* constructed on working relationships between professional scholars and community activists, our text is collaborative.[3] As Clifford observes regarding collaborative ethnography: "This possibly suggests an alternative text and strategy, a utopia of plural authorship that accords to collaborators not merely the status of independent enunciators but that of writers."[4]

The Intended Audience

Like most texts, this one has more than one audience. In my own previous work, I have been cognizant of writing for dual audiences—both for a larger, multiethnic audience and for a Mexican-American audience. I have always believed that as "ethnic American writers," we must direct our narratives both outwardly and inwardly. In other words, we need to educate and inform the dominant white population about our particular experiences and to position our texts within an American-based historical discourse. At the same time, given the historical amnesia (what David Blight calls "collective forgetting") whereby racial minorities have been mostly written out of American history and

3. See, for example, Nell Irvin Painter, *The Narrative of Hosea Hudson: His Life as a Negro Communist in the South* (Cambridge: Harvard University Press, 1979); Elisabeth Burgos-Debray, *I, Rigoberta Menchú: An Indian Woman in Guatemala* (London: Verso, 1984); and Dorothy Healey and Maurice Isserman, *Dorothy Healey Remembers: A Life in the American Communist Party* (New York: Oxford University Press, 1990).

4. James Clifford, *The Predicament of Culture: Twentieth-Century Ethnography, Literature, and Art* (Cambridge: Harvard University Press, 1986), p. 51. Anthropologist Ruth Behar suggests that in producing/writing a *testimonio,* the scholar is transformed from being a listener to being a storyteller ("Rage and Redemption: Reading the Life Story of a Mexican Marketing Woman," *Feminist Studies* 16 [Summer 1990]: 228).

culture, it is also important that we educate and inform minority audiences in the hope that our texts will help to empower our communities.[5] In this sense, this text is also positioned within the discourse of the Mexican-American experience.

Because Corona's narrative involves a type of dual authorship, or "double voice," are there also competing audiences? I don't believe so. In responding to my questions, Corona, although addressing me personally, was in fact also addressing the same dual audience I had in mind. His narrative in a larger sense is an American story, a story of growing up and coming of age as a Mexican-American in the United States. It is a story of both individual and collective struggles against injustice. It is also the story of those successes and victories—never complete—that oppositional struggles, or what George Lipsitz refers to as "social contestations," produce.[6]

Corona's culture of opposition, while never fully transforming the exploitative relationships that affect Mexican-Americans, nevertheless has achieved certain positive changes and empowerment for Chicanos. As Lipsitz notes: "Thus even when aggrieved populations fail to seize power or to fashion autonomous spheres of opposition, they still influence the exercise of power in this society."[7] Corona's narrative is intended to deconstruct American history both to reveal breaks in the traditional textual or mythological notion of American progress and justice for all and, at the same time, to redefine, to rewrite, to decenter American history to include the presence, contributions, successes, and failures of previously marginalized racial minorities such as Mexican-Americans.

5. David W. Blight, " 'For Something Beyond the Battlefield': Frederick Douglass and the Memory of the Civil War," *Journal of American History* 75 (March 1989): 1173. Chicano cultural critic Guillermo Gómez-Peña notes: "The U.S. suffers from a severe case of amnesia. In its obsessive quest to 'construct the future,' it tends to forget or erase the past. Fortunately, the so-called disenfranchised groups who don't feel part of this national project have been meticulously documenting these histories. Latinos, blacks, Asians, women, gays, experimental artists and non-aligned intellectuals have used inventive languages to record the other history from a multicentric perspective" ("The Multicultural Paradigm: An Open Letter to the National Arts Community," *High Performance* [September 1989]: 22).

6. George Lipsitz, *A Life in the Struggle: Ivory Perry and the Culture of Opposition* (Philadelphia: Temple University Press, 1988), p. 9.

7. Ibid., p. 13.

In attempting to do this, Corona's narrative is intended not just for export. It is also intended to empower Mexican-American audiences through an additional revelation about the history of Chicanos, especially their quest for social justice. "Perhaps now we can understand the voices of Mexican-American autobiography in yet another way," Nericcio observes, "as a voice in search for not only identity but also access to the realm of power. . . . To transform the world means to conceptualize that world. Hence, access to words equals access to history."[8] Over the past two decades, we have reconstructed a good deal of this history, but much more needs to be done. Corona's narrative helps to accomplish this.

The Collective Self

In examining some of the literature on both autobiography and the Latin American *testimonio,* one finds a distinct division between a Western, male-centered version of autobiography and a more contestatory version of Third World and women's autobiography and narrative. (In this context, I use the category Third World to include racial minority groups in the United States.) At the risk of essentializing, it might be said that the more traditional form of autobiography, which (at least since the Renaissance) largely deals with the lives and exploits of white males, takes as its central theme the fulfillment of what is referred to as the "unified self." Paul John Eakin describes this as the mythology of the "completed self" and the "autonomous self"; Doris Sommer discusses the "singular subject." When he defines the genre, Philippe Lejeune regards autobiography along individualist lines "as the retrospective prose narrative that someone writes concerning *his* own existence, where the focus is *his* individual life, in particular the story of *his* personality" (my emphasis). What Lejeune terms the "autobiographical pact" between author and reader is still largely singular in scope in that it stresses the effort by the author not to recompose historical exactitude but to sincerely come to terms with his or her own life.[9]

8. William Anthony Nericcio, "Autobiographies at *La Frontera:* The Quest for Mexican-American Narrative," *Americas Review* 16 (Fall-Winter 1988): 174.

9. See Paul John Eakin, "Malcolm X and the Limits of Autobiography," in *Autobiography: Essays Theoretical and Critical,* ed. James Olney (Princeton:

Shari Benstock notes that the traditional autobiography serves as a means to create an image of "self" or to recapture the self and to find a singular "voice." According to Georges Gusdorf: "Autobiography . . . requires a *man* to reconstitute *himself* in the focus of *his* special unity and identity across time" (my emphasis). For Gusdorf, the cultural precondition for autobiography is a previous concept of individualism, "a conscious awareness of the singularity of each individual life." Sommer asserts that in traditional Western autobiography a separation or a gap always exists between the public and the private spheres—that is, between the individual and the community or the masses. One hears a resonance with Richard Rodríguez's lamentation about his perception of the split between Spanish as a "private" language and English as a "public" language. Although traditional autobiography addresses the public, it does so largely to reflect back on the primacy of the individual self. As Ramón Saldívar writes of Richard Rodríguez's text: "Social and political events gain meaning in Rodríguez's life *only* because of their connection with his private life" (his emphasis).[10]

In contrast, African-American autobiography (including slave narratives), women's autobiography, and the Latin American *testimonio* appear to be less individually centered. In postmodernist fashion, these revisions of the traditional autobiographical genre decenter the subject to frame instead what Eakin refers to as the "split subject."[11] Yet the subject and the author do not disappear, as some postmodernist critics argue. In these more oppositional narratives, the subjects—and they are

Princeton University Press, 1980), p. 183; Doris Sommer, " 'Not Just a Personal Story': Women's *Testimonios* and the Plural Self," in *Life/Lines: Theorizing Women's Autobiography,* ed. Bella Brodzki and Celeste Schenck (Ithaca: Cornell University Press, 1988), p. 107; and Lejeune, *On Autobiography,* pp. viii and ix. See also Arnold Krupat, *For Those Who Come After: A Study of Native American Autobiography* (Berkeley and Los Angeles: University of California Press, 1985), p. xxii.

10. Shari Benstock, ed., *The Private Self: Theory and Practice of Women's Autobiographical Writings* (Chapel Hill: University of North Carolina Press, 1988), p. 5; Gusdorf is quoted in ibid., pp. 14–15; Sommer, " 'Not Just a Personal Story,' " p. 111; Rodríguez, *Hunger of Memory,* pp. 11–40; Saldívar, *Chicano Narrative,* p. 159.

11. See Paul John Eakin's foreword in Krupat, *For Those Who Come After,* p. xii.

indeed very central subjects—exist in a diverse world of subjects, although not without reference to hierarchical power relations. The white, male great figures of history are pushed aside to include a myriad of other, perhaps more central, subjects.

In place of the unified subject (meaning the alleged secure identity of particular white males), Third World and women's autobiographical narratives argue for a collective self, described by Doris Sommer as the "plural self."[12] This concept recognizes that members of these communities cannot be understood or interpreted without regard for the community itself or a sense of collective identity. With respect to African-American autobiography, many critics seem to agree that most African-American autobiographical texts position the role of the individual within a community context (with certain exceptions, perhaps such as Booker T. Washington's middle-class–oriented *Up from Slavery*). That identity and that struggle with and for the collective good provide the inspiration for one's identity and sense of history.[13]

The concept of the collective self is vividly brought to our attention in the recent wave of Latin American testimonial literature centered on people's responses to oppression. John Beverley and Marc Zimmerman observe that "testimonio is not so much concerned with the life of a 'problematic hero' . . . as with a problematic collective social situation that the narrator lives with or alongside others." Based on collective struggles, the *testimonio* constitutes a "nonfictional, popular-democratic form of epic narrative." Each *testimonio* articulates not a singular voice but a choir of voices in what Beverley and Zimmerman—borrowing from the Russian literary theorist Mikhail Bakhtin—term the "polyphonic testimonio." As Rigoberta Menchú stresses in her popular testimonial: "This is my testimony. I didn't learn it from a book and I didn't learn it alone. I'd like to stress that it's not only my life, it's also the testimony of my people."[14]

12. Sommer, " 'Not Just a Personal Story.' " Also see Samuel Schrager, "What Is Social in Oral History?" *International Journal of Oral History* 4, no. 2 (June 1983): 76–98.

13. See Stephen Butterfield, *Black Autobiography in America* (Amherst: University of Massachusetts Press, 1974). Also see Roger Rosenblatt, "Black Autobiography: Life as the Death Weapon," in Olney, *Autobiography*, pp. 179–180.

14. John Beverley and Marc Zimmerman, *Literature and Politics in the Central American Revolutions* (Austin: University of Texas Press, 1990), pp. 174–178. Rigoberta Menchú is quoted in ibid., p. 174.

If it were to be removed from the collective experience, Beverley and Zimmerman believe that the *testimonio* would revert to the more traditional autobiography centered on the individual "I." Echoing this same theme, Doris Sommer categorizes *testimonios* as "public events," or what Margaret Randall calls *"testimonio para si."* Miguel Barnet, who more than any other scholar has promoted the literary and historical value of *testimonios*, stresses that the main objective of the *testimonio "debe contribuir a articular la memoria collectiva, el* nosotros *y no el yo"* (should be to articulate a collective memory, the *we* not the *I*) (his emphasis).[15]

This manifestation of the collective self finds expression in the narrative of Bert Corona. Although he is an exemplary individual, Corona nevertheless always frames his life history in relationship to the larger Mexican-American community and especially to the struggles of Mexican-Americans to achieve social justice. Corona centers his narrative not on his own accomplishments and successes but on the collective efforts of his community, including both the leadership of numerous less well known Mexican-Americans and the efforts of the rank and file.

Community Intellectual

Through his engagement in social contestation and through his leadership in the Mexican-American community, Corona emerges, in my opinion, as someone who can be classified as a "community intellectual." To understand this, we must refer to the notion of the "organic intellectual" as first conceptualized by Antonio Gramsci and later elaborated by others. From the perspective of post–World War I Europe, Gramsci suggested that in the evolution of Western culture two types of intellectuals had emerged. The first type he termed "traditional intellectuals." These were professional intellectuals, literary and scientific types—that is, those whom we normally perceive as intellectuals

15. Beverley and Zimmerman, *Literature and Politics,* pp. 177–178; Sommer, " 'Not Just a Personal Story,' " p. 118. Margaret Randall is quoted in Jorge Narvaez, "El Testimonio 1972–1982: Transformaciones en el Sistema Literario," in *Testimonio y Literatura,* ed. Rene Jara and Hernan Vidal (Edina, Minn.: Society for the Study of Contemporary Hispanic and Lusophone Revolutionary Literatures, 1986), p. 239. See Miguel Barnet, "La Novela Testimonio: Socio-Literatura," in Jara and Vidal, *Testimonio y Literatura,* p. 294.

(writers, professors, scientists, artists, and so on). Gramsci also suggested that a second type, called "organic intellectuals," had emerged from the ranks of specific social groups, especially from developing industrial or economic groups.

Rather than functioning in the abstract world of ideas, organic intellectuals provide indirect intellectual and moral direction through their activities in organizing particular economic functions. As examples of organic intellectuals, Gramsci focused on factory technicians (later termed the "new managerial class"). He wrote: "In the modern world, technical education, closely bound to industrial labor even at the most primitive and unqualified level, must form the basis of the new type of intellectual." Yet it would appear that Gramsci had in mind not simply intermediate managers but in fact all leading elements, including industrial capitalists and working-class revolutionaries, who, as Quintin Hoare notes, through their function direct "the ideas and aspirations of the class to which they organically belong."[16]

Although organic intellectuals have often been regarded as elements within the progressive or left working-class and radical movements, in fact Gramsci's description of organic intellectuals places them more in the realm of the dominant bourgeois class. As John Cammett observes of Gramsci's emphasis on this point: "The interests of the organic intellectual are, however, more nearly identical with those of the dominant class of the time than the traditional intellectual's."[17] Gramsci lamented this situation and hoped that organic intellectuals would likewise emerge from the ranks of the new industrial proletarians. Hoare elaborates: "The working class, like the bourgeoisie before it, is capable of developing from within its ranks its own organic intellectuals."[18]

Post-Gramsci intellectuals, particularly on the left, have been drawn to the concept of the organic intellectual as a way of linking in a more syncretic way the role of traditional intellectuals and the working class. In the recent period, for example, the new Chicano intellectuals emerging from the Chicano movement stress the need for this new intelli-

16. See Quintin Hoare's introduction in Antonio Gramsci, *Selections from the Prison Notebooks* (New York: International Publishers, 1971), pp. 3, 9.

17. John W. Cammett, *Antonio Gramsci and the Origins of Italian Communism* (Stanford: Stanford University Press, 1967), p. 202.

18. Hoare, in Gramsci, *Selections from the Prison Notebooks*, p. 4.

gentsia to become organic intellectuals, although, ironically, without necessarily giving up their roles and positions in the universities as traditional intellectuals.

It would appear that what Gramsci had in mind was the emergence out of the proletariat itself of those workers who, through their examples of struggle against capitalist exploitation, would help to develop and inspire the consciousness of their co-workers toward revolutionary, or at least oppositional, goals. Here it is useful to refer to a recent work by George Lipsitz, *A Life in the Struggle: Ivory Perry and the Culture of Opposition.* Analyzing the life and activities of community and working-class activist Ivory Perry in St. Louis during the civil rights struggles of the 1950s and 1960s, Lipsitz concludes that Perry is a good, if not perfect, example of what Gramsci meant by an organic intellectual, at least from the perspective of the working class. Although he had little education, Perry, through his participation in social contestation, not only acquired his own political education but also educated and directed other poor African-Americans concerning the nature of their oppression as both a racial and a class group.

"Organic intellectuals learn about the world by trying to change it," according to Lipsitz, "and they change the world by learning about it from the perspective of the needs and aspirations of their social group."[19] Oppositional ideas flow from social action. Hence, Lipsitz observes of Perry: "On picket lines and marches, at mass meetings and rallies, in the streets and in jail, Perry has functioned as the quintessential organic intellectual."[20]

Drawing from the concept of the organic intellectual as I understand it, I suggest that Bert Corona represents a revised version of this construct. In my view, Corona combines aspects of a traditional intellectual with those of an organic intellectual. Although Corona is not a professional intellectual (by virtue of advanced education), nor is intellectual work the central focus of his life, he nevertheless did attend college for a year—an astonishing achievement for a Mexican-American in the 1930s. More important, Corona, unlike Perry, is a self-taught intellectual, with wide reading experience in history and

19. Lipsitz, *A Life in the Struggle,* p. 10. Also see Jerome Karabel, "Revolutionary Contradictions: Antonio Gramsci and the Problem of Intellectuals," *Politics and Society* 6, no. 1 (1976): 123–172.

20. Lipsitz, *A Life in the Struggle,* p. 11.

politics. Indeed, beginning in the late 1960s, with the development of Chicano Studies programs in California, Corona was invited to teach courses on Chicano politics, community organizing, and immigration issues at several universities, including California State University, Los Angeles; San Diego State University; the University of California, Berkeley; and the University of California, Santa Barbara.

At the same time, although he is from a middle-class background in El Paso, Corona, like Perry, emerged as a working-class organic intellectual through his involvement in the late 1930s with the CIO. Unlike Perry, however, Corona came to his role as an organic intellectual with considerably more formal education as well as more self-education. He already held some developed ideas and an analysis of American society and culture. Moreover, Perry represents the rank-and-file activist rather than the leadership of community-based groups. In contrast, Corona became a leader of both the union movement and Mexican-American community organizations. And Corona's leadership is positioned not only with blue-collar, working-class groups but also with white-collar, middle-class organizations such as CSO and MAPA.

Yet, of course, like Perry, Corona made his main contributions as a type of organic intellectual through social contestation and oppositional struggles. "Ideas become important," Carl Boggs notes of the role of organic intellectuals, "only when they can be translated into collective social and political forces."[21] But because of the complex characteristics that Corona brings to the concept of the organic intellectual—certainly in contrast to Lipsitz's portrayal of Ivory Perry—I believe that it might be more correct to interpret Corona as a "community intellectual."

But one might ask how effectively Corona has functioned as a community intellectual. How have his community-based activities, along with his own ideological perspectives, influenced others, especially those within the Mexican-American communities? Both his participation in community struggles and his speaking out over the years on a variety of issues together characterize him, in my opinion, as a community intellectual. Given this, I would single out three key intellectual and political principles that Corona has embodied and that he has attempted to pass on to others.

21. Carl Boggs, *Gramsci's Marxism* (London: Pluto Press, 1976), p. 33.

The first I would categorize as the principle of historical agency. Through his example as a labor and community leader and his outspoken opposition to exploitation and discrimination, especially against Mexican-Americans and Latinos, Corona has influenced other Mexican-Americans to believe in themselves and in their own abilities to effect changes in their lives. Chicanos can and do make history and empower themselves through a process of social struggle. After joining the CIO in the late 1930s, for example, Corona and other labor leaders convinced hundreds of fellow workers to join the Longshoremen's Union for their own self-protection and even to go on strike to combat wage discrimination and win concessions from the bosses.

In building MAPA in the 1960s, to offer another example, Corona and others empowered Mexican-American political activists by helping them to perceive themselves as independent political actors, not beholden to patronage dispensers, especially within the Democratic Party. Building from a more independent perspective, Corona and MAPA further projected the image of Mexican-Americans as national political actors, which raised their own expectations as well as their sense of influencing national policy.

Still another example of Corona's promotion of historical agency can be seen in his more recent work with undocumented immigrants. His leadership and that of the Hermandad Mexicana Nacional have empowered immigrant workers, one of the most exploited sectors in American society, to organize among themselves, to believe in their human and constitutional rights, and to successfully struggle against injustice and for new policies.

A second principle flowing from Corona's history of community struggle concerns the importance of organization in bringing about social change. For Corona, organization is the key to combatting social ills. Without effective and broad-based organization, nothing is achievable, despite any lofty ideals one might possess. Throughout his career, Corona has consistently passed on to others the critical nature of organization. Learning this principle from his early years with the CIO, he has always interpreted organization not from the perspective of an elite vanguard but from the need to organize broadly at the community level—to serve the base and to develop organic leadership from that base.

Whether working with the CIO unions or later with groups such as

CSO, ANMA, MAPA, and the Hermandad Mexicana Nacional, Corona has always stressed the importance of organizing around the concept of the family. Only by involving all family members, he believes, can a really effective community-based organization succeed. This stress on securing what liberation theologists in the context of popular Latin American struggles refer to as *comunidades de base*—the base communities—is something Corona tried to stress to members of the younger Chicano Generation of the 1960s and 1970s who, he believed, were too impatient to achieve social change and in their impatience neglected to effectively organize at the grassroots level.

Finally, I would suggest that a third principle embodied by Corona concerns his unfettered optimism and belief in the ultimate success of social change, despite setbacks and partial reforms. Part of this optimism is Corona's deep and persistent commitment to struggle. As he noted more than once, there are no shortcuts to achieving social justice. "Hegemonizing," Stuart Hall asserts, "is hard work." The construction of a more just and democratic America, which involves building what Michael Denning refers to as new "hegemonic formations," is not only a matter of ideas, according to Denning, but "also an issue of participation, in the sense of involving people both in cultural institutions—schools, churches, sporting events—and in long-term historic projects."[22]

But all this takes dedication and lots of hard work. These qualities Corona has certainly possessed. By his personal example, he has influenced his colleagues and those who have known him to keep faith in the ultimate success of social protest. It is struggle—the struggle for justice—that has given meaning to Corona's life. Yet it is also his commitment and his example, his belief in *la lucha,* the struggle, that has given meaning to others.

These are only some of the ideological influences that emanate from Corona's role as a community intellectual. These influences directly and indirectly have affected the views and perspectives—the so-called worldviews—of many of his *compañeros* and *compañeras,* his colleagues in struggle.

22. Both Hall and Denning are quoted from Michael Denning, "The End of Mass Culture," *International Labor and Working-Class History* 32 (Spring 1990): 14.

Index

Compositor:	Com Com
Text:	10/13 Sabon
Display:	Sabon
Printer:	Haddon Craftsmen, Inc.
Binder:	Haddon Craftsmen, Inc.